Judd Winick
J. Calafiore
Writers

Tom Fowler
Ron Garney
Ron Lim
Paul Lee
Pencillers

Dan Davis
Rodney Ramos
Bill Reinhold
Inkers

Guy Major
Colorist

Rob Leigh
Pat Brosseau
Phil Balsman
Jared K. Fletcher
Letterers

GREEN ARROW

HEADING INTO THE LIGHT

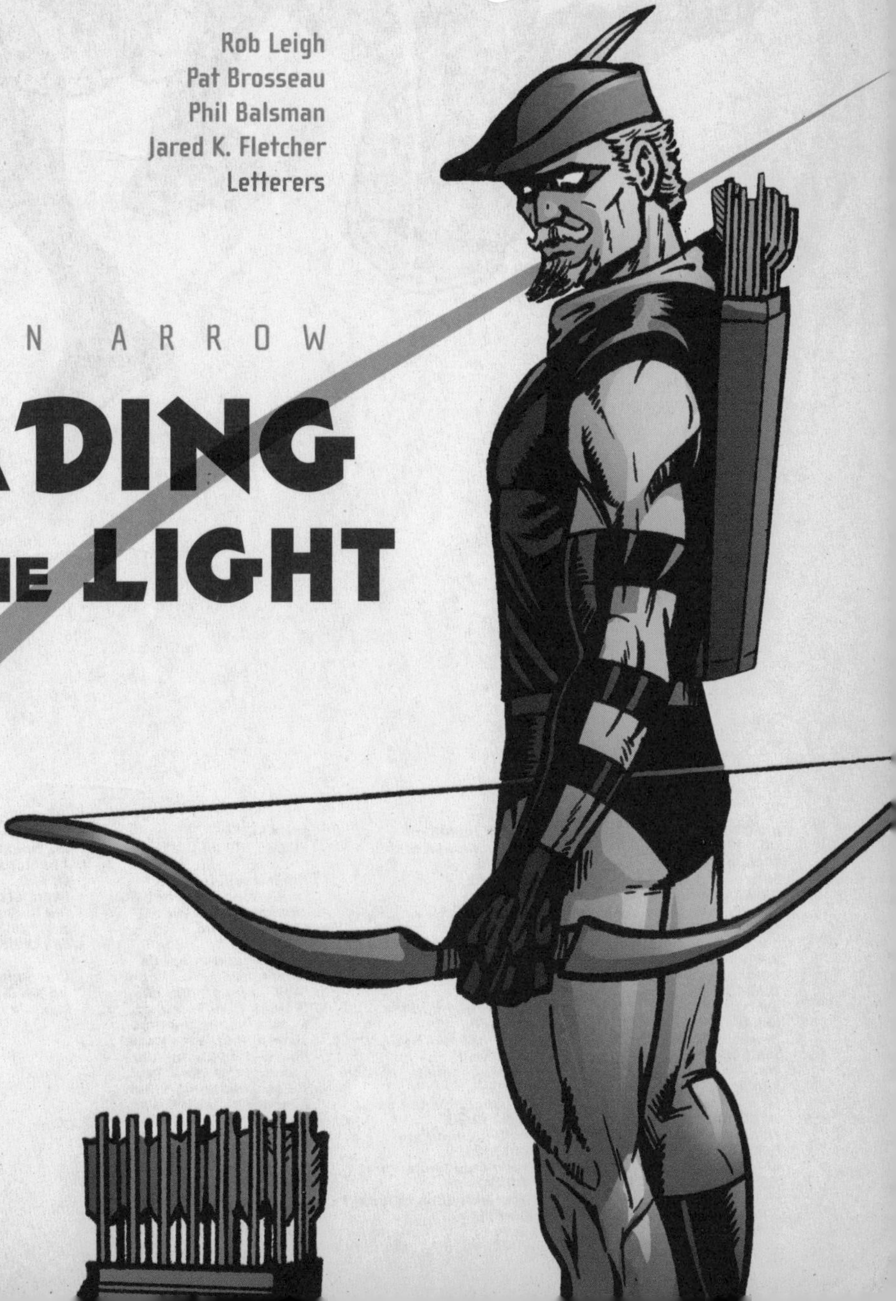

DAN DIDIO
Senior VP-Executive Editor
BOB SCHRECK
Editor-original series
MICHAEL WRIGHT
Associate Editor-original series
BRANDON MONTCLARE
Assistant Editor-original series
BOB HARRAS
Group Editor-collected edition
ROBBIN BROSTERMAN
Senior Art Director
PAUL LEVITZ
President & Publisher
GEORG BREWER
VP-Design & DC Direct Creative
RICHARD BRUNING
Senior VP-Creative Director
PATRICK CALDON
Executive VP-Finance & Operations
CHRIS CARAMALIS
VP-Finance
JOHN CUNNINGHAM
VP-Marketing
TERRI CUNNINGHAM
VP-Managing Editor

STEPHANIE FIERMAN
Senior VP-Sales & Marketing
ALISON GILL
VP-Manufacturing
RICH JOHNSON
VP-Book Trade Sales
HANK KANALZ
VP-General Manager, WildStorm
LILLIAN LASERSON
Senior VP & General Counsel
JIM LEE
Editorial Director-WildStorm
PAULA LOWITT
Senior VP-Business & Legal Affairs
DAVID MCKILLIPS
VP-Advertising & Custom Publishing
JOHN NEE
VP-Business Development
GREGORY NOVECK
Senior VP-Creative Affairs
CHERYL RUBIN
Senior VP-Brand Management
JEFF TROJAN
VP-Business Development, DC Direct
BOB WAYNE
VP-Sales

GREEN ARROW:
HEADING INTO THE LIGHT

DC Comics, 1700 Broadway,
New York, NY 10019
A Warner Bros. Entertainment
Company
Printed in Canada.
First Printing.
ISBN: 1-4012-1094-5
ISBN 13: 978-1-4012-1094-6

Cover illustration by Scott McDaniel
and Andy Owens.
Cover color by Guy Major.

HE STORY THUS FAR...

Despite his misgivings, Oliver Queen is persuaded to allow young Mia Dearden, former runaway and now ward of the Emerald Archer, to join the Green Team. Reinventing herself as Green Arrow's new-and-improved sidekick Speedy, her life is given new meaning and purpose after she is diagnosed HIV positive. Green Arrow sends Speedy on a crash course training mission with the Teen Titans in order to test her mettle. At Titans Tower, rigorous training reveals her impressive maturity and natural skill as a crimefighter.

Roy Harper, Green Arrow's former sidekick, the formidable Arsenal, disapproves of Green Arrow's plan, fearful that Mia is too young and inexperienced for life behind the mask.

When disaster strikes Star City, with the appearance of adversaries Brick and the Duke of Oil, Mia gets the opportunity to show what a true asset she can be. But, before the Green Team can get even a moment's rest, the diminutive but deadly Constantine Drakon enters the scene seeking revenge against Ollie by kidnapping Arsenal.

Connor Hawke, Green Arrow's son, joins in the mission that succeeds in rescuing Arsenal. But just as Ollie's "family" is reunited, tragedy strikes as their home explodes in a ferocious fireball.

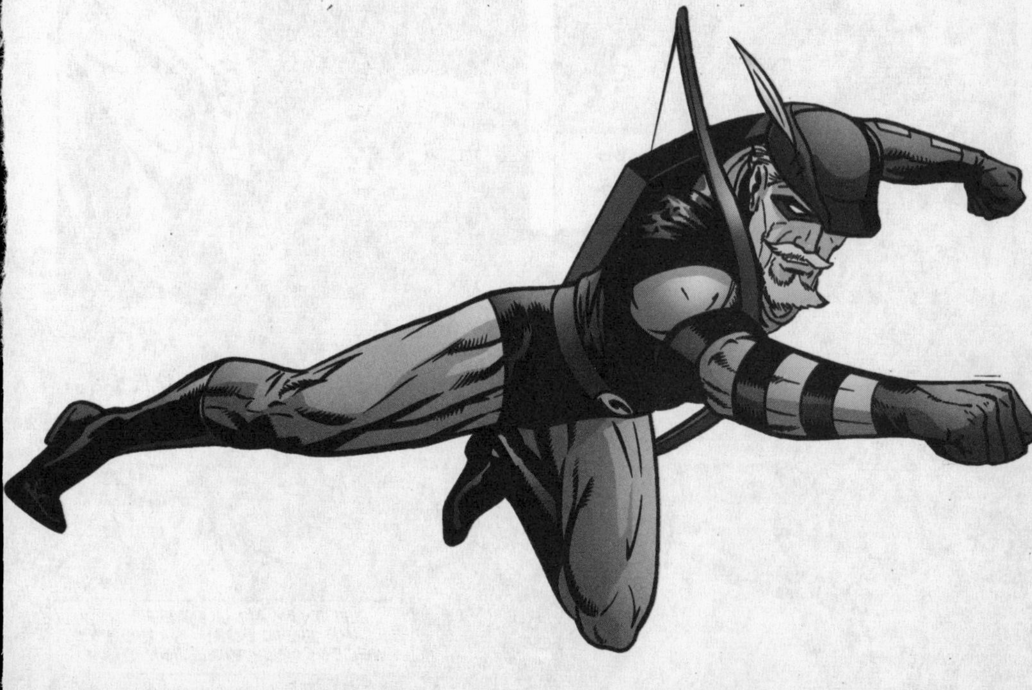

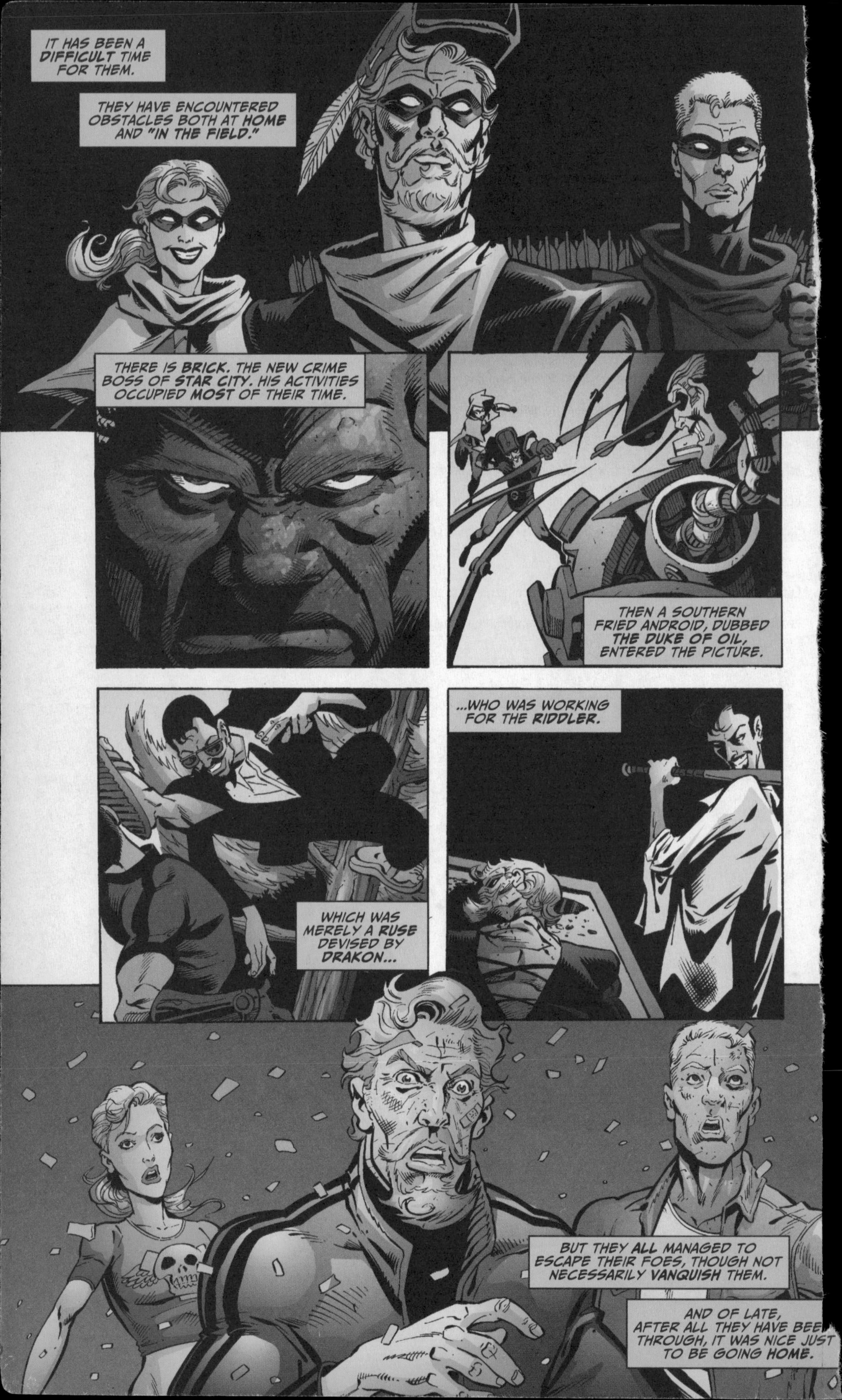
IT HAS BEEN A DIFFICULT TIME FOR THEM.
THEY HAVE ENCOUNTERED OBSTACLES BOTH AT HOME AND "IN THE FIELD."
THERE IS BRICK. THE NEW CRIME BOSS OF STAR CITY. HIS ACTIVITIES OCCUPIED MOST OF THEIR TIME.
THEN A SOUTHERN FRIED ANDROID, DUBBED THE DUKE OF OIL, ENTERED THE PICTURE.
WHICH WAS MERELY A RUSE DEVISED BY DRAKON...
...WHO WAS WORKING FOR THE RIDDLER.
BUT THEY ALL MANAGED TO ESCAPE THEIR FOES, THOUGH NOT NECESSARILY VANQUISH THEM.
AND OF LATE, AFTER ALL THEY HAVE BEE THROUGH, IT WAS NICE JUST TO BE GOING HOME.

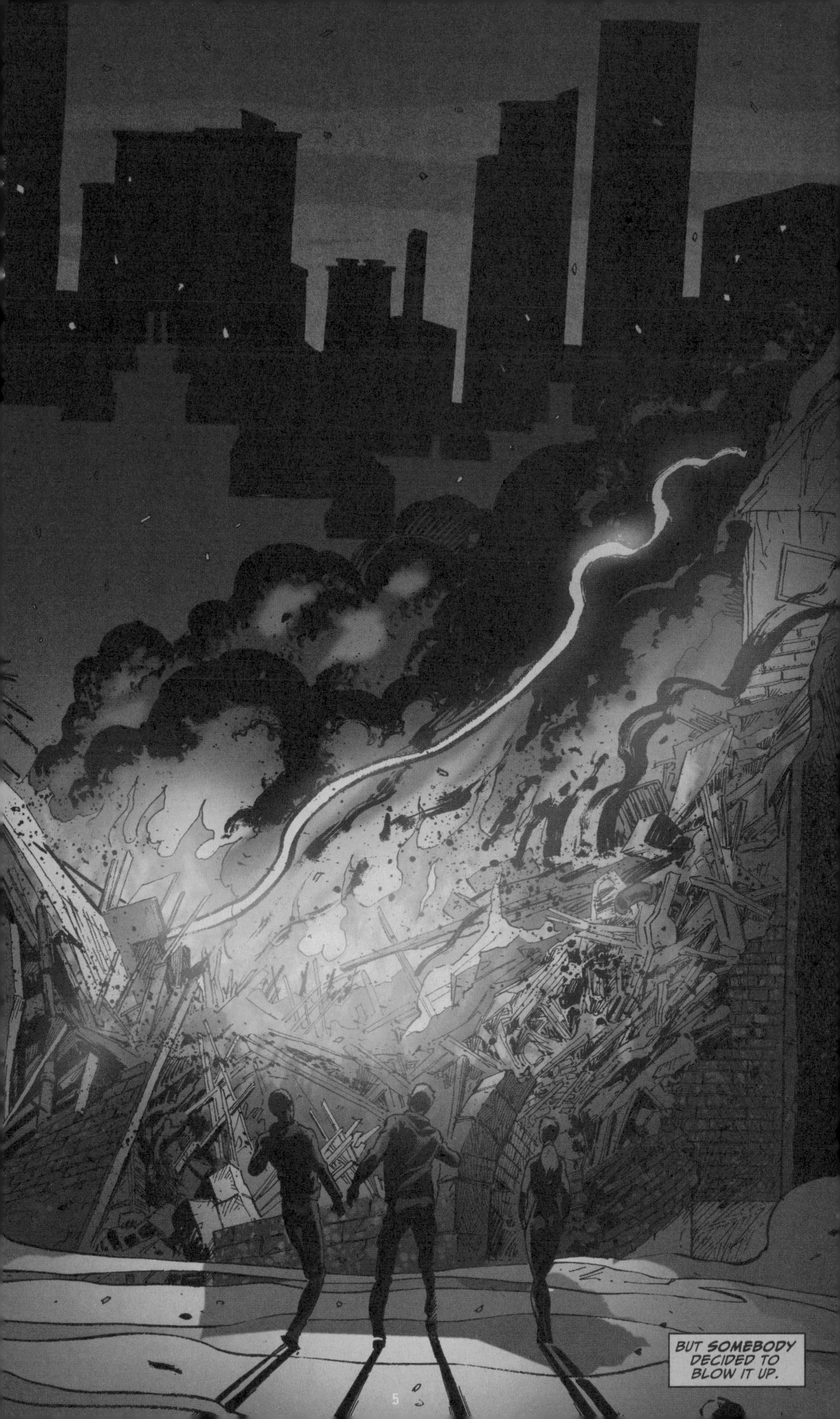
BUT SOMEBODY DECIDED TO BLOW IT UP.

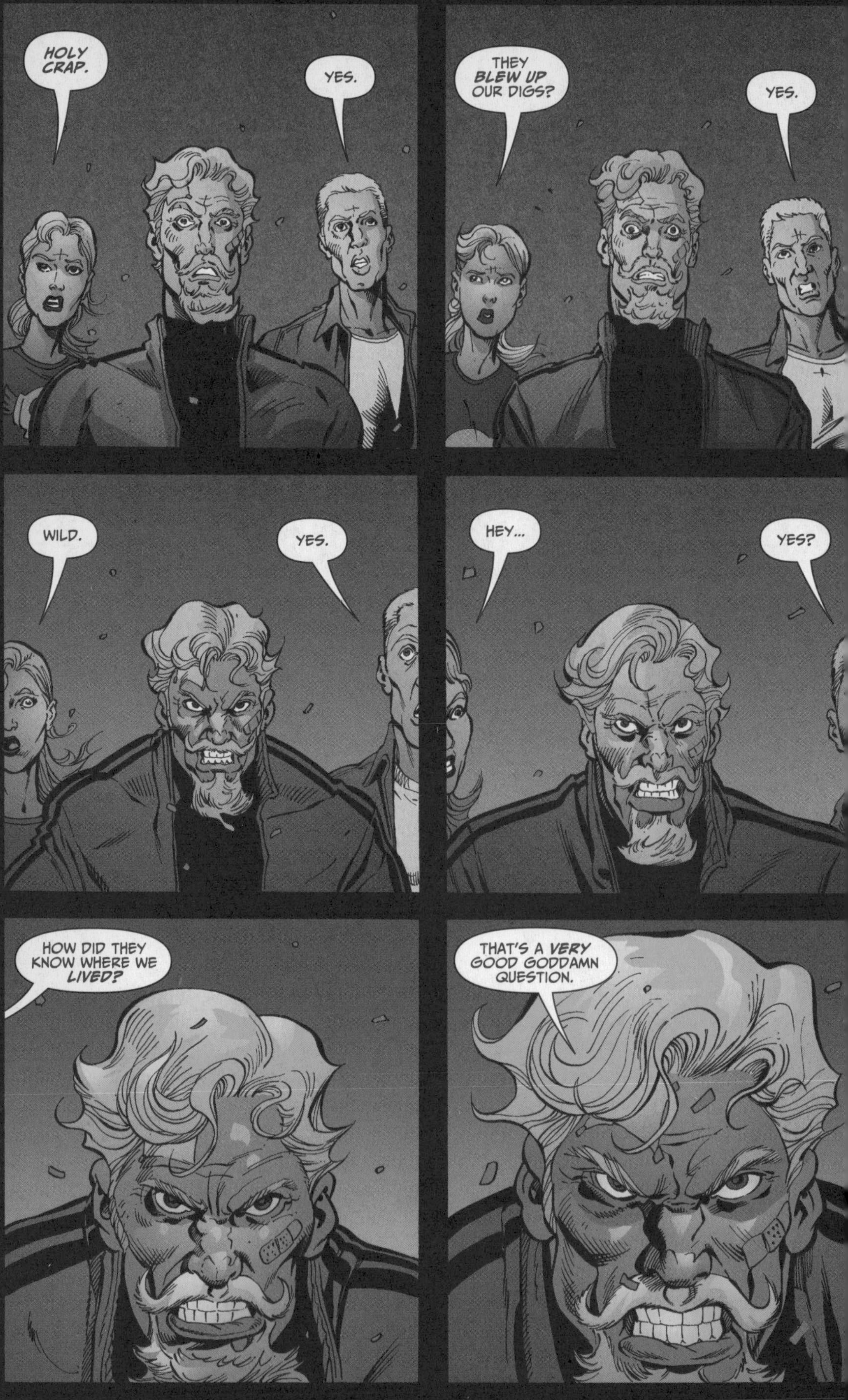

HOLY CRAP.
YES.
THEY BLEW UP OUR DIGS?
YES.
WILD.
YES.
HEY...
YES?
HOW DID THEY KNOW WHERE WE LIVED?
THAT'S A VERY GOOD GODDAMN QUESTION.

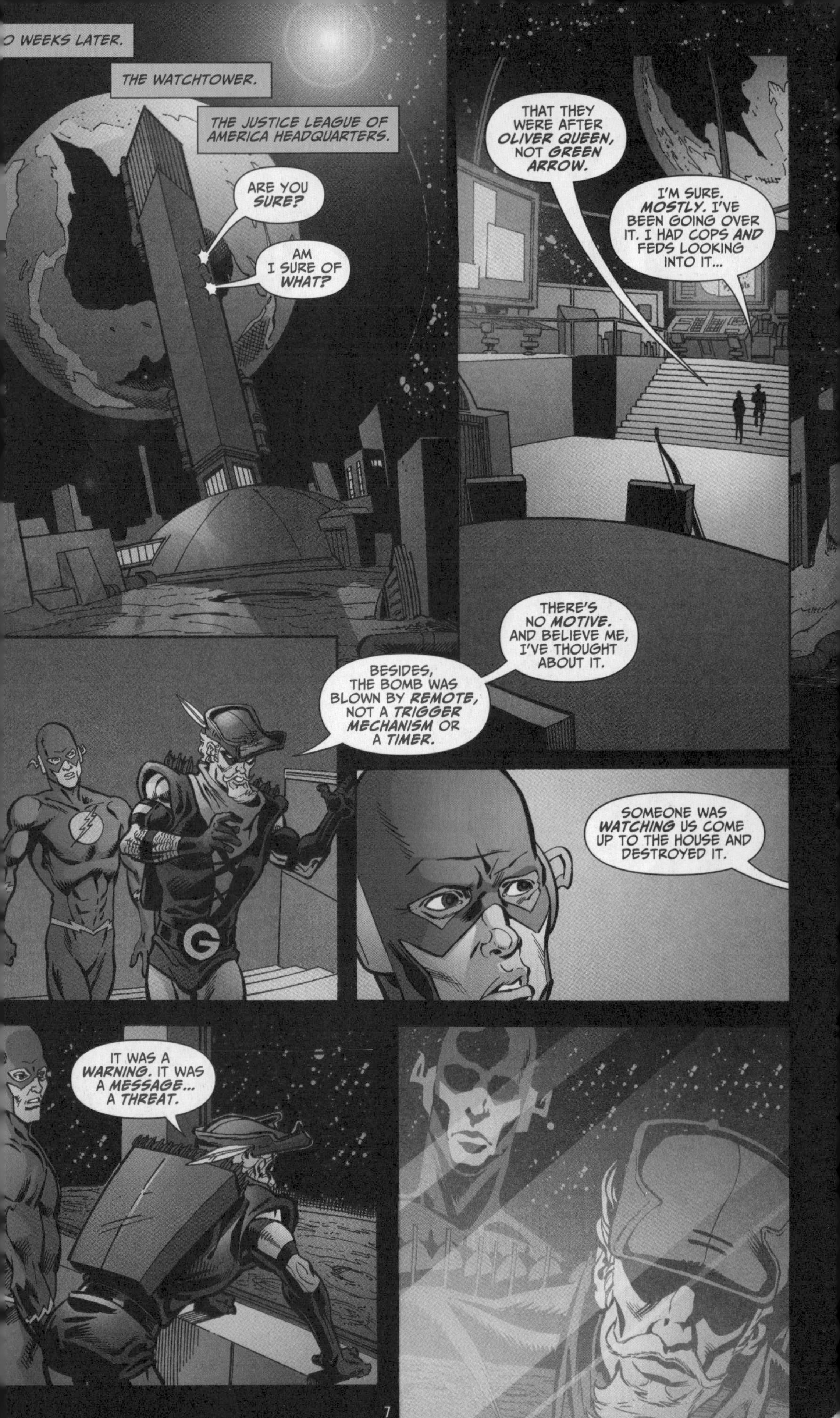
O WEEKS LATER.
THE WATCHTOWER.
THE JUSTICE LEAGUE OF AMERICA HEADQUARTERS.
ARE YOU SURE?
AM I SURE OF WHAT?
THAT THEY WERE AFTER OLIVER QUEEN, NOT GREEN ARROW.
I'M SURE. MOSTLY. I'VE BEEN GOING OVER IT. I HAD COPS AND FEDS LOOKING INTO IT...
THERE'S NO MOTIVE. AND BELIEVE ME, I'VE THOUGHT ABOUT IT.
BESIDES, THE BOMB WAS BLOWN BY REMOTE, NOT A TRIGGER MECHANISM OR A TIMER.
SOMEONE WAS WATCHING US COME UP TO THE HOUSE AND DESTROYED IT.
IT WAS A WARNING. IT WAS A MESSAGE... A THREAT.

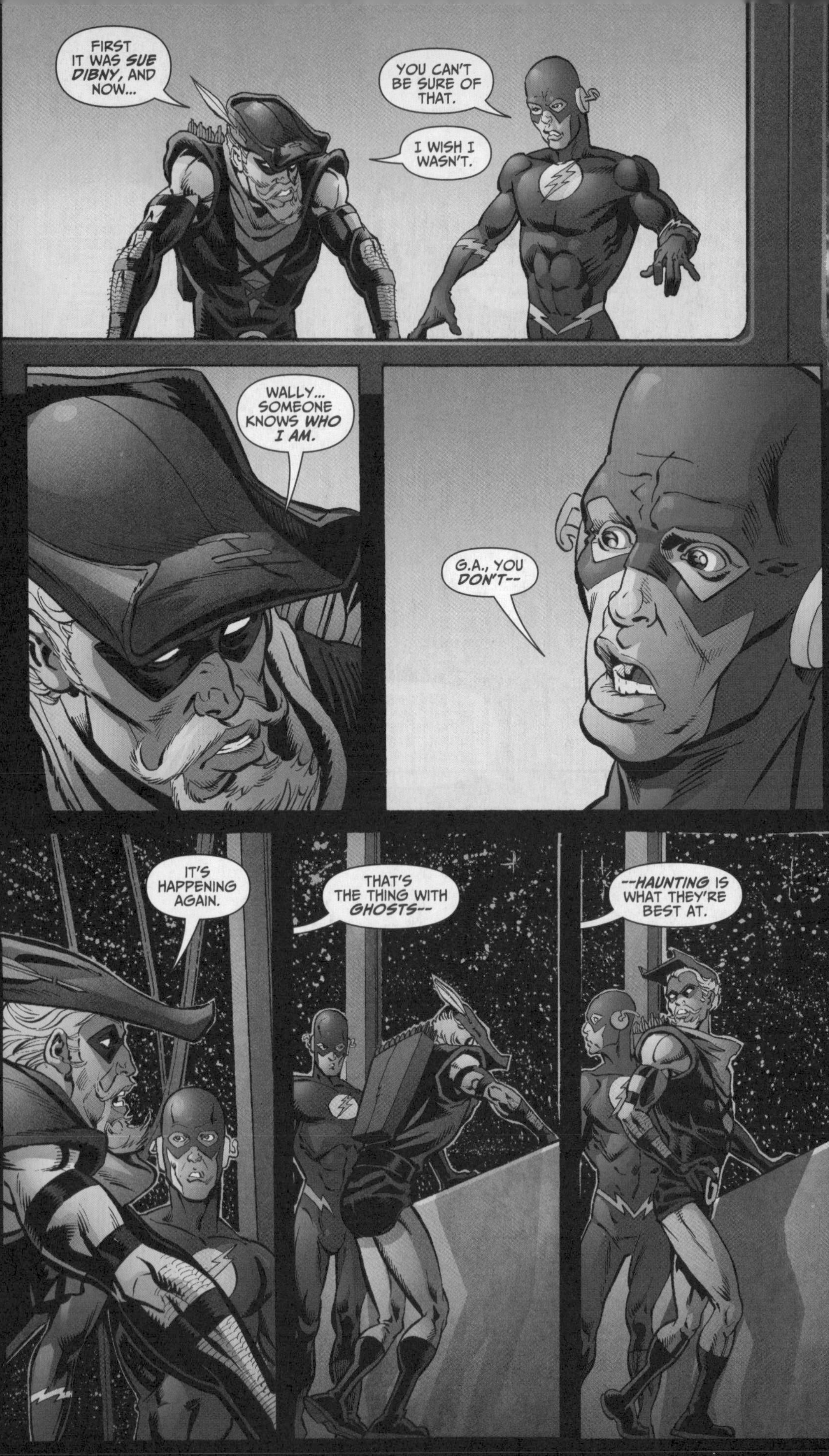
FIRST IT WAS *SUE DIBNY*, AND NOW...
YOU CAN'T BE SURE OF THAT.
I WISH I WASN'T.
WALLY... SOMEONE KNOWS *WHO I AM.*
G.A., YOU *DON'T*--
IT'S HAPPENING AGAIN.
THAT'S THE THING WITH *GHOSTS*--
--*HAUNTING* IS WHAT THEY'RE BEST AT.

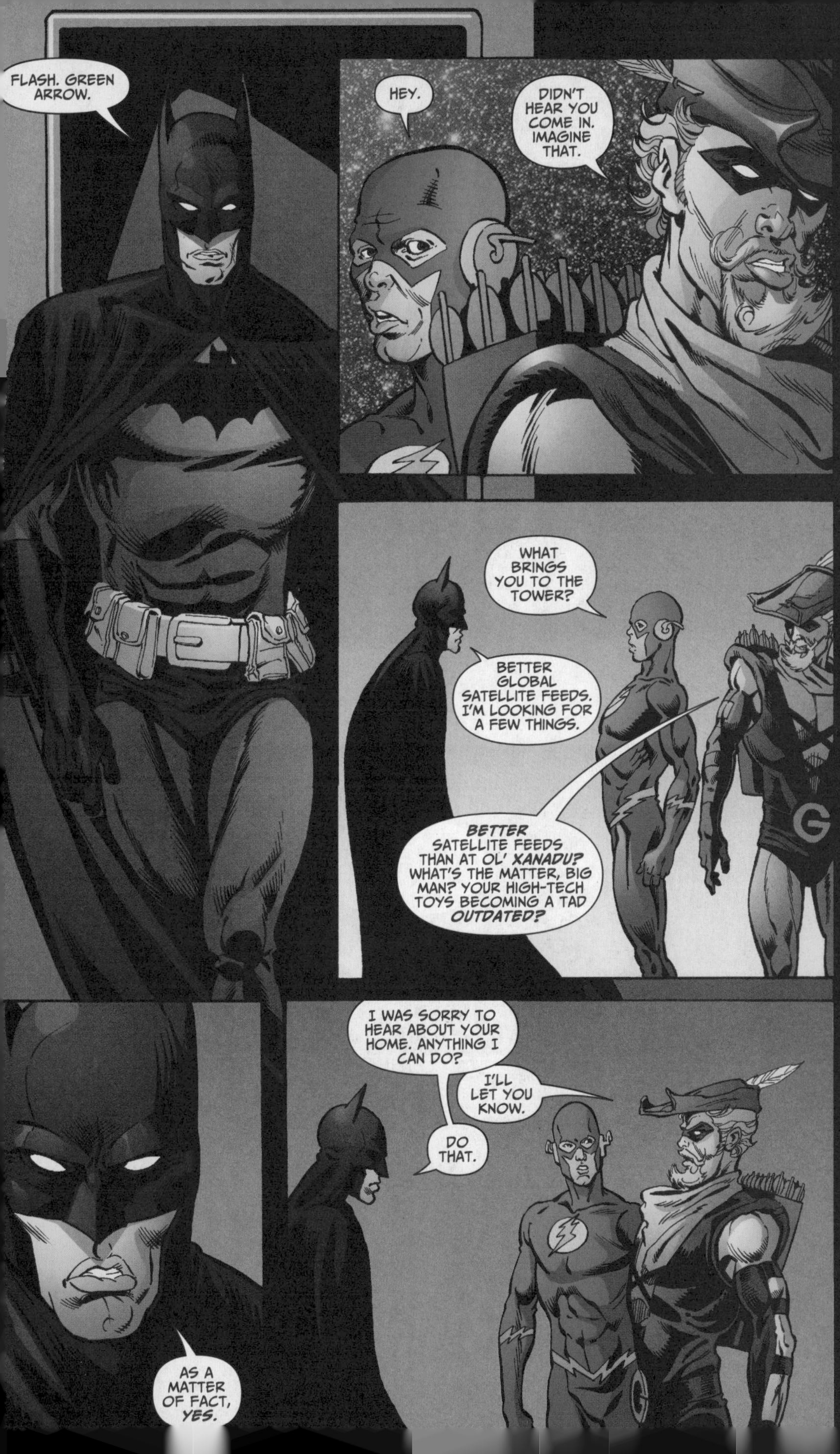
FLASH. GREEN ARROW.
HEY.
DIDN'T HEAR YOU COME IN. IMAGINE THAT.
WHAT BRINGS YOU TO THE TOWER?
BETTER GLOBAL SATELLITE FEEDS. I'M LOOKING FOR A FEW THINGS.
BETTER SATELLITE FEEDS THAN AT OL' *XANADU?* WHAT'S THE MATTER, BIG MAN? YOUR HIGH-TECH TOYS BECOMING A TAD *OUTDATED?*
AS A MATTER OF FACT, *YES.*
I WAS SORRY TO HEAR ABOUT YOUR HOME. ANYTHING I CAN DO?
I'LL LET YOU KNOW.
DO THAT.

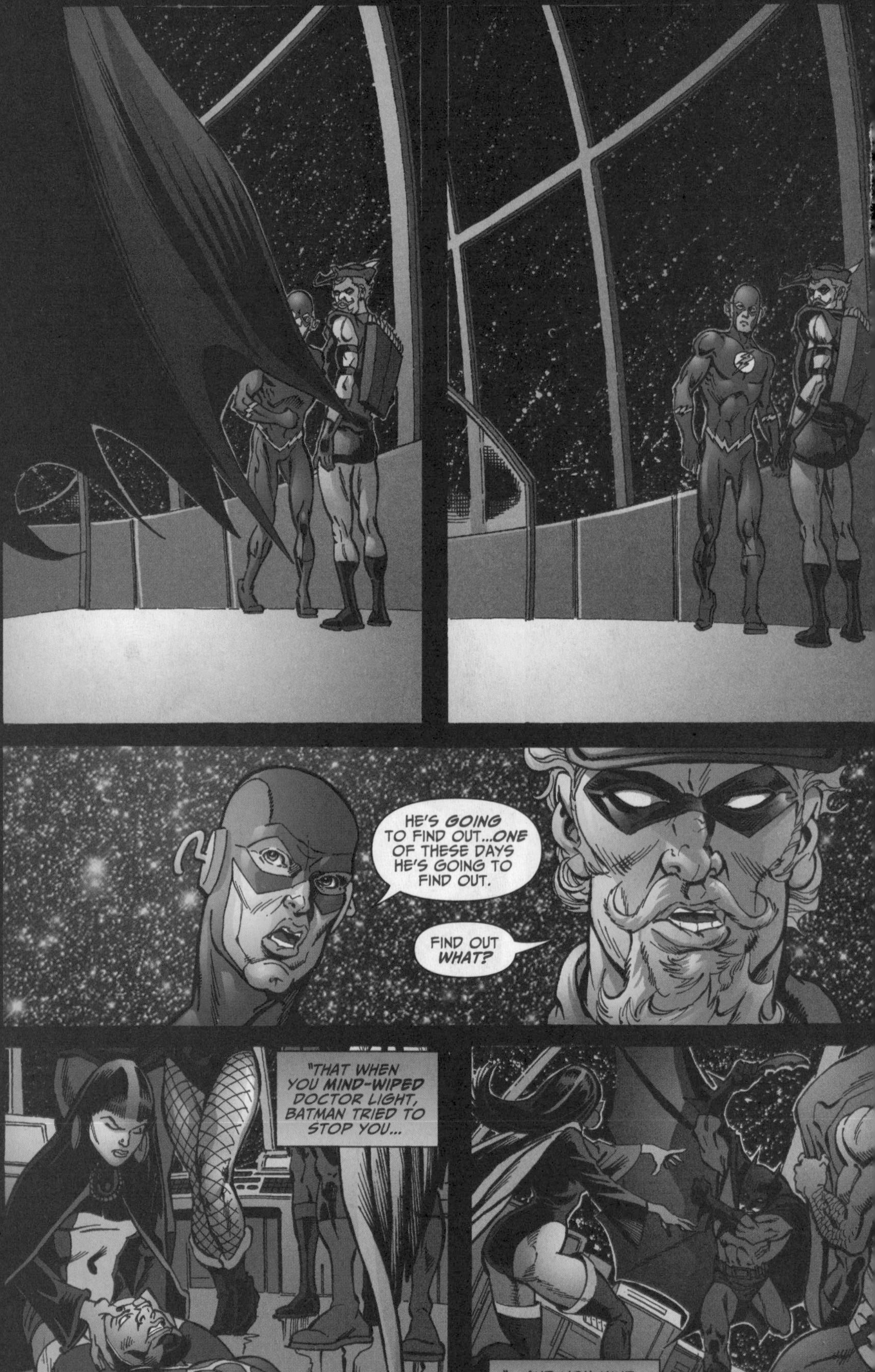
HE'S GOING TO FIND OUT...ONE OF THESE DAYS HE'S GOING TO FIND OUT.
FIND OUT WHAT?
"THAT WHEN YOU MIND-WIPED DOCTOR LIGHT, BATMAN TRIED TO STOP YOU...
"...AND YOU MIND-WIPED HIM, TOO."

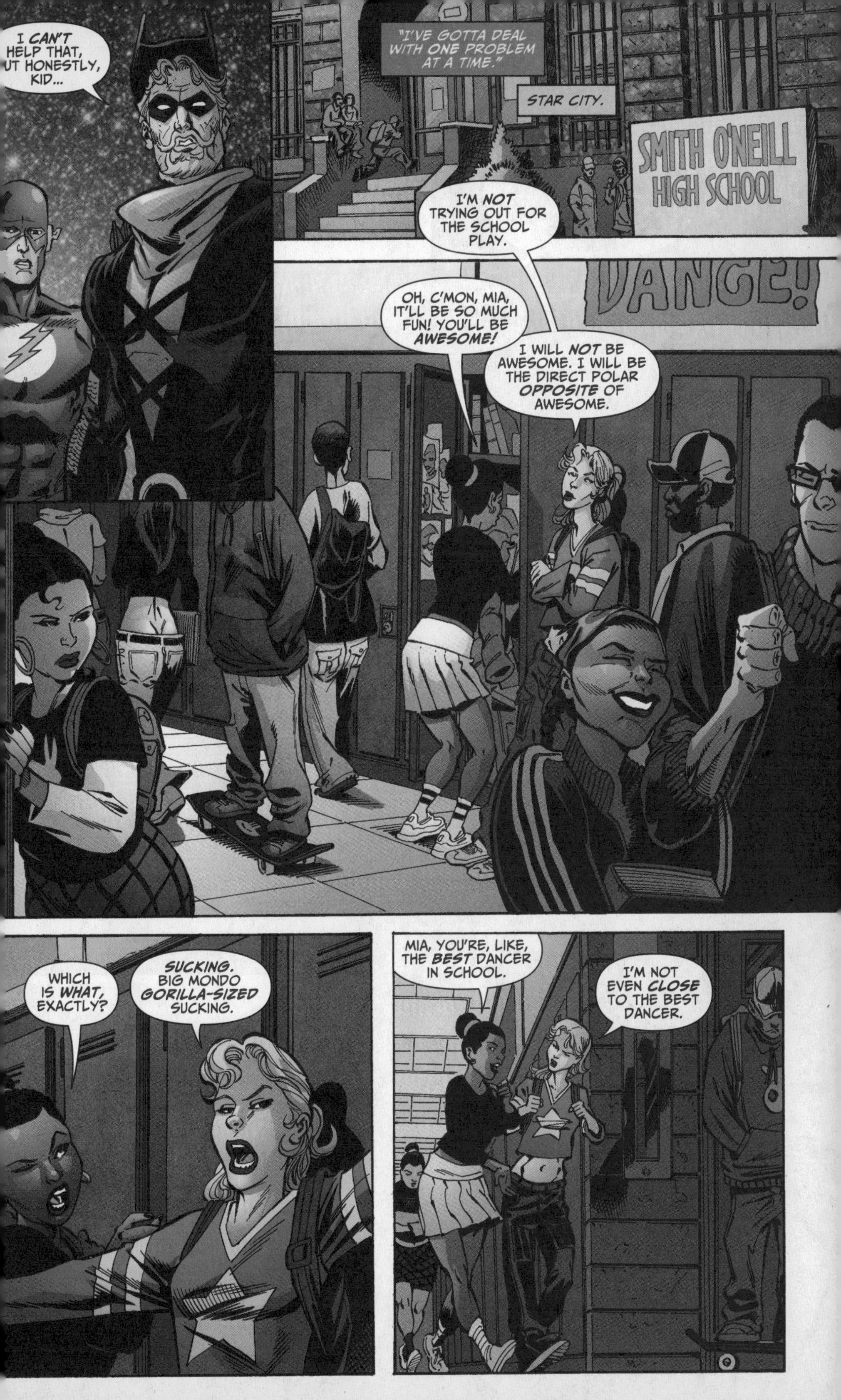

I CAN'T HELP THAT, BUT HONESTLY, KID...
"I'VE GOTTA DEAL WITH ONE PROBLEM AT A TIME."
STAR CITY.
SMITH O'NEILL HIGH SCHOOL
I'M NOT TRYING OUT FOR THE SCHOOL PLAY.
DANCE!
OH, C'MON, MIA, IT'LL BE SO MUCH FUN! YOU'LL BE AWESOME!
I WILL NOT BE AWESOME. I WILL BE THE DIRECT POLAR OPPOSITE OF AWESOME.
WHICH IS WHAT, EXACTLY?
SUCKING. BIG MONDO GORILLA-SIZED SUCKING.
MIA, YOU'RE, LIKE, THE BEST DANCER IN SCHOOL.
I'M NOT EVEN CLOSE TO THE BEST DANCER.

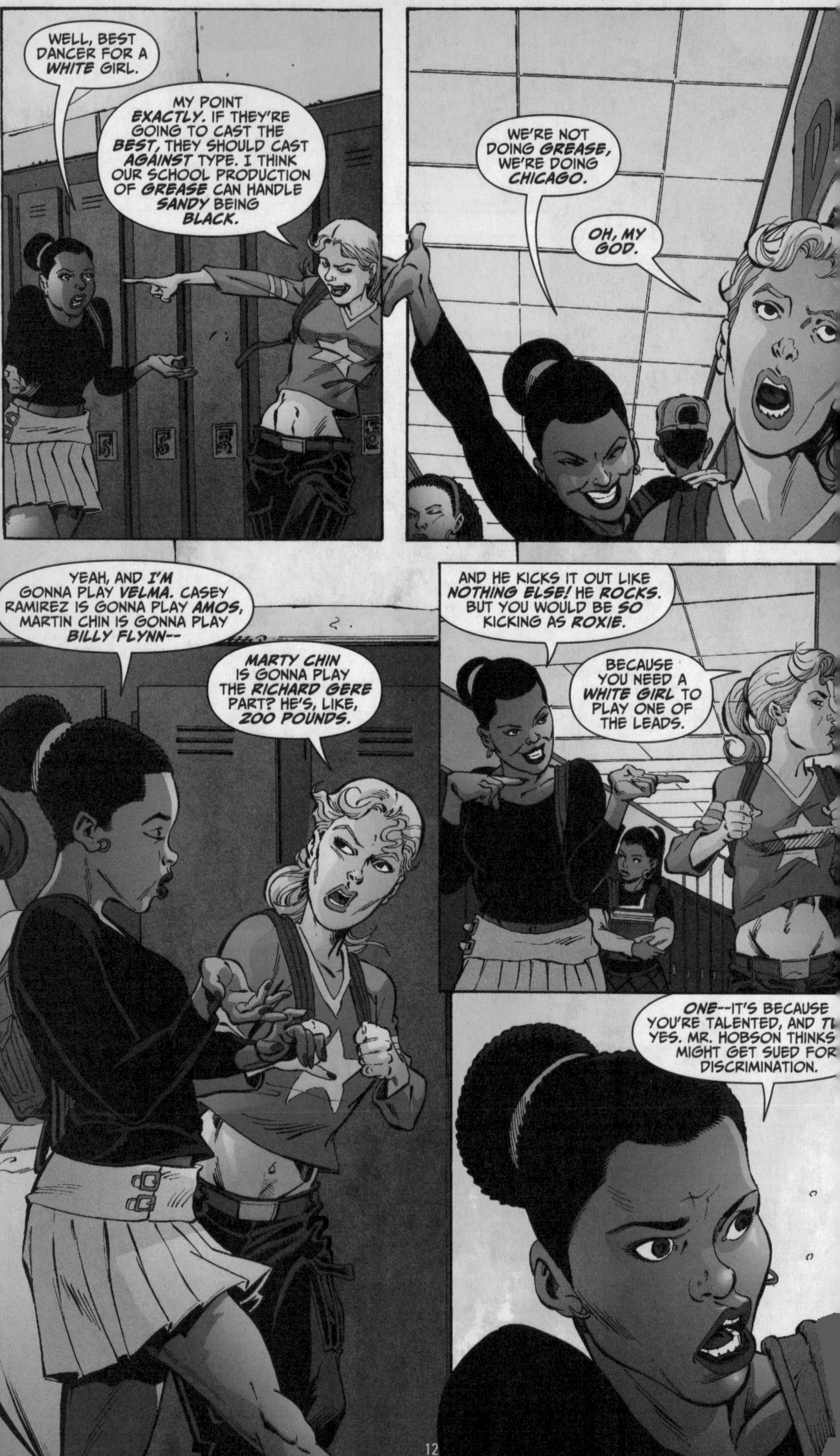
WELL, BEST DANCER FOR A WHITE GIRL.
MY POINT EXACTLY. IF THEY'RE GOING TO CAST THE BEST, THEY SHOULD CAST AGAINST TYPE. I THINK OUR SCHOOL PRODUCTION OF GREASE CAN HANDLE SANDY BEING BLACK.
WE'RE NOT DOING GREASE, WE'RE DOING CHICAGO.
OH, MY GOD.
YEAH, AND I'M GONNA PLAY VELMA. CASEY RAMIREZ IS GONNA PLAY AMOS, MARTIN CHIN IS GONNA PLAY BILLY FLYNN--
MARTY CHIN IS GONNA PLAY THE RICHARD GERE PART? HE'S, LIKE, 200 POUNDS.
AND HE KICKS IT OUT LIKE NOTHING ELSE! HE ROCKS. BUT YOU WOULD BE SO KICKING AS ROXIE.
BECAUSE YOU NEED A WHITE GIRL TO PLAY ONE OF THE LEADS.
ONE--IT'S BECAUSE YOU'RE TALENTED, AND T YES. MR. HOBSON THINKS MIGHT GET SUED FOR DISCRIMINATION.

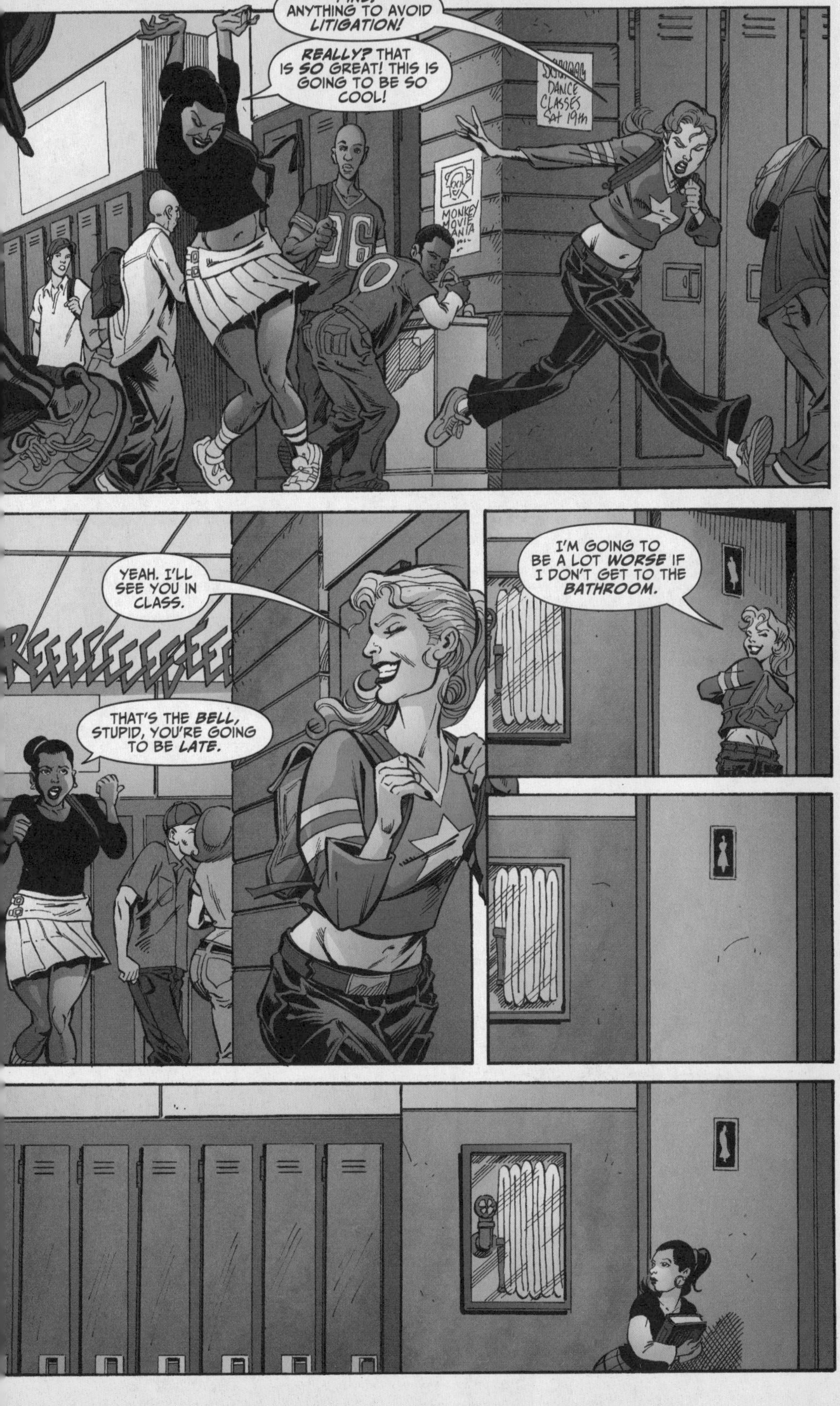
FINE! ANYTHING TO AVOID LITIGATION!
REALLY? THAT IS SO GREAT! THIS IS GOING TO BE SO COOL!
DANCE CLASSES Sat 19th
MONKEY MOVIE MANIA
YEAH. I'LL SEE YOU IN CLASS.
THAT'S THE BELL, STUPID, YOU'RE GOING TO BE LATE.
I'M GOING TO BE A LOT WORSE IF I DON'T GET TO THE BATHROOM.

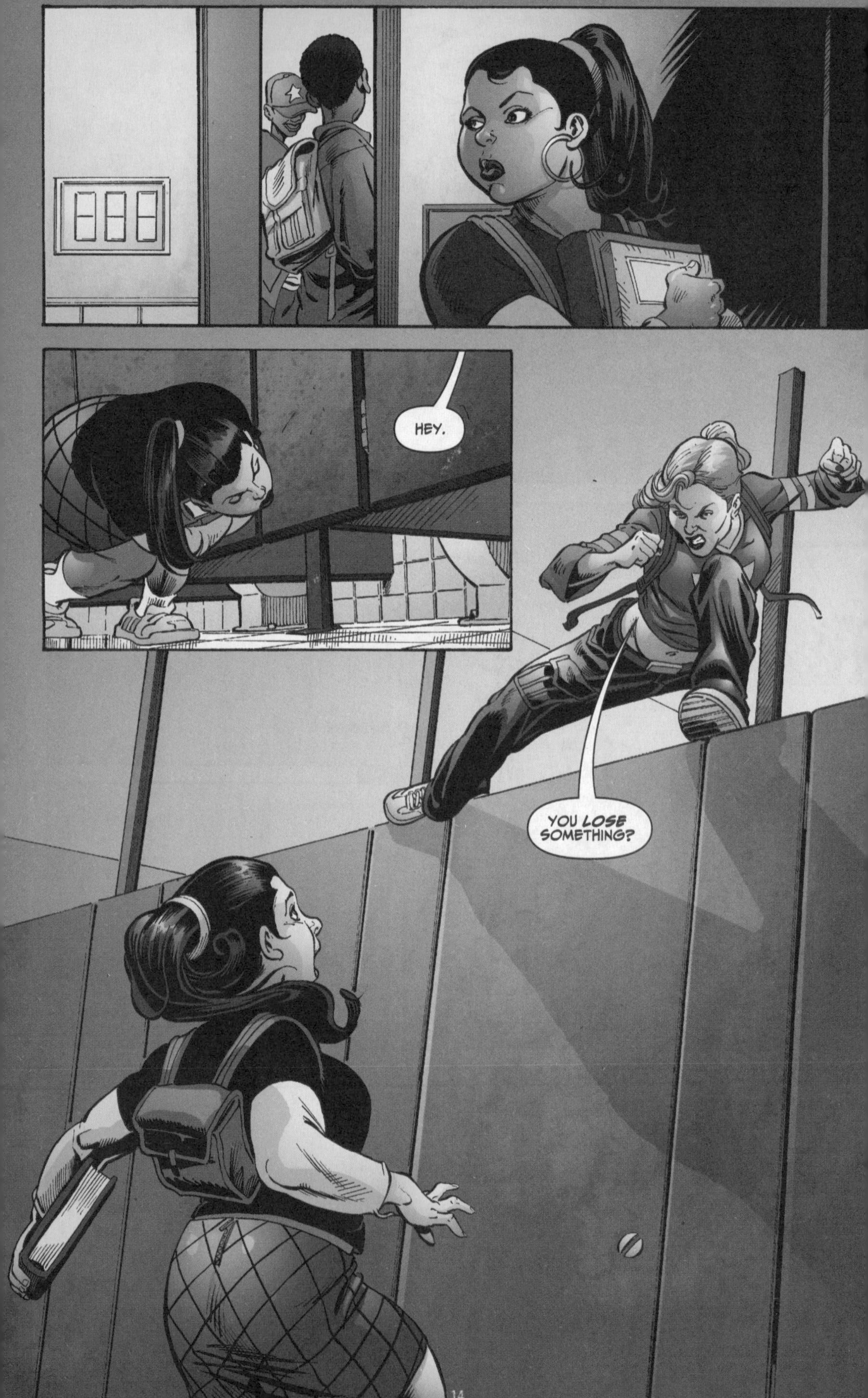
HEY.
YOU LOSE SOMETHING?

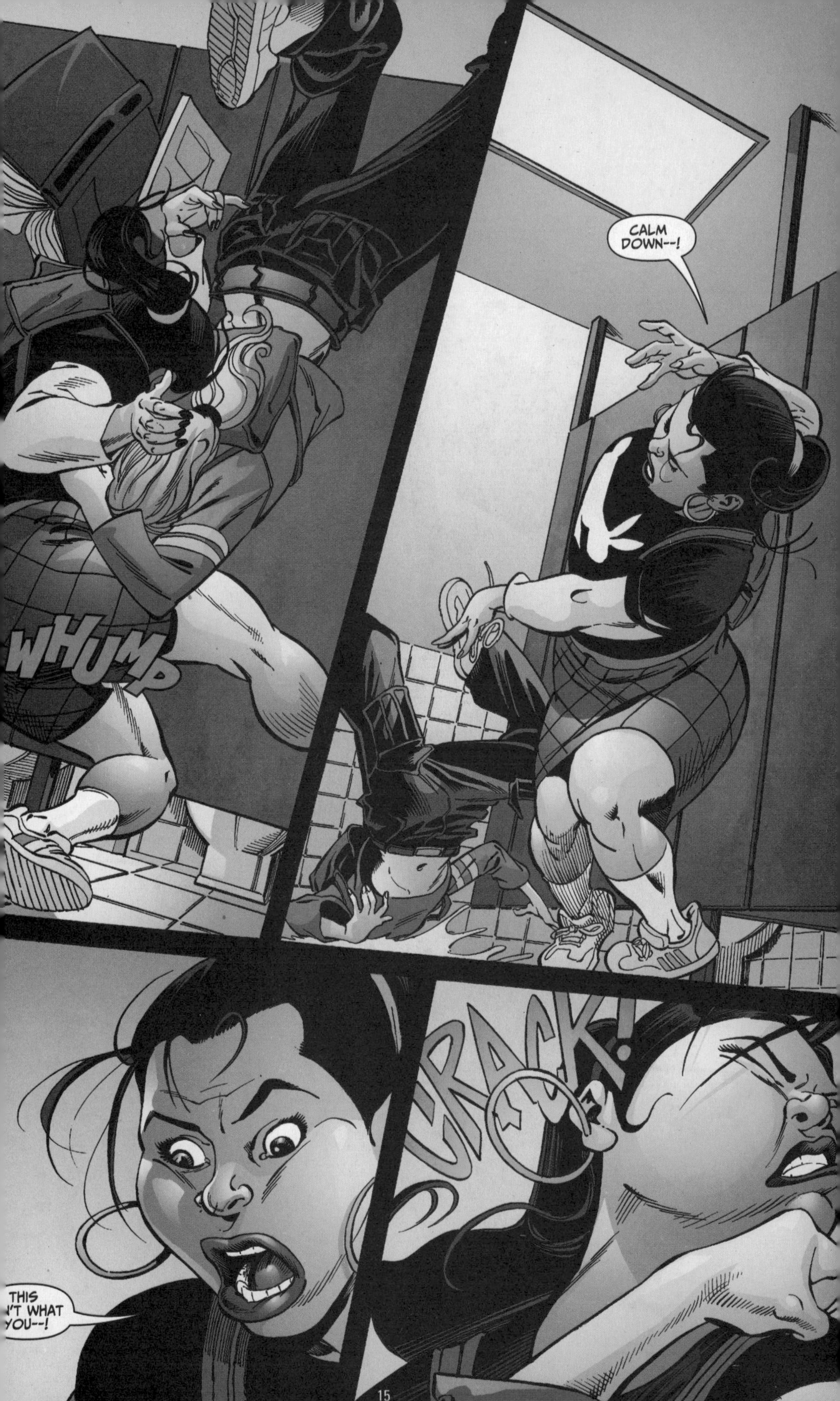
CALM DOWN--!
WHUMP
CRACK!
THIS
'T WHAT
YOU--!

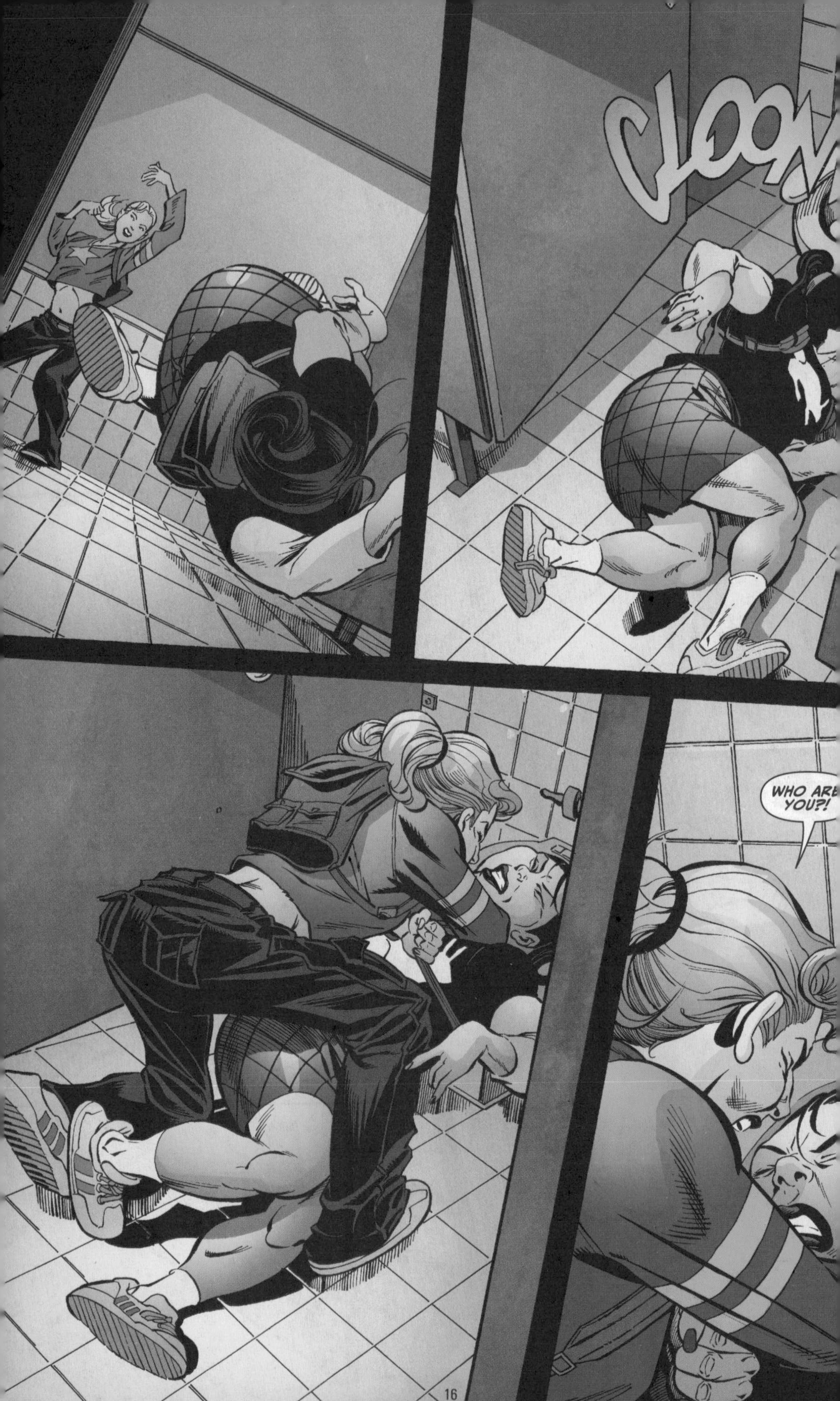
CLOOM
WHO ARE YOU?!

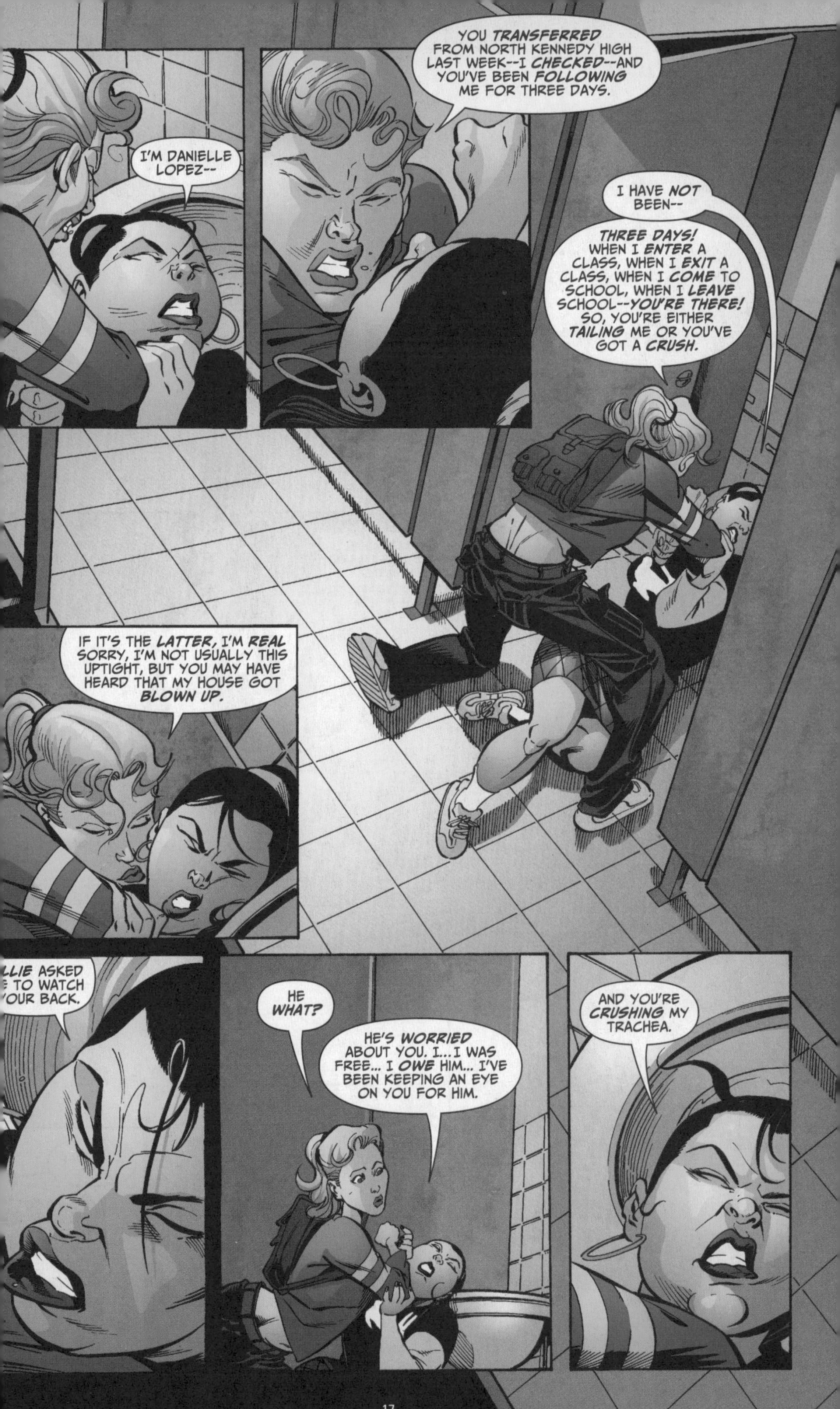
I'M DANIELLE LOPEZ--
YOU TRANSFERRED FROM NORTH KENNEDY HIGH LAST WEEK--I CHECKED--AND YOU'VE BEEN FOLLOWING ME FOR THREE DAYS.
I HAVE NOT BEEN--
THREE DAYS! WHEN I ENTER A CLASS, WHEN I EXIT A CLASS, WHEN I COME TO SCHOOL, WHEN I LEAVE SCHOOL--YOU'RE THERE! SO, YOU'RE EITHER TAILING ME OR YOU'VE GOT A CRUSH.
IF IT'S THE LATTER, I'M REAL SORRY, I'M NOT USUALLY THIS UPTIGHT, BUT YOU MAY HAVE HEARD THAT MY HOUSE GOT BLOWN UP.
LLIE ASKED E TO WATCH OUR BACK.
HE WHAT?
HE'S WORRIED ABOUT YOU. I... I WAS FREE... I OWE HIM... I'VE BEEN KEEPING AN EYE ON YOU FOR HIM.
AND YOU'RE CRUSHING MY TRACHEA.

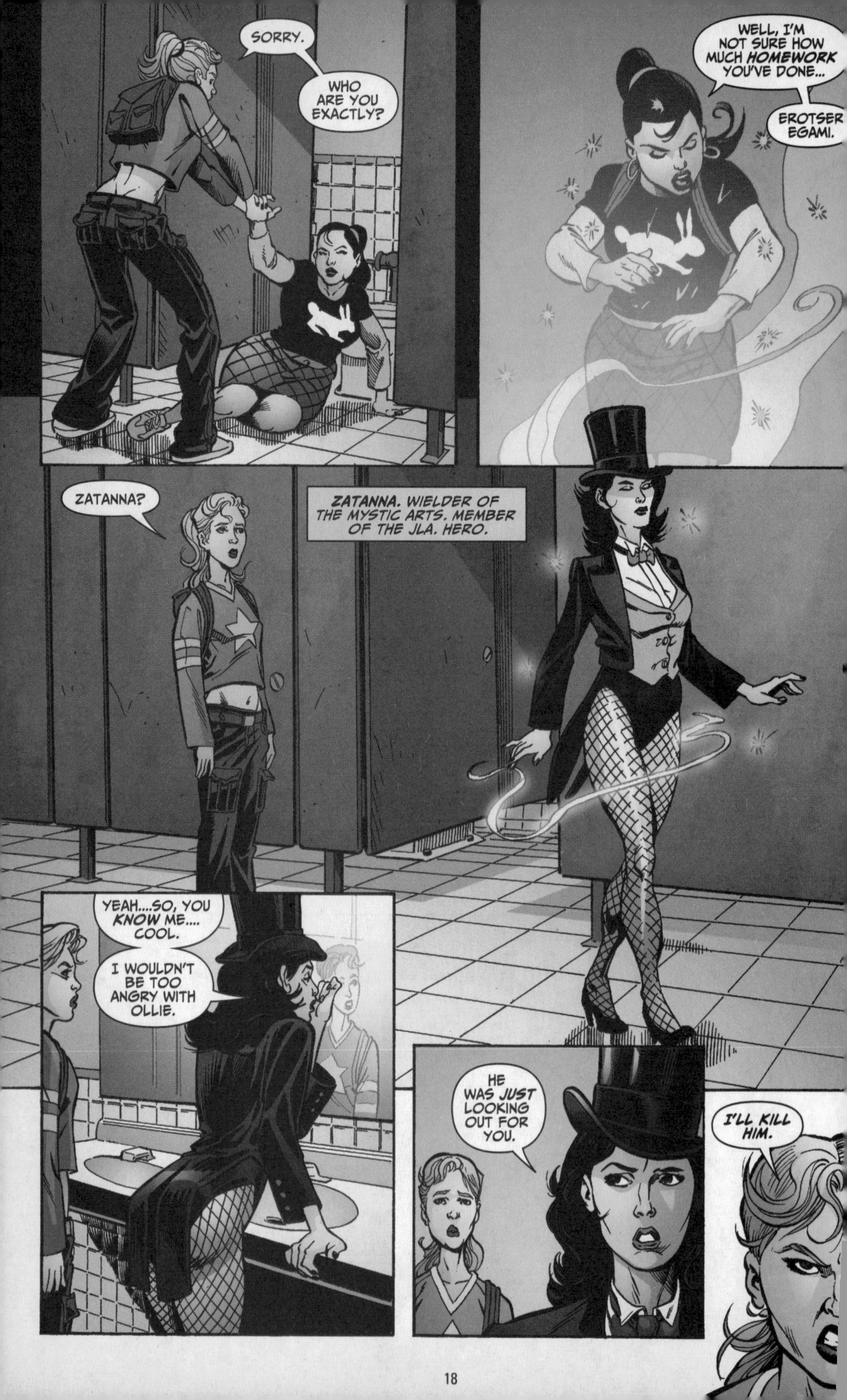

SORRY.
WHO ARE YOU EXACTLY?
WELL, I'M NOT SURE HOW MUCH HOMEWORK YOU'VE DONE...
EROTSER EGAMI.
ZATANNA?
ZATANNA. WIELDER OF THE MYSTIC ARTS. MEMBER OF THE JLA. HERO.
YEAH....SO, YOU KNOW ME.... COOL.
I WOULDN'T BE TOO ANGRY WITH OLLIE.
HE WAS JUST LOOKING OUT FOR YOU.
I'LL KILL HIM.

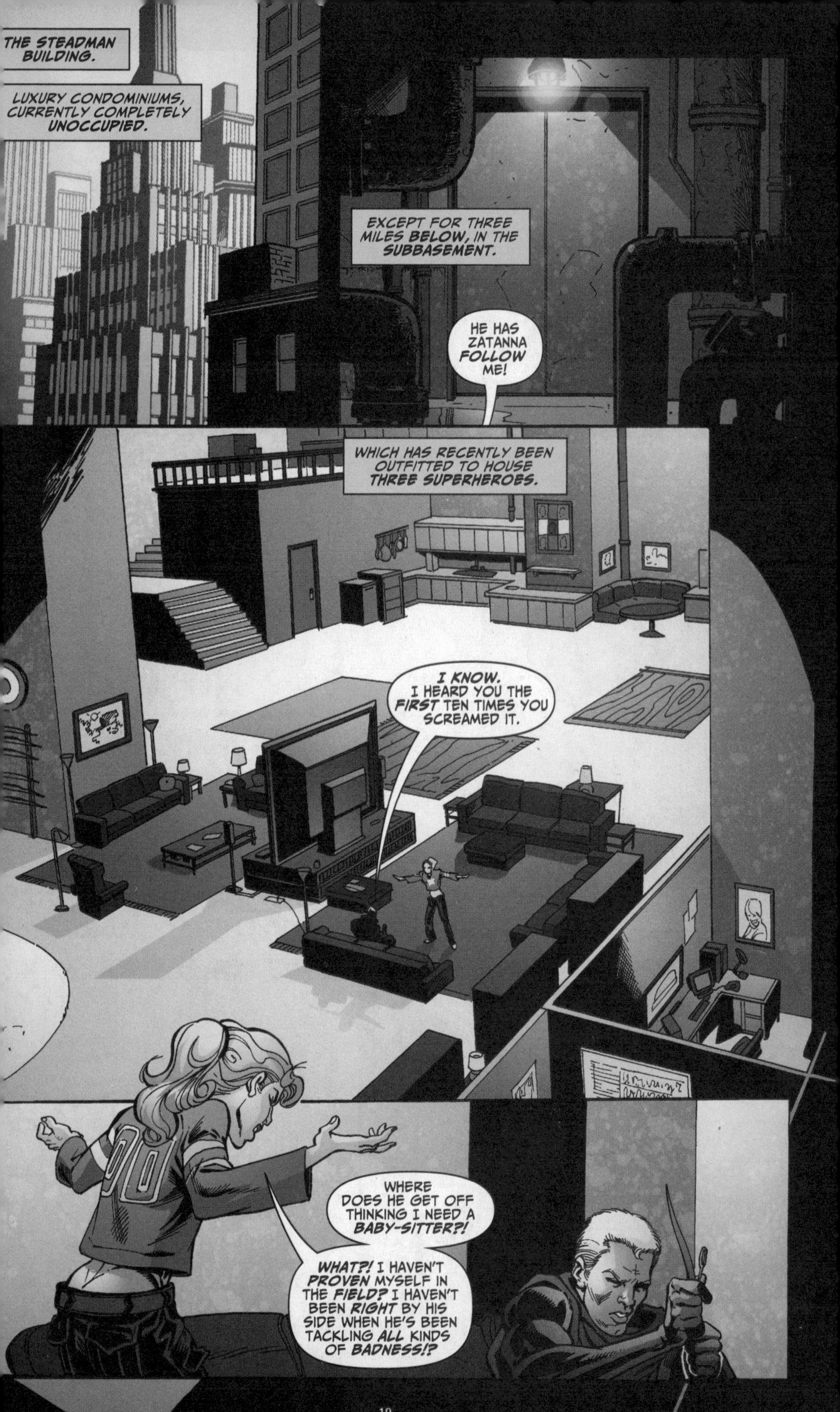

THE STEADMAN BUILDING.
LUXURY CONDOMINIUMS, CURRENTLY COMPLETELY UNOCCUPIED.
EXCEPT FOR THREE MILES BELOW, IN THE SUBBASEMENT.
HE HAS ZATANNA FOLLOW ME!
WHICH HAS RECENTLY BEEN OUTFITTED TO HOUSE THREE SUPERHEROES.
I KNOW. I HEARD YOU THE FIRST TEN TIMES YOU SCREAMED IT.
WHERE DOES HE GET OFF THINKING I NEED A BABY-SITTER?!
WHAT?! I HAVEN'T PROVEN MYSELF IN THE FIELD? I HAVEN'T BEEN RIGHT BY HIS SIDE WHEN HE'S BEEN TACKLING ALL KINDS OF BADNESS!?

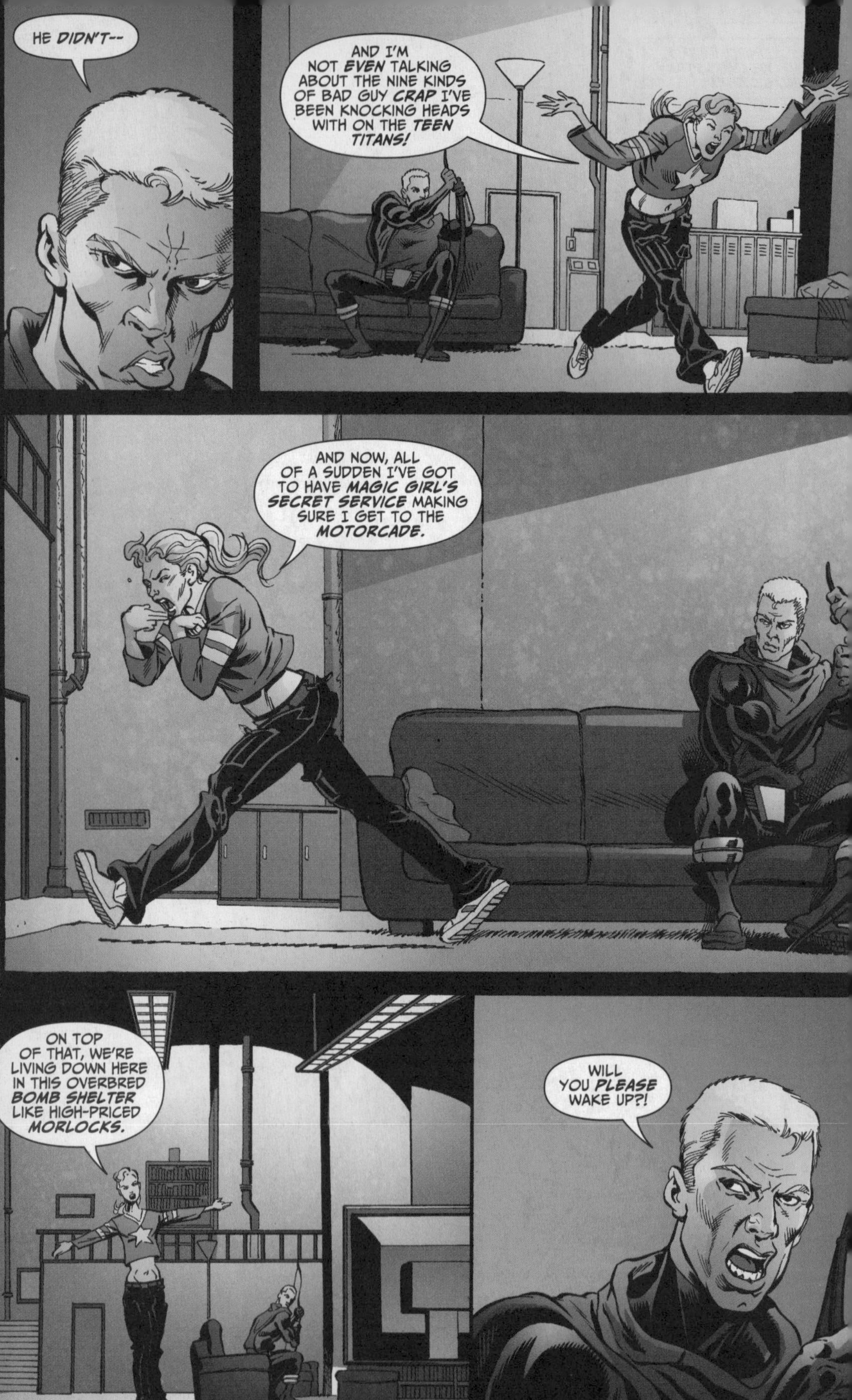
HE DIDN'T--
AND I'M NOT EVEN TALKING ABOUT THE NINE KINDS OF BAD GUY CRAP I'VE BEEN KNOCKING HEADS WITH ON THE TEEN TITANS!
AND NOW, ALL OF A SUDDEN I'VE GOT TO HAVE MAGIC GIRL'S SECRET SERVICE MAKING SURE I GET TO THE MOTORCADE.
ON TOP OF THAT, WE'RE LIVING DOWN HERE IN THIS OVERBRED BOMB SHELTER LIKE HIGH-PRICED MORLOCKS.
WILL YOU PLEASE WAKE UP?!

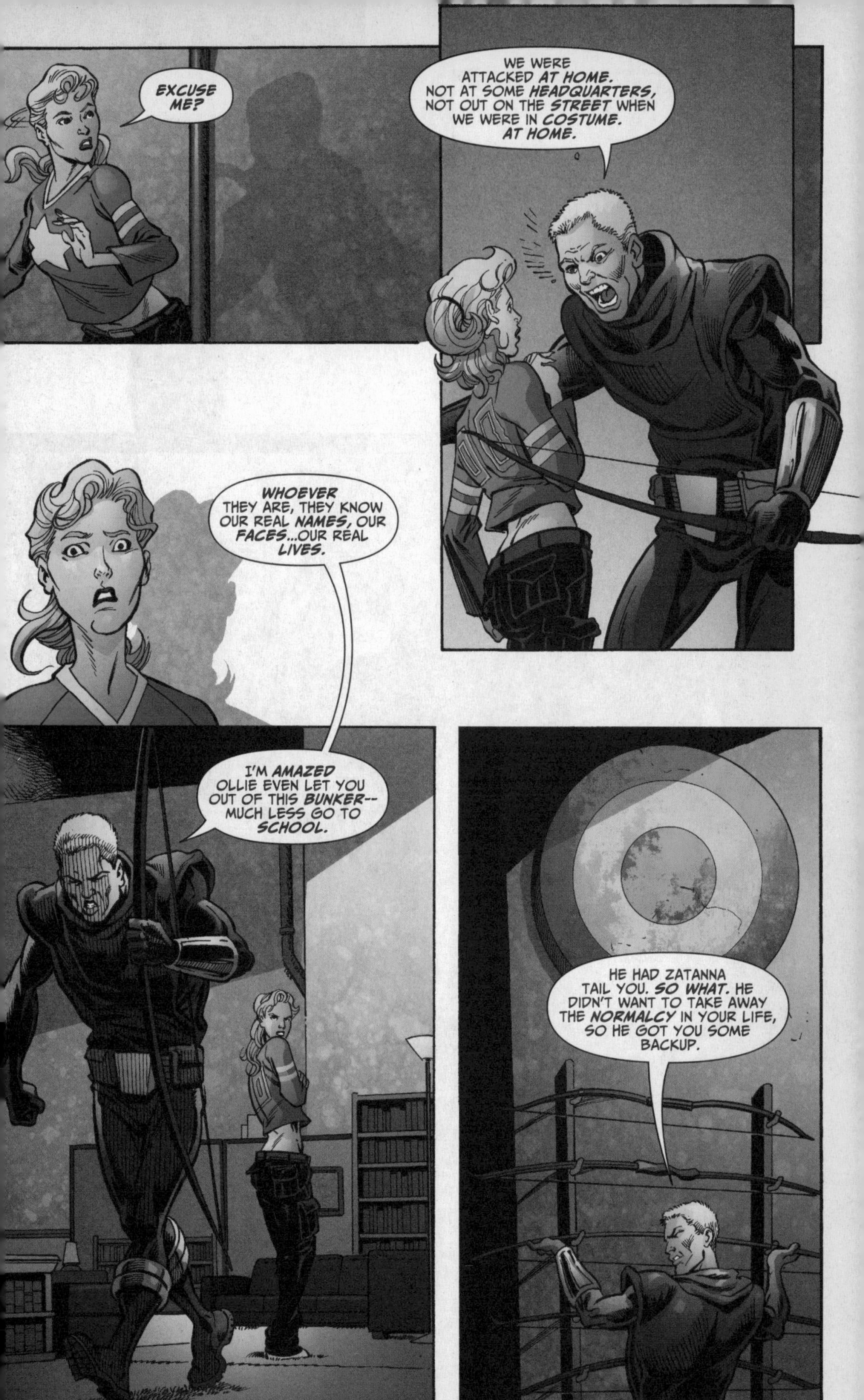
EXCUSE ME?
WE WERE ATTACKED AT HOME. NOT AT SOME HEADQUARTERS, NOT OUT ON THE STREET WHEN WE WERE IN COSTUME. AT HOME.
WHOEVER THEY ARE, THEY KNOW OUR REAL NAMES, OUR FACES...OUR REAL LIVES.
I'M AMAZED OLLIE EVEN LET YOU OUT OF THIS BUNKER-- MUCH LESS GO TO SCHOOL.
HE HAD ZATANNA TAIL YOU. SO WHAT. HE DIDN'T WANT TO TAKE AWAY THE NORMALCY IN YOUR LIFE, SO HE GOT YOU SOME BACKUP.

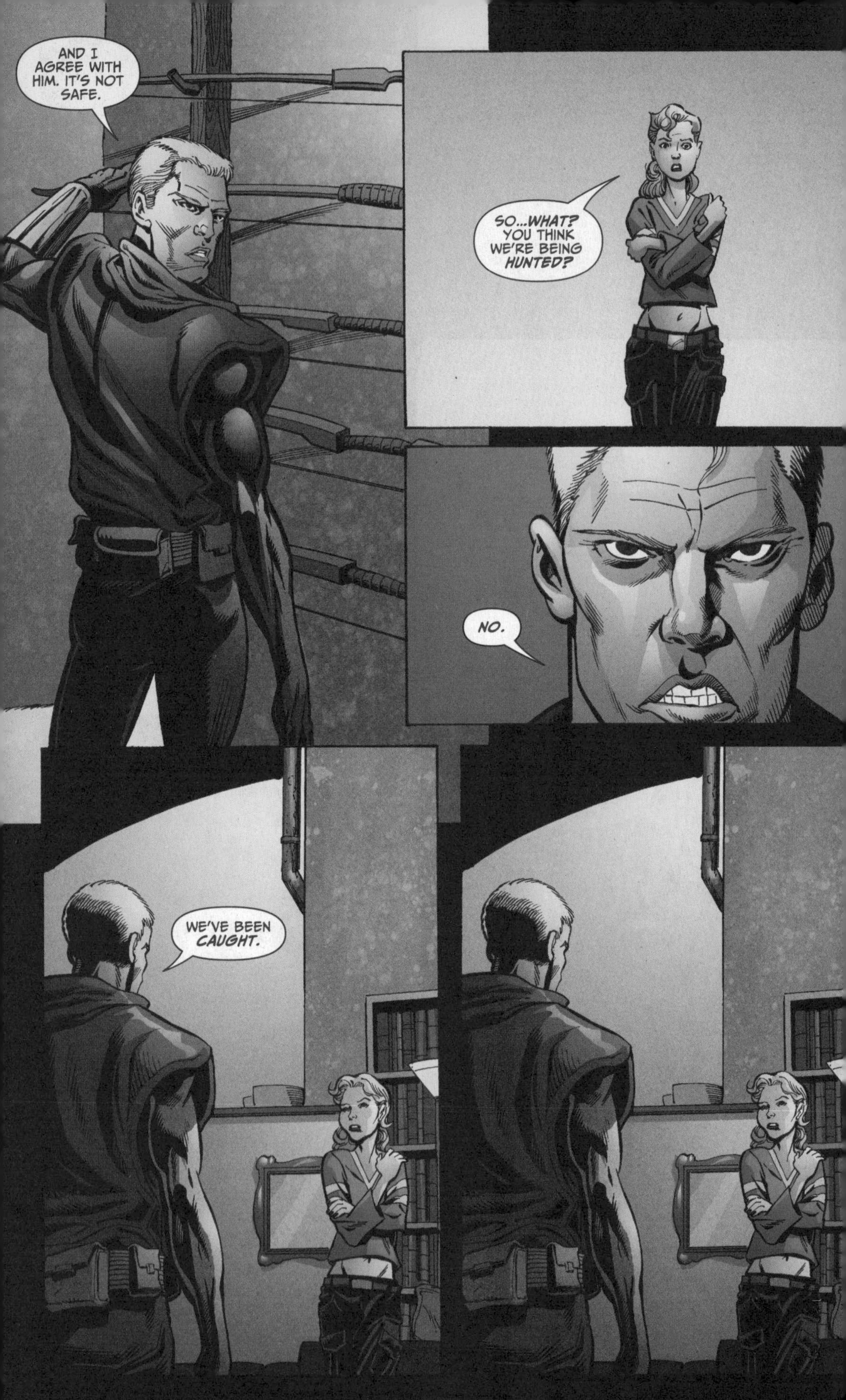
AND I AGREE WITH HIM. IT'S NOT SAFE.
SO...WHAT? YOU THINK WE'RE BEING HUNTED?
NO.
WE'VE BEEN CAUGHT.

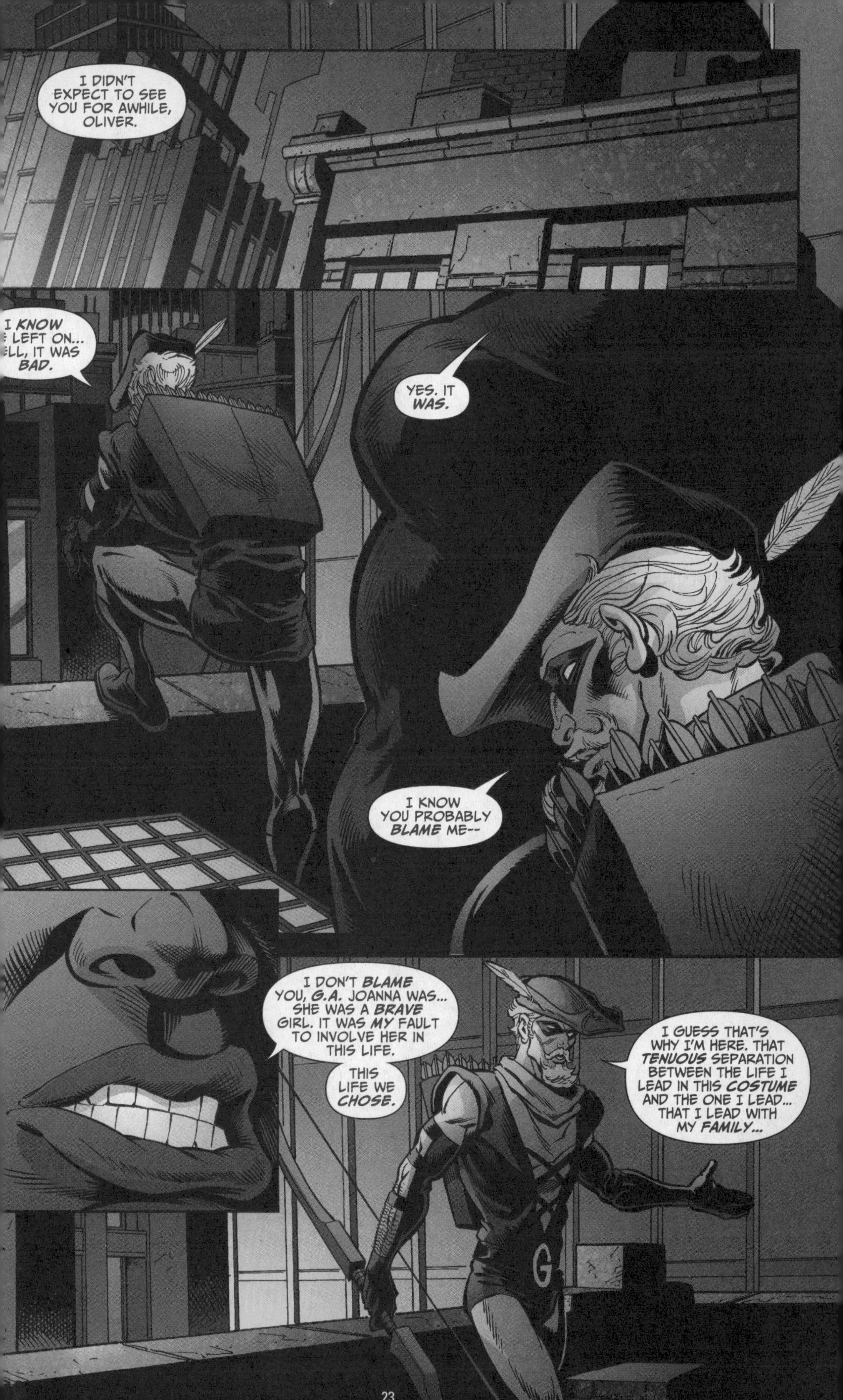

I DIDN'T EXPECT TO SEE YOU FOR AWHILE, OLIVER.
I KNOW E LEFT ON... ELL, IT WAS BAD.
YES. IT WAS.
I KNOW YOU PROBABLY BLAME ME--
I DON'T BLAME YOU, G.A. JOANNA WAS... SHE WAS A BRAVE GIRL. IT WAS MY FAULT TO INVOLVE HER IN THIS LIFE.
THIS LIFE WE CHOSE.
I GUESS THAT'S WHY I'M HERE. THAT TENUOUS SEPARATION BETWEEN THE LIFE I LEAD IN THIS COSTUME AND THE ONE I LEAD... THAT I LEAD WITH MY FAMILY...

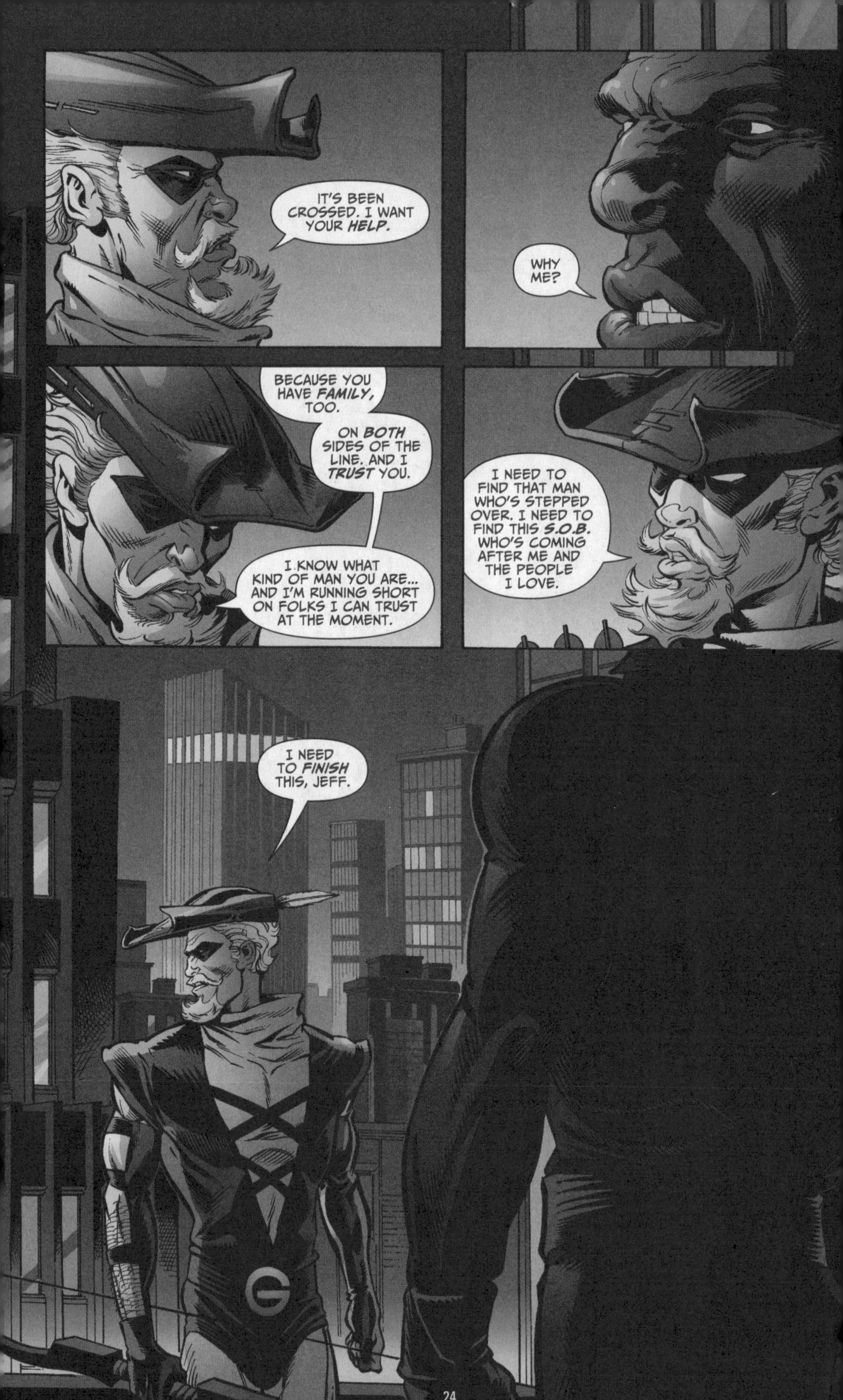

IT'S BEEN CROSSED. I WANT YOUR HELP.
WHY ME?
BECAUSE YOU HAVE FAMILY, TOO.
ON BOTH SIDES OF THE LINE. AND I TRUST YOU.
I KNOW WHAT KIND OF MAN YOU ARE... AND I'M RUNNING SHORT ON FOLKS I CAN TRUST AT THE MOMENT.
I NEED TO FIND THAT MAN WHO'S STEPPED OVER. I NEED TO FIND THIS S.O.B. WHO'S COMING AFTER ME AND THE PEOPLE I LOVE.
I NEED TO FINISH THIS, JEFF.

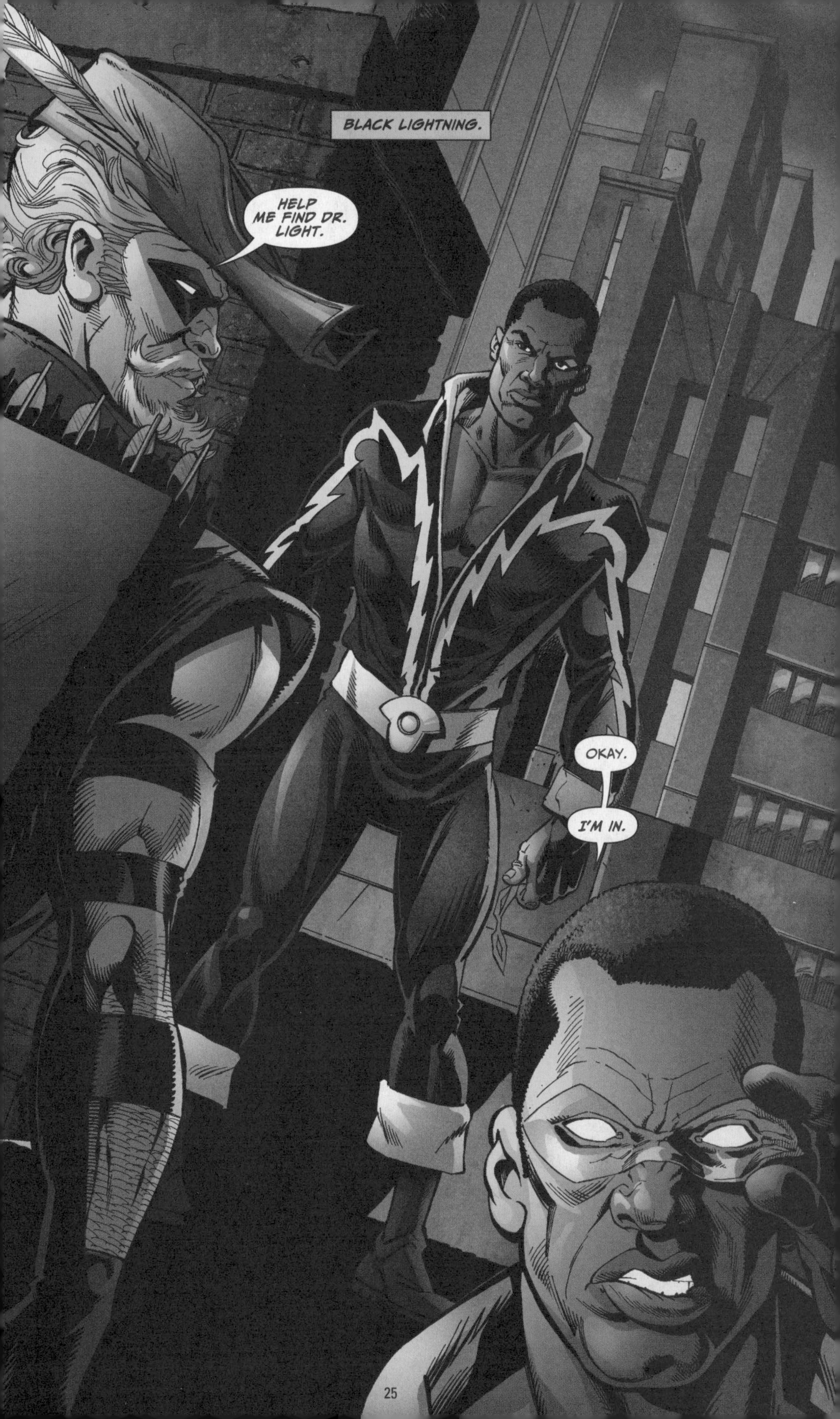

BLACK LIGHTNING.
HELP ME FIND DR. LIGHT.
OKAY.
I'M IN.

THIS HOW YOU WANT TO DO THIS?

SURE.

IT'S JUST NOT THE MOST EFFICIENT WAY--

WE'RE LOOKING FOR A BAD GUY. THIS IS HOW WE SHOULD *LOOK* FOR THE BAD GUY.

SEVERAL MILES BELOW STREET LEVEL. GREEN ARROW'S NEW HOME. SAFE FROM PRYING EYES.

THE NEW HOME OF OLIVER QUEEN.

BLACK LIGHTNING. FORMER SECRETARY OF EDUCATION UNDER THE LUTHOR ADMINISTRATION. AND CURRENTLY, A CRIME FIGHTER.

IT'S JUST A LITTLE LOW-TECH.

THIS IS A G.P.S. TRACKING DEVICE.

YES, AND I'VE SEEN BETTER STUFF AT A CHEAPO RETAIL ELECTRONICS STORE.

THIS IS MILITARY GRADE.

SURE, *TEN* YEARS AGO. WE *COULD* GET SOME HELP.

WHAT ABOU ORACLE, O EVEN THE JLA?

NO. TOO MANY RED FLAGS... THERE'S TOO MUCH LOOSE TALK...TOO MANY LEAKS OF LATE...NO ONE CAN KNOW BUT *US*.

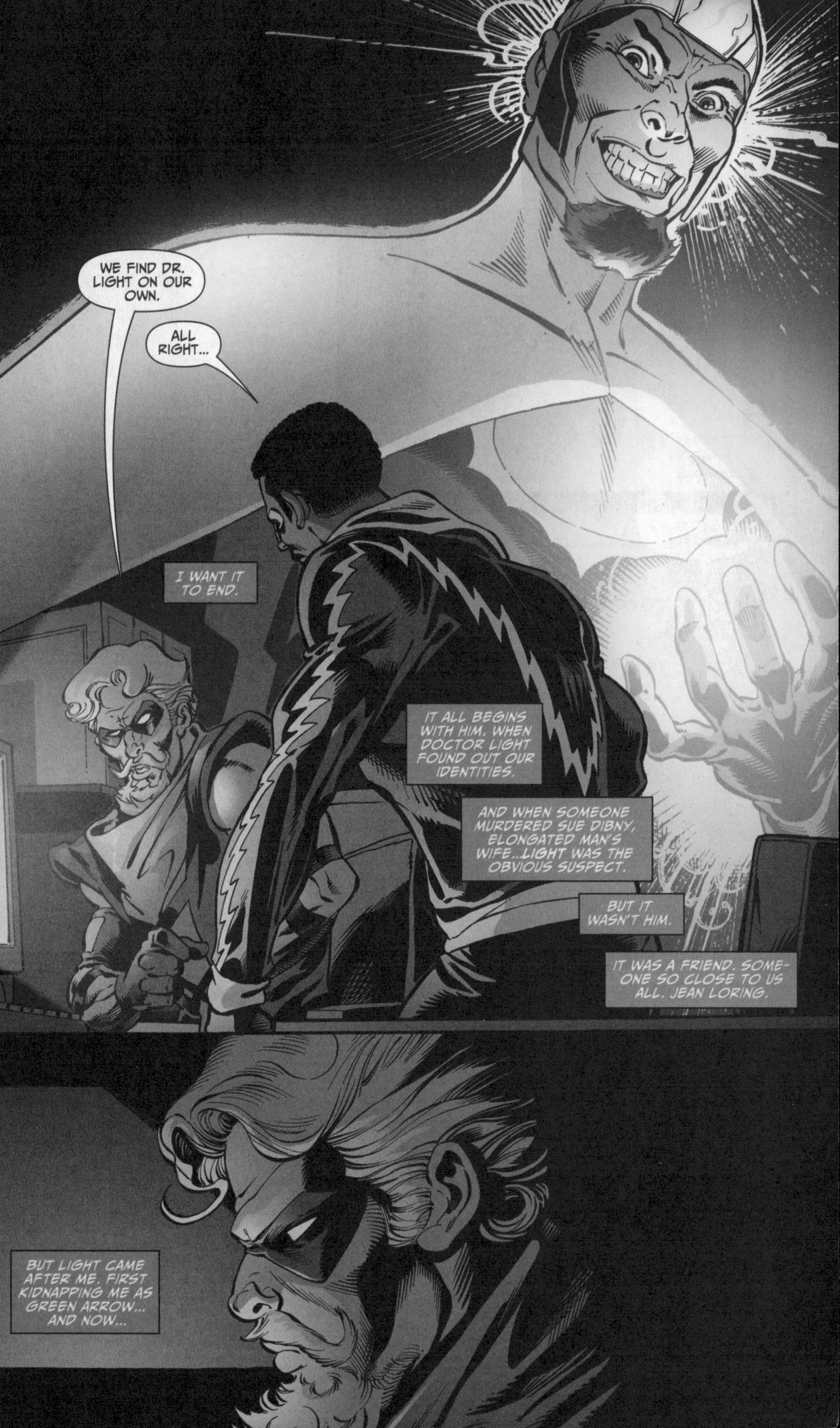

WE FIND DR. LIGHT ON OUR OWN.
ALL RIGHT...
I WANT IT TO END.
IT ALL BEGINS WITH HIM. WHEN DOCTOR LIGHT FOUND OUT OUR IDENTITIES.
AND WHEN SOMEONE MURDERED SUE DIBNY, ELONGATED MAN'S WIFE...LIGHT WAS THE OBVIOUS SUSPECT.
BUT IT WASN'T HIM.
IT WAS A FRIEND. SOME-ONE SO CLOSE TO US ALL. JEAN LORING.
BUT LIGHT CAME AFTER ME. FIRST KIDNAPPING ME AS GREEN ARROW... AND NOW...

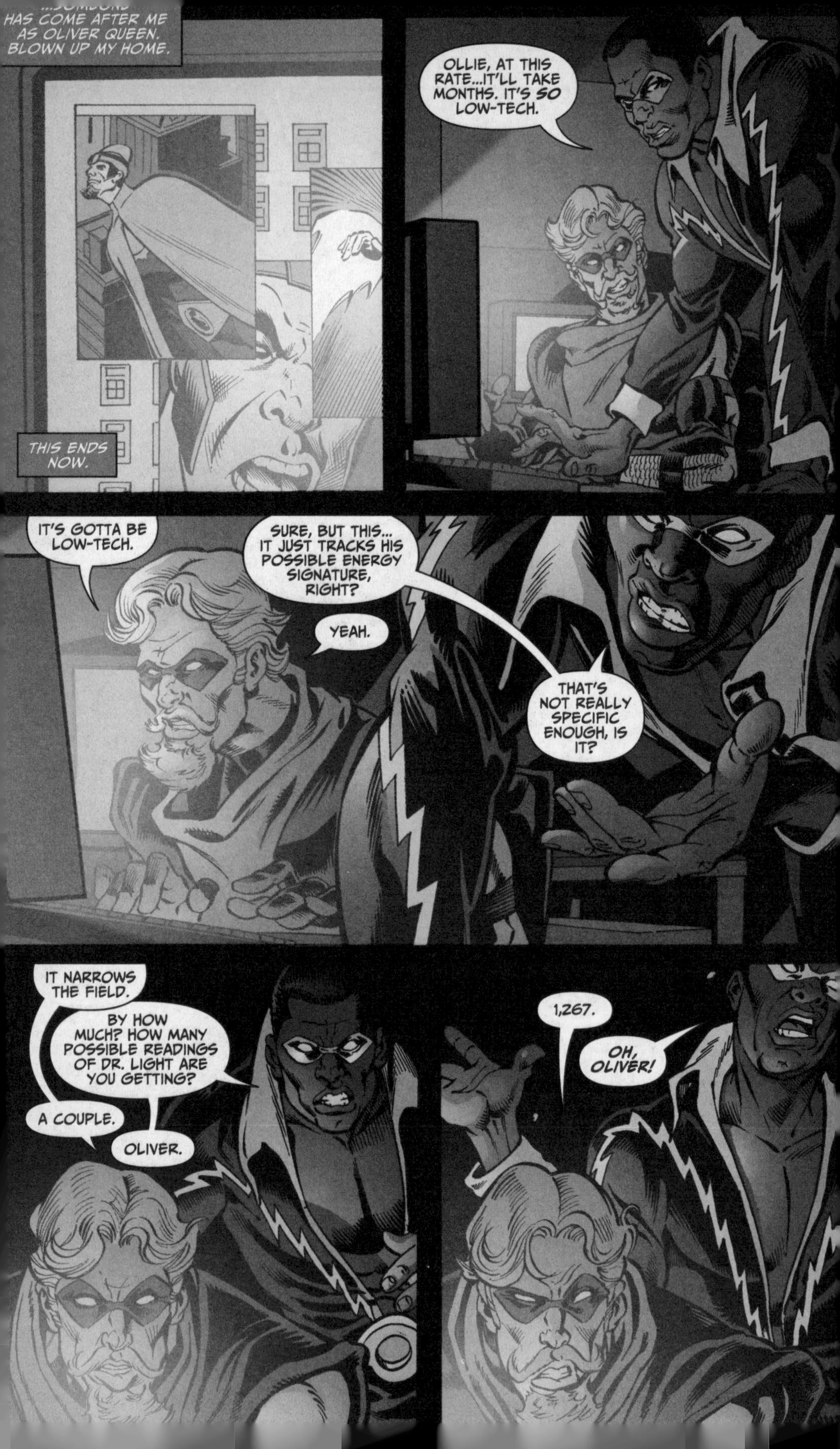
...SOMEONE HAS COME AFTER ME AS OLIVER QUEEN. BLOWN UP MY HOME.
THIS ENDS NOW.
OLLIE, AT THIS RATE...IT'LL TAKE MONTHS. IT'S SO LOW-TECH.
IT'S GOTTA BE LOW-TECH.
SURE, BUT THIS... IT JUST TRACKS HIS POSSIBLE ENERGY SIGNATURE, RIGHT?
YEAH.
THAT'S NOT REALLY SPECIFIC ENOUGH, IS IT?
IT NARROWS THE FIELD.
BY HOW MUCH? HOW MANY POSSIBLE READINGS OF DR. LIGHT ARE YOU GETTING?
A COUPLE.
OLIVER.
1,267.
OH, OLIVER!

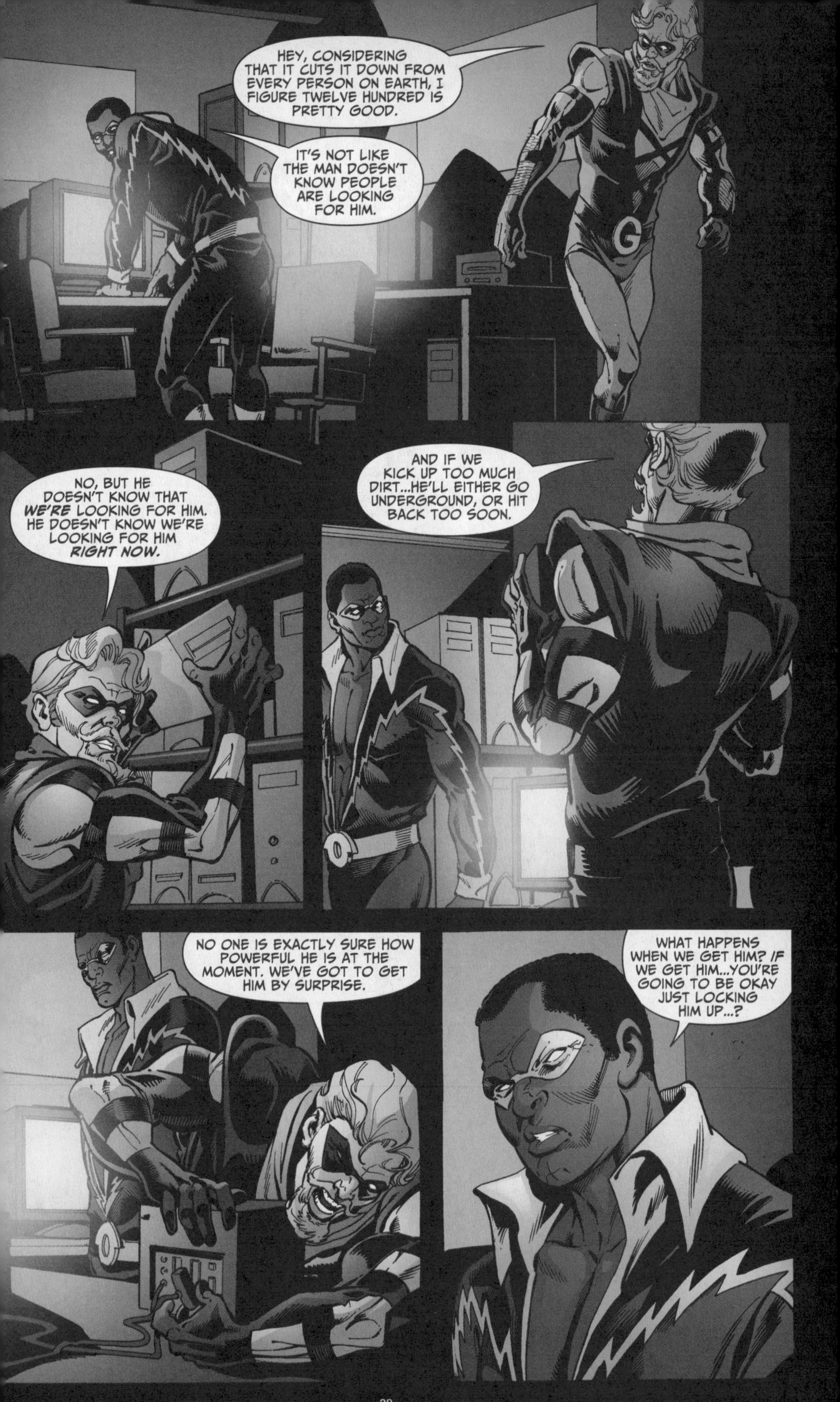
HEY, CONSIDERING THAT IT CUTS IT DOWN FROM EVERY PERSON ON EARTH, I FIGURE TWELVE HUNDRED IS PRETTY GOOD.
IT'S NOT LIKE THE MAN DOESN'T KNOW PEOPLE ARE LOOKING FOR HIM.
NO, BUT HE DOESN'T KNOW THAT *WE'RE* LOOKING FOR HIM. HE DOESN'T KNOW WE'RE LOOKING FOR HIM *RIGHT NOW.*
AND IF WE KICK UP TOO MUCH DIRT...HE'LL EITHER GO UNDERGROUND, OR HIT BACK TOO SOON.
NO ONE IS EXACTLY SURE HOW POWERFUL HE IS AT THE MOMENT. WE'VE GOT TO GET HIM BY SURPRISE.
WHAT HAPPENS WHEN WE GET HIM? *IF* WE GET HIM...YOU'RE GOING TO BE OKAY JUST LOCKING HIM UP...?

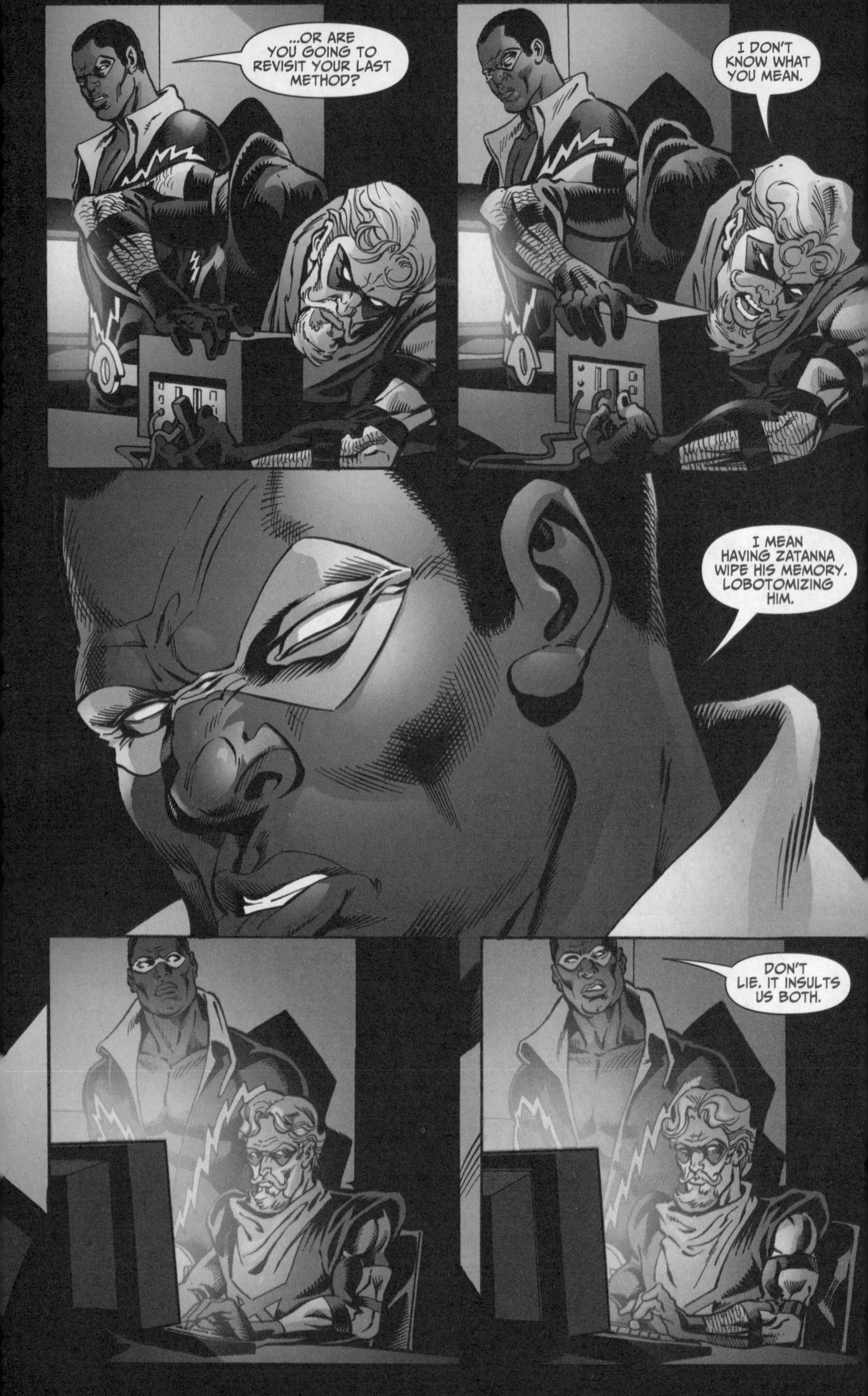
...OR ARE YOU GOING TO REVISIT YOUR LAST METHOD?
I DON'T KNOW WHAT YOU MEAN.
I MEAN HAVING ZATANNA WIPE HIS MEMORY. LOBOTOMIZING HIM.
DON'T LIE. IT INSULTS US BOTH.

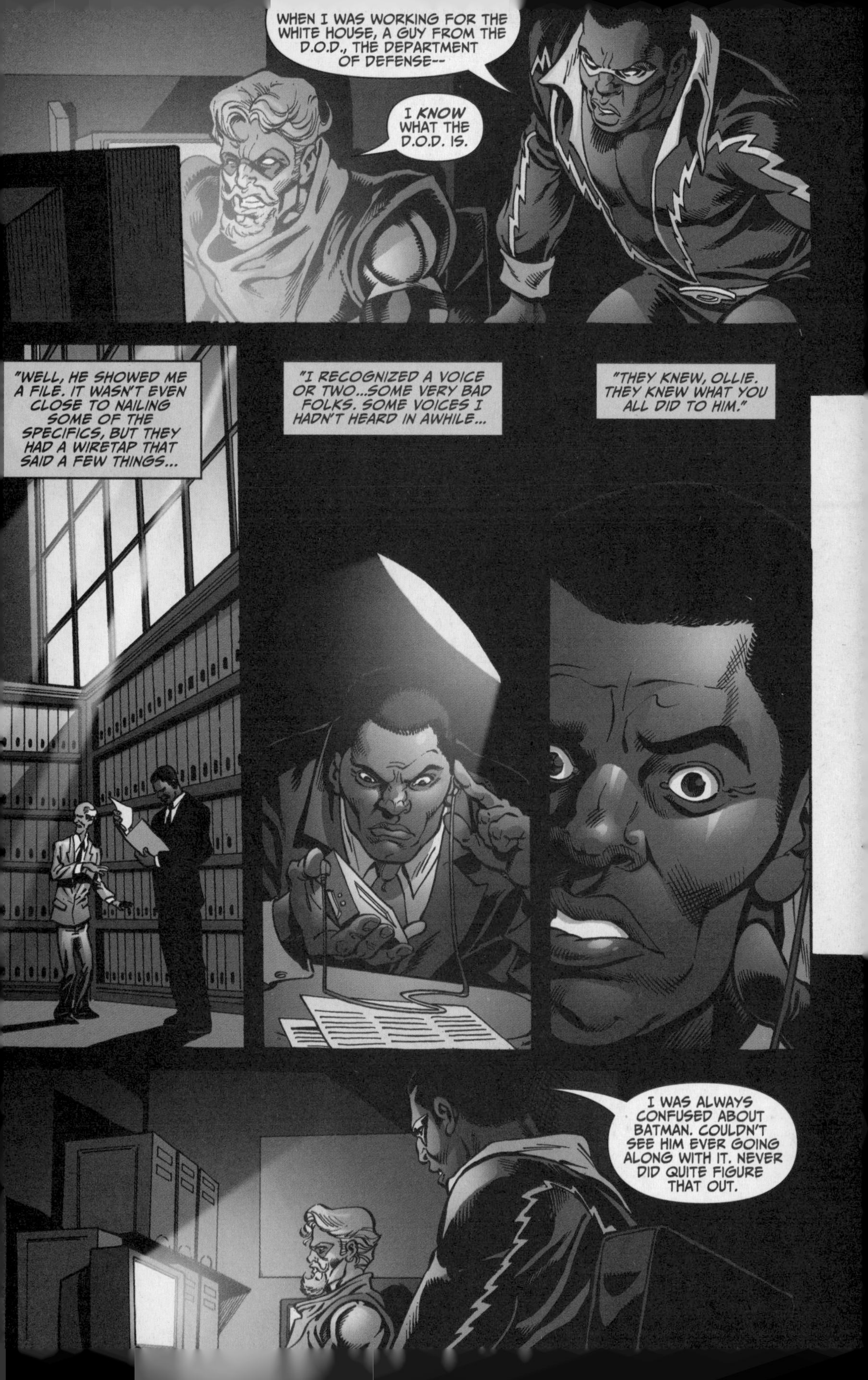
WHEN I WAS WORKING FOR THE WHITE HOUSE, A GUY FROM THE D.O.D., THE DEPARTMENT OF DEFENSE--
I KNOW WHAT THE D.O.D. IS.
"WELL, HE SHOWED ME A FILE. IT WASN'T EVEN CLOSE TO NAILING SOME OF THE SPECIFICS, BUT THEY HAD A WIRETAP THAT SAID A FEW THINGS...
"I RECOGNIZED A VOICE OR TWO...SOME VERY BAD FOLKS. SOME VOICES I HADN'T HEARD IN AWHILE...
"THEY KNEW, OLLIE. THEY KNEW WHAT YOU ALL DID TO HIM."
I WAS ALWAYS CONFUSED ABOUT BATMAN. COULDN'T SEE HIM EVER GOING ALONG WITH IT. NEVER DID QUITE FIGURE THAT OUT.

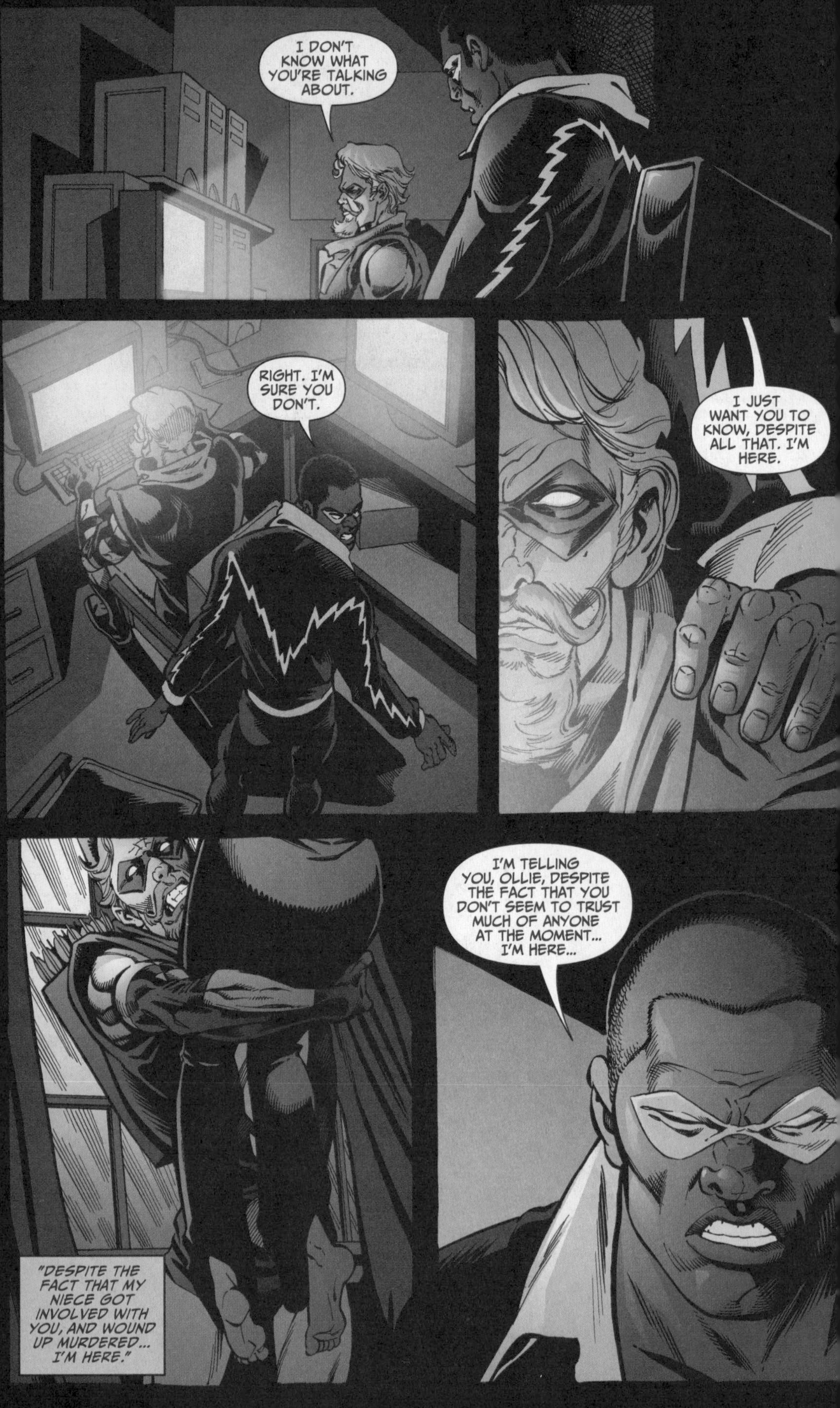
I DON'T KNOW WHAT YOU'RE TALKING ABOUT.
RIGHT. I'M SURE YOU DON'T.
I JUST WANT YOU TO KNOW, DESPITE ALL THAT. I'M HERE.
"DESPITE THE FACT THAT MY NIECE GOT INVOLVED WITH YOU, AND WOUND UP MURDERED... I'M HERE."
I'M TELLING YOU, OLLIE, DESPITE THE FACT THAT YOU DON'T SEEM TO TRUST MUCH OF ANYONE AT THE MOMENT... I'M HERE...

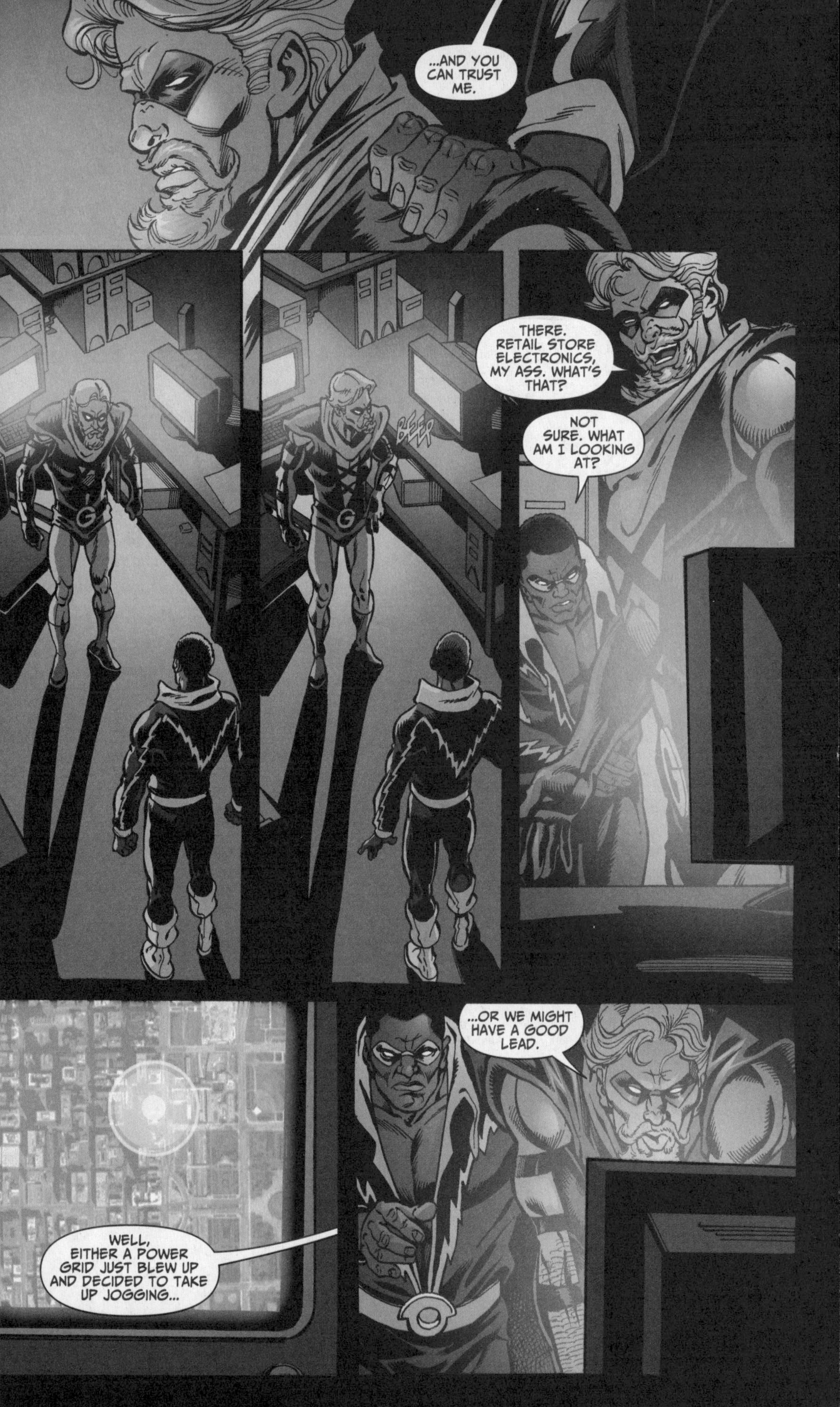
...AND YOU CAN TRUST ME.
BEEP
THERE. RETAIL STORE ELECTRONICS, MY ASS. WHAT'S THAT?
NOT SURE. WHAT AM I LOOKING AT?
WELL, EITHER A POWER GRID JUST BLEW UP AND DECIDED TO TAKE UP JOGGING...
...OR WE MIGHT HAVE A GOOD LEAD.

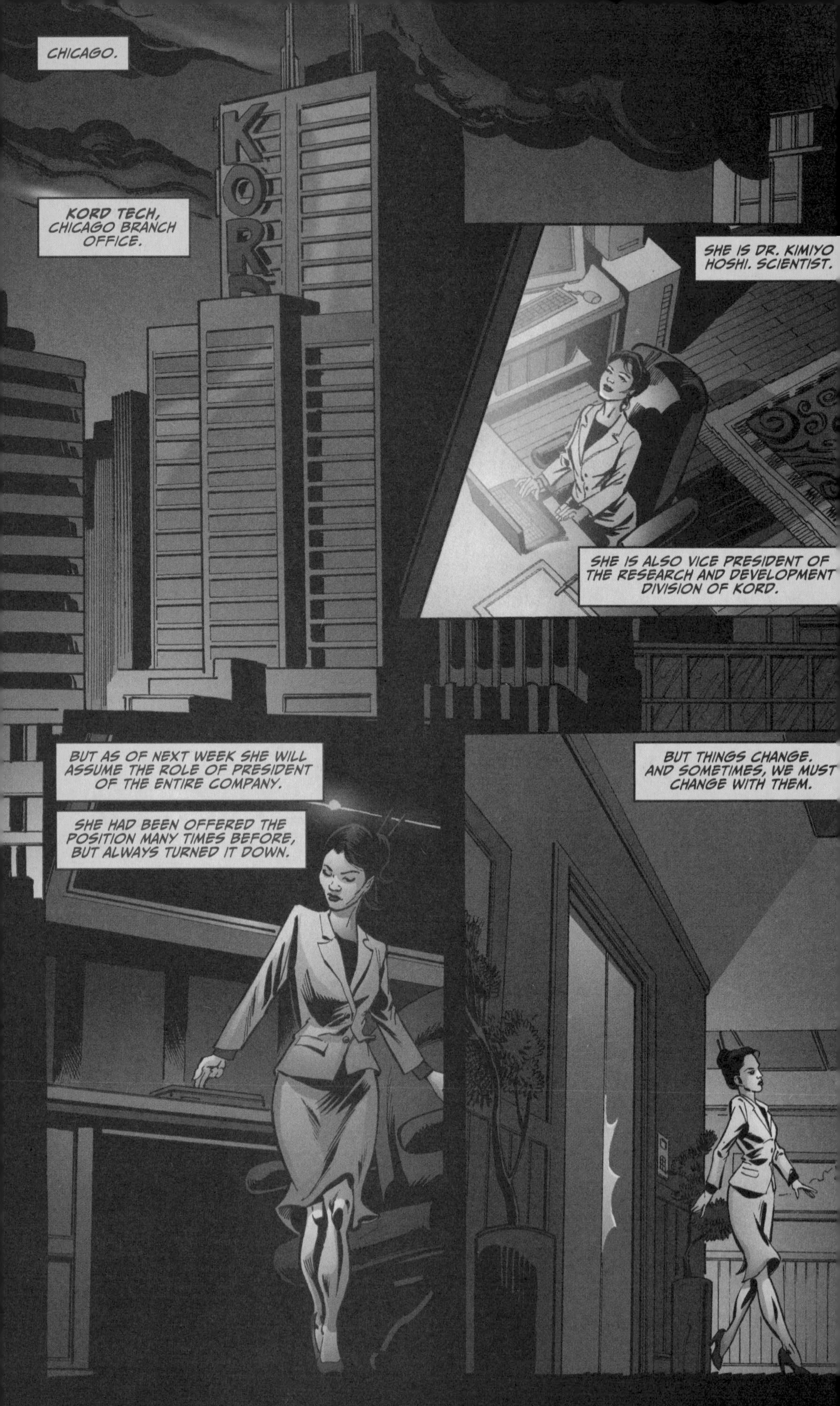
CHICAGO.
KORD TECH, CHICAGO BRANCH OFFICE.
KORD
SHE IS DR. KIMIYO HOSHI. SCIENTIST.
SHE IS ALSO VICE PRESIDENT OF THE RESEARCH AND DEVELOPMENT DIVISION OF KORD.
BUT AS OF NEXT WEEK SHE WILL ASSUME THE ROLE OF PRESIDENT OF THE ENTIRE COMPANY.
SHE HAD BEEN OFFERED THE POSITION MANY TIMES BEFORE, BUT ALWAYS TURNED IT DOWN.
BUT THINGS CHANGE. AND SOMETIMES, WE MUST CHANGE WITH THEM.

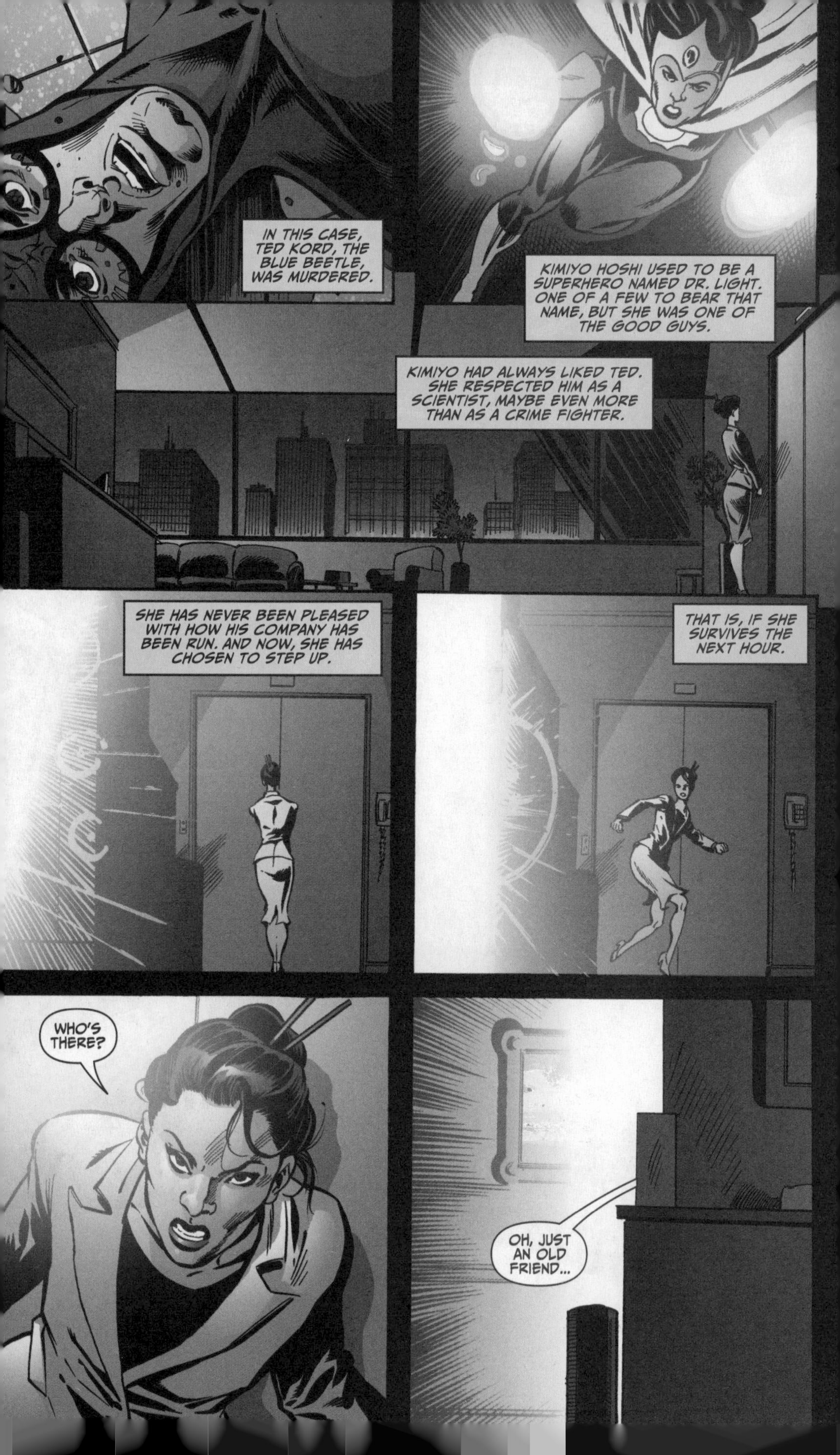
IN THIS CASE, TED KORD, THE BLUE BEETLE, WAS MURDERED.
KIMIYO HOSHI USED TO BE A SUPERHERO NAMED DR. LIGHT. ONE OF A FEW TO BEAR THAT NAME, BUT SHE WAS ONE OF THE GOOD GUYS.
KIMIYO HAD ALWAYS LIKED TED. SHE RESPECTED HIM AS A SCIENTIST, MAYBE EVEN MORE THAN AS A CRIME FIGHTER.
SHE HAS NEVER BEEN PLEASED WITH HOW HIS COMPANY HAS BEEN RUN. AND NOW, SHE HAS CHOSEN TO STEP UP.
THAT IS, IF SHE SURVIVES THE NEXT HOUR.
WHO'S THERE?
OH, JUST AN OLD FRIEND...

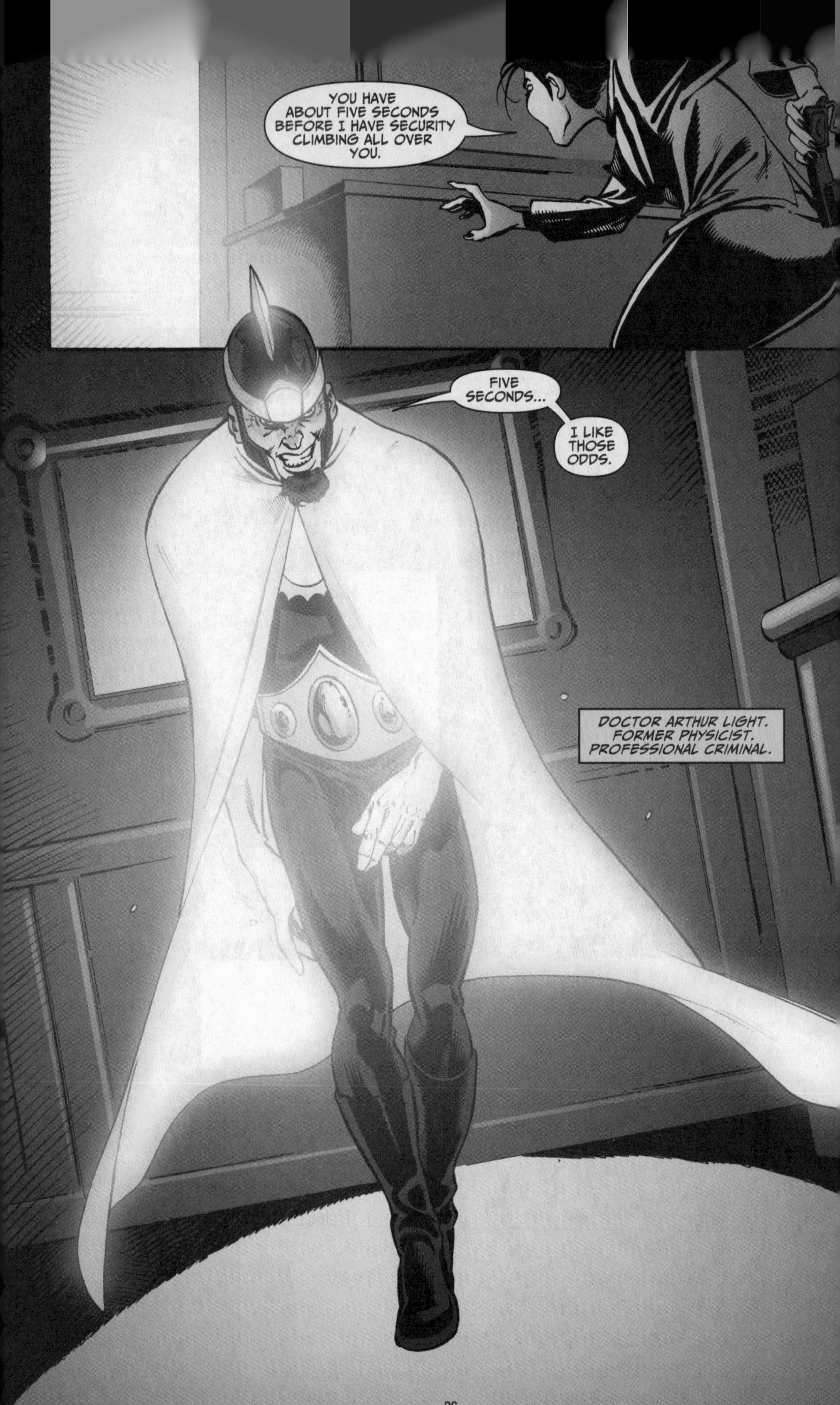
YOU HAVE ABOUT FIVE SECONDS BEFORE I HAVE SECURITY CLIMBING ALL OVER YOU.
FIVE SECONDS...
I LIKE THOSE ODDS.
DOCTOR ARTHUR LIGHT. FORMER PHYSICIST. PROFESSIONAL CRIMINAL.

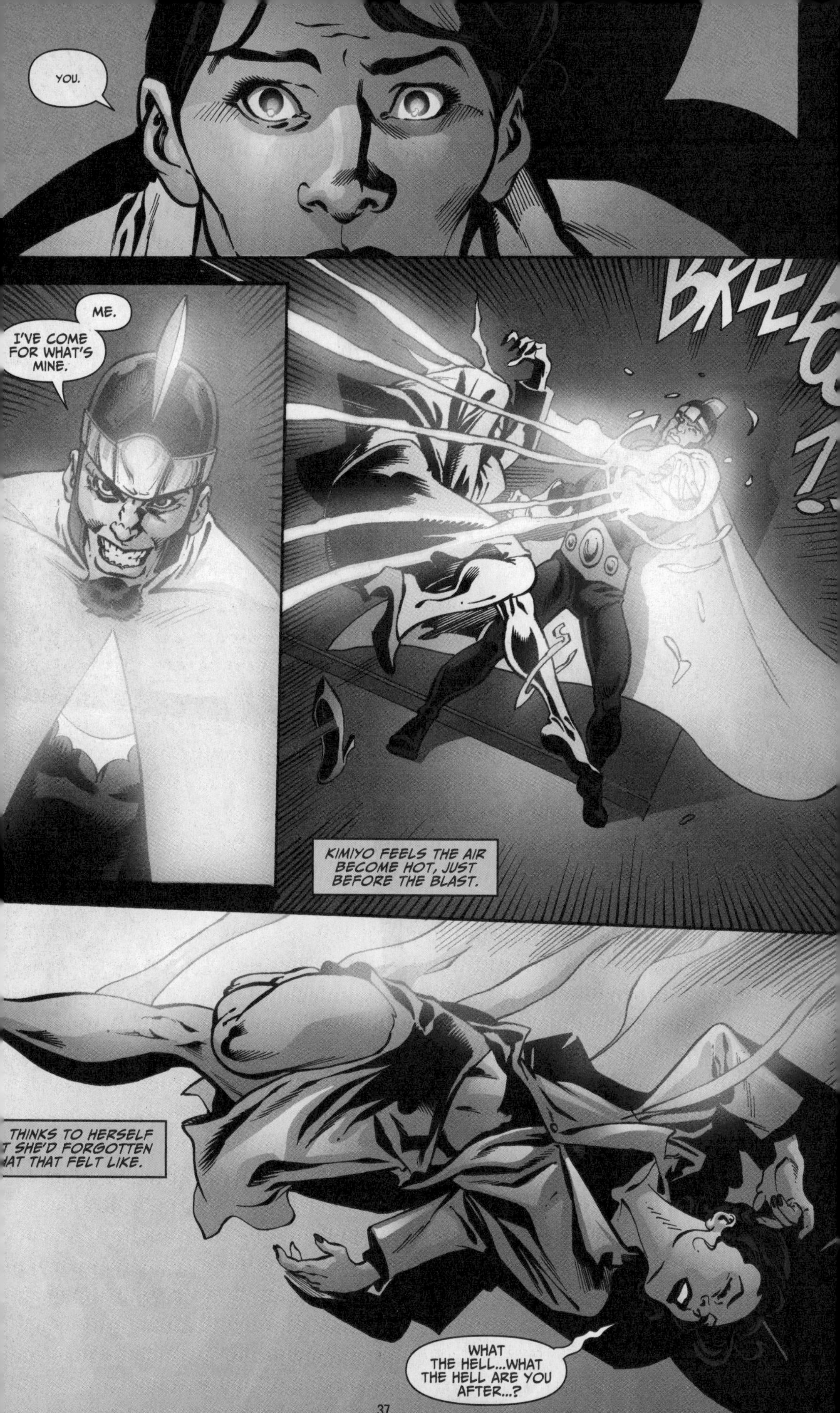
YOU.
ME.
I'VE COME FOR WHAT'S MINE.
BREE...
KIMIYO FEELS THE AIR BECOME HOT, JUST BEFORE THE BLAST.
THINKS TO HERSELF
T SHE'D FORGOTTEN
HAT THAT FELT LIKE.
WHAT THE HELL...WHAT THE HELL ARE YOU AFTER...?

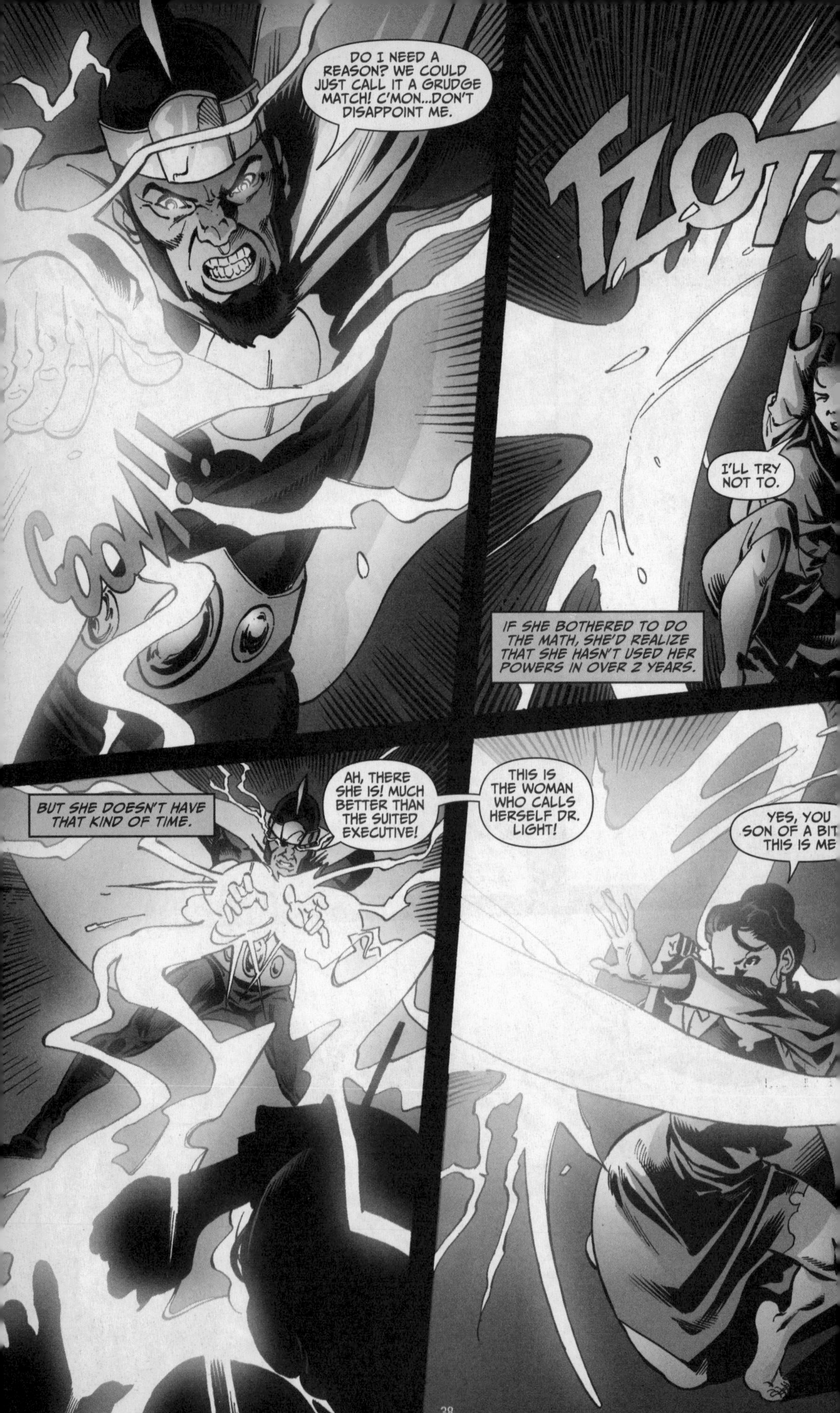
DO I NEED A REASON? WE COULD JUST CALL IT A GRUDGE MATCH! C'MON...DON'T DISAPPOINT ME.
GOOM!
FZOT!
I'LL TRY NOT TO.
IF SHE BOTHERED TO DO THE MATH, SHE'D REALIZE THAT SHE HASN'T USED HER POWERS IN OVER 2 YEARS.
BUT SHE DOESN'T HAVE THAT KIND OF TIME.
AH, THERE SHE IS! MUCH BETTER THAN THE SUITED EXECUTIVE!
THIS IS THE WOMAN WHO CALLS HERSELF DR. LIGHT!
YES, YOU SON OF A BIT THIS IS ME

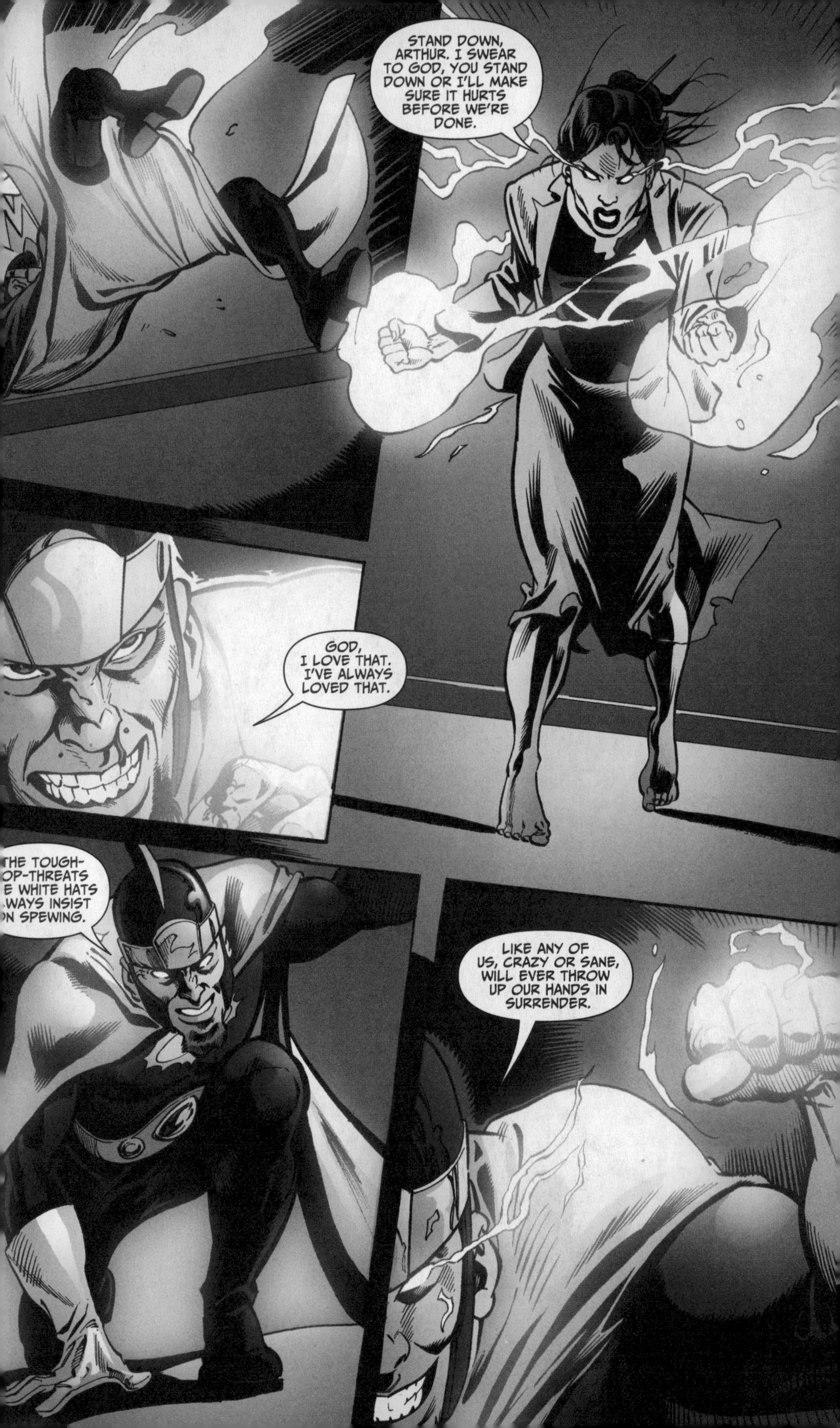
STAND DOWN, ARTHUR. I SWEAR TO GOD, YOU STAND DOWN OR I'LL MAKE SURE IT HURTS BEFORE WE'RE DONE.
GOD, I LOVE THAT. I'VE ALWAYS LOVED THAT.
THE TOUGH-
OP-THREATS
E WHITE HATS
WAYS INSIST
N SPEWING.
LIKE ANY OF US, CRAZY OR SANE, WILL EVER THROW UP OUR HANDS IN SURRENDER.

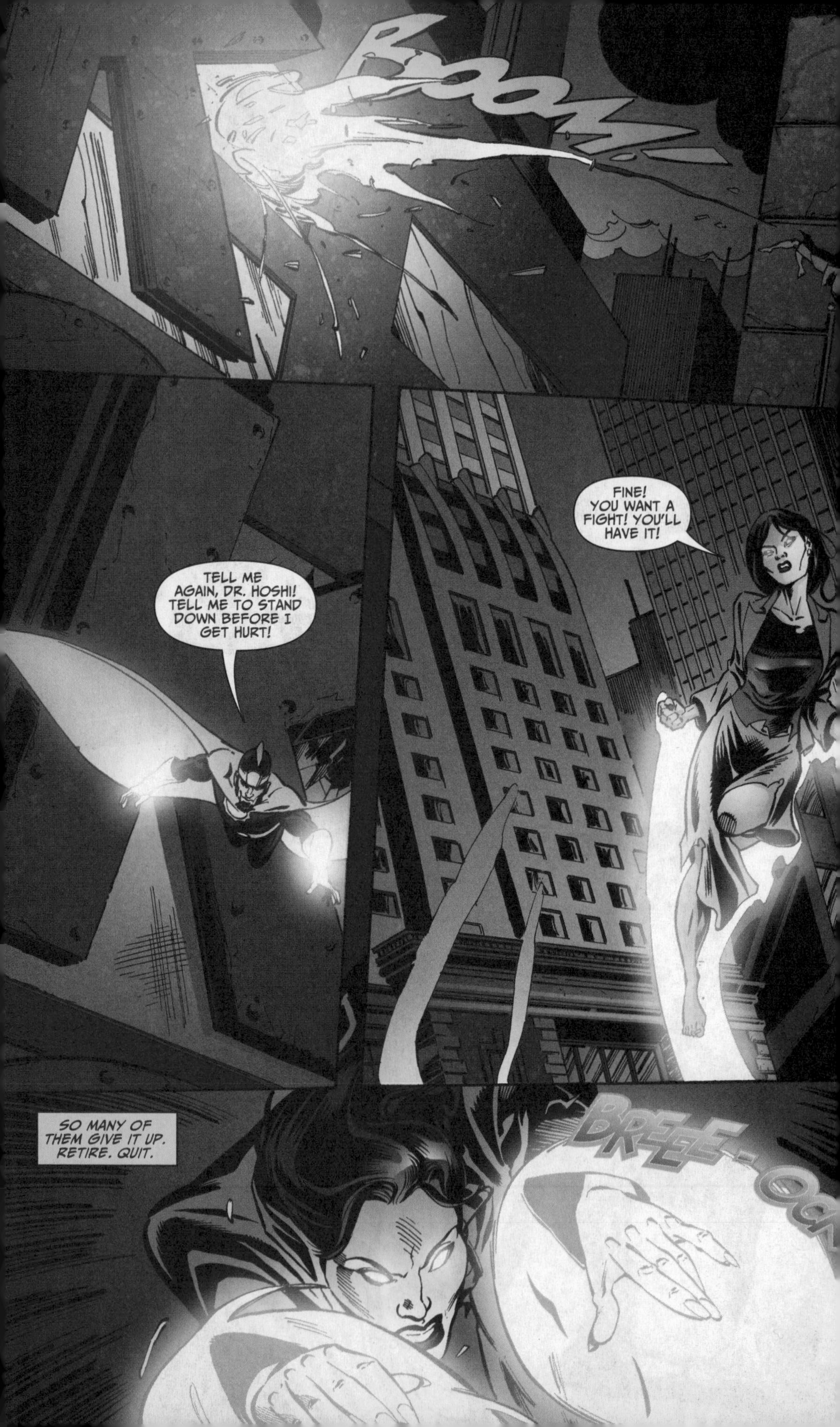
BOOM!
TELL ME AGAIN, DR. HOSHI! TELL ME TO STAND DOWN BEFORE I GET HURT!
FINE! YOU WANT A FIGHT! YOU'LL HAVE IT!
SO MANY OF THEM GIVE IT UP. RETIRE. QUIT.
BREEE-OOM

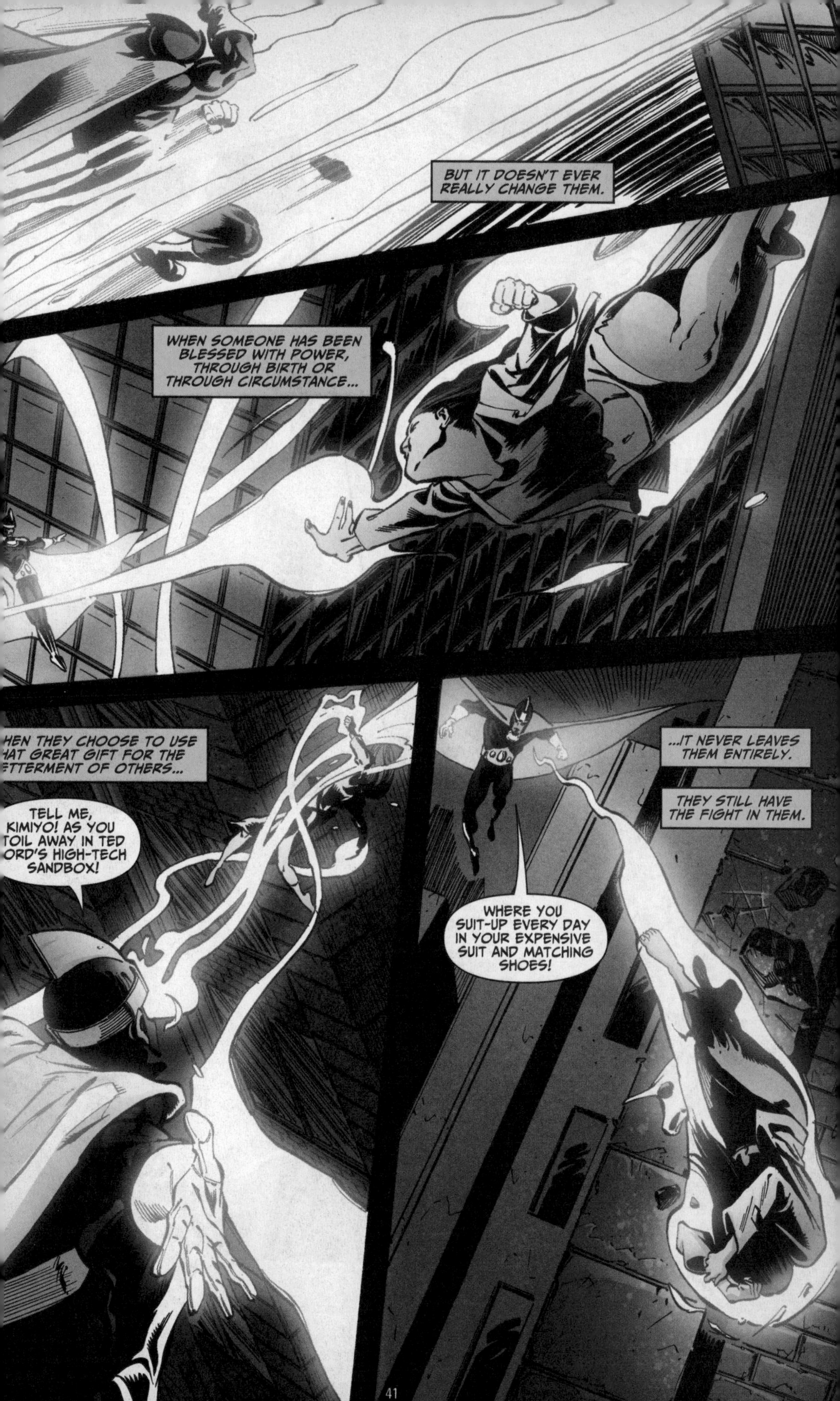
BUT IT DOESN'T EVER REALLY CHANGE THEM.
WHEN SOMEONE HAS BEEN BLESSED WITH POWER, THROUGH BIRTH OR THROUGH CIRCUMSTANCE...
HEN THEY CHOOSE TO USE HAT GREAT GIFT FOR THE ETTERMENT OF OTHERS...
TELL ME, KIMIYO! AS YOU TOIL AWAY IN TED ORD'S HIGH-TECH SANDBOX!
...IT NEVER LEAVES THEM ENTIRELY.
THEY STILL HAVE THE FIGHT IN THEM.
WHERE YOU SUIT-UP EVERY DAY IN YOUR EXPENSIVE SUIT AND MATCHING SHOES!

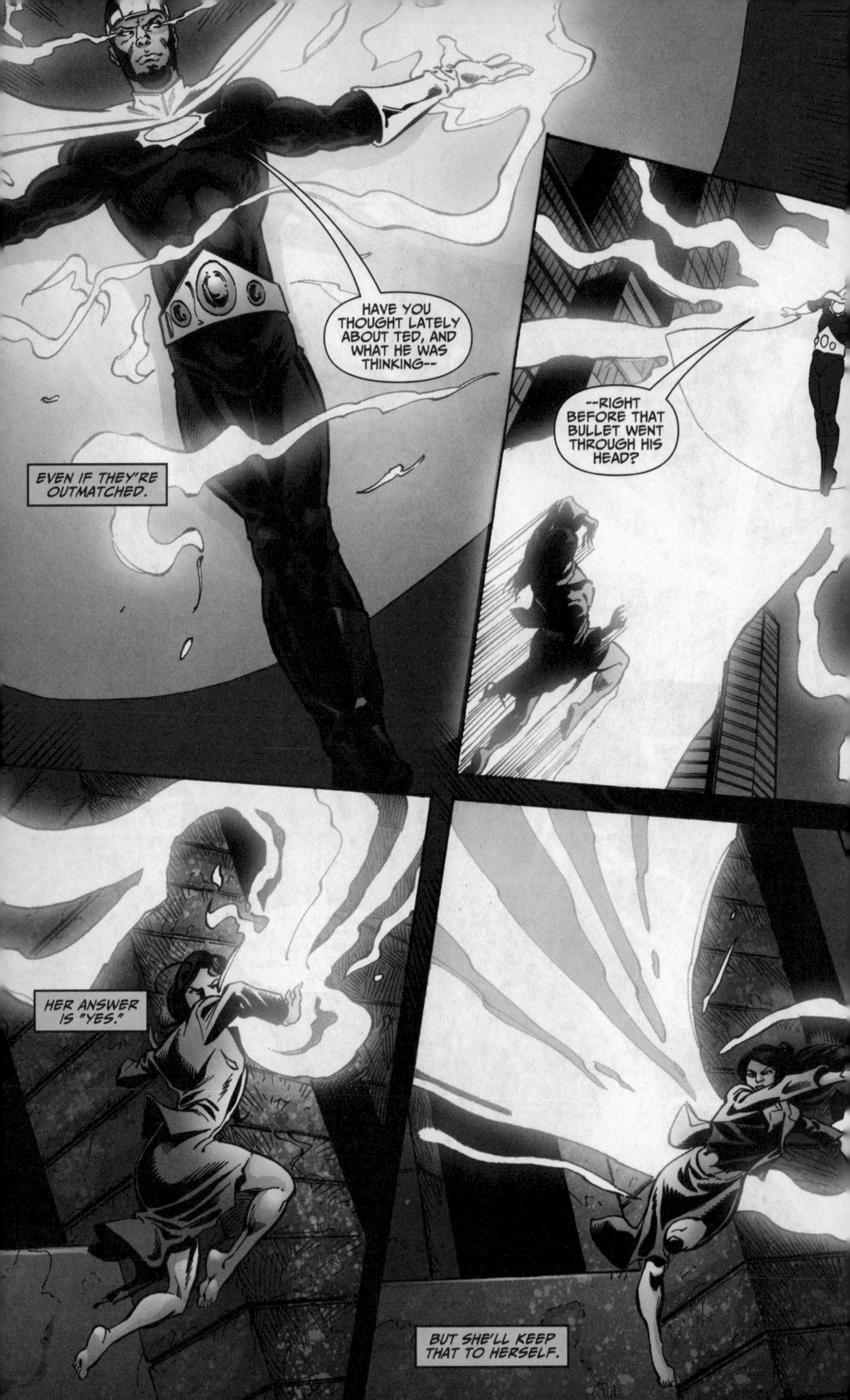
HAVE YOU THOUGHT LATELY ABOUT TED, AND WHAT HE WAS THINKING--
--RIGHT BEFORE THAT BULLET WENT THROUGH HIS HEAD?
EVEN IF THEY'RE OUTMATCHED.
HER ANSWER IS "YES."
BUT SHE'LL KEEP THAT TO HERSELF.

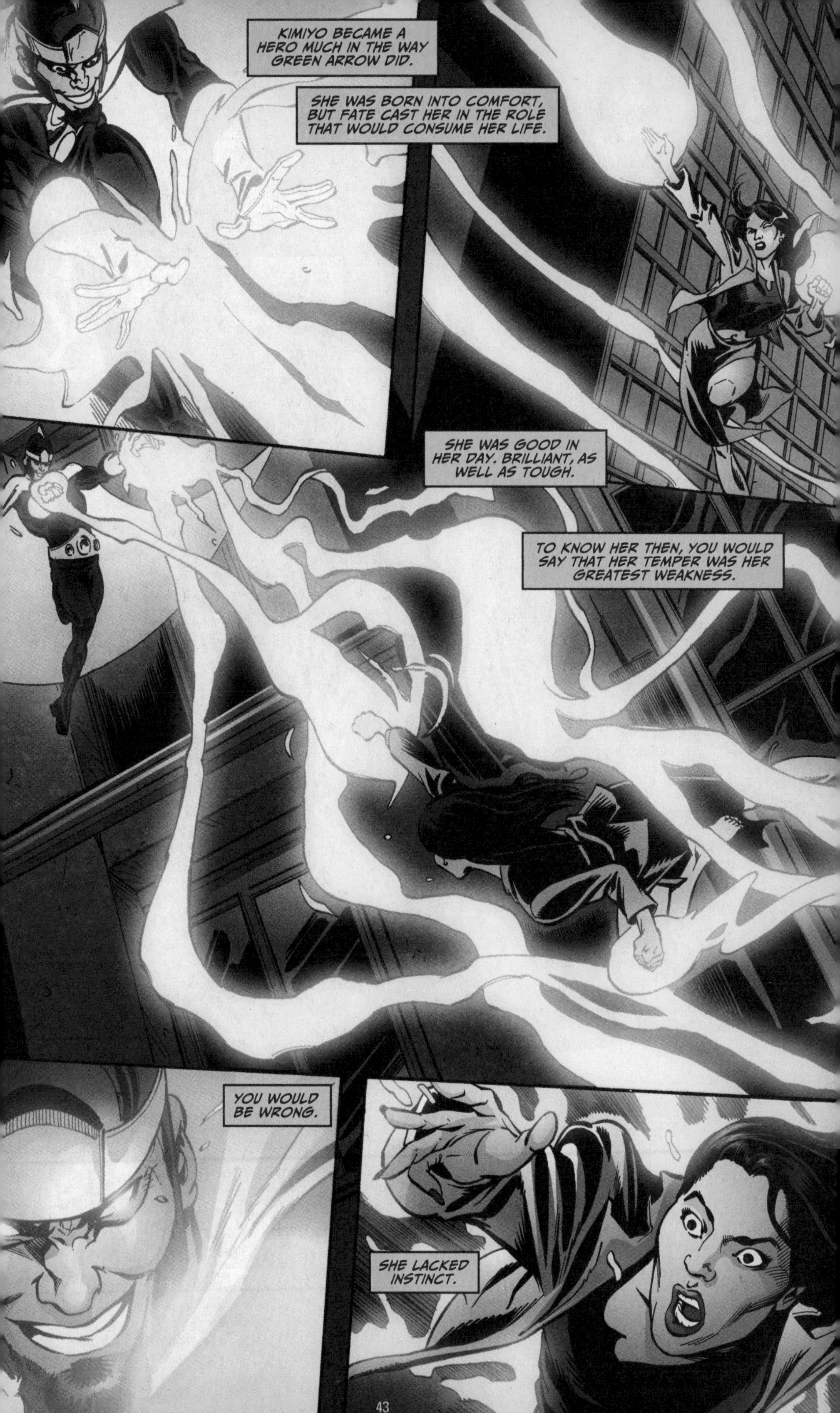
KIMIYO BECAME A HERO MUCH IN THE WAY GREEN ARROW DID.
SHE WAS BORN INTO COMFORT, BUT FATE CAST HER IN THE ROLE THAT WOULD CONSUME HER LIFE.
SHE WAS GOOD IN HER DAY. BRILLIANT, AS WELL AS TOUGH.
TO KNOW HER THEN, YOU WOULD SAY THAT HER TEMPER WAS HER GREATEST WEAKNESS.
YOU WOULD BE WRONG.
SHE LACKED INSTINCT.

INSTINCT, IN THIS CASE, THAT WOULD HAVE TOLD HER THAT DR. LIGHT WAS NOT HERE TO FIGHT HER.

BUT, JUST AS HE SAID, "I'VE COME FOR WHAT'S MINE."

"WHAT'S HIS BEING THE STARLIGHT HER POWE

MY... THAT FEELS... WONDERFUL...

THANK YOU, DEAR... EVERY LITTLE BIT HELPS...

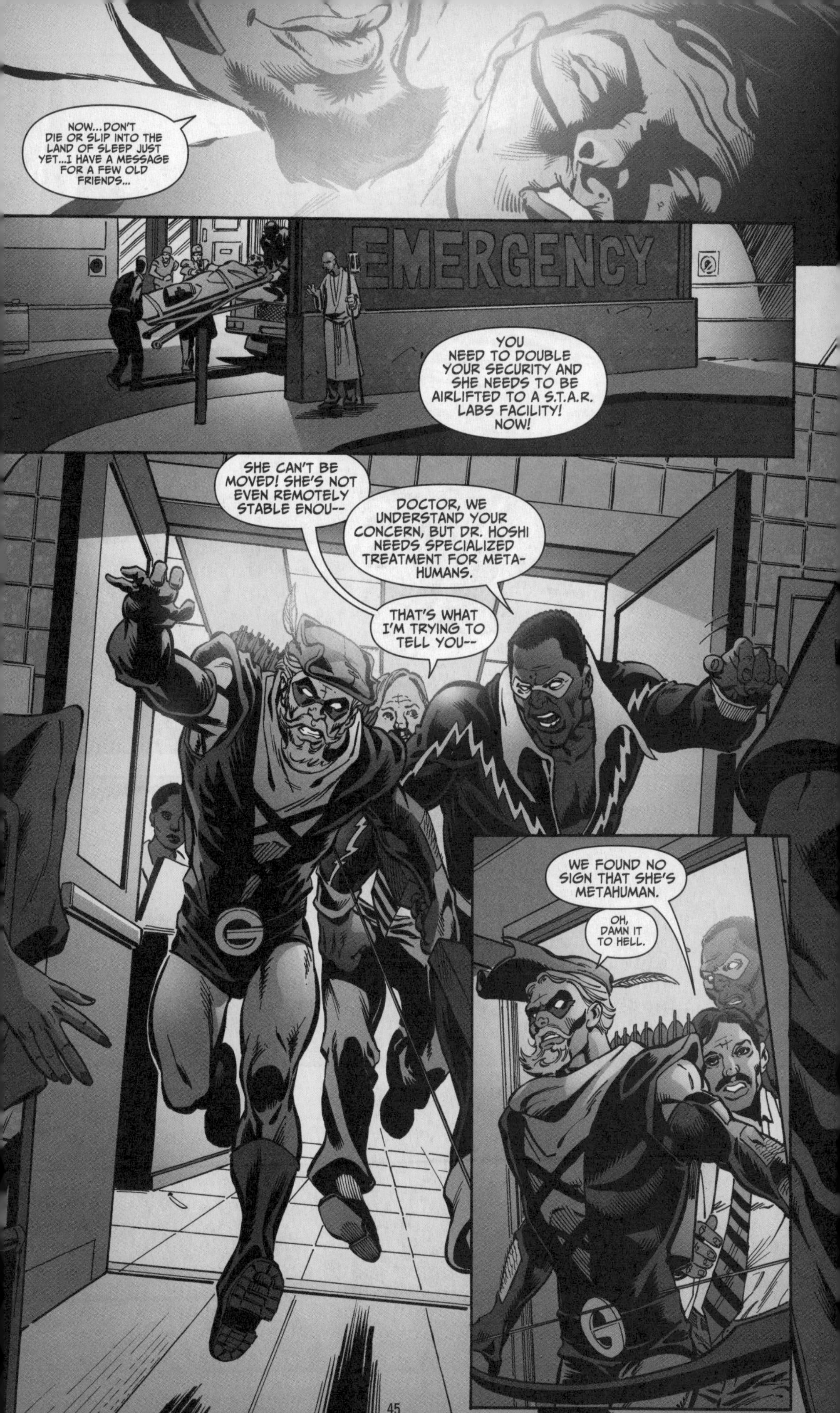
NOW...DON'T DIE OR SLIP INTO THE LAND OF SLEEP JUST YET...I HAVE A MESSAGE FOR A FEW OLD FRIENDS...
EMERGENCY
YOU NEED TO DOUBLE YOUR SECURITY AND SHE NEEDS TO BE AIRLIFTED TO A S.T.A.R. LABS FACILITY! NOW!
SHE CAN'T BE MOVED! SHE'S NOT EVEN REMOTELY STABLE ENOU--
DOCTOR, WE UNDERSTAND YOUR CONCERN, BUT DR. HOSHI NEEDS SPECIALIZED TREATMENT FOR META-HUMANS.
THAT'S WHAT I'M TRYING TO TELL YOU--
WE FOUND NO SIGN THAT SHE'S METAHUMAN.
OH, DAMN IT TO HELL.

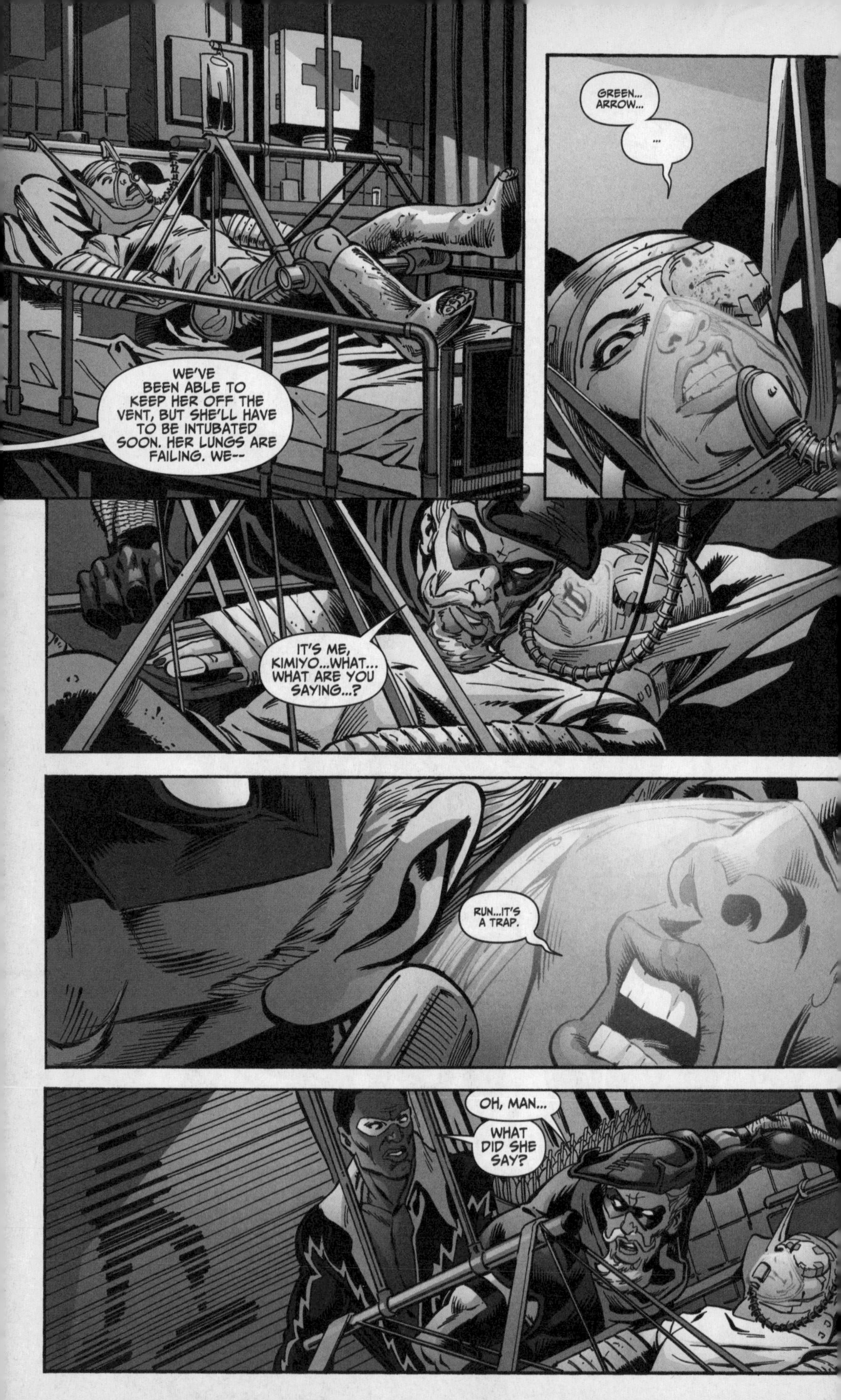
WE'VE BEEN ABLE TO KEEP HER OFF THE VENT, BUT SHE'LL HAVE TO BE INTUBATED SOON. HER LUNGS ARE FAILING. WE--
GREEN... ARROW...
...
IT'S ME, KIMIYO...WHAT... WHAT ARE YOU SAYING...?
RUN...IT'S A TRAP.
OH, MAN...
WHAT DID SHE SAY?

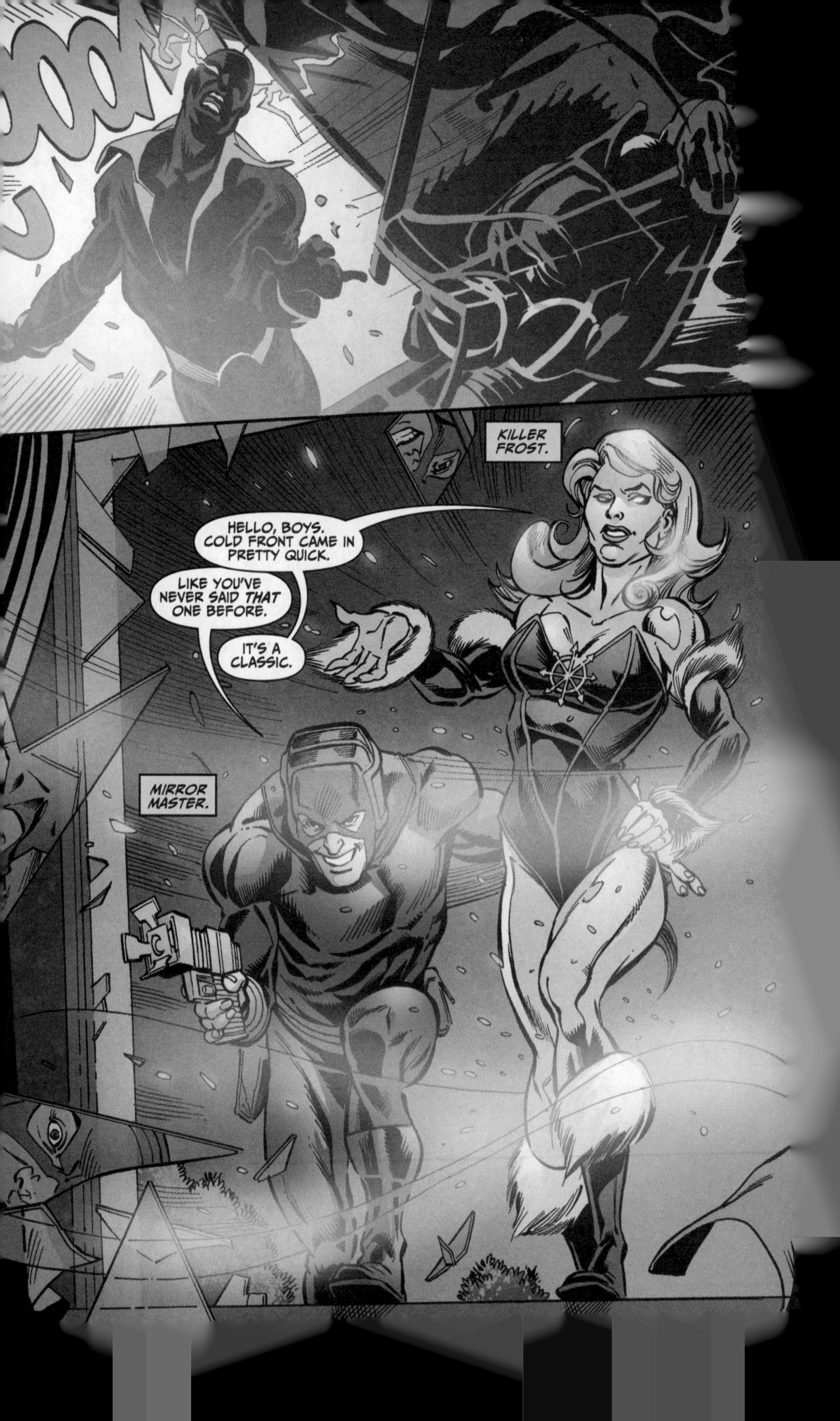
KILLER FROST.
HELLO, BOYS. COLD FRONT CAME IN PRETTY QUICK.
LIKE YOU'VE NEVER SAID *THAT* ONE BEFORE.
IT'S A CLASSIC.
MIRROR MASTER.

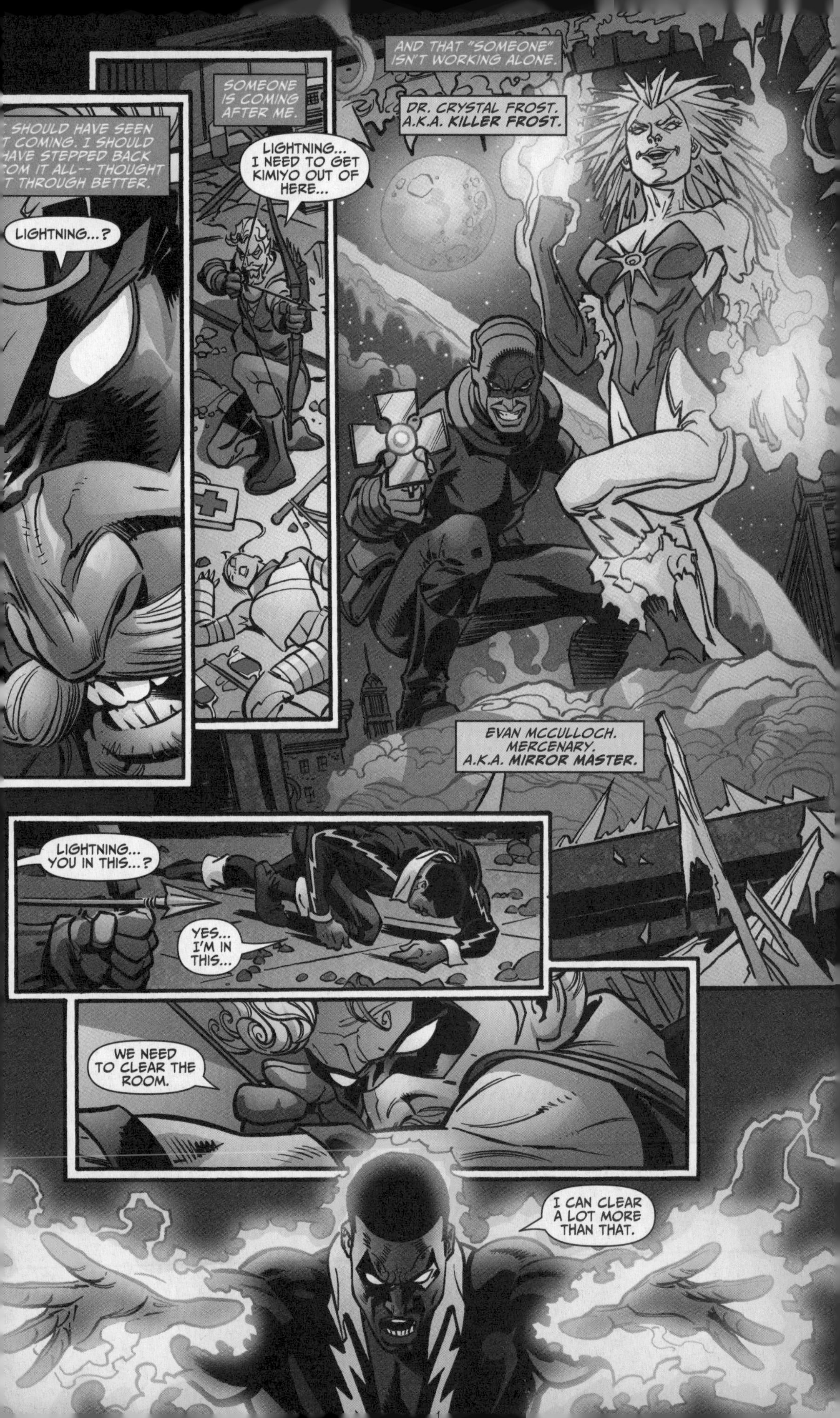

SOMEONE IS COMING AFTER ME.
AND THAT "SOMEONE" ISN'T WORKING ALONE.
DR. CRYSTAL FROST. A.K.A. KILLER FROST.
SHOULD HAVE SEEN COMING. I SHOULD HAVE STEPPED BACK ROM IT ALL-- THOUGHT T THROUGH BETTER.
LIGHTNING...?
LIGHTNING... I NEED TO GET KIMIYO OUT OF HERE...
EVAN MCCULLOCH. MERCENARY. A.K.A. MIRROR MASTER.
LIGHTNING... YOU IN THIS...?
YES... I'M IN THIS...
WE NEED TO CLEAR THE ROOM.
I CAN CLEAR A LOT MORE THAN THAT.

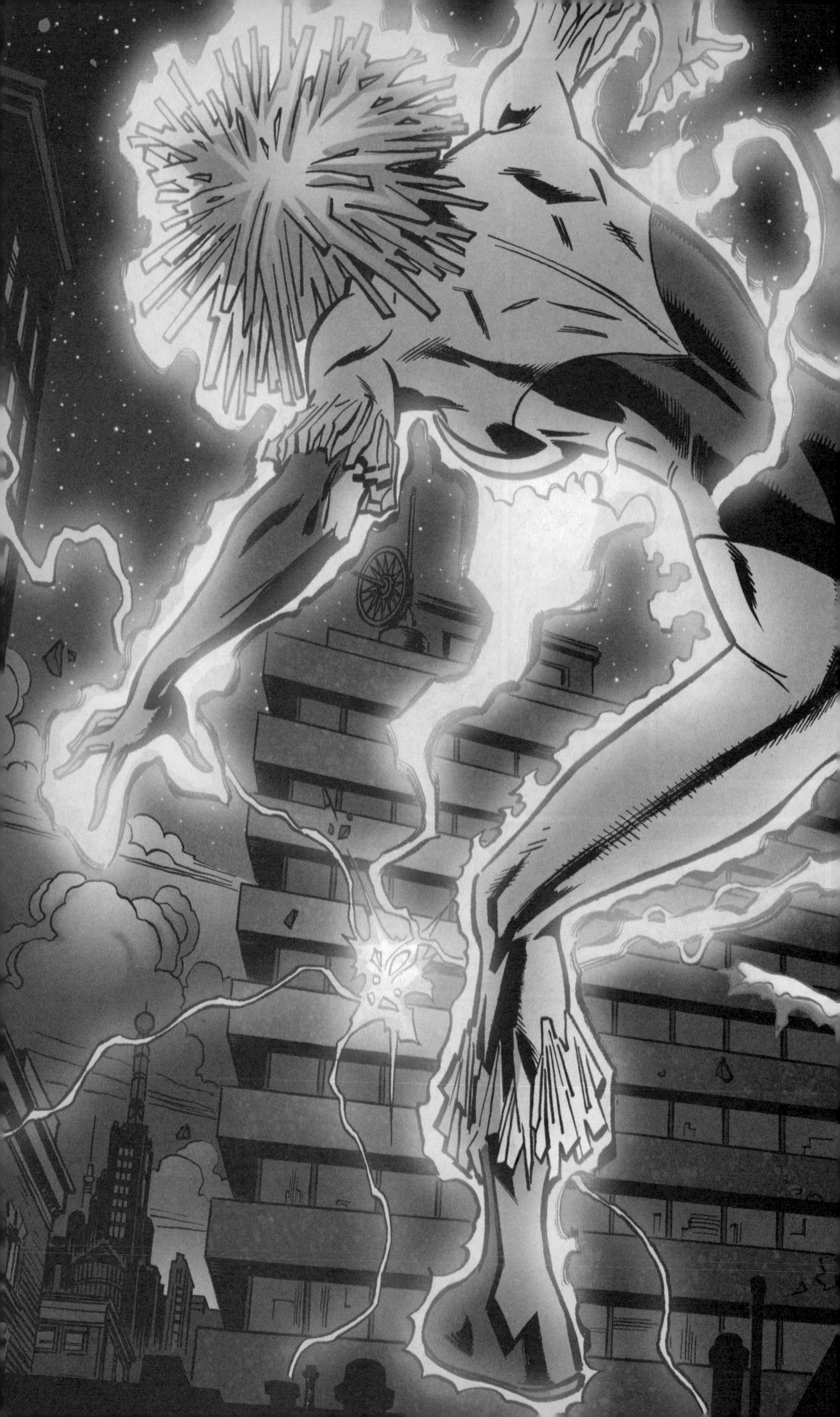

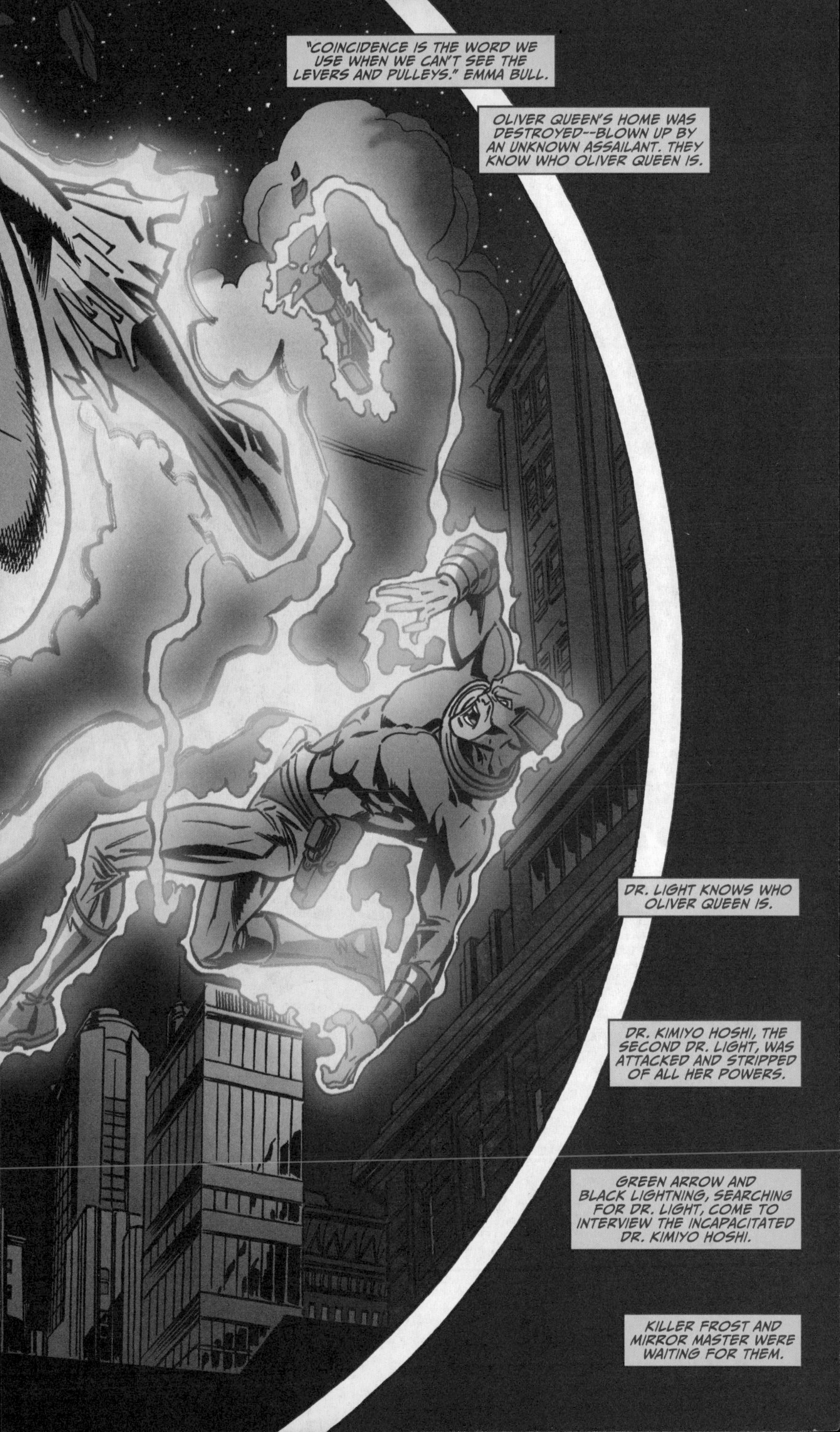
"COINCIDENCE IS THE WORD WE USE WHEN WE CAN'T SEE THE LEVERS AND PULLEYS." EMMA BULL.
OLIVER QUEEN'S HOME WAS DESTROYED--BLOWN UP BY AN UNKNOWN ASSAILANT. THEY KNOW WHO OLIVER QUEEN IS.
DR. LIGHT KNOWS WHO OLIVER QUEEN IS.
DR. KIMIYO HOSHI, THE SECOND DR. LIGHT, WAS ATTACKED AND STRIPPED OF ALL HER POWERS.
GREEN ARROW AND BLACK LIGHTNING, SEARCHING FOR DR. LIGHT, COME TO INTERVIEW THE INCAPACITATED DR. KIMIYO HOSHI.
KILLER FROST AND MIRROR MASTER WERE WAITING FOR THEM.

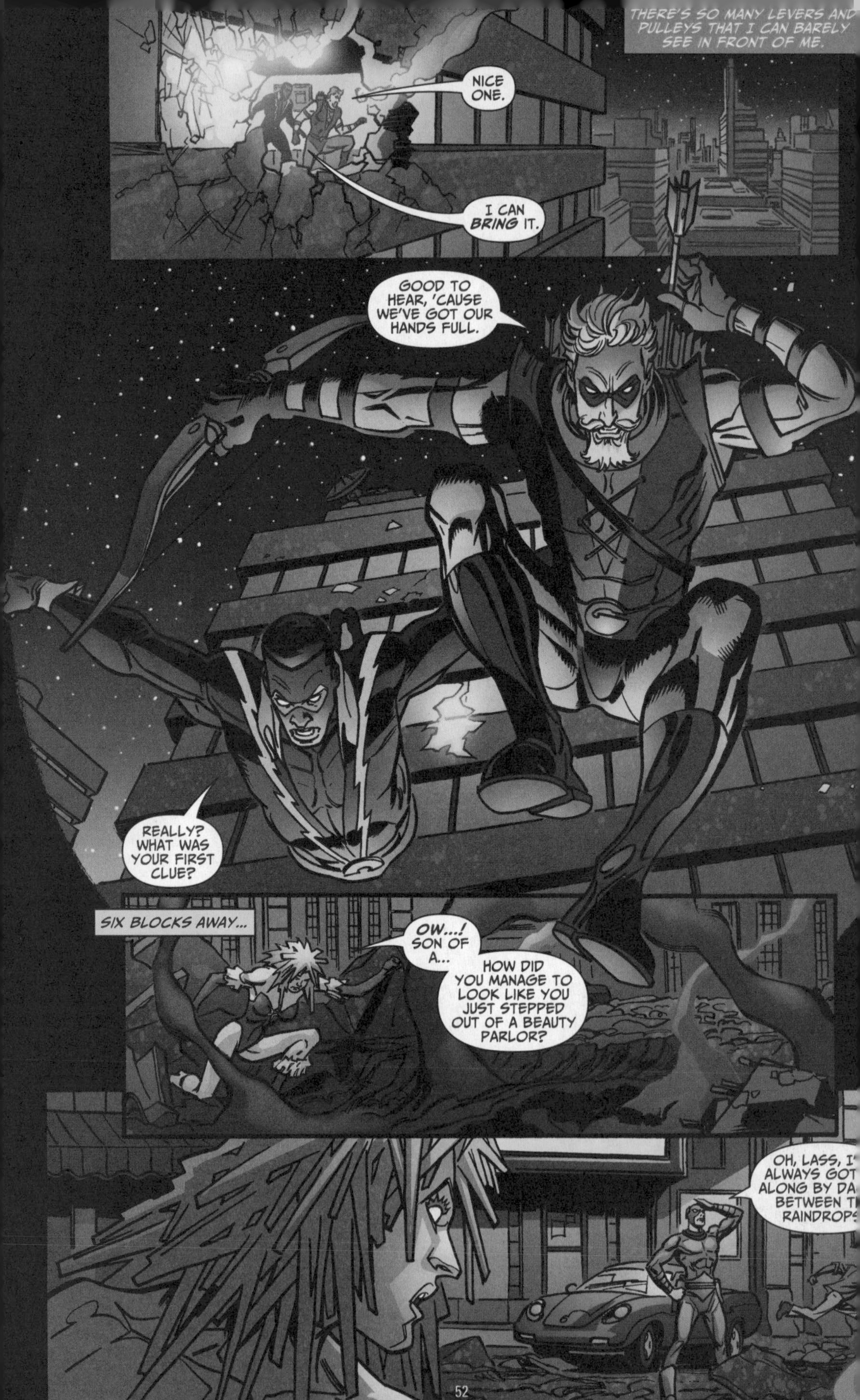

THERE'S SO MANY LEVERS AND PULLEYS THAT I CAN BARELY SEE IN FRONT OF ME.
NICE ONE.
I CAN BRING IT.
GOOD TO HEAR, 'CAUSE WE'VE GOT OUR HANDS FULL.
REALLY? WHAT WAS YOUR FIRST CLUE?
SIX BLOCKS AWAY...
OW...! SON OF A...
HOW DID YOU MANAGE TO LOOK LIKE YOU JUST STEPPED OUT OF A BEAUTY PARLOR?
OH, LASS, I ALWAYS GOT ALONG BY DA BETWEEN T RAINDROPS

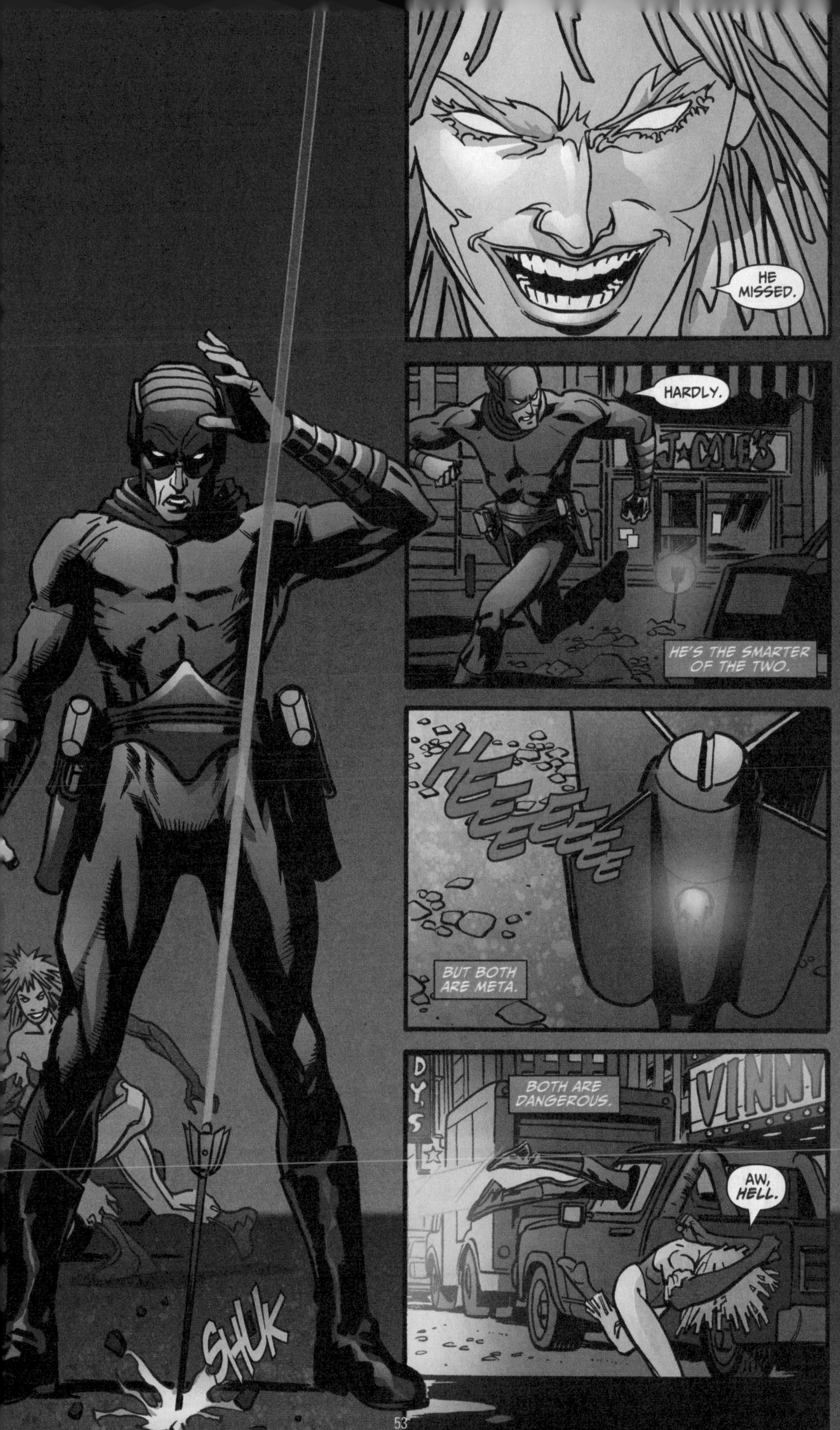
HE MISSED.
HARDLY.
J. COLE'S
HE'S THE SMARTER OF THE TWO.
HEEEEEEE
BUT BOTH ARE META.
BOTH ARE DANGEROUS.
VINNY
AW, HELL.
SHUK

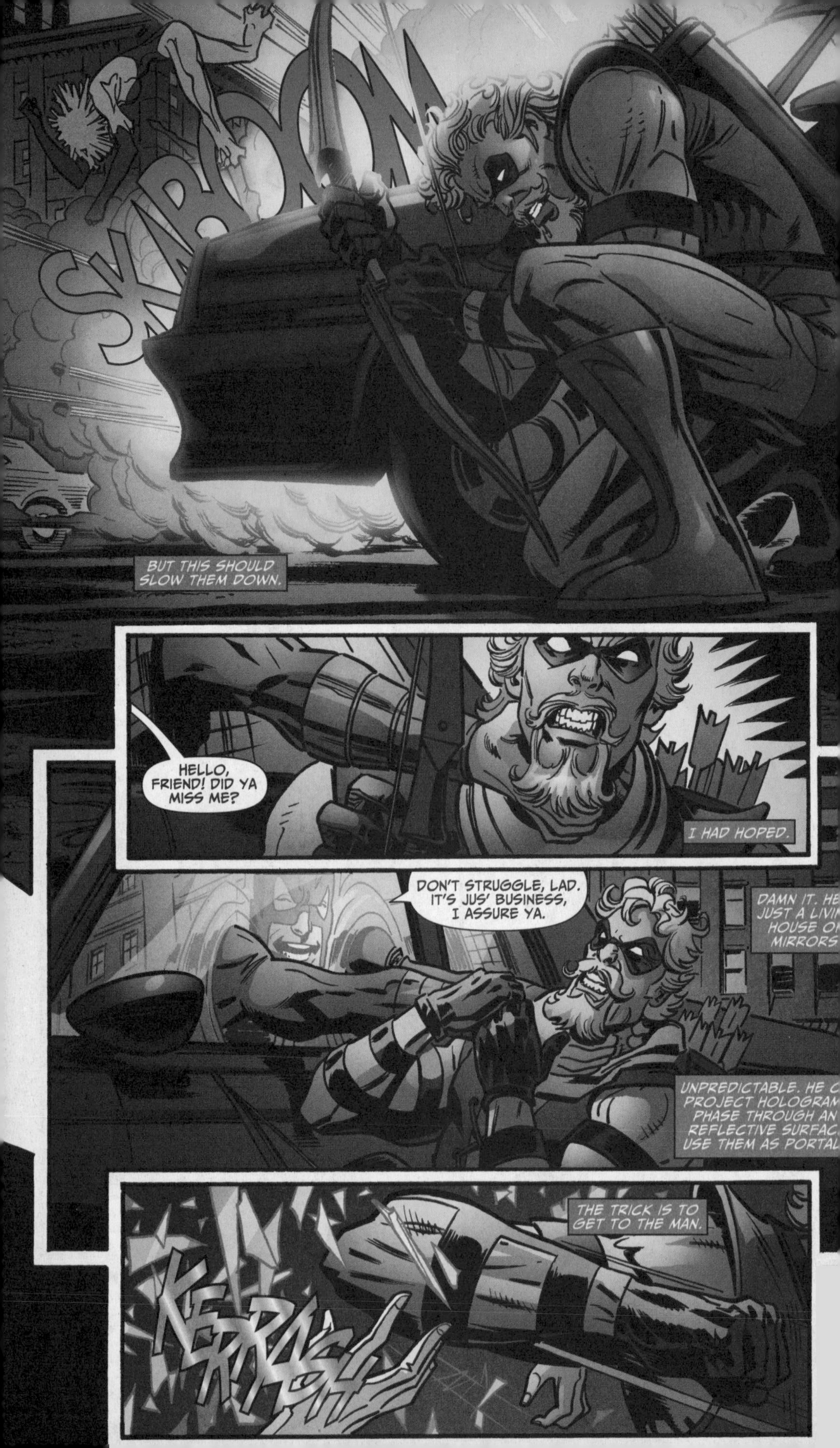

SKRBOOOM
BUT THIS SHOULD SLOW THEM DOWN.
HELLO, FRIEND! DID YA MISS ME?
I HAD HOPED.
DON'T STRUGGLE, LAD. IT'S JUS' BUSINESS, I ASSURE YA.
DAMN IT. HE
JUST A LIVI
HOUSE O
MIRRORS
UNPREDICTABLE. HE C
PROJECT HOLOGRAM
PHASE THROUGH AN
REFLECTIVE SURFAC
USE THEM AS PORTAL
THE TRICK IS TO GET TO THE MAN.
KERRASSH

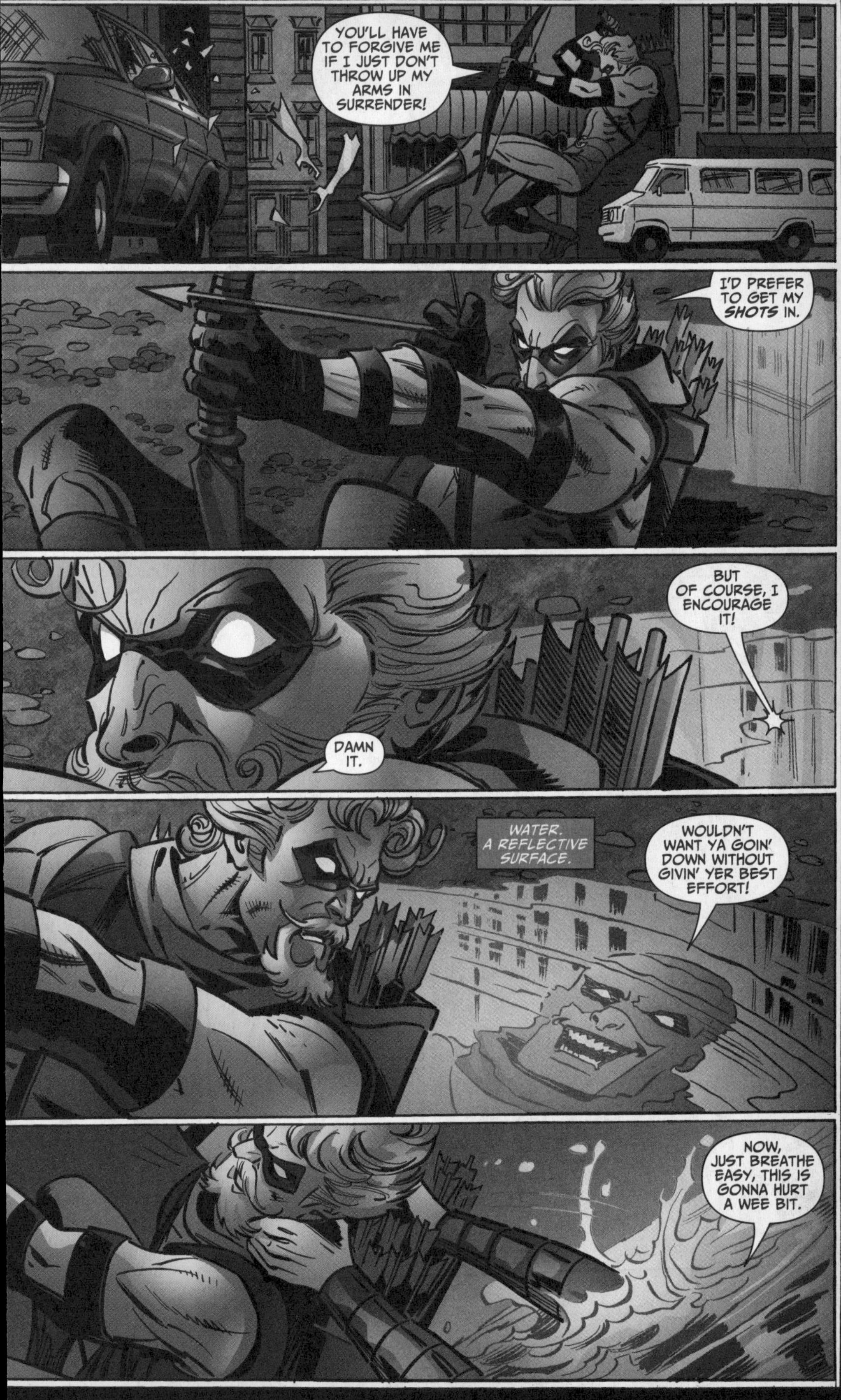

YOU'LL HAVE TO FORGIVE ME IF I JUST DON'T THROW UP MY ARMS IN SURRENDER!
I'D PREFER TO GET MY SHOTS IN.
BUT OF COURSE, I ENCOURAGE IT!
DAMN IT.
WATER. A REFLECTIVE SURFACE.
WOULDN'T WANT YA GOIN' DOWN WITHOUT GIVIN' YER BEST EFFORT!
NOW, JUST BREATHE EASY, THIS IS GONNA HURT A WEE BIT.

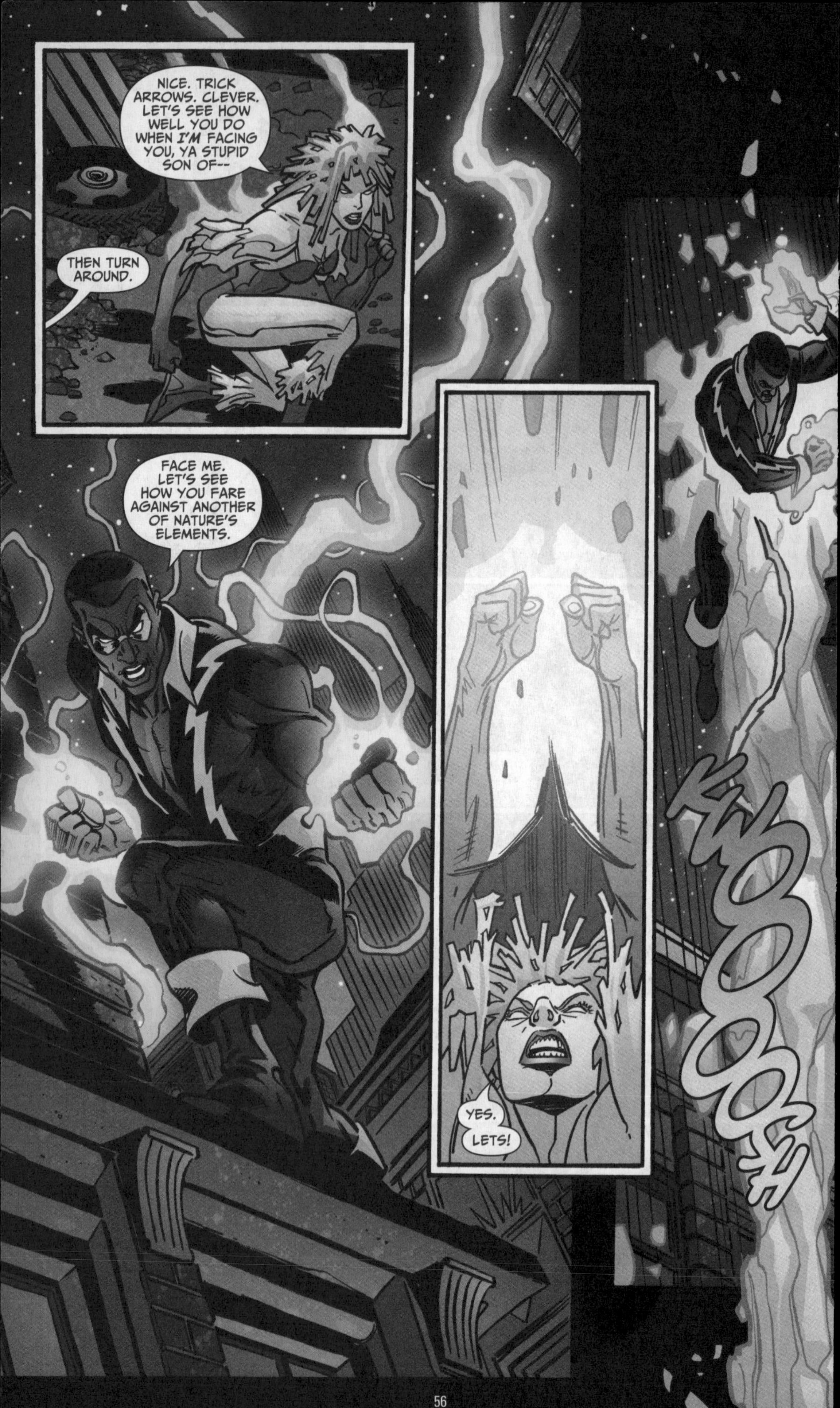
NICE. TRICK ARROWS. CLEVER. LET'S SEE HOW WELL YOU DO WHEN I'M FACING YOU, YA STUPID SON OF--
THEN TURN AROUND.
FACE ME. LET'S SEE HOW YOU FARE AGAINST ANOTHER OF NATURE'S ELEMENTS.
YES.
LETS!
KWOOOOOOM

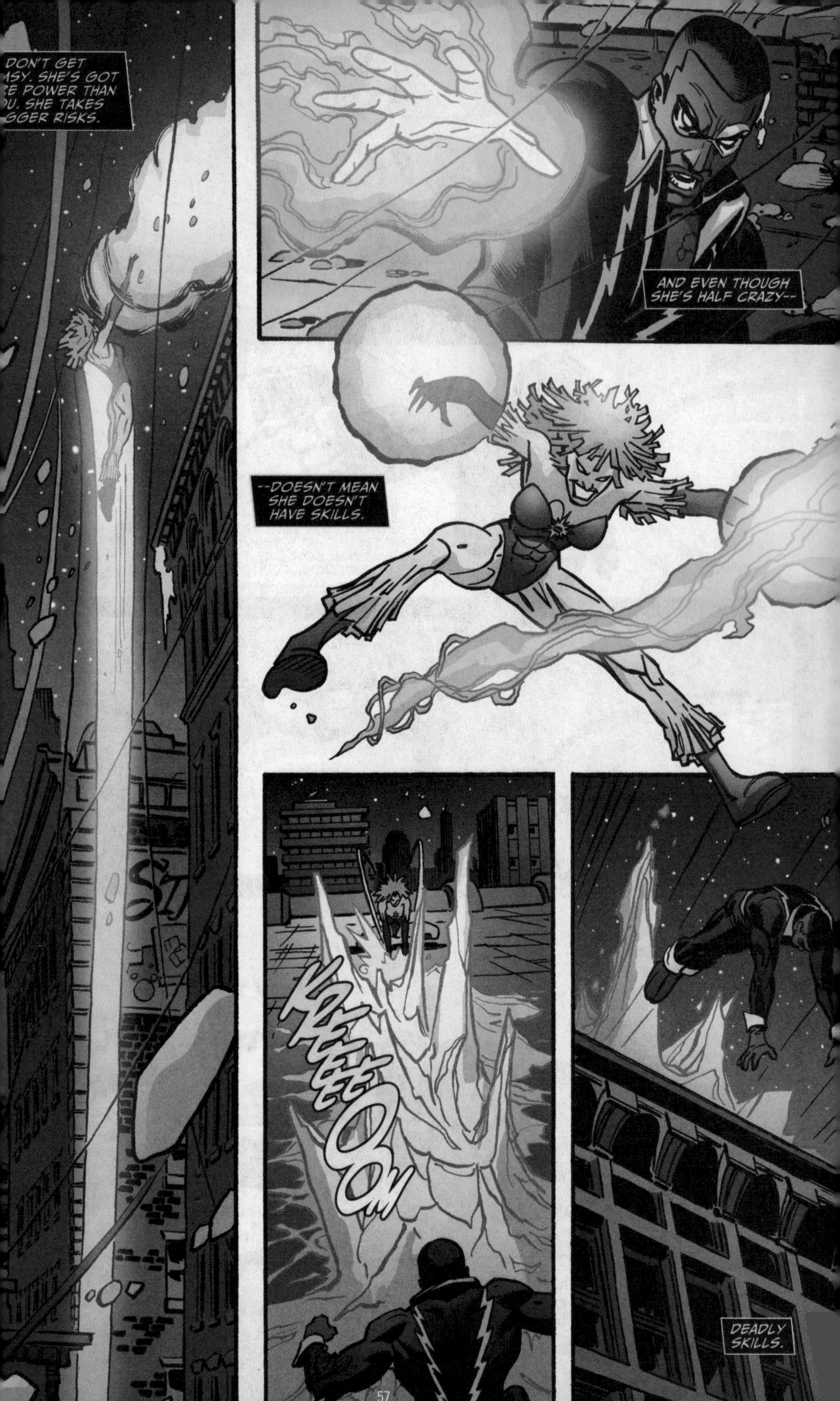
DON'T GET
MSY. SHE'S GOT
E POWER THAN
OU. SHE TAKES
GGER RISKS.
AND EVEN THOUGH SHE'S HALF CRAZY--
--DOESN'T MEAN SHE DOESN'T HAVE SKILLS.
KRKEEEOOOM
DEADLY SKILLS.

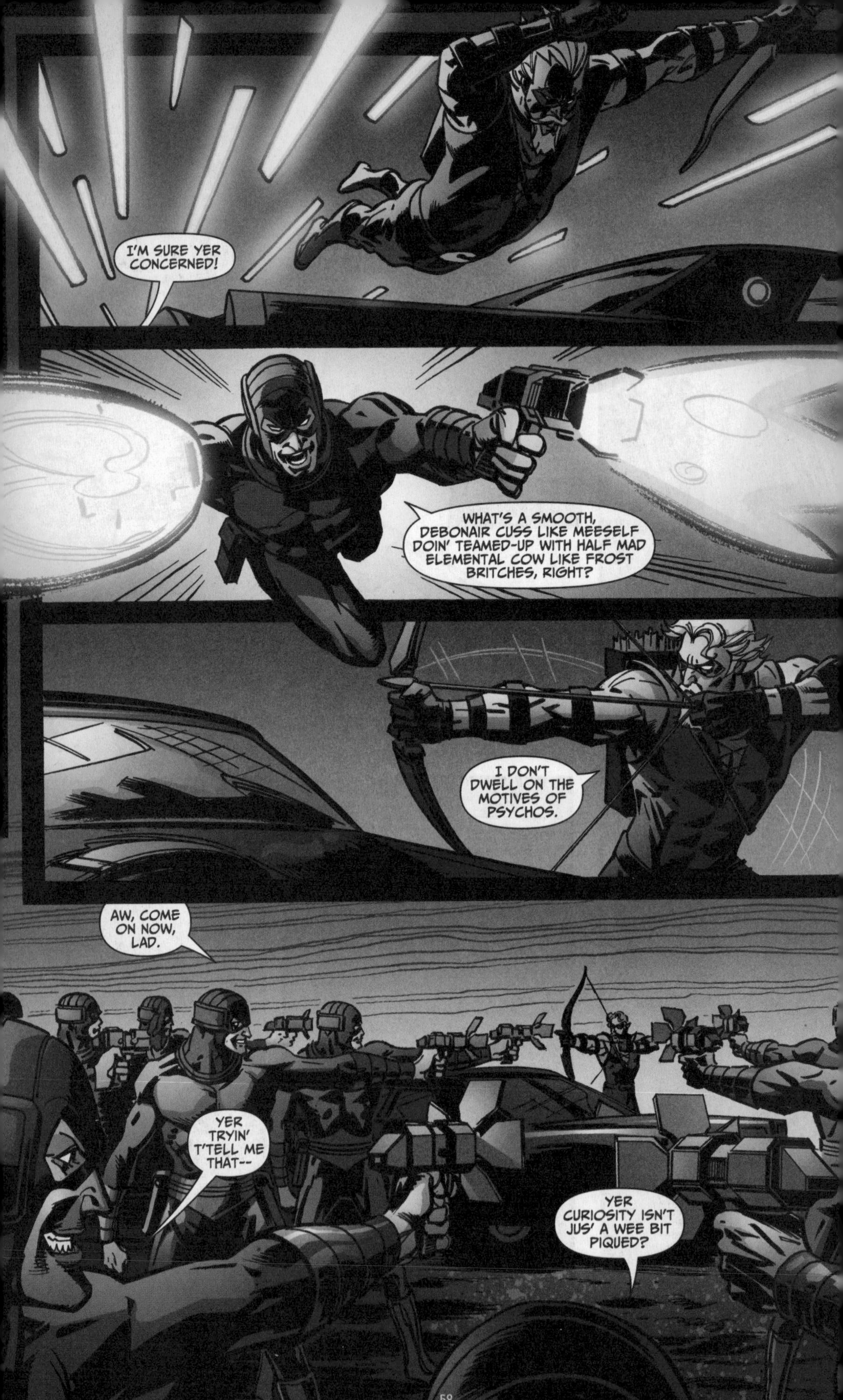
I'M SURE YER CONCERNED!
WHAT'S A SMOOTH, DEBONAIR CUSS LIKE MEESELF DOIN' TEAMED-UP WITH HALF MAD ELEMENTAL COW LIKE FROST BRITCHES, RIGHT?
I DON'T DWELL ON THE MOTIVES OF PSYCHOS.
AW, COME ON NOW, LAD.
YER TRYIN' T'TELL ME THAT--
YER CURIOSITY ISN'T JUS' A WEE BIT PIQUED?

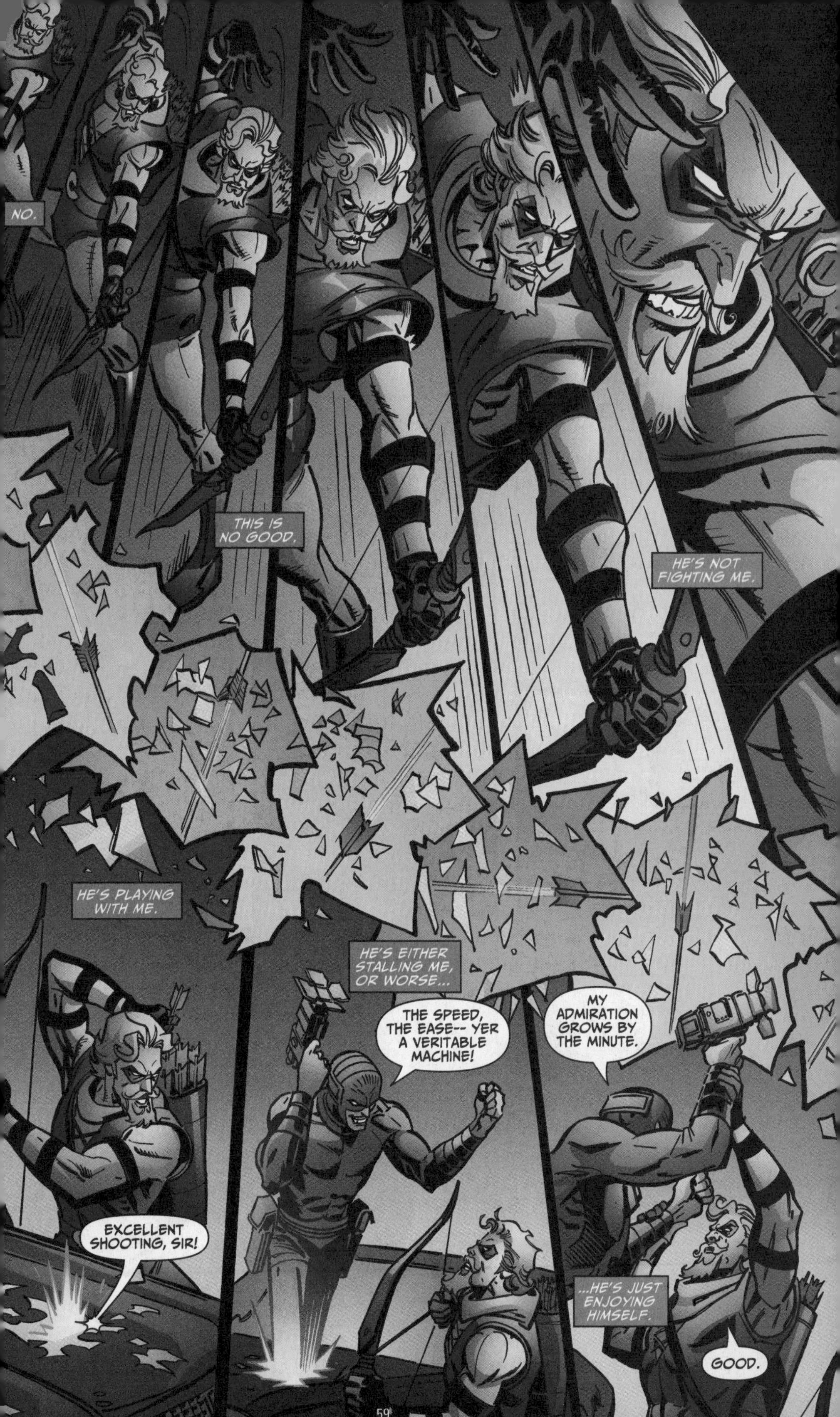
NO.
THIS IS NO GOOD.
HE'S NOT FIGHTING ME.
HE'S PLAYING WITH ME.
HE'S EITHER STALLING ME, OR WORSE...
EXCELLENT SHOOTING, SIR!
THE SPEED, THE EASE-- YER A VERITABLE MACHINE!
MY ADMIRATION GROWS BY THE MINUTE.
...HE'S JUST ENJOYING HIMSELF.
GOOD.

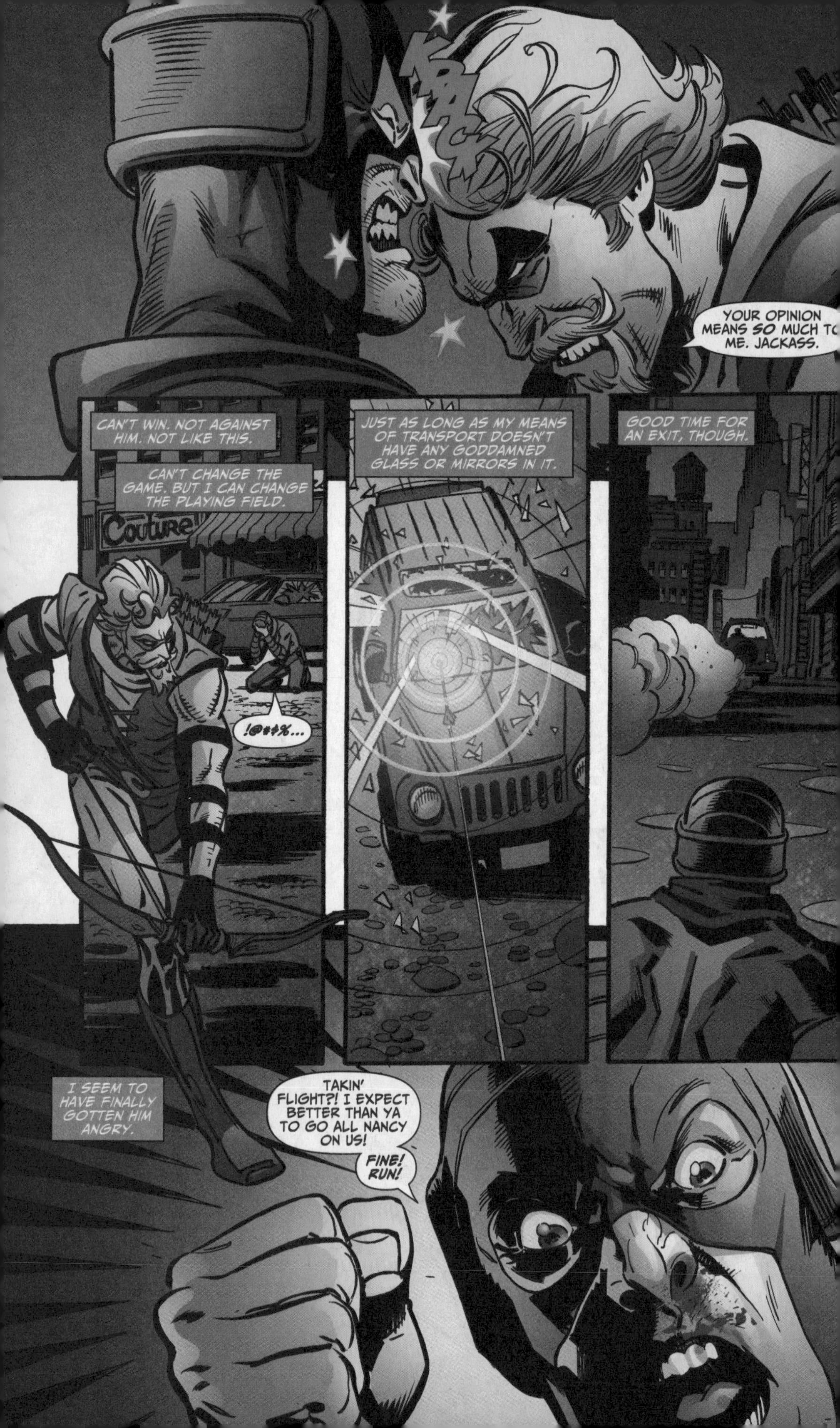
KRACK
YOUR OPINION MEANS SO MUCH TO ME. JACKASS.
CAN'T WIN. NOT AGAINST HIM. NOT LIKE THIS.
CAN'T CHANGE THE GAME. BUT I CAN CHANGE THE PLAYING FIELD.
Couture
!@##%...
JUST AS LONG AS MY MEANS OF TRANSPORT DOESN'T HAVE ANY GODDAMNED GLASS OR MIRRORS IN IT.
GOOD TIME FOR AN EXIT, THOUGH.
I SEEM TO HAVE FINALLY GOTTEN HIM ANGRY.
TAKIN' FLIGHT?! I EXPECT BETTER THAN YA TO GO ALL NANCY ON US!
FINE! RUN!

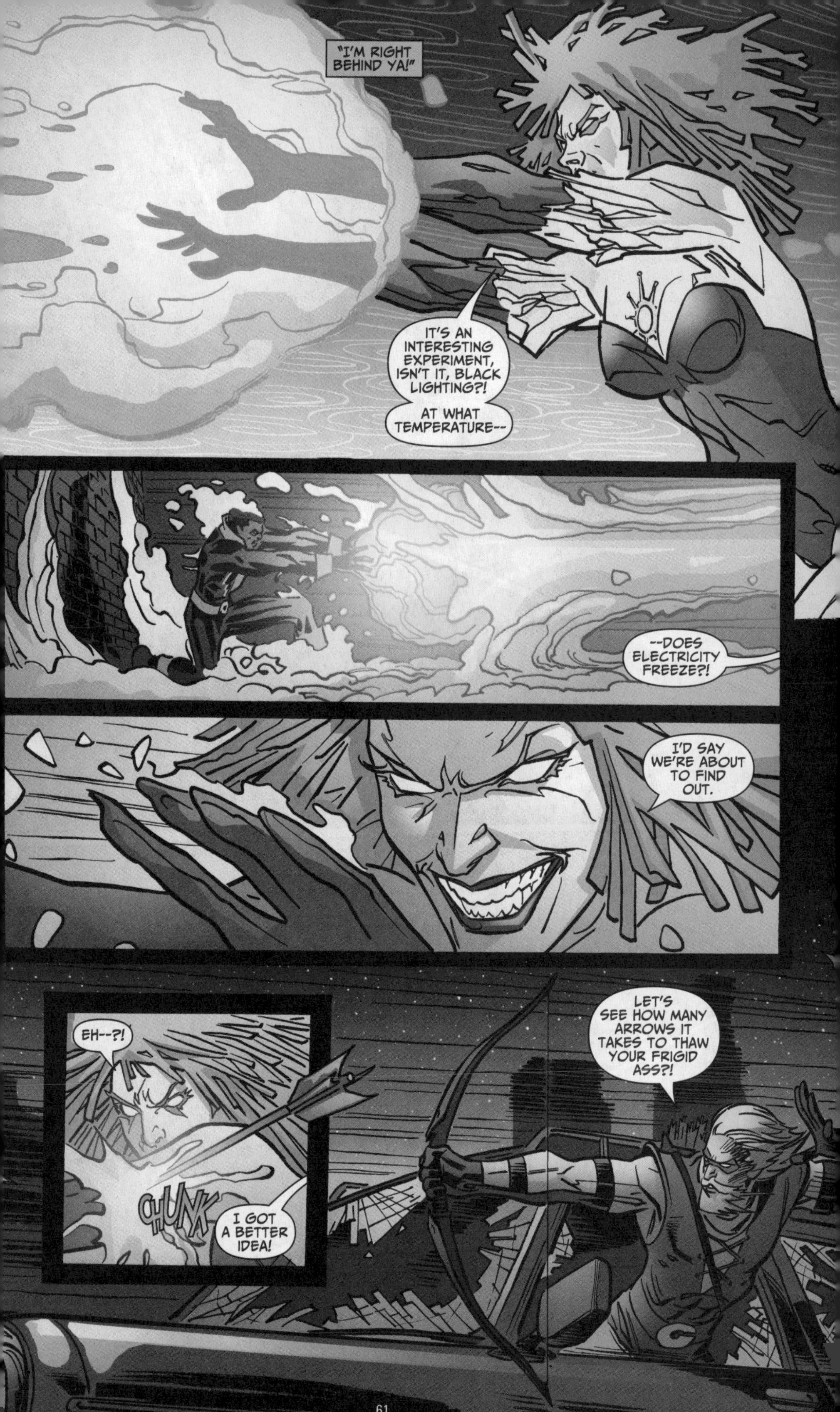
"I'M RIGHT BEHIND YA!"
IT'S AN INTERESTING EXPERIMENT, ISN'T IT, BLACK LIGHTING?!
AT WHAT TEMPERATURE--
--DOES ELECTRICITY FREEZE?!
I'D SAY WE'RE ABOUT TO FIND OUT.
EH--?!
CHUNK
I GOT A BETTER IDEA!
LET'S SEE HOW MANY ARROWS IT TAKES TO THAW YOUR FRIGID ASS?!

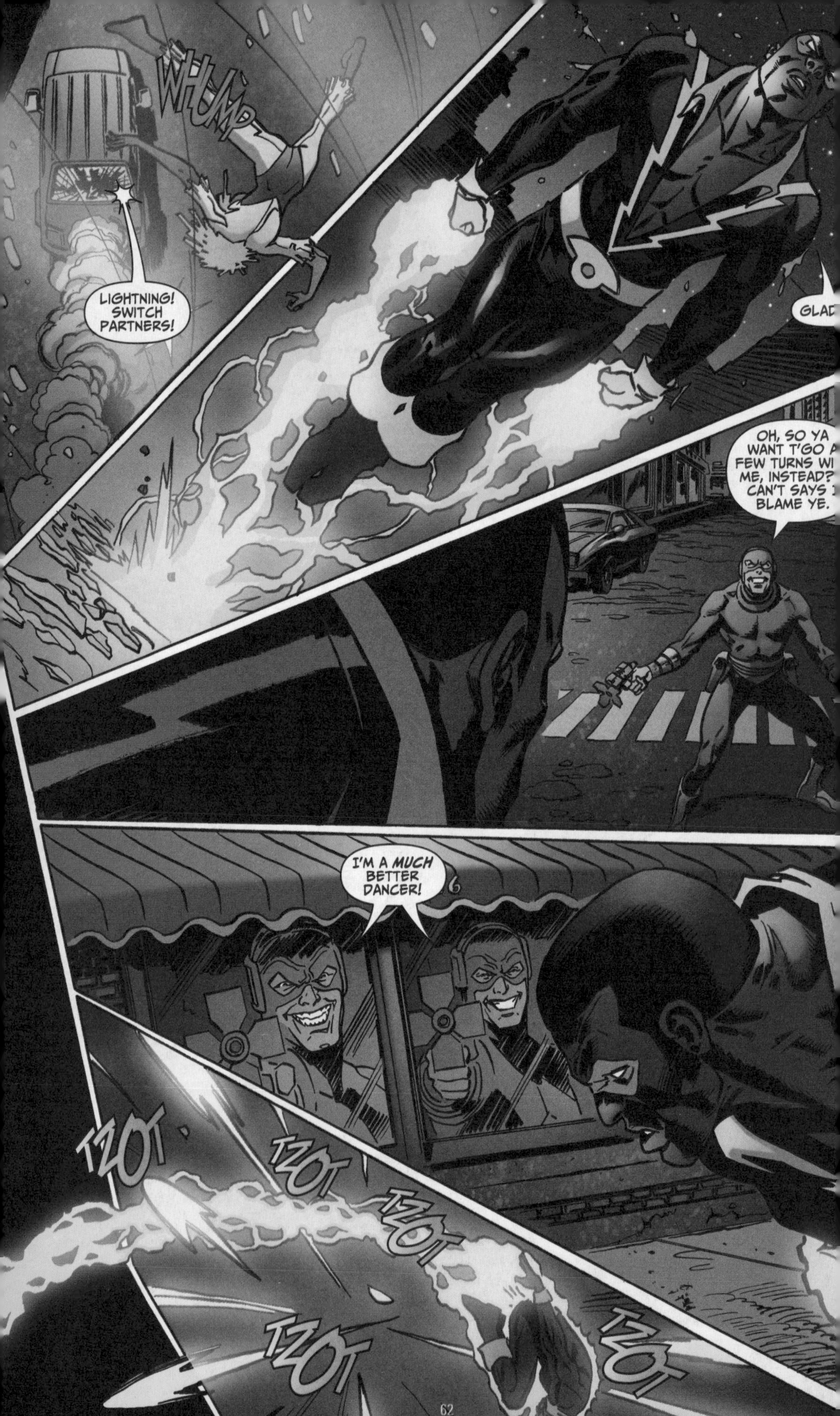
WHUMP
LIGHTNING! SWITCH PARTNERS!
GLAD
OH, SO YA WANT T'GO A FEW TURNS WI ME, INSTEAD? CAN'T SAYS I BLAME YE.
I'M A *MUCH* BETTER DANCER!
TZOT
TZOT
TZOT
TZOT
TZOT

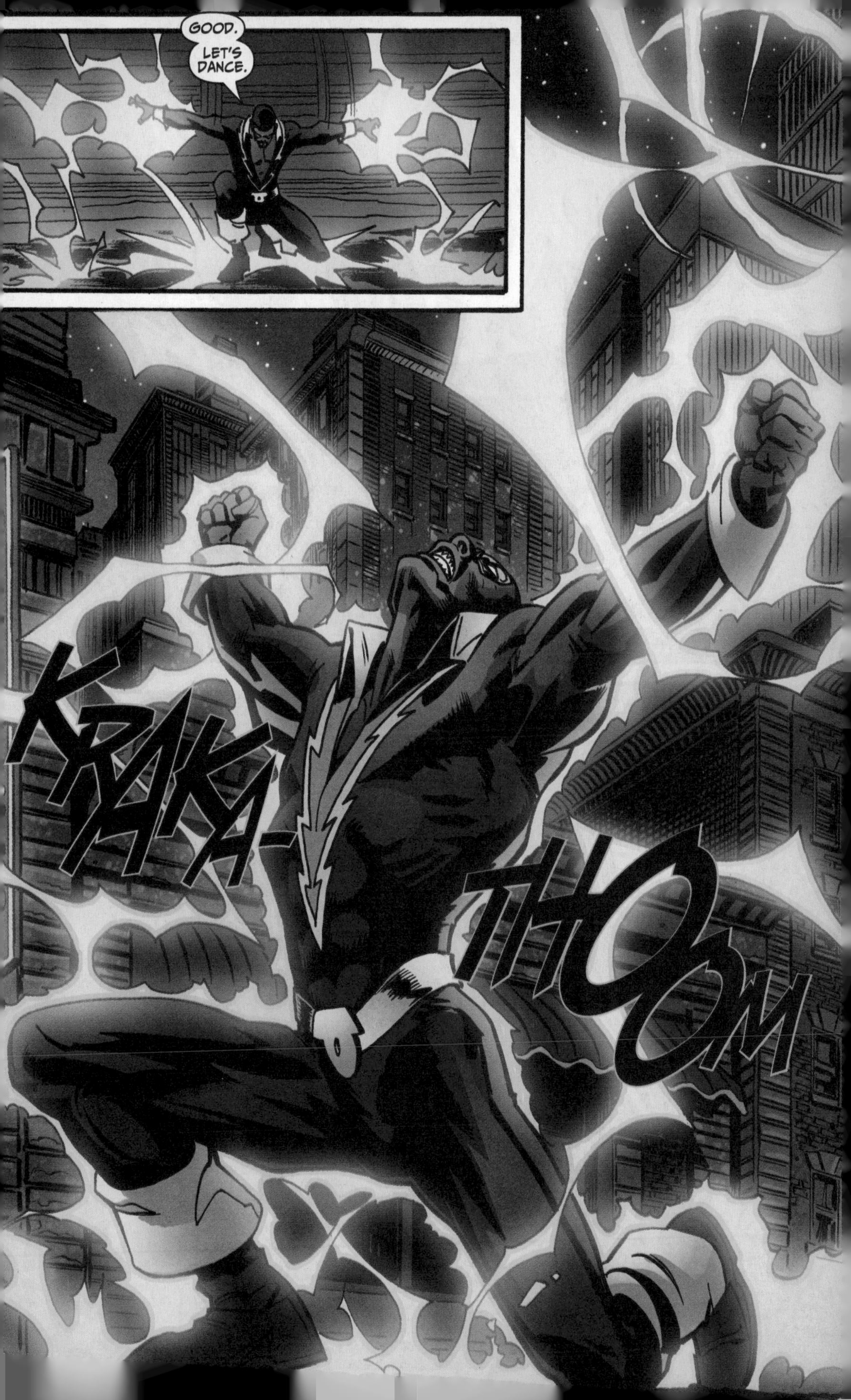
GOOD. LET'S DANCE.
KRAKA-KA-THOOM

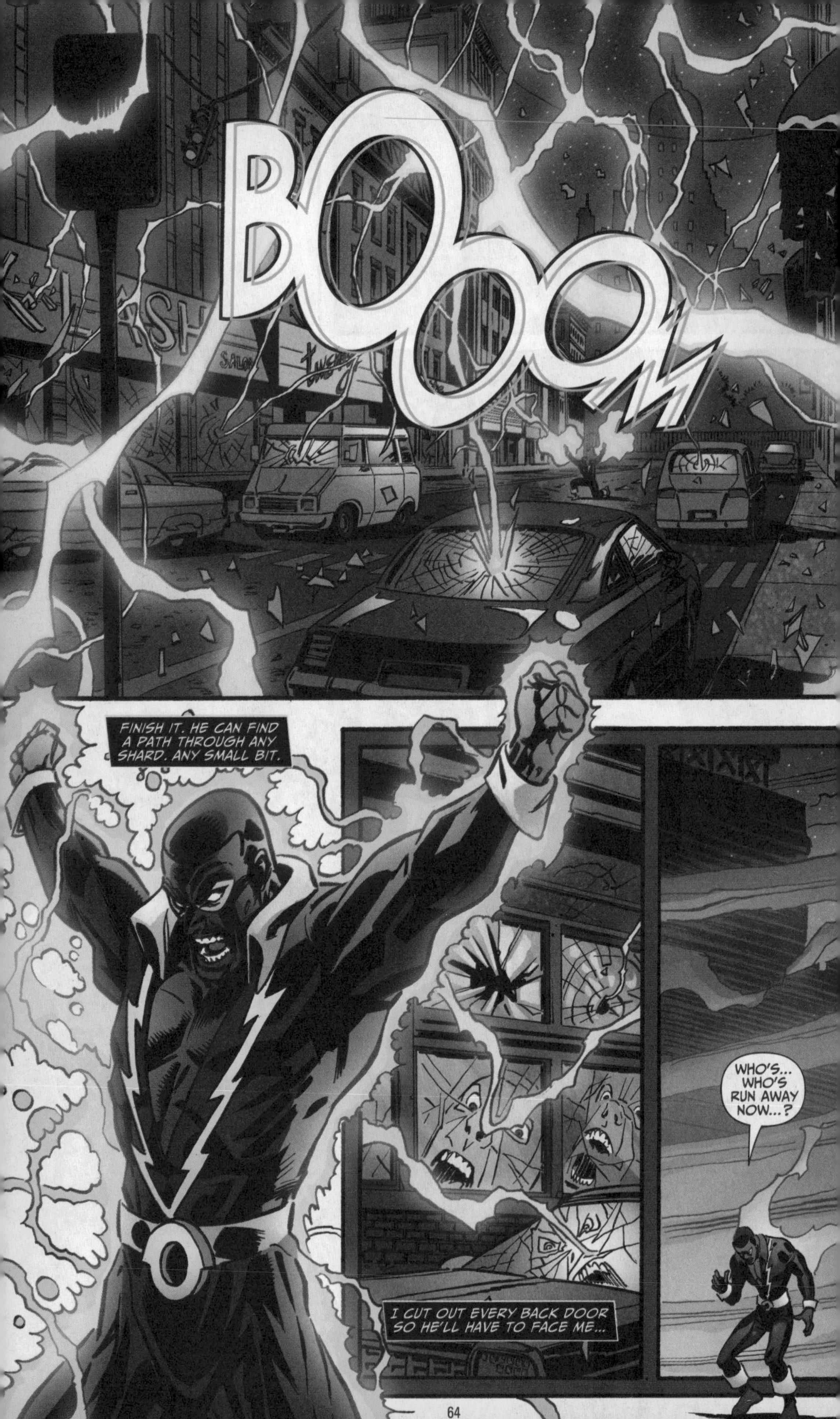
BOOOOM
FINISH IT. HE CAN FIND A PATH THROUGH ANY SHARD. ANY SMALL BIT.
I CUT OUT EVERY BACK DOOR SO HE'LL HAVE TO FACE ME...
WHO'S... WHO'S RUN AWAY NOW...?

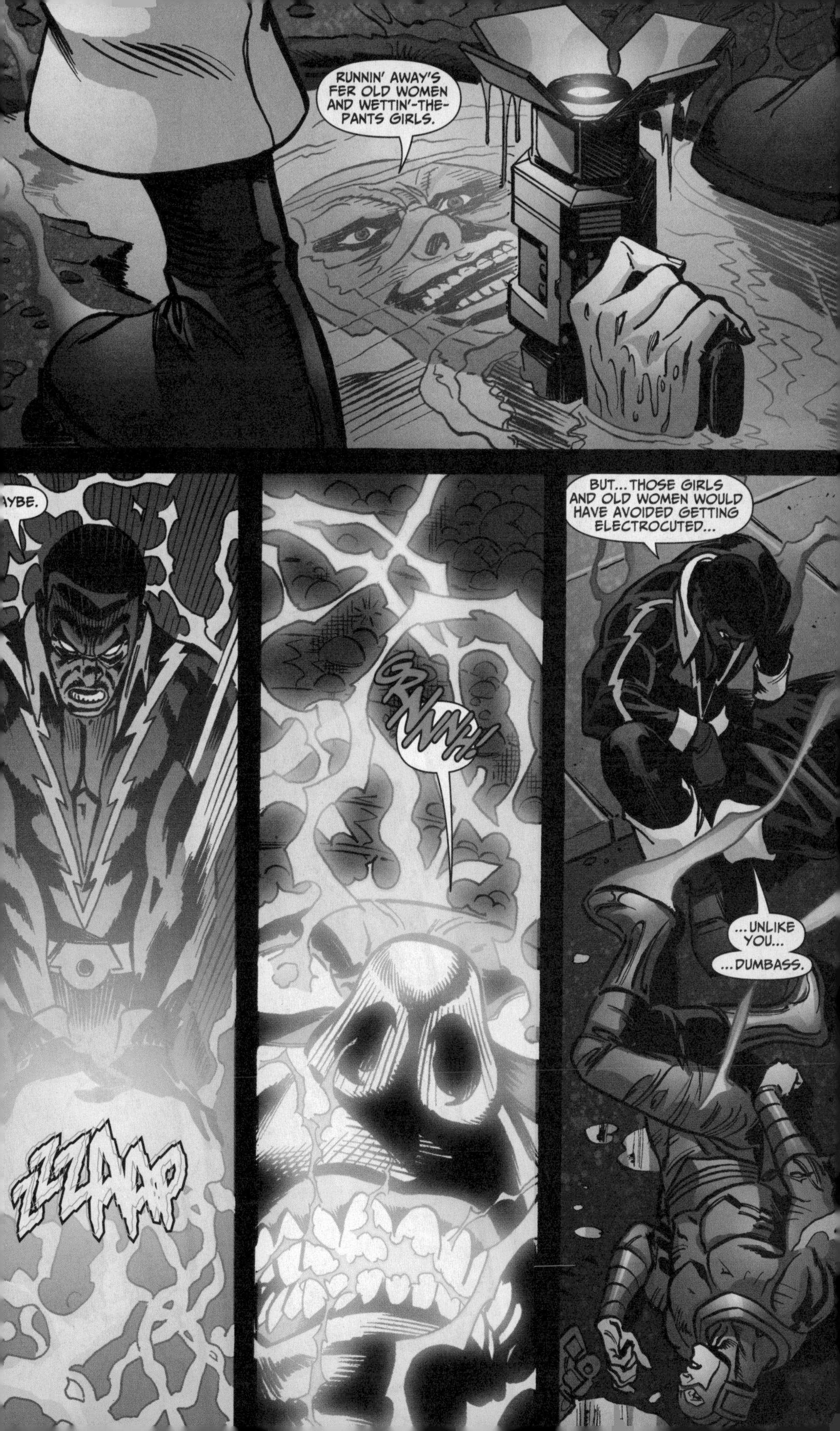
RUNNIN' AWAY'S FER OLD WOMEN AND WETTIN'-THE-PANTS GIRLS.
AYBE.
ZZZAAP
GRNNNH!
BUT...THOSE GIRLS AND OLD WOMEN WOULD HAVE AVOIDED GETTING ELECTROCUTED...
...UNLIKE YOU...
...DUMBASS.

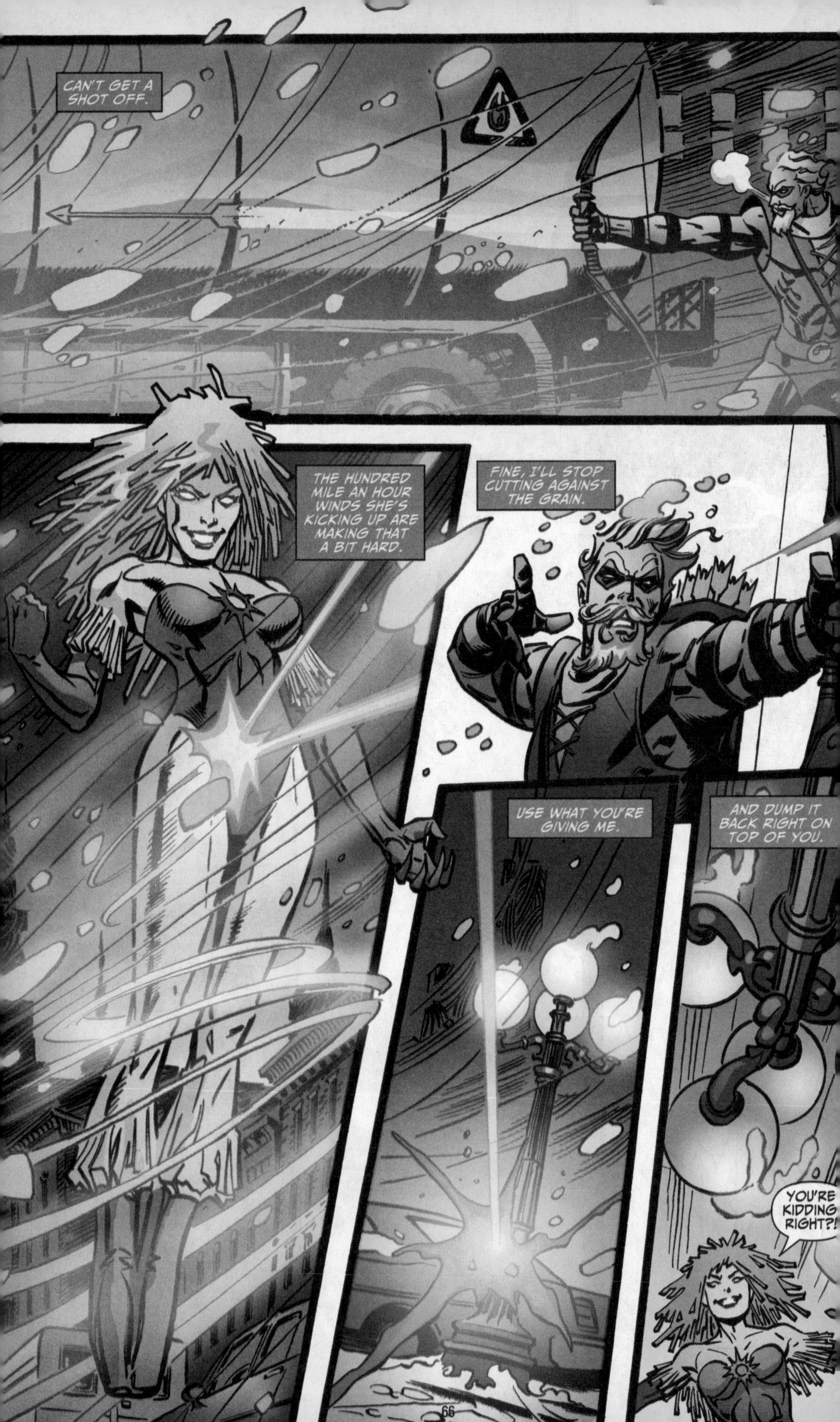
CAN'T GET A SHOT OFF.
THE HUNDRED MILE AN HOUR WINDS SHE'S KICKING UP ARE MAKING THAT A BIT HARD.
FINE, I'LL STOP CUTTING AGAINST THE GRAIN.
USE WHAT YOU'RE GIVING ME.
AND DUMP IT BACK RIGHT ON TOP OF YOU.
YOU'RE KIDDING RIGHT?!

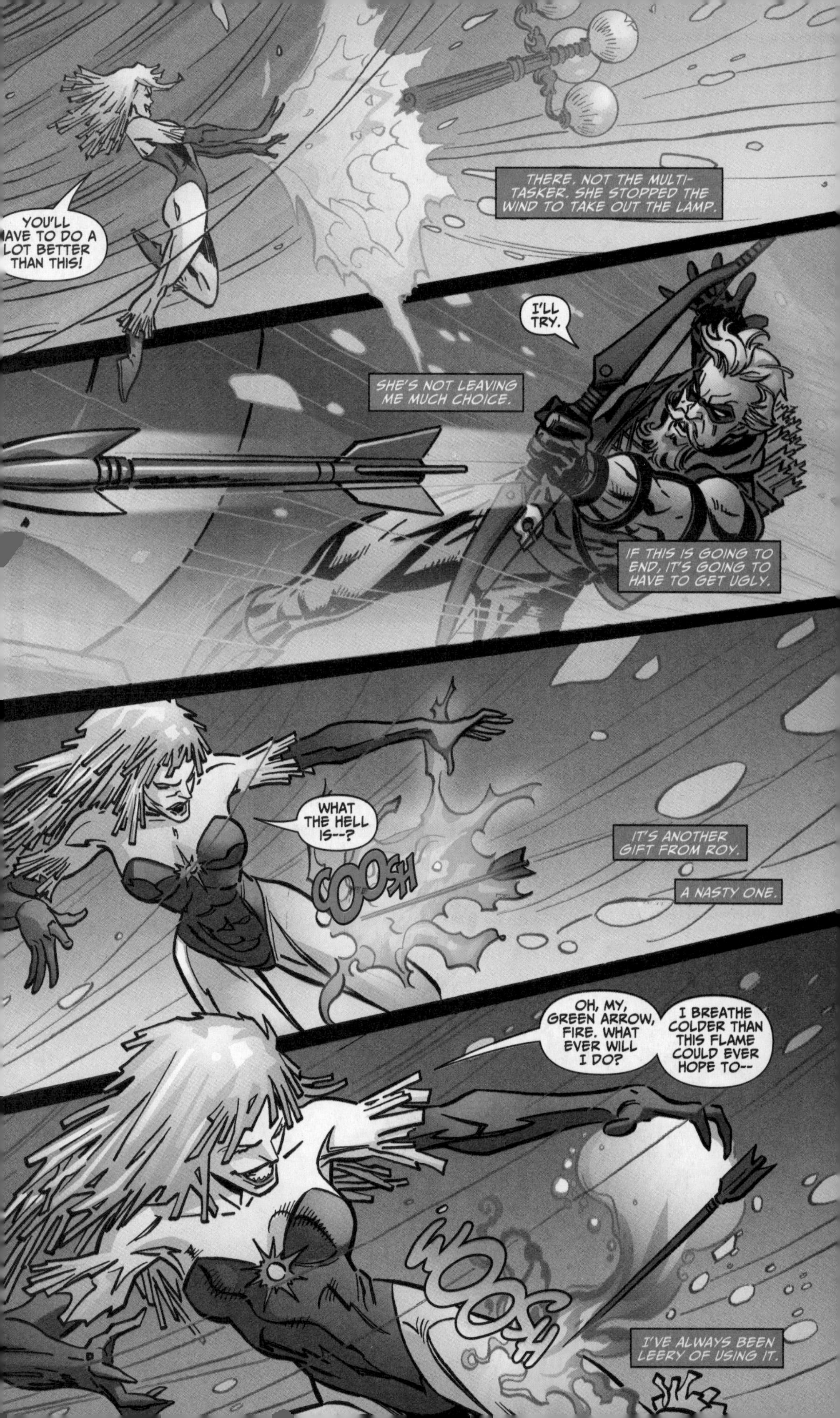
YOU'LL HAVE TO DO A LOT BETTER THAN THIS!
THERE. NOT THE MULTI-TASKER. SHE STOPPED THE WIND TO TAKE OUT THE LAMP.
I'LL TRY.
SHE'S NOT LEAVING ME MUCH CHOICE.
IF THIS IS GOING TO END, IT'S GOING TO HAVE TO GET UGLY.
WHAT THE HELL IS--?
COOSH
IT'S ANOTHER GIFT FROM ROY.
A NASTY ONE.
OH, MY, GREEN ARROW, FIRE. WHAT EVER WILL I DO?
I BREATHE COLDER THAN THIS FLAME COULD EVER HOPE TO--
WOOSH
I'VE ALWAYS BEEN LEERY OF USING IT.

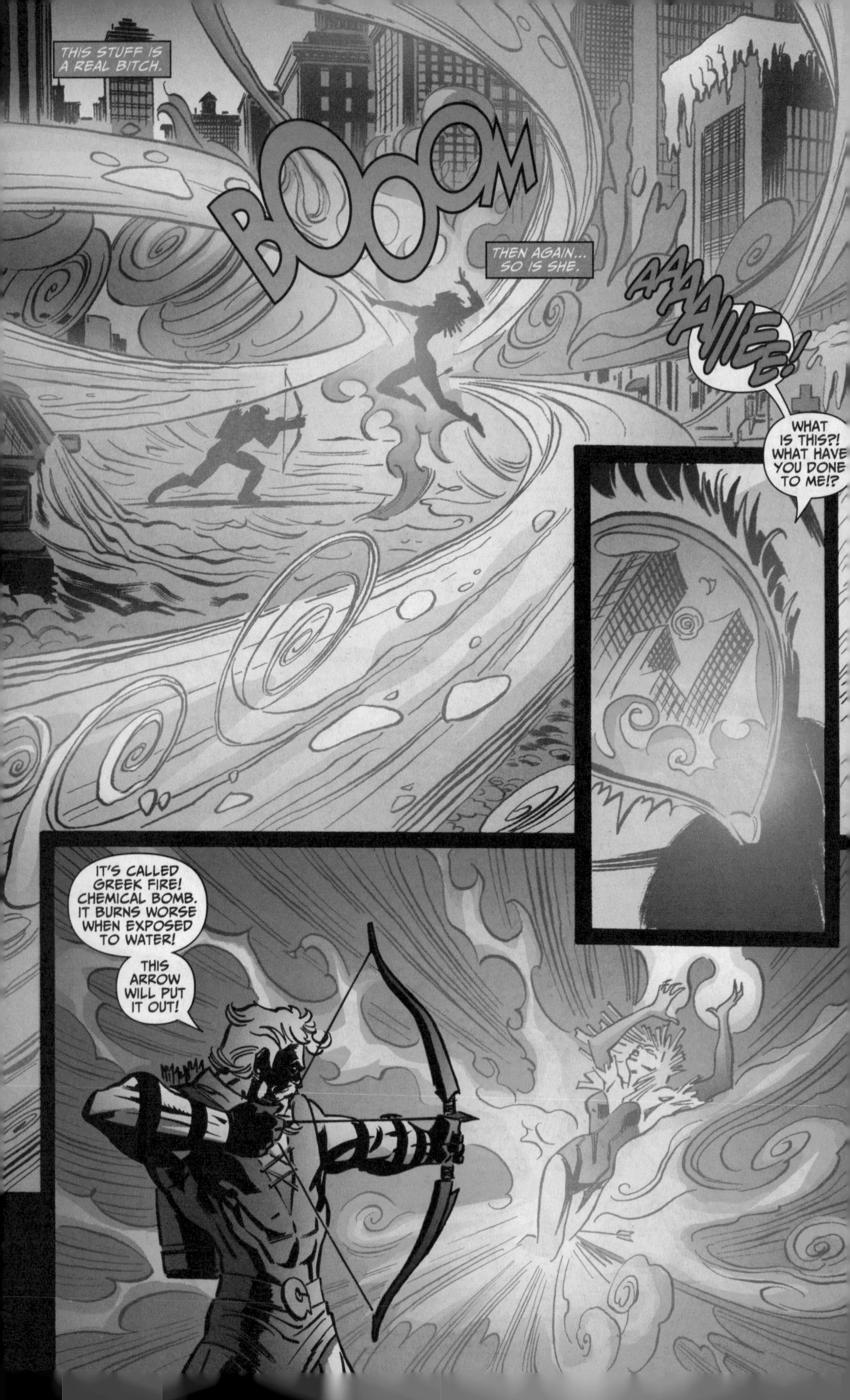
THIS STUFF IS A REAL BITCH.
BOOOM
THEN AGAIN... SO IS SHE.
AAAAIIEE!
WHAT IS THIS?! WHAT HAVE YOU DONE TO ME!?
IT'S CALLED GREEK FIRE! CHEMICAL BOMB. IT BURNS WORSE WHEN EXPOSED TO WATER!
THIS ARROW WILL PUT IT OUT!

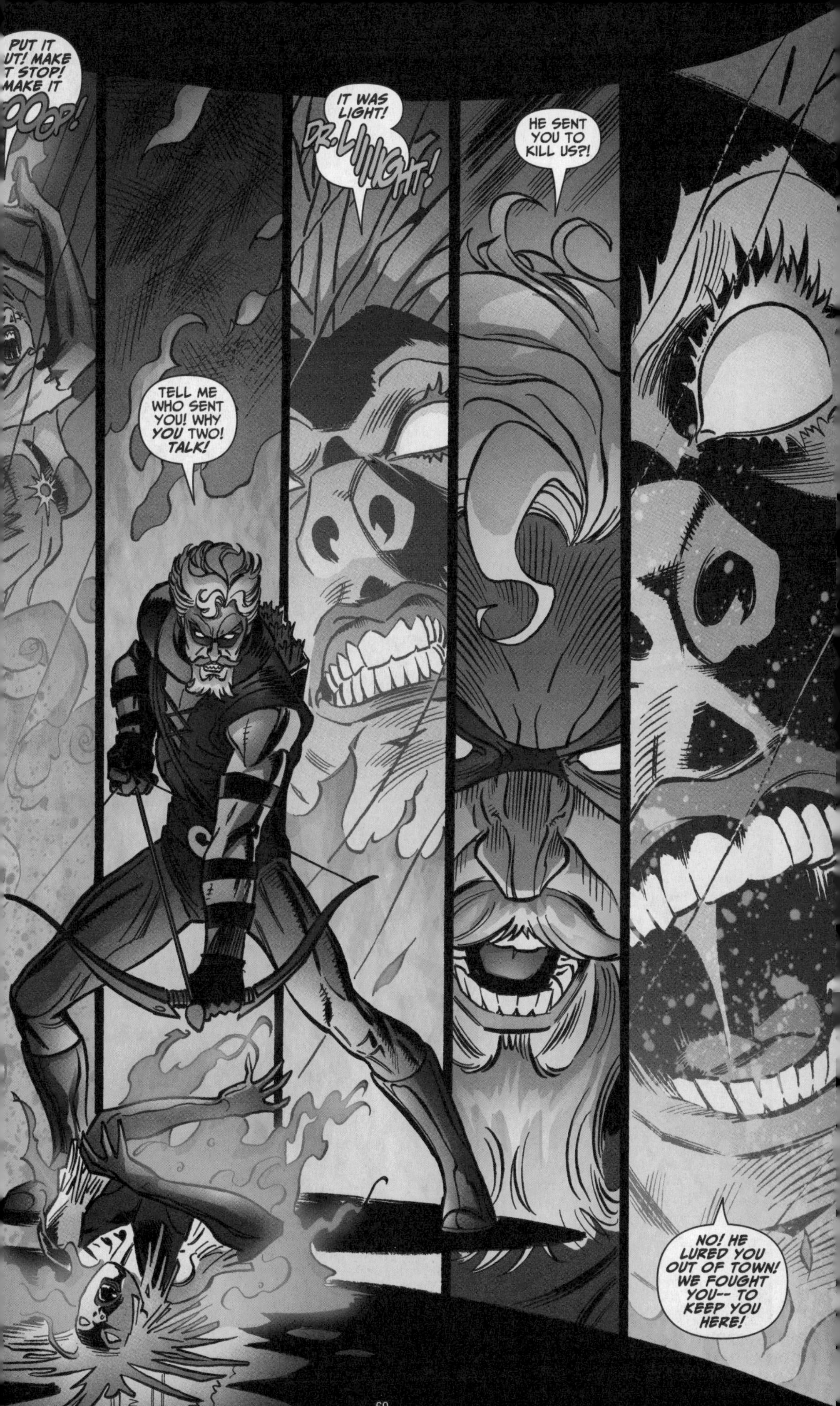
PUT IT OUT! MAKE IT STOP! MAKE IT STOOOP!
TELL ME WHO SENT YOU! WHY YOU TWO! TALK!
IT WAS LIGHT! DR. LIIIIGHT!
HE SENT YOU TO KILL US?!
NO! HE LURED YOU OUT OF TOWN! WE FOUGHT YOU-- TO KEEP YOU HERE!

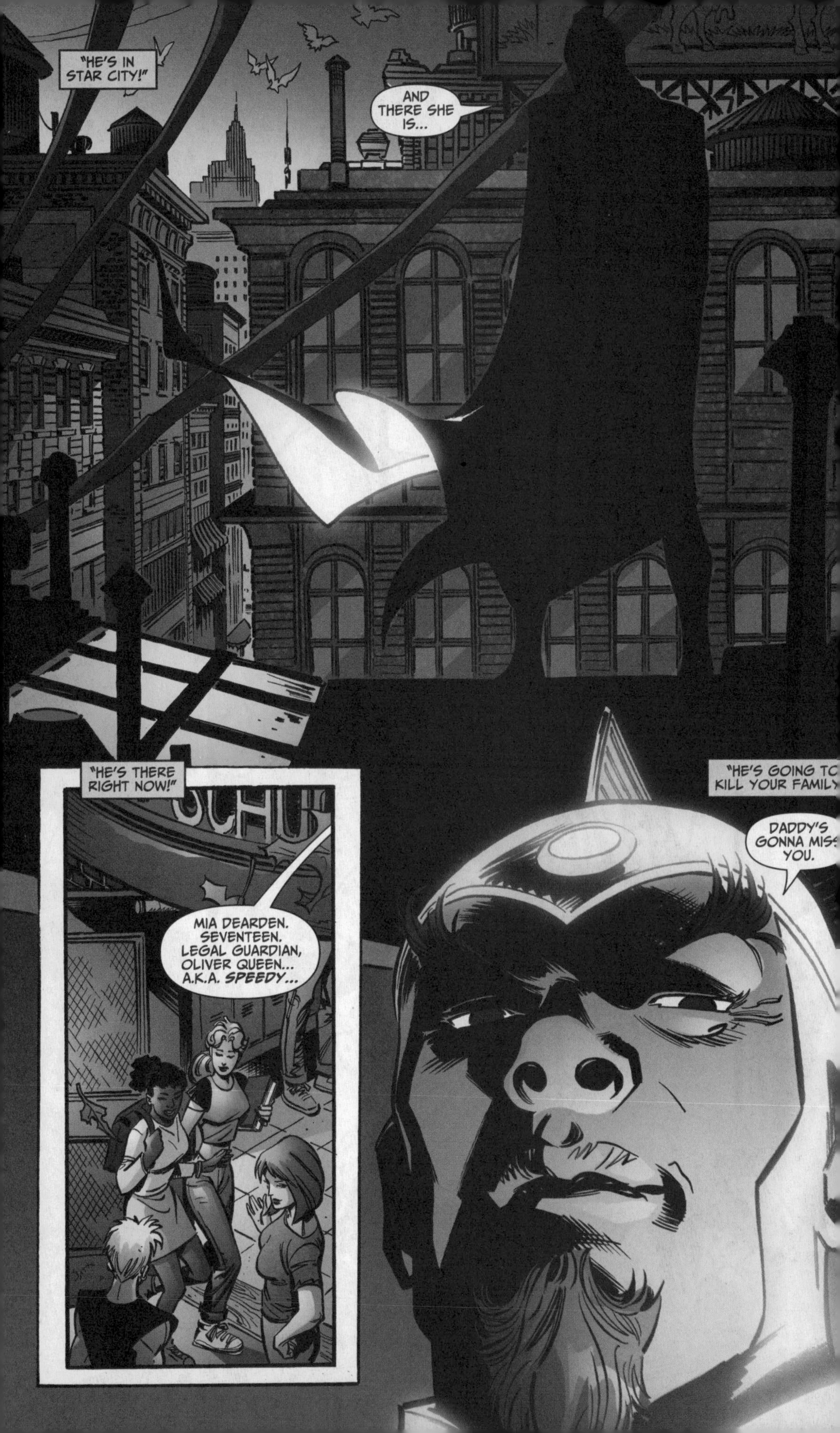
"HE'S IN STAR CITY!"
AND THERE SHE IS...
"HE'S THERE RIGHT NOW!"
MIA DEARDEN. SEVENTEEN. LEGAL GUARDIAN, OLIVER QUEEN... A.K.A. SPEEDY...
"HE'S GOING TO KILL YOUR FAMILY
DADDY'S GONNA MISS YOU.

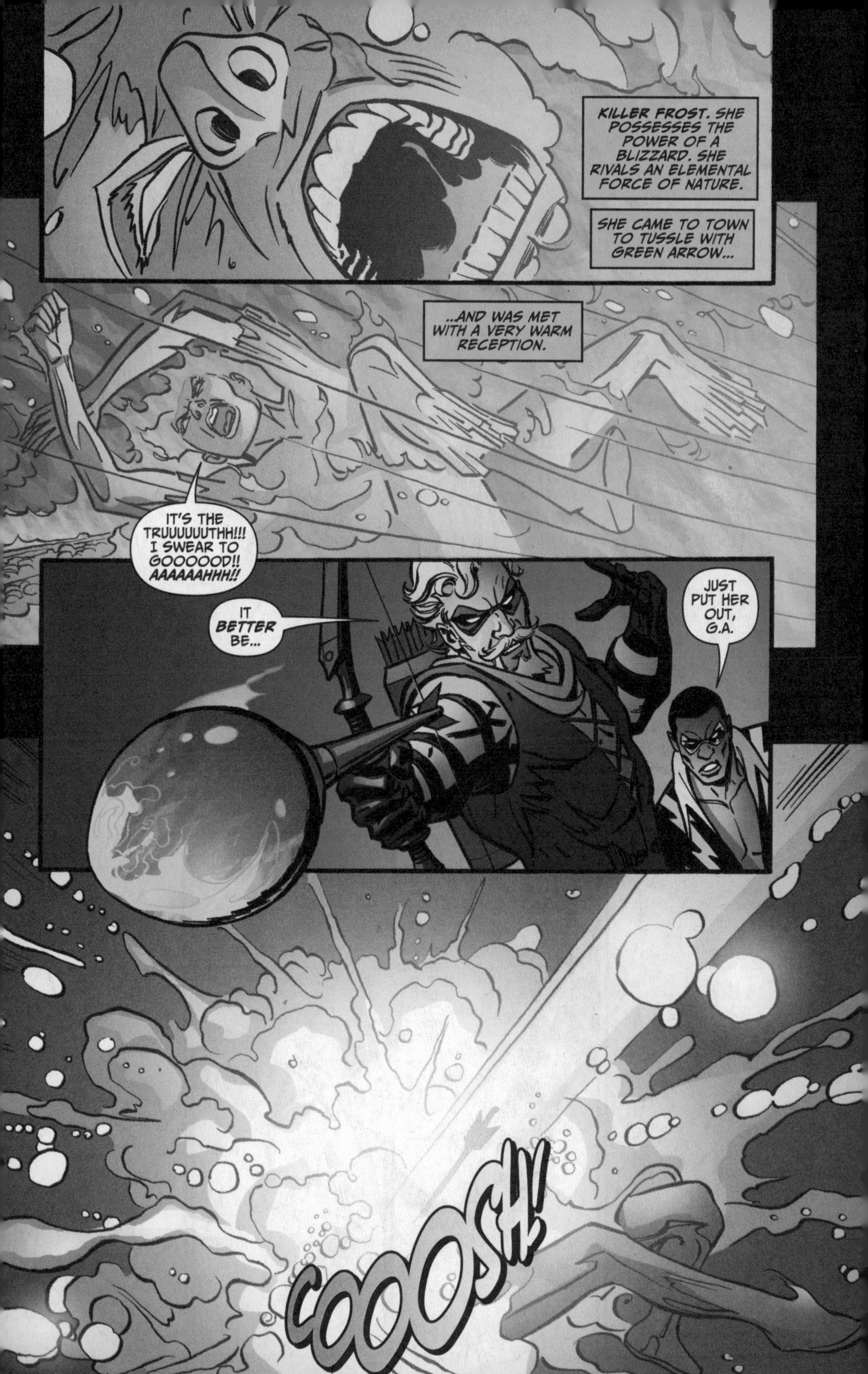
KILLER FROST. SHE POSSESSES THE POWER OF A BLIZZARD. SHE RIVALS AN ELEMENTAL FORCE OF NATURE.
SHE CAME TO TOWN TO TUSSLE WITH GREEN ARROW...
...AND WAS MET WITH A VERY WARM RECEPTION.
IT'S THE TRUUUUUUTHH!!! I SWEAR TO GOOOOOD!! AAAAAAHHH!!
IT BETTER BE...
JUST PUT HER OUT, G.A.
COOOSH!!

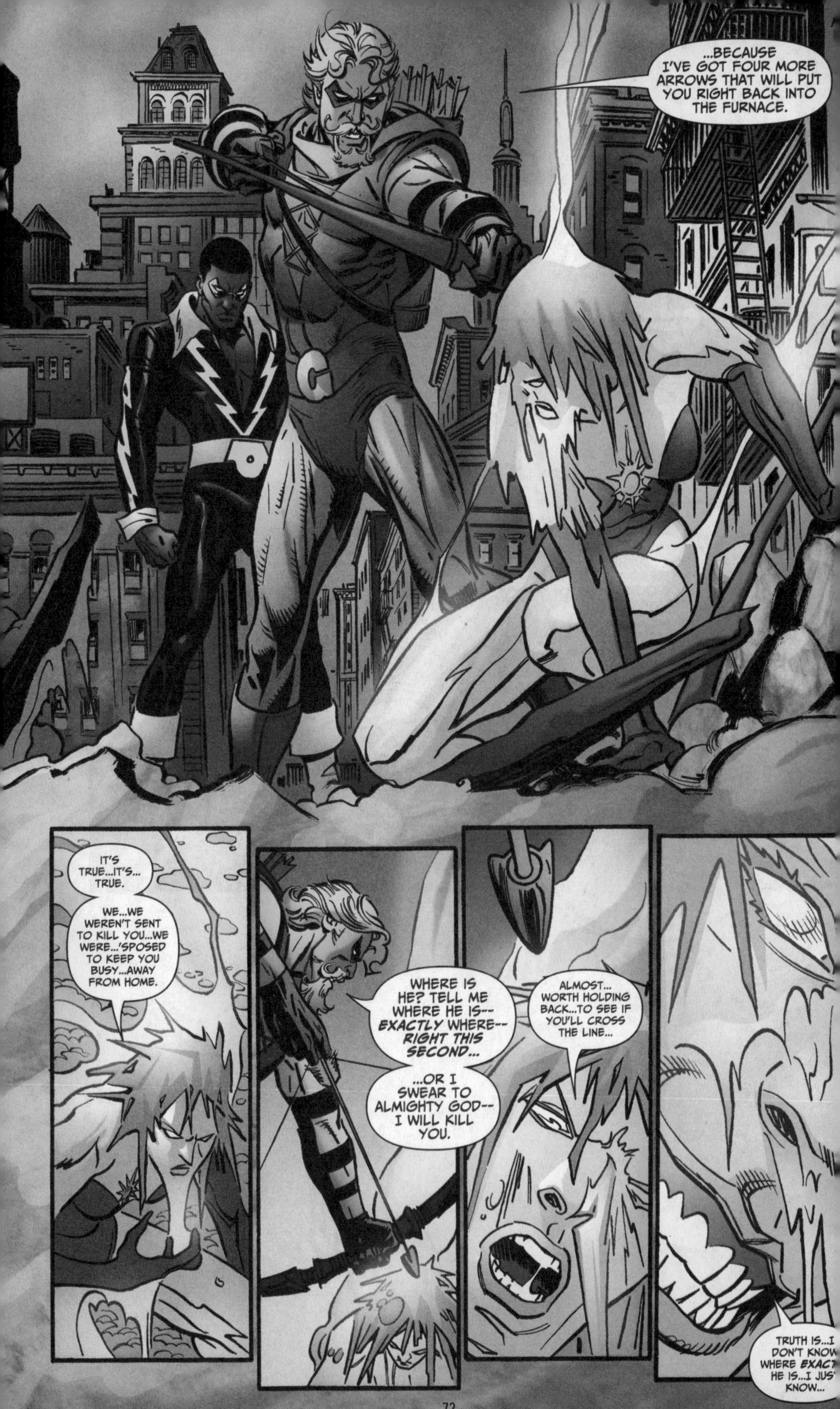
...BECAUSE I'VE GOT FOUR MORE ARROWS THAT WILL PUT YOU RIGHT BACK INTO THE FURNACE.
IT'S TRUE...IT'S... TRUE.
WE...WE WEREN'T SENT TO KILL YOU...WE WERE...'SPOSED TO KEEP YOU BUSY...AWAY FROM HOME.
WHERE IS HE? TELL ME WHERE HE IS-- EXACTLY WHERE-- RIGHT THIS SECOND...
...OR I SWEAR TO ALMIGHTY GOD-- I WILL KILL YOU.
ALMOST... WORTH HOLDING BACK...TO SEE IF YOU'LL CROSS THE LINE...
TRUTH IS...I DON'T KNOW WHERE EXACT HE IS...I JUS KNOW...

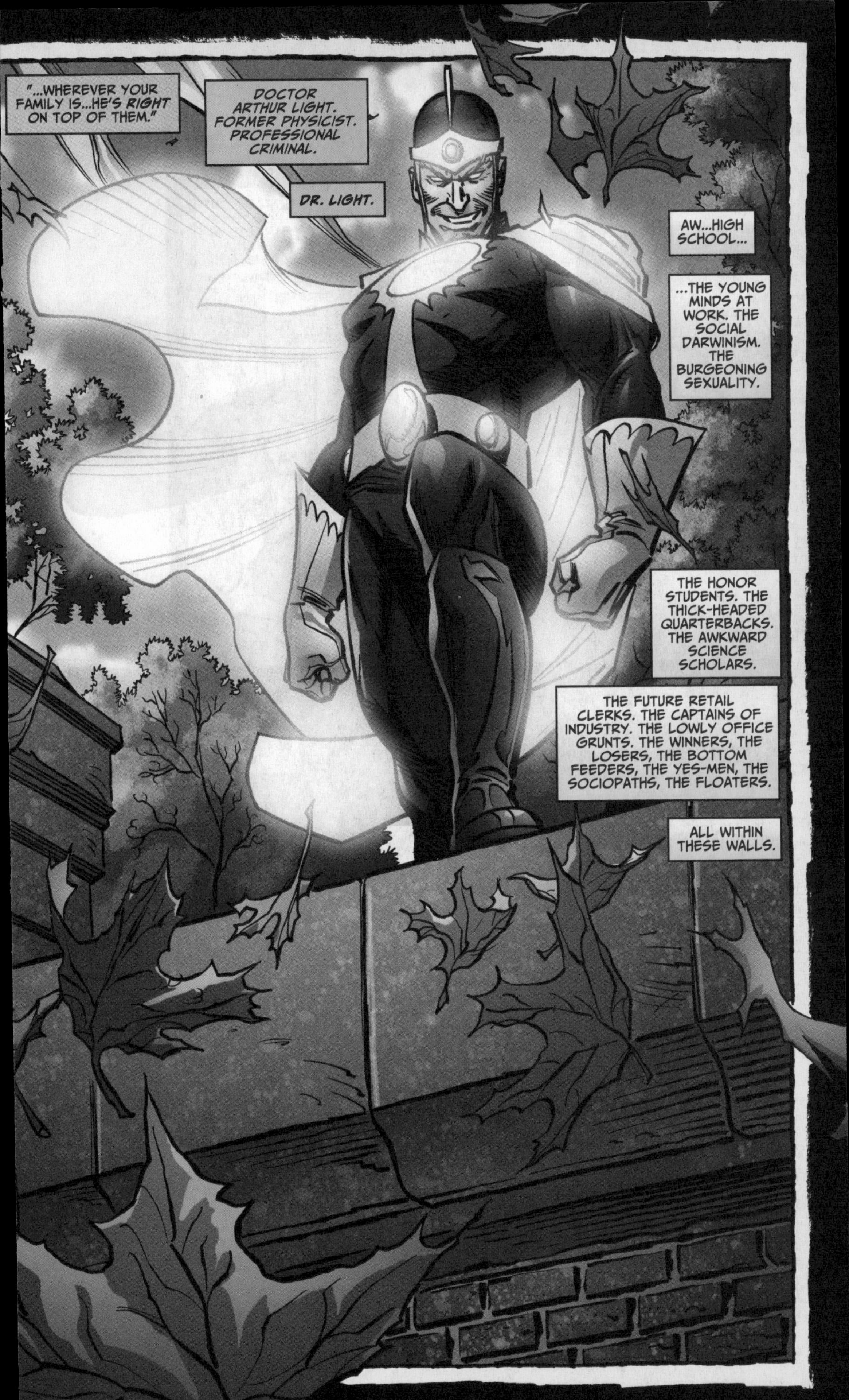

"...WHEREVER YOUR FAMILY IS...HE'S *RIGHT* ON TOP OF THEM."
DOCTOR ARTHUR LIGHT. FORMER PHYSICIST. PROFESSIONAL CRIMINAL.
DR. LIGHT.
AW...HIGH SCHOOL...
...THE YOUNG MINDS AT WORK. THE SOCIAL DARWINISM. THE BURGEONING SEXUALITY.
THE HONOR STUDENTS. THE THICK-HEADED QUARTERBACKS. THE AWKWARD SCIENCE SCHOLARS.
THE FUTURE RETAIL CLERKS. THE CAPTAINS OF INDUSTRY. THE LOWLY OFFICE GRUNTS. THE WINNERS, THE LOSERS, THE BOTTOM FEEDERS, THE YES-MEN, THE SOCIOPATHS, THE FLOATERS.
ALL WITHIN THESE WALLS.

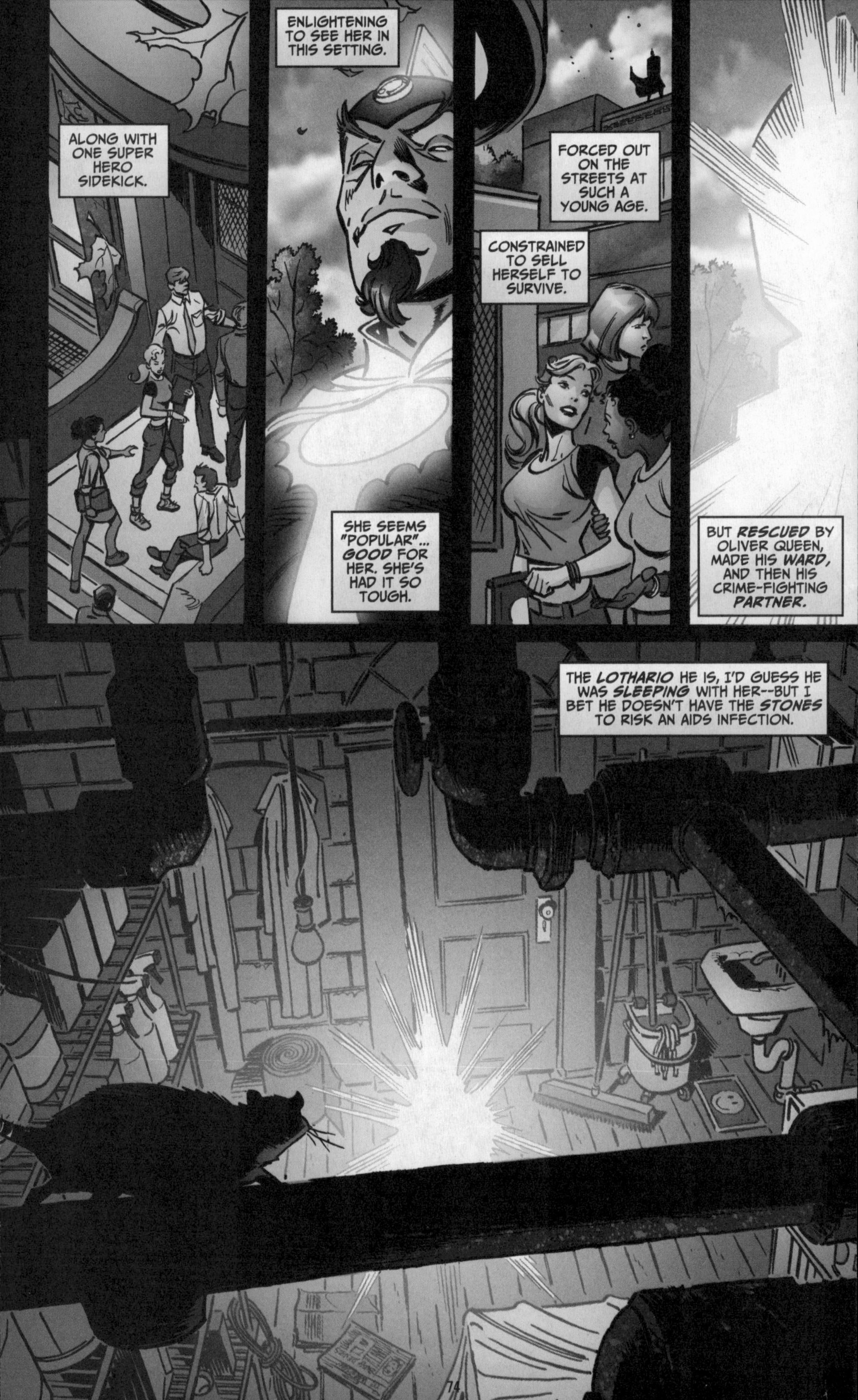
ALONG WITH ONE SUPER HERO SIDEKICK.
ENLIGHTENING TO SEE HER IN THIS SETTING.
SHE SEEMS "POPULAR"... GOOD FOR HER. SHE'S HAD IT SO TOUGH.
FORCED OUT ON THE STREETS AT SUCH A YOUNG AGE.
CONSTRAINED TO SELL HERSELF TO SURVIVE.
BUT RESCUED BY OLIVER QUEEN, MADE HIS WARD, AND THEN HIS CRIME-FIGHTING PARTNER.
THE LOTHARIO HE IS, I'D GUESS HE WAS SLEEPING WITH HER--BUT I BET HE DOESN'T HAVE THE STONES TO RISK AN AIDS INFECTION.

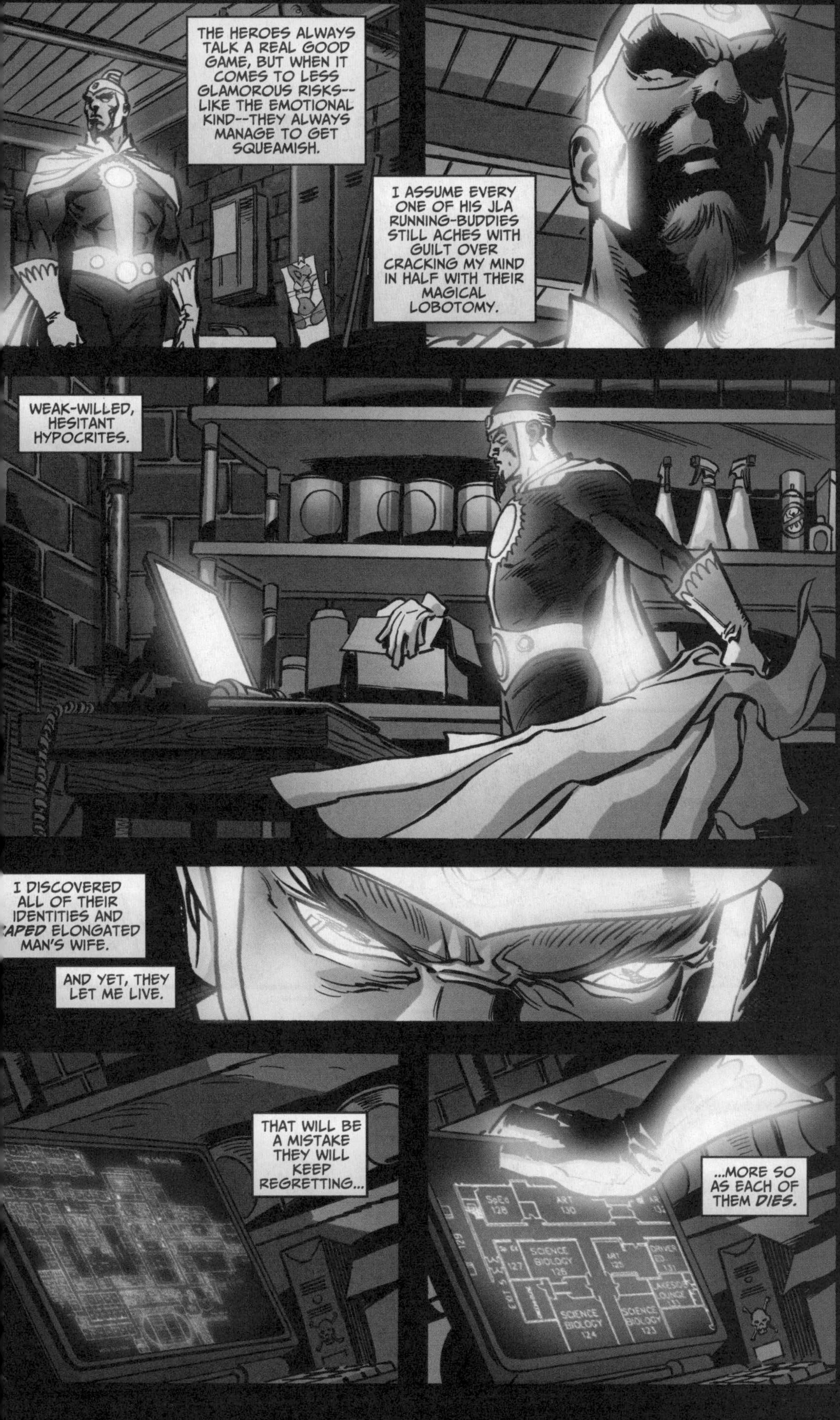
THE HEROES ALWAYS TALK A REAL GOOD GAME, BUT WHEN IT COMES TO LESS GLAMOROUS RISKS-- LIKE THE EMOTIONAL KIND--THEY ALWAYS MANAGE TO GET SQUEAMISH.
I ASSUME EVERY ONE OF HIS JLA RUNNING-BUDDIES STILL ACHES WITH GUILT OVER CRACKING MY MIND IN HALF WITH THEIR MAGICAL LOBOTOMY.
WEAK-WILLED, HESITANT HYPOCRITES.
I DISCOVERED ALL OF THEIR IDENTITIES AND *RAPED* ELONGATED MAN'S WIFE.
AND YET, THEY LET ME LIVE.
THAT WILL BE A MISTAKE THEY WILL KEEP REGRETTING...
...MORE SO AS EACH OF THEM *DIES*.

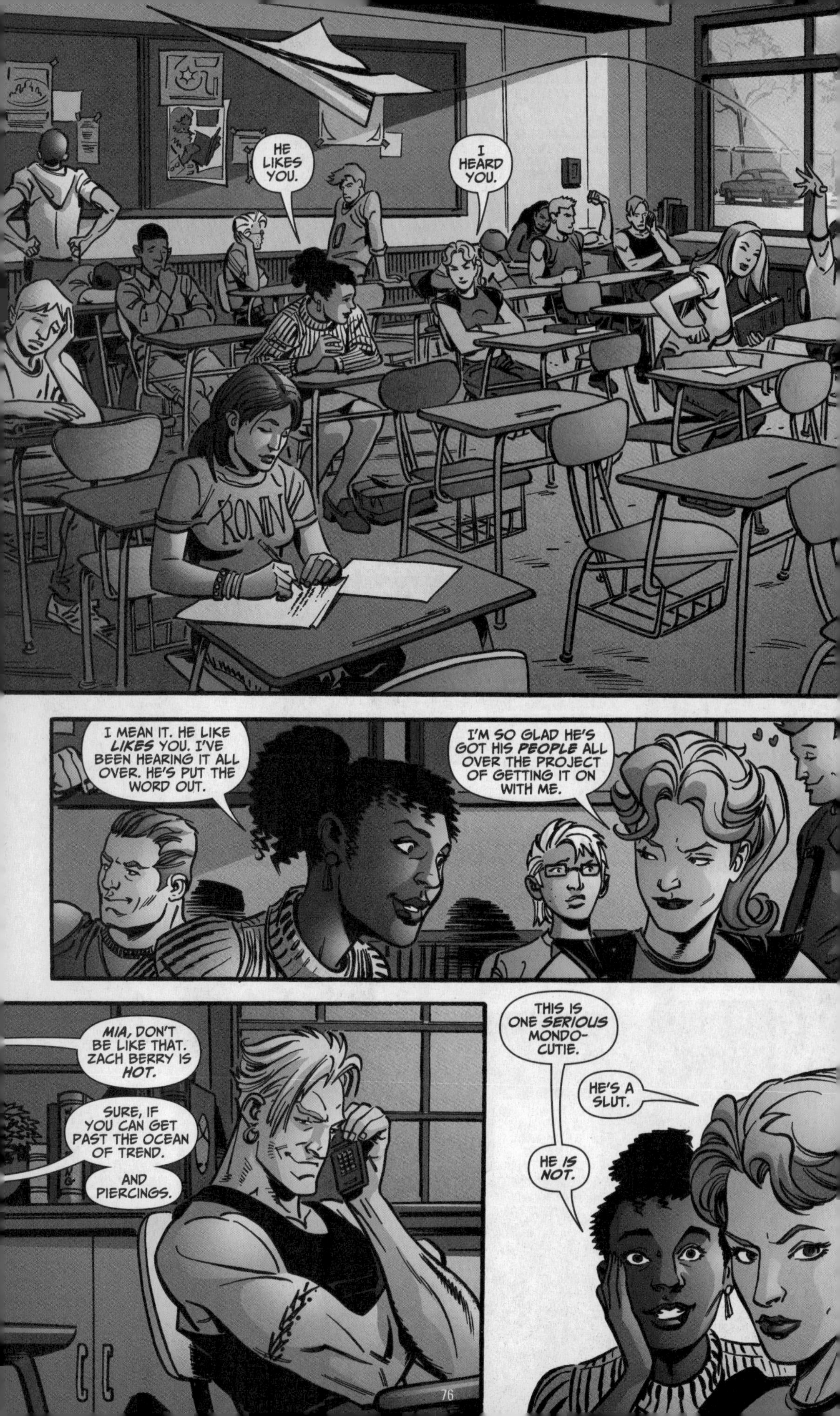
RONIN
HE LIKES YOU.
I HEARD YOU.
I MEAN IT. HE LIKE *LIKES* YOU. I'VE BEEN HEARING IT ALL OVER. HE'S PUT THE WORD OUT.
I'M SO GLAD HE'S GOT HIS *PEOPLE* ALL OVER THE PROJECT OF GETTING IT ON WITH ME.
MIA, DON'T BE LIKE THAT. ZACH BERRY IS *HOT.*
SURE, IF YOU CAN GET PAST THE OCEAN OF TREND.
AND PIERCINGS.
THIS IS ONE *SERIOUS* MONDO-CUTIE.
HE'S A SLUT.
HE *IS NOT.*

GINA, HE'S MESSED AROUND WITH HALF THE 11TH GRADE. AND I'M GUESSING THE ENTIRE 10TH GRADE, AS WELL.

SURE, POPULAR IN THE NAKED-EXCHANGES-OF-SWEAT-AND-FLUID KIND OF WAY. YOU GOT WITH HIM, TOO.

THAT'S *JUST* NOT TRUE. HE'S JUST POPULAR.

ONCE.

WHAT ABOUT THAT PARTY AT MONICA'S?

GREAT GATSBY — WORK IMAGERY RD. 7G. 15-30

A LITTLE QUIET, PLEASE...

FINE, THREE TIMES. DOESN'T MEAN YOU SHOULDN'T GET YOURS.

I'M NOT INTERESTED IN *GETTING* MINE. AND IF I WAS, IT WOULDN'T BE WITH "ZACH THE OCTOPUS."

WE'RE GOING TO WATCH THE SECOND HALF OF THE FILM VERSION OF THE *GREAT GATSBY.*

GATSBY — WORKSHEET IMAGERY 5-60

AGAIN, THIS IS MY ATTEMPT TO *TRAP* YOU. THE MOVIE AND THE BOOK ARE DIFFERENT.

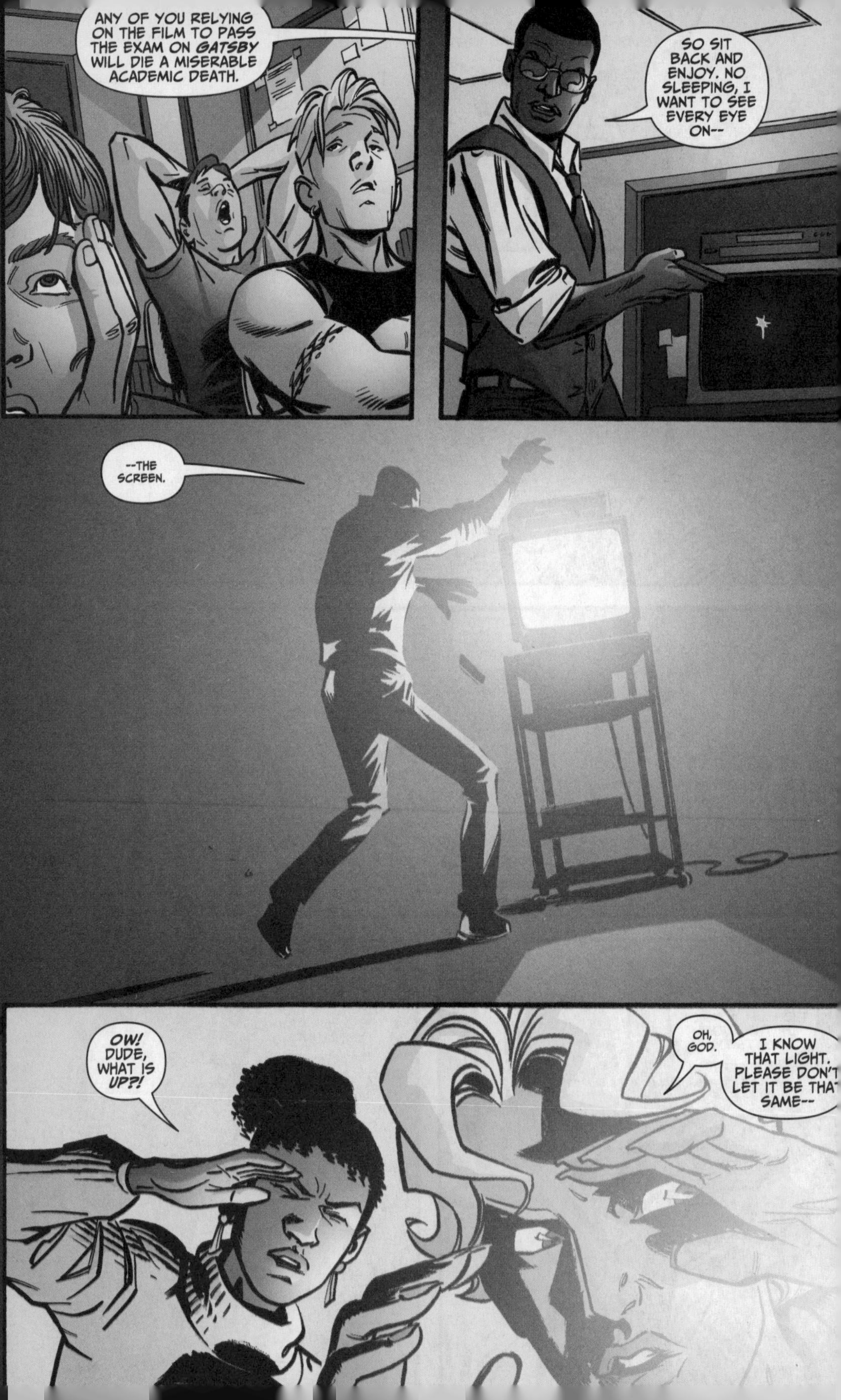
ANY OF YOU RELYING ON THE FILM TO PASS THE EXAM ON *GATSBY* WILL DIE A MISERABLE ACADEMIC DEATH.
SO SIT BACK AND ENJOY. NO SLEEPING, I WANT TO SEE EVERY EYE ON--
--THE SCREEN.
OW! DUDE, WHAT IS *UP?!*
OH, GOD.
I KNOW THAT LIGHT. PLEASE DON'T LET IT BE THAT SAME--

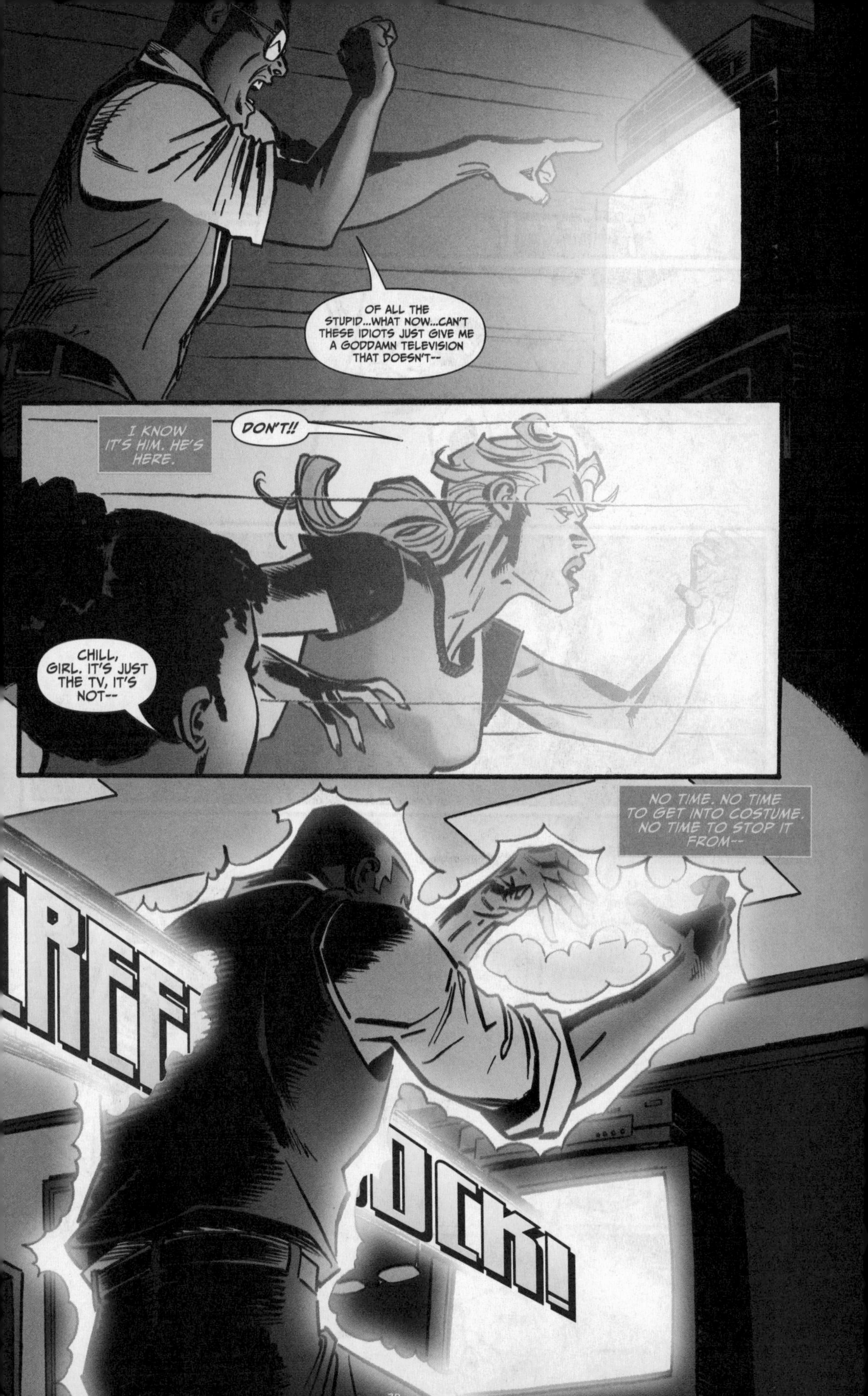
OF ALL THE STUPID...WHAT NOW...CAN'T THESE IDIOTS JUST GIVE ME A GODDAMN TELEVISION THAT DOESN'T--
I KNOW IT'S HIM. HE'S HERE.
DON'T!!
CHILL, GIRL. IT'S JUST THE TV, IT'S NOT--
NO TIME. NO TIME TO GET INTO COSTUME. NO TIME TO STOP IT FROM--

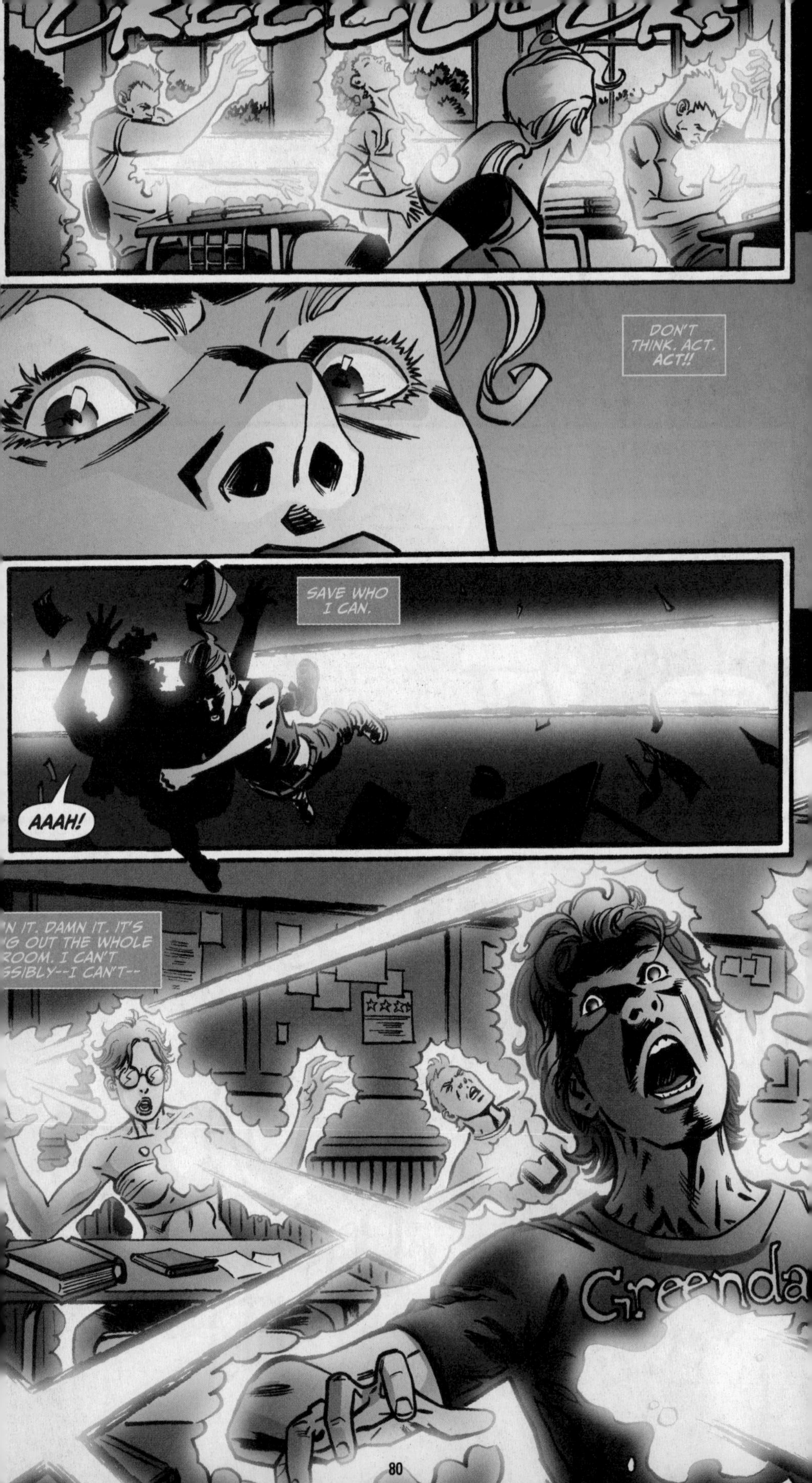
DON'T THINK. ACT. ACT!!
SAVE WHO I CAN.
AAAH!
N IT. DAMN IT. IT'S G OUT THE WHOLE ROOM. I CAN'T SSIBLY--I CAN'T--
Greenda

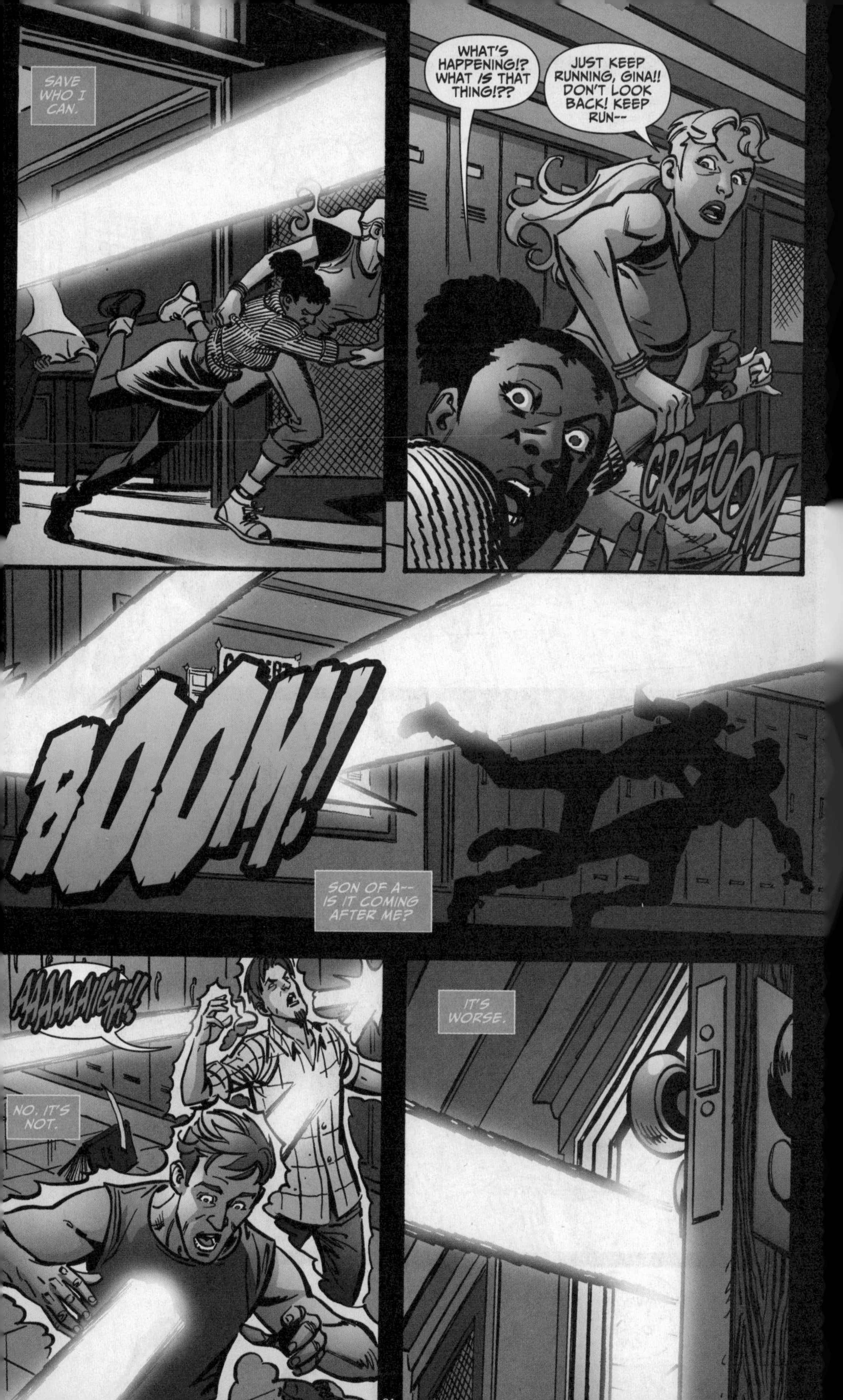

SAVE WHO I CAN.
WHAT'S HAPPENING!? WHAT IS THAT THING!??
JUST KEEP RUNNING, GINA!! DON'T LOOK BACK! KEEP RUN--
CREEOOM
BOOM!!
SON OF A-- IS IT COMING AFTER ME?
AAAAAAAIIGH!!
IT'S WORSE.
NO. IT'S NOT.

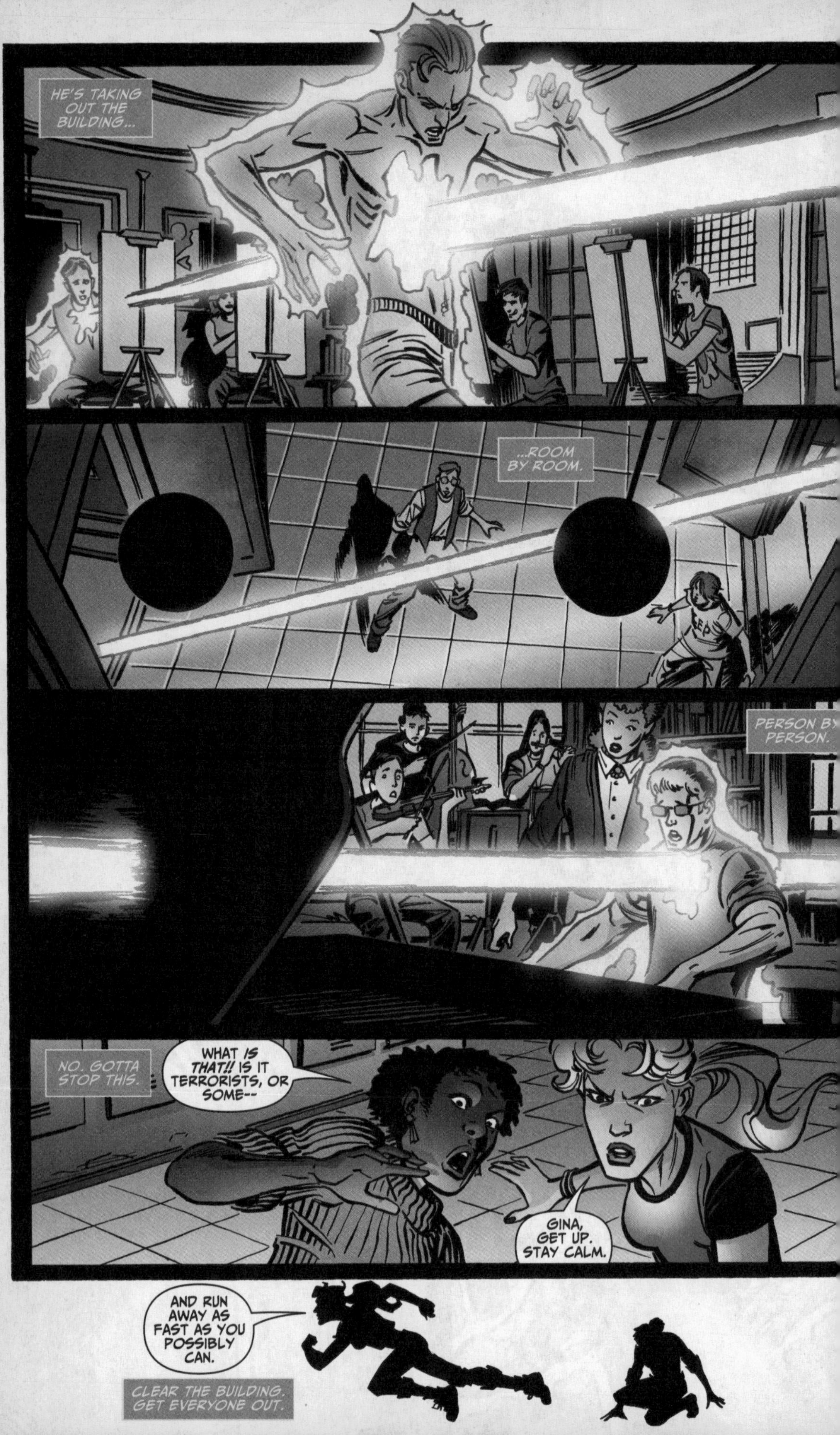
HE'S TAKING OUT THE BUILDING...
...ROOM BY ROOM.
PERSON BY PERSON.
NO. GOTTA STOP THIS.
WHAT IS THAT!! IS IT TERRORISTS, OR SOME--
GINA, GET UP. STAY CALM.
AND RUN AWAY AS FAST AS YOU POSSIBLY CAN.
CLEAR THE BUILDING. GET EVERYONE OUT.

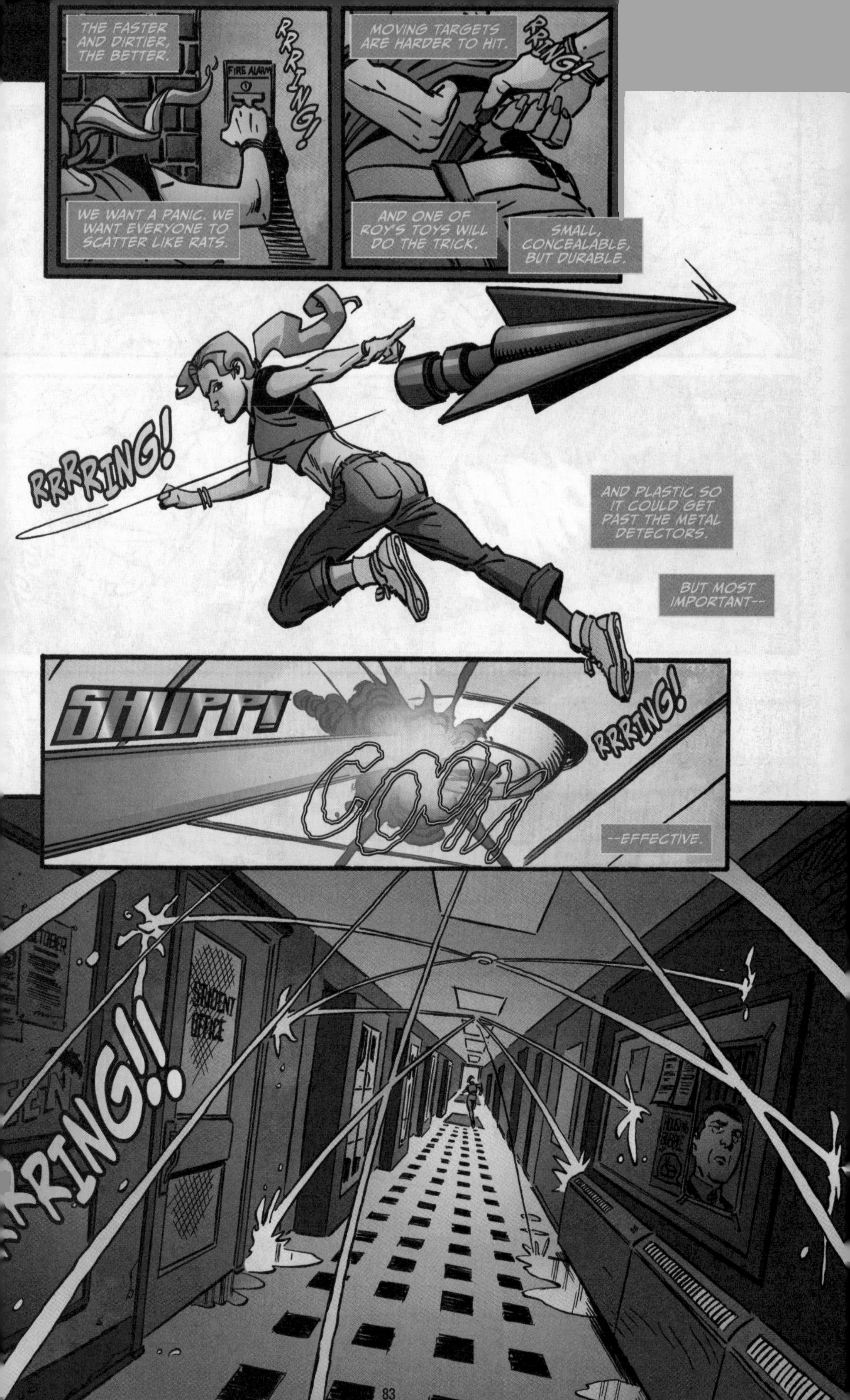

THE FASTER AND DIRTIER, THE BETTER.
FIRE ALARM
RRRING!
WE WANT A PANIC. WE WANT EVERYONE TO SCATTER LIKE RATS.
MOVING TARGETS ARE HARDER TO HIT.
RRING!
AND ONE OF ROY'S TOYS WILL DO THE TRICK.
SMALL, CONCEALABLE, BUT DURABLE.
RRRRING!
AND PLASTIC SO IT COULD GET PAST THE METAL DETECTORS.
BUT MOST IMPORTANT--
SHUPP!
RRRING!
COOM
--EFFECTIVE.
STUDENT OFFICE
RRING!!

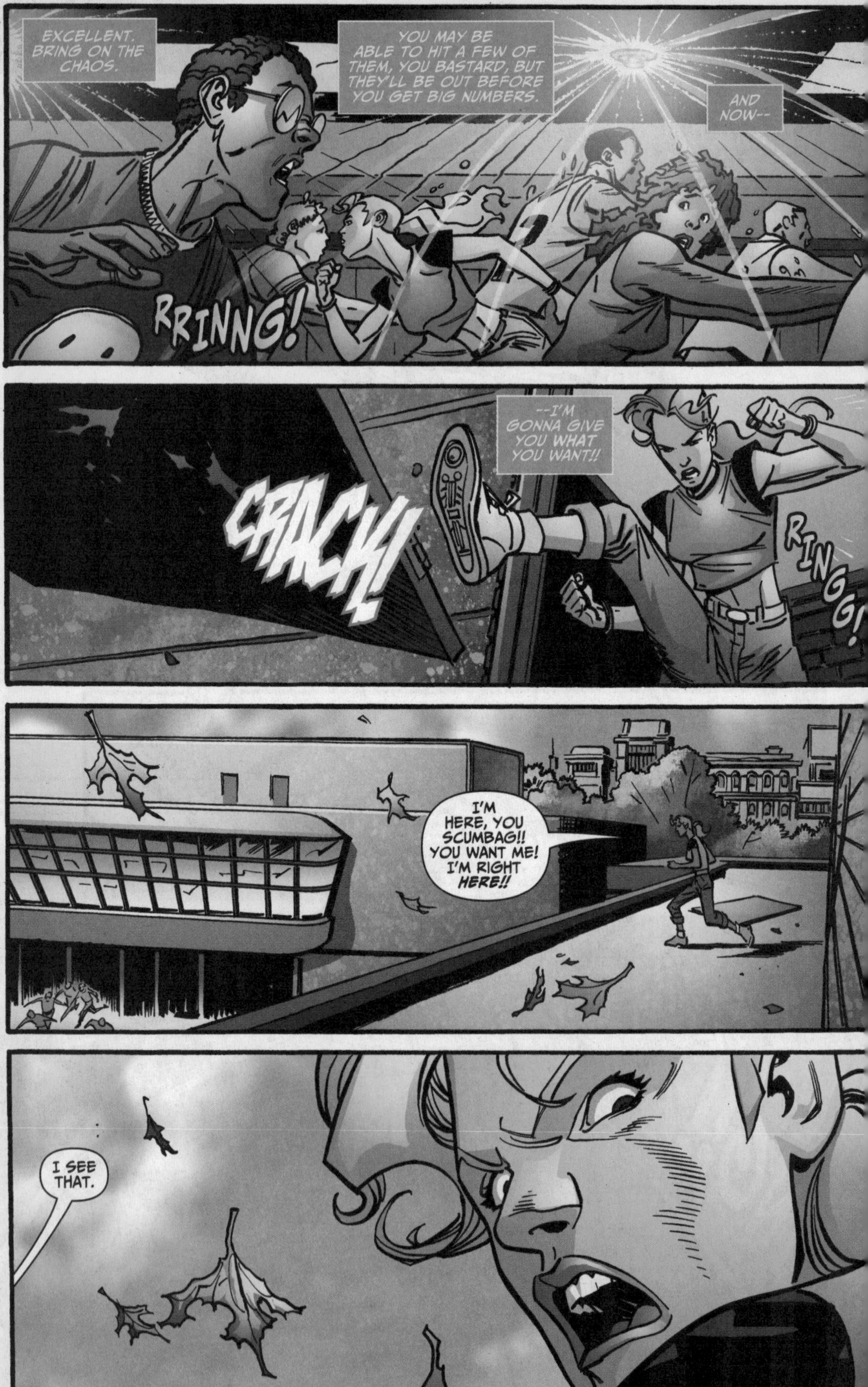
EXCELLENT. BRING ON THE CHAOS.
YOU MAY BE ABLE TO HIT A FEW OF THEM, YOU BASTARD, BUT THEY'LL BE OUT BEFORE YOU GET BIG NUMBERS.
AND NOW--
RRINNG!
--I'M GONNA GIVE YOU WHAT YOU WANT!!
CRACK!
RINGG!
I'M HERE, YOU SCUMBAG!! YOU WANT ME! I'M RIGHT HERE!!
I SEE THAT.

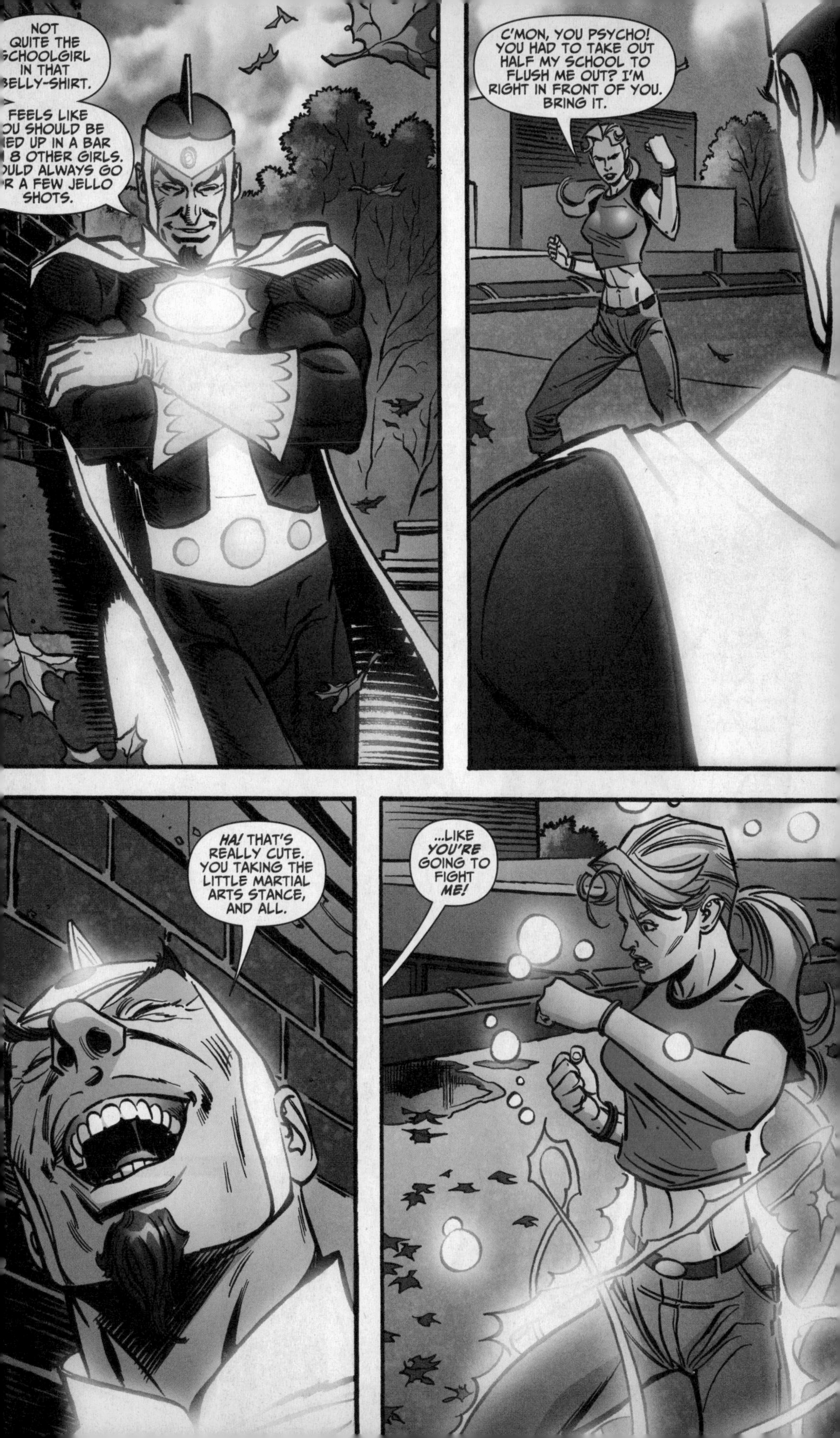
NOT QUITE THE SCHOOLGIRL IN THAT BELLY-SHIRT.
FEELS LIKE YOU SHOULD BE ...ED UP IN A BAR ... 8 OTHER GIRLS. ...OULD ALWAYS GO ...R A FEW JELLO SHOTS.
C'MON, YOU PSYCHO! YOU HAD TO TAKE OUT HALF MY SCHOOL TO FLUSH ME OUT? I'M RIGHT IN FRONT OF YOU. BRING IT.
HA! THAT'S REALLY CUTE. YOU TAKING THE LITTLE MARTIAL ARTS STANCE, AND ALL.
...LIKE YOU'RE GOING TO FIGHT ME!

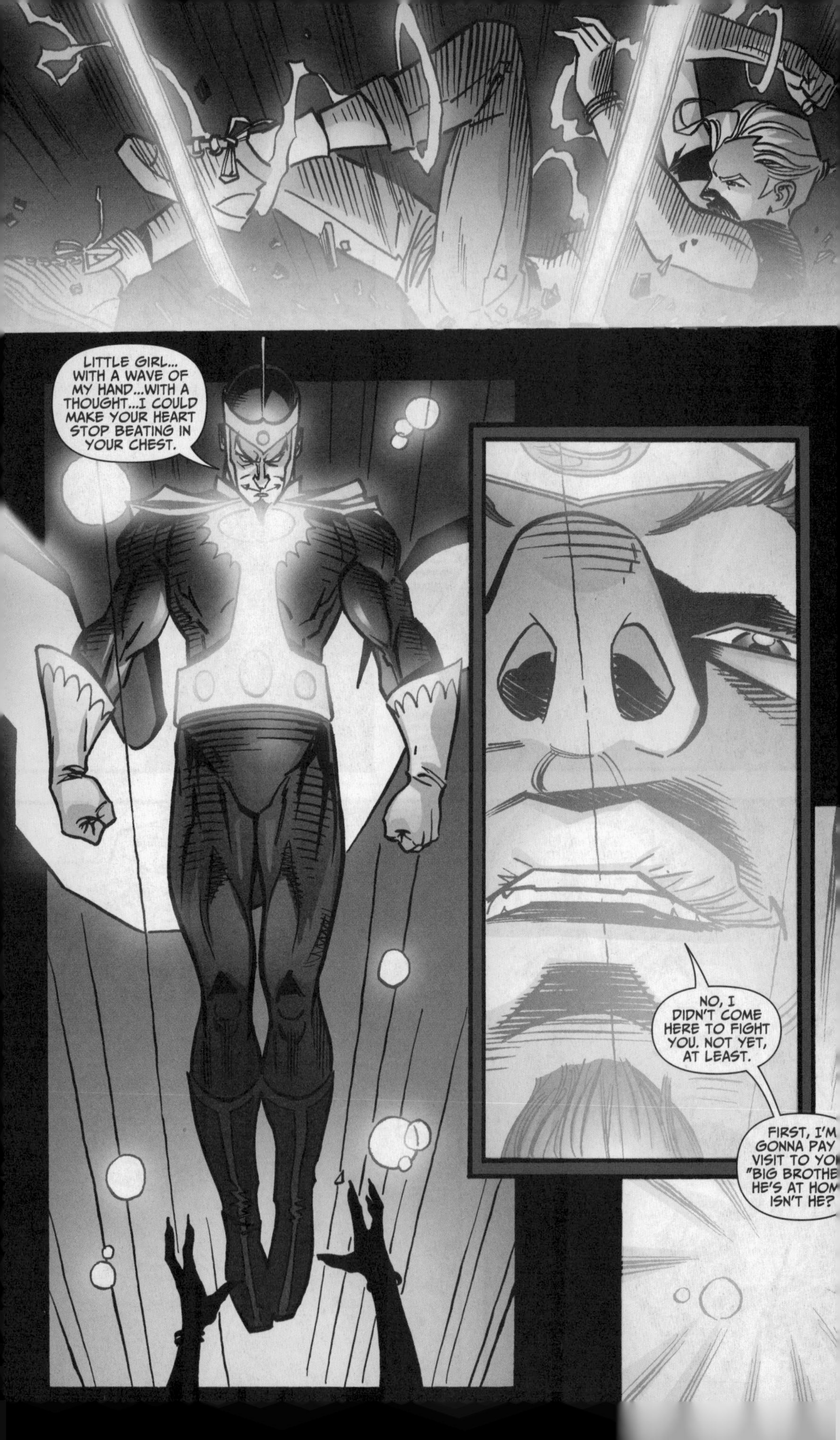
LITTLE GIRL... WITH A WAVE OF MY HAND...WITH A THOUGHT...I COULD MAKE YOUR HEART STOP BEATING IN YOUR CHEST.
NO, I DIDN'T COME HERE TO FIGHT YOU. NOT YET, AT LEAST.
FIRST, I'M GONNA PAY VISIT TO YO "BIG BROTHE HE'S AT HOM ISN'T HE?

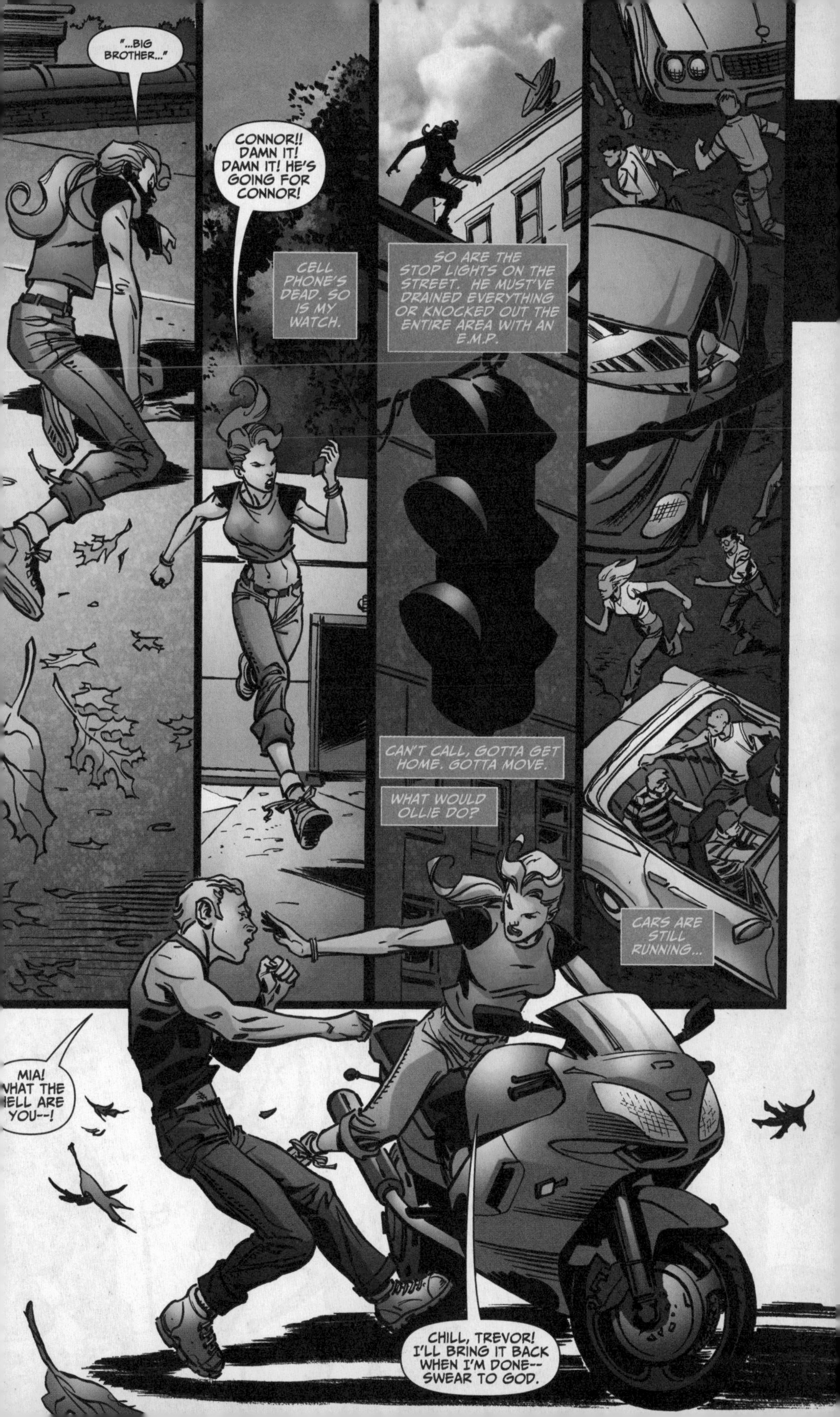

"...BIG BROTHER..."
CONNOR!! DAMN IT! DAMN IT! HE'S GOING FOR CONNOR!
CELL PHONE'S DEAD. SO IS MY WATCH.
SO ARE THE STOP LIGHTS ON THE STREET. HE MUST'VE DRAINED EVERYTHING OR KNOCKED OUT THE ENTIRE AREA WITH AN E.M.P.
CAN'T CALL, GOTTA GET HOME. GOTTA MOVE.
WHAT WOULD OLLIE DO?
CARS ARE STILL RUNNING...
MIA! WHAT THE HELL ARE YOU--!
CHILL, TREVOR! I'LL BRING IT BACK WHEN I'M DONE-- SWEAR TO GOD.

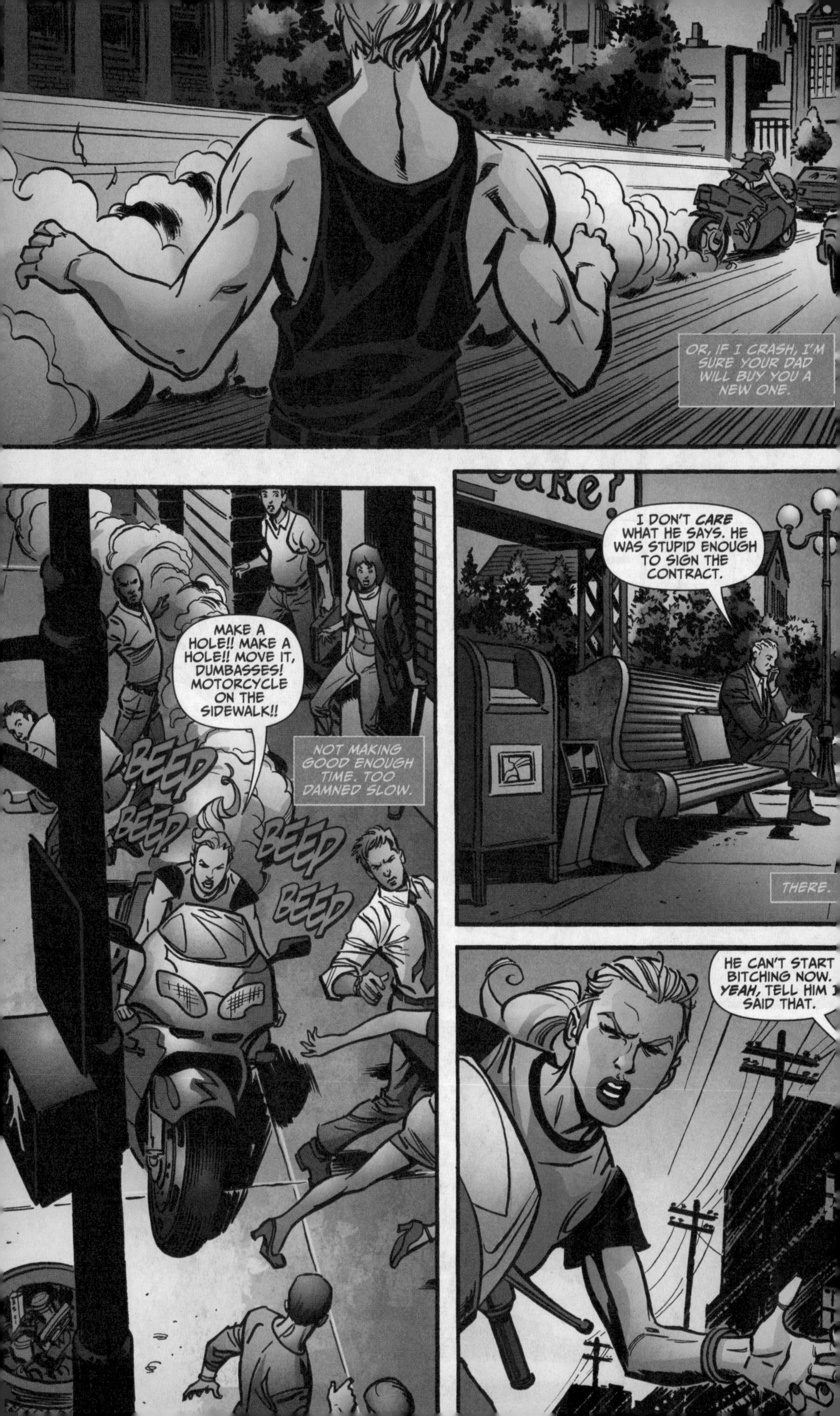
OR, IF I CRASH, I'M SURE YOUR DAD WILL BUY YOU A NEW ONE.
MAKE A HOLE!! MAKE A HOLE!! MOVE IT, DUMBASSES! MOTORCYCLE ON THE SIDEWALK!!
NOT MAKING GOOD ENOUGH TIME. TOO DAMNED SLOW.
BEEP BEEP
BEEP BEEP
I DON'T CARE WHAT HE SAYS. HE WAS STUPID ENOUGH TO SIGN THE CONTRACT.
THERE.
HE CAN'T START BITCHING NOW. YEAH, TELL HIM SAID THAT.

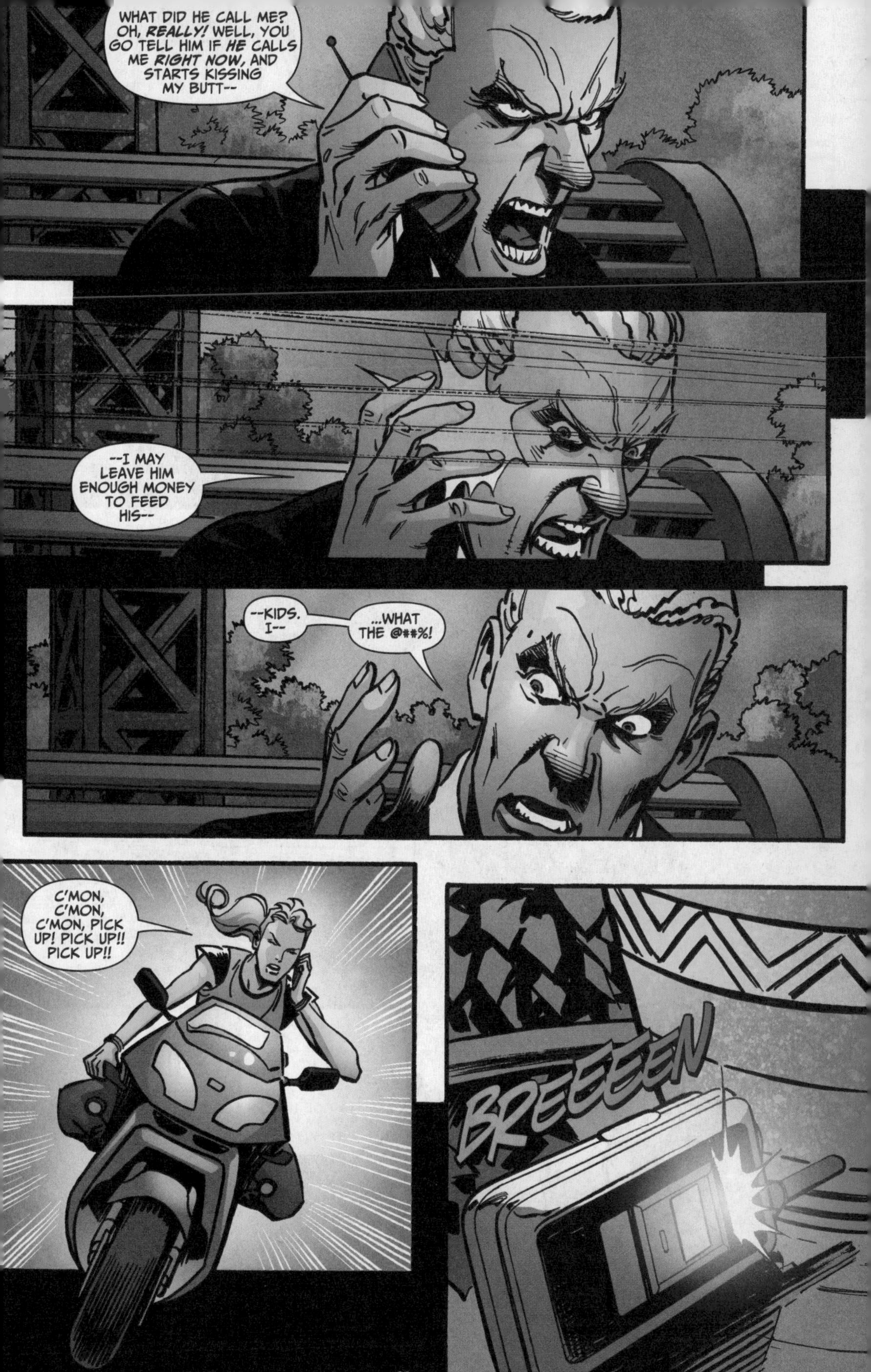
WHAT DID HE CALL ME? OH, REALLY! WELL, YOU GO TELL HIM IF HE CALLS ME RIGHT NOW, AND STARTS KISSING MY BUTT--
--I MAY LEAVE HIM ENOUGH MONEY TO FEED HIS--
--KIDS. I--
...WHAT THE @##%!
C'MON, C'MON, C'MON, PICK UP! PICK UP!! PICK UP!!
BREEEEN

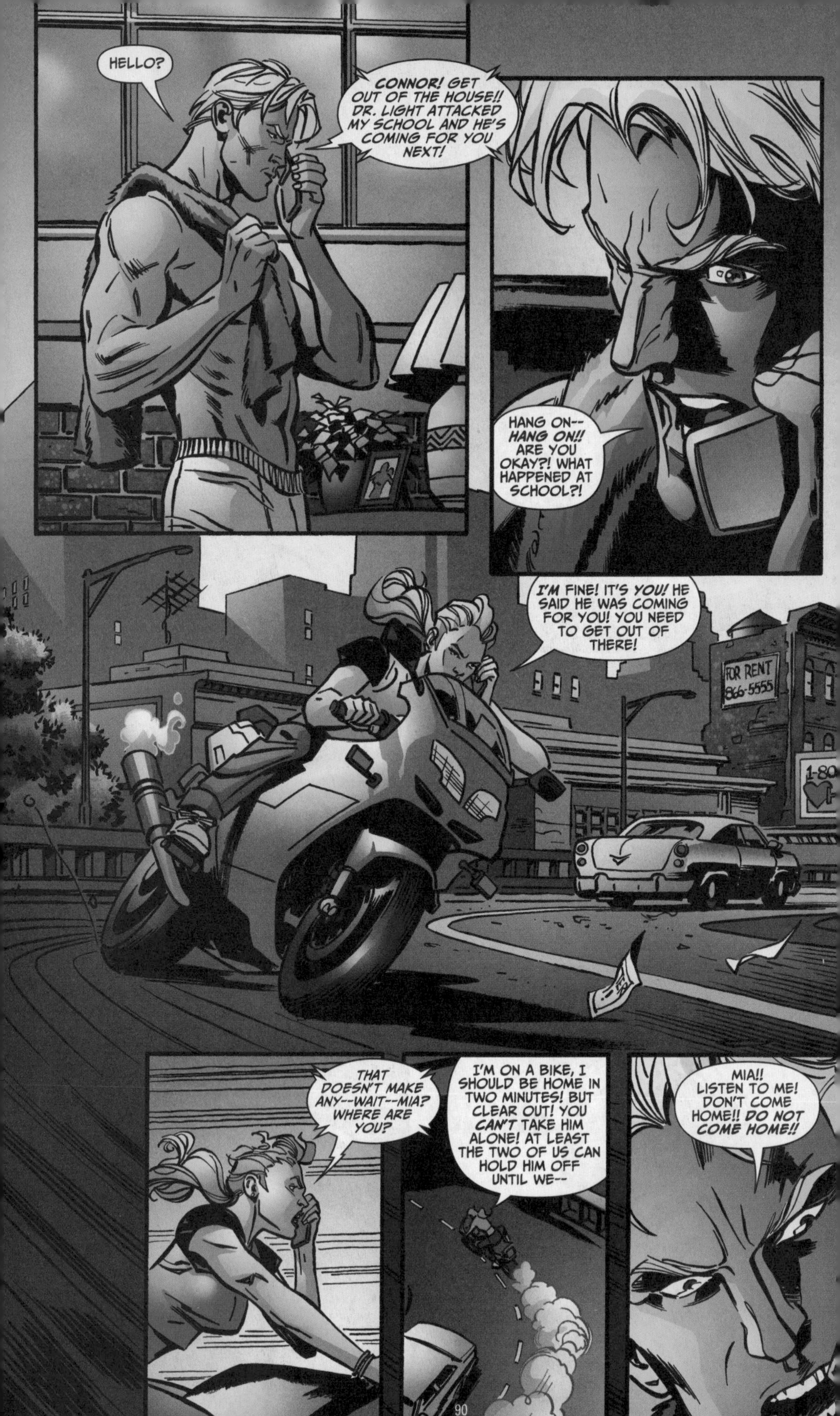
HELLO?
CONNOR! GET OUT OF THE HOUSE!! DR. LIGHT ATTACKED MY SCHOOL AND HE'S COMING FOR YOU NEXT!
HANG ON-- HANG ON!! ARE YOU OKAY?! WHAT HAPPENED AT SCHOOL?!
I'M FINE! IT'S YOU! HE SAID HE WAS COMING FOR YOU! YOU NEED TO GET OUT OF THERE!
FOR RENT 866-5555
THAT DOESN'T MAKE ANY--WAIT--MIA? WHERE ARE YOU?
I'M ON A BIKE, I SHOULD BE HOME IN TWO MINUTES! BUT CLEAR OUT! YOU CAN'T TAKE HIM ALONE! AT LEAST THE TWO OF US CAN HOLD HIM OFF UNTIL WE--
MIA!! LISTEN TO ME! DON'T COME HOME!! DO NOT COME HOME!!

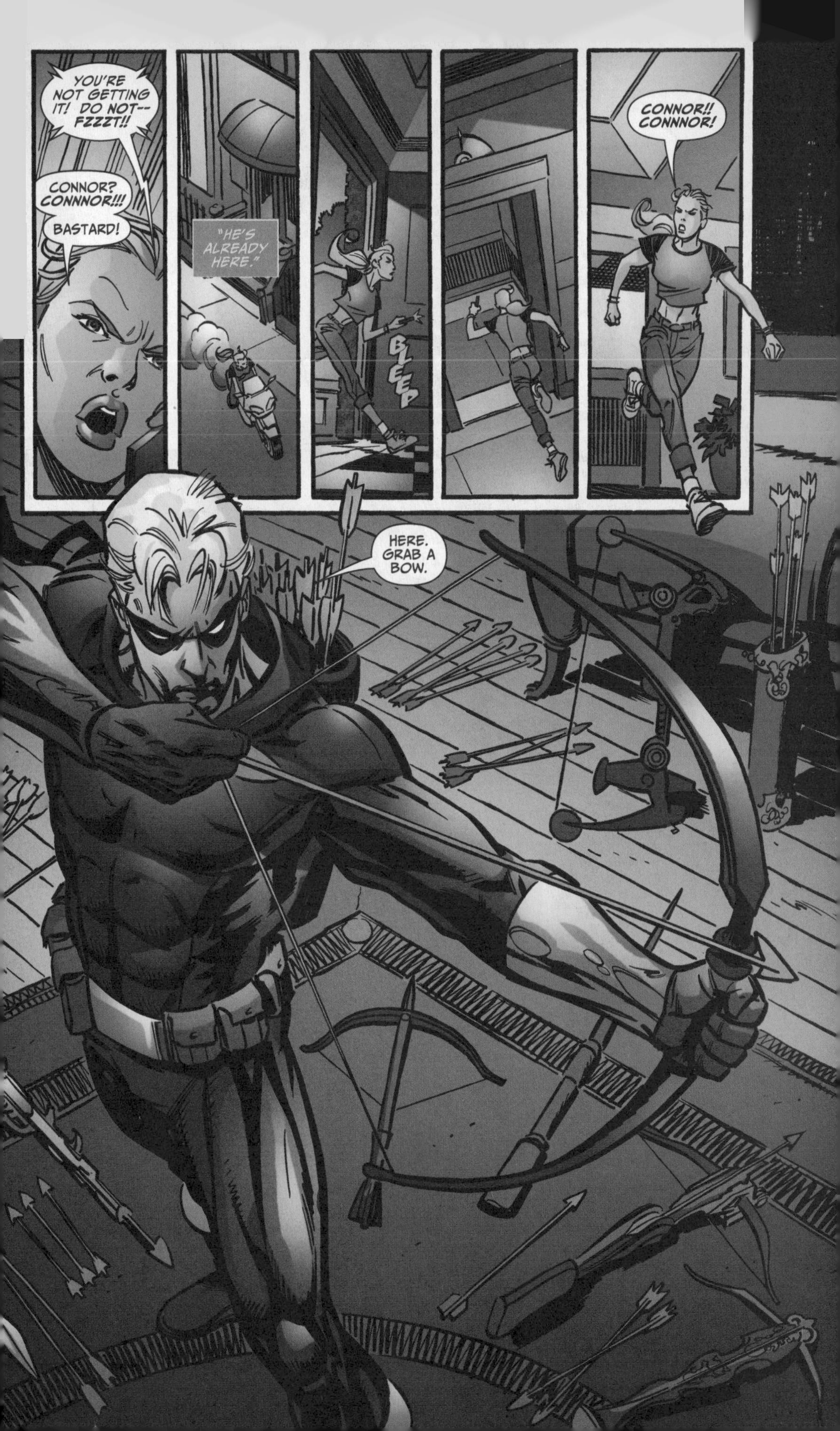

YOU'RE NOT GETTING IT! DO NOT-- FZZZT!!
CONNOR? CONNOR!!!
BASTARD!
"HE'S ALREADY HERE."
BLEEP
CONNOR!! CONNOR!
HERE. GRAB A BOW.

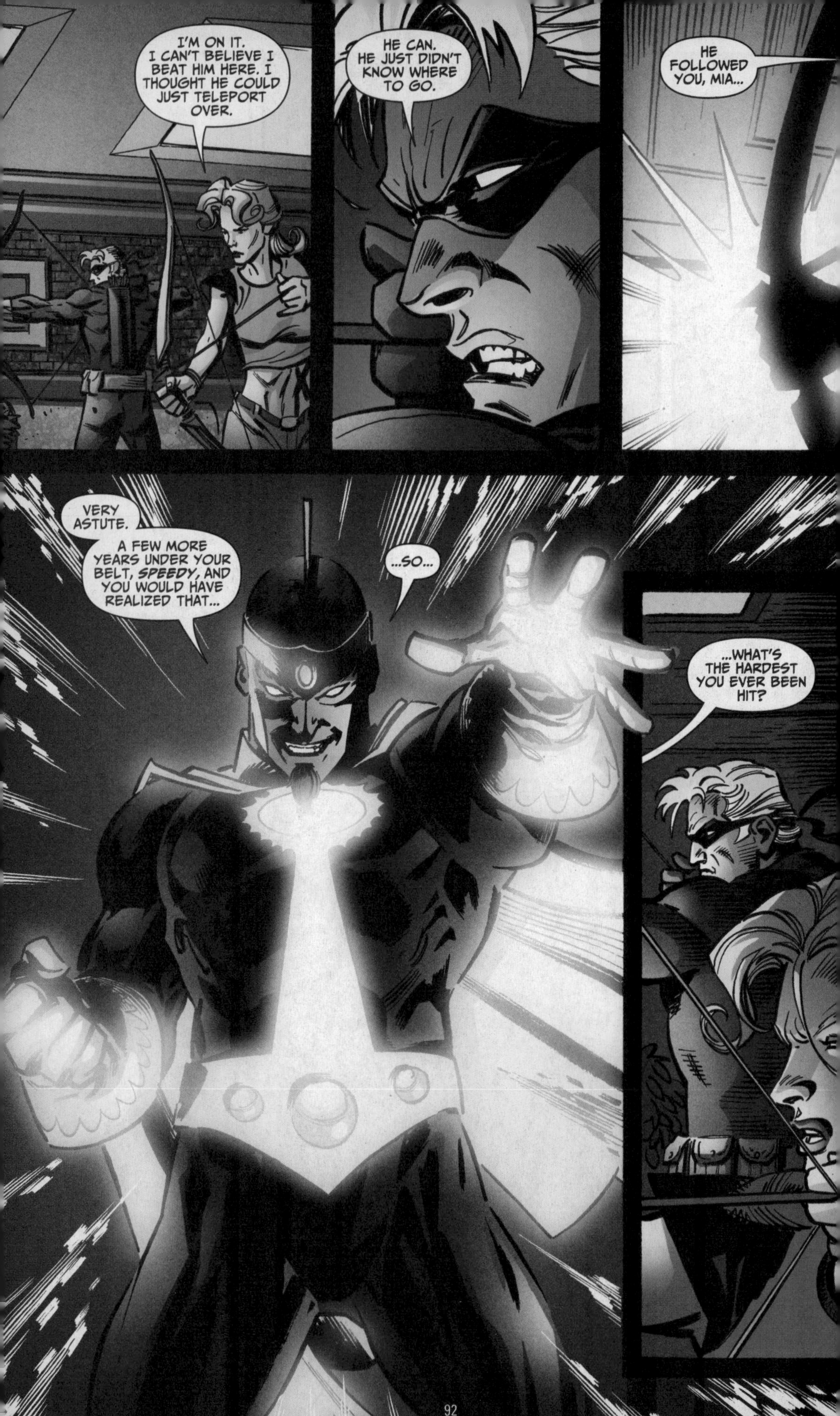
I'M ON IT. I CAN'T BELIEVE I BEAT HIM HERE. I THOUGHT HE COULD JUST TELEPORT OVER.
HE CAN. HE JUST DIDN'T KNOW WHERE TO GO.
HE FOLLOWED YOU, MIA...
VERY ASTUTE.
A FEW MORE YEARS UNDER YOUR BELT, *SPEEDY,* AND YOU WOULD HAVE REALIZED THAT...
...SO...
...WHAT'S THE HARDEST YOU EVER BEEN HIT?

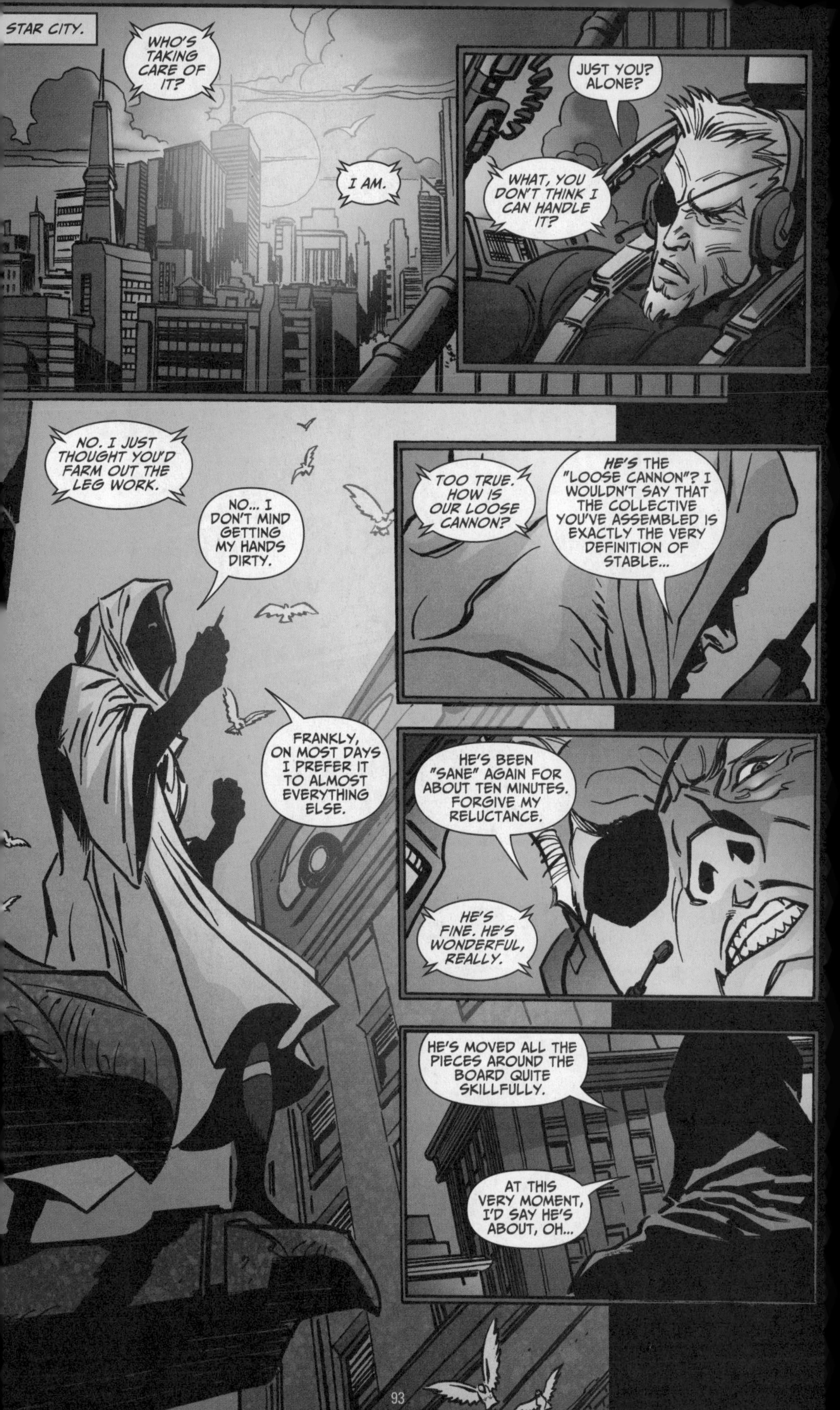
STAR CITY.
WHO'S TAKING CARE OF IT?
I AM.
JUST YOU? ALONE?
WHAT, YOU DON'T THINK I CAN HANDLE IT?
NO. I JUST THOUGHT YOU'D FARM OUT THE LEG WORK.
NO... I DON'T MIND GETTING MY HANDS DIRTY.
FRANKLY, ON MOST DAYS I PREFER IT TO ALMOST EVERYTHING ELSE.
TOO TRUE. HOW IS OUR LOOSE CANNON?
HE'S THE "LOOSE CANNON"? I WOULDN'T SAY THAT THE COLLECTIVE YOU'VE ASSEMBLED IS EXACTLY THE VERY DEFINITION OF STABLE...
HE'S BEEN "SANE" AGAIN FOR ABOUT TEN MINUTES. FORGIVE MY RELUCTANCE.
HE'S FINE. HE'S WONDERFUL, REALLY.
HE'S MOVED ALL THE PIECES AROUND THE BOARD QUITE SKILLFULLY.
AT THIS VERY MOMENT, I'D SAY HE'S ABOUT, OH...

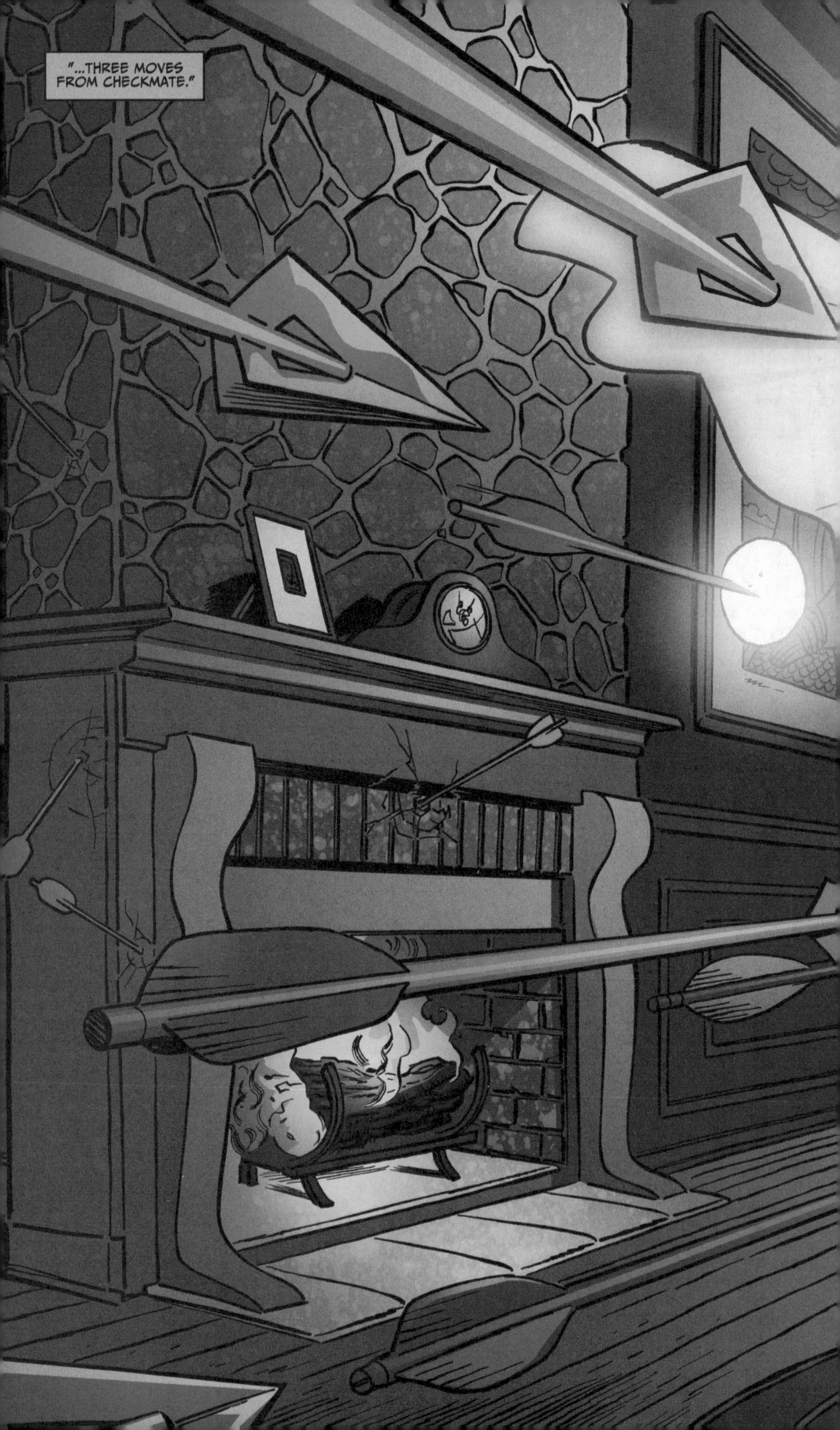
"...THREE MOVES FROM CHECKMATE."

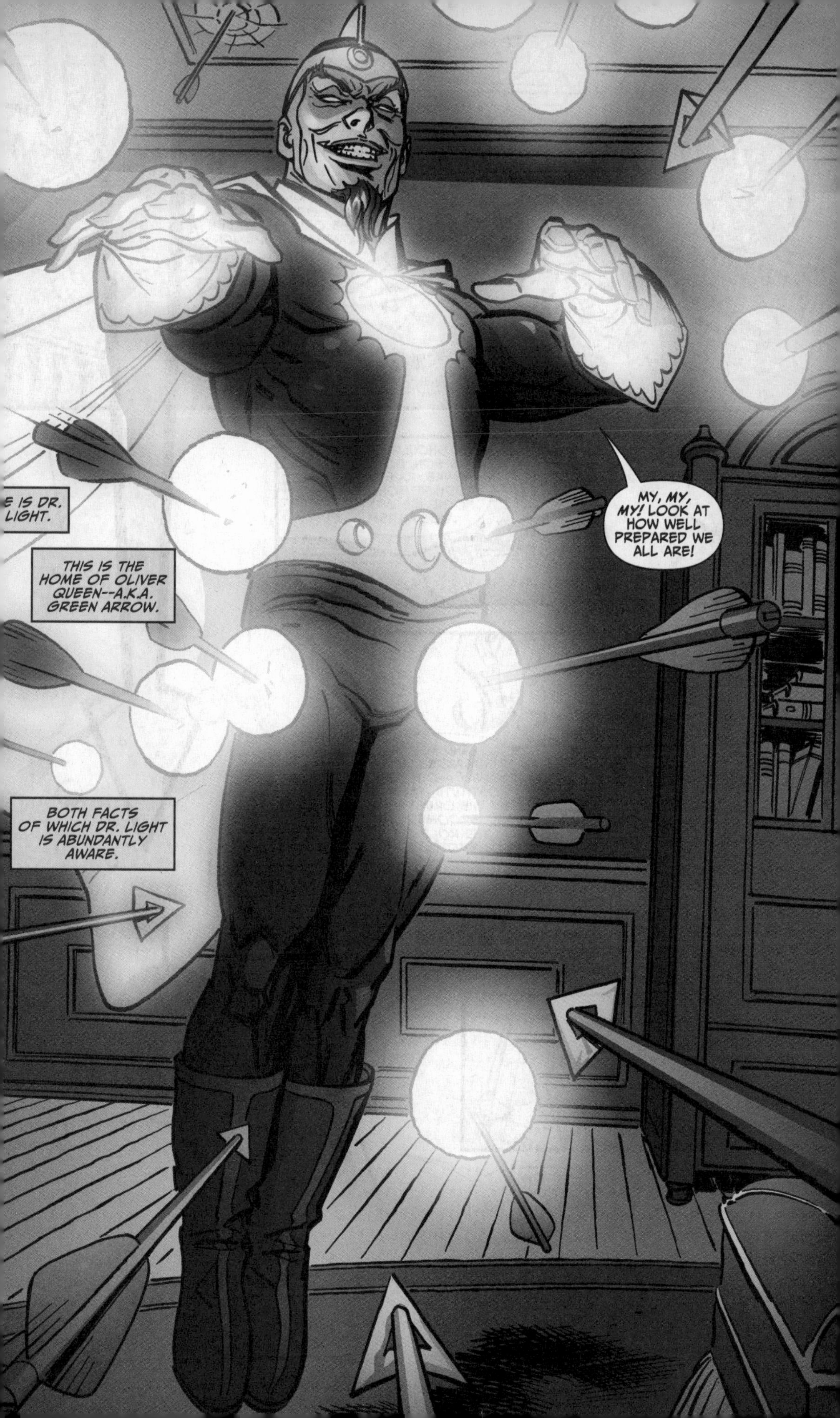
E IS DR. LIGHT.
THIS IS THE HOME OF OLIVER QUEEN--A.K.A. GREEN ARROW.
MY, MY, MY! LOOK AT HOW WELL PREPARED WE ALL ARE!
BOTH FACTS OF WHICH DR. LIGHT IS ABUNDANTLY AWARE.

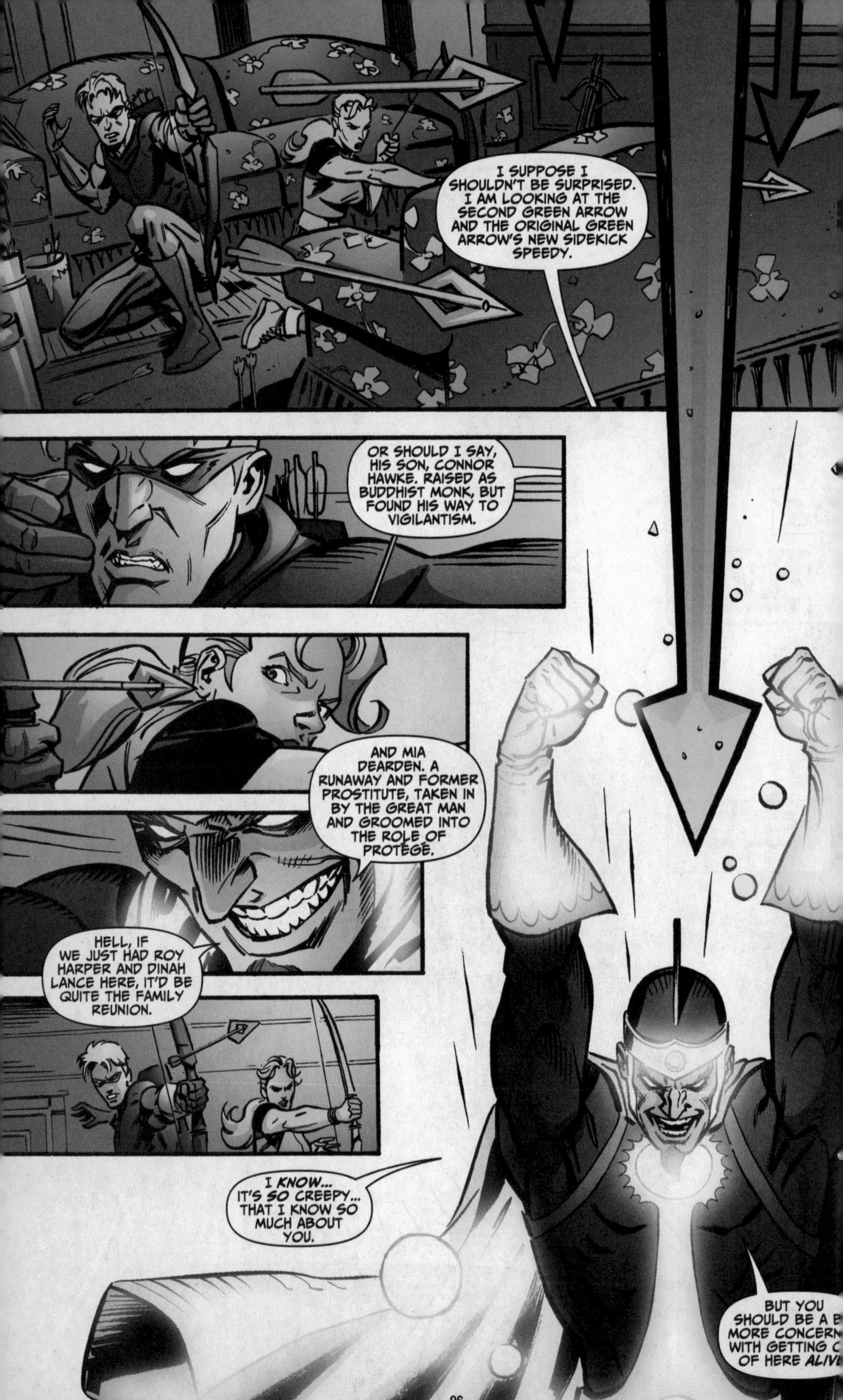
I SUPPOSE I SHOULDN'T BE SURPRISED. I AM LOOKING AT THE SECOND GREEN ARROW AND THE ORIGINAL GREEN ARROW'S NEW SIDEKICK SPEEDY.
OR SHOULD I SAY, HIS SON, CONNOR HAWKE. RAISED AS BUDDHIST MONK, BUT FOUND HIS WAY TO VIGILANTISM.
AND MIA DEARDEN. A RUNAWAY AND FORMER PROSTITUTE, TAKEN IN BY THE GREAT MAN AND GROOMED INTO THE ROLE OF PROTEGE.
HELL, IF WE JUST HAD ROY HARPER AND DINAH LANCE HERE, IT'D BE QUITE THE FAMILY REUNION.
I KNOW... IT'S SO CREEPY... THAT I KNOW SO MUCH ABOUT YOU.
BUT YOU SHOULD BE A B MORE CONCERN WITH GETTING O OF HERE ALIVE

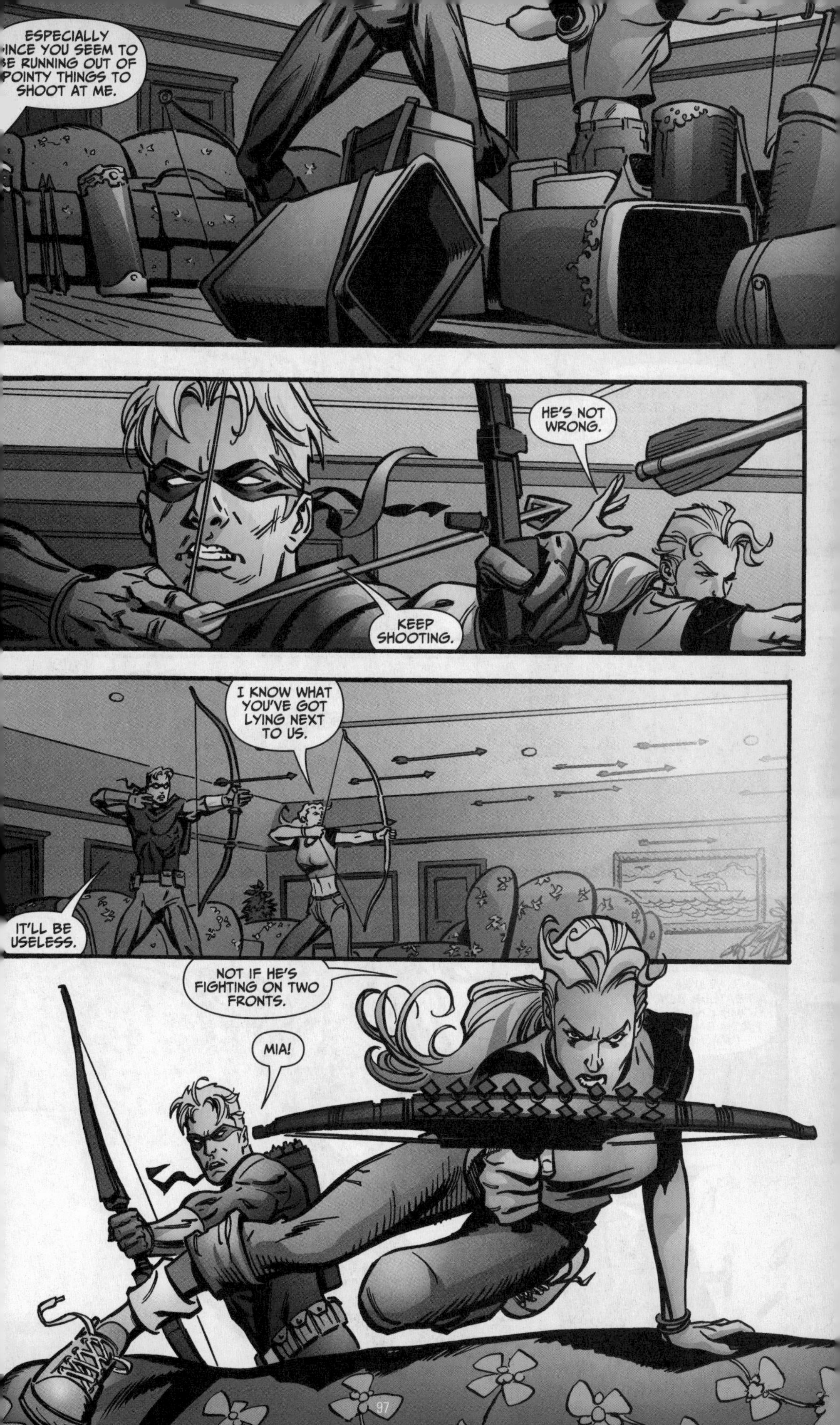
ESPECIALLY SINCE YOU SEEM TO BE RUNNING OUT OF POINTY THINGS TO SHOOT AT ME.
HE'S NOT WRONG.
KEEP SHOOTING.
I KNOW WHAT YOU'VE GOT LYING NEXT TO US.
IT'LL BE USELESS.
NOT IF HE'S FIGHTING ON TWO FRONTS.
MIA!

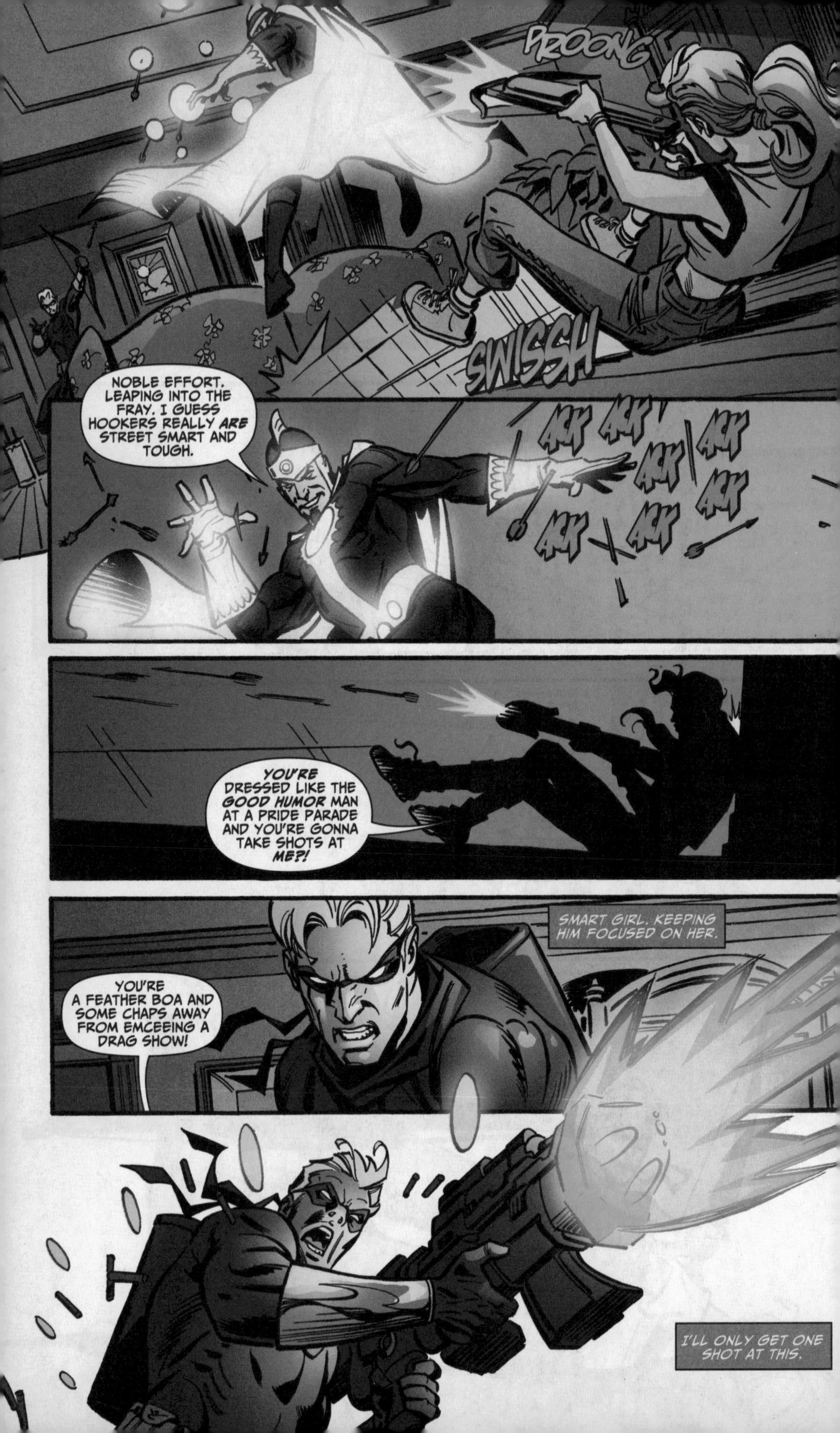
PROOONG
SWISSH
NOBLE EFFORT. LEAPING INTO THE FRAY. I GUESS HOOKERS REALLY *ARE* STREET SMART AND TOUGH.
ACK ACK ACK ACK ACK ACK ACK ACK
YOU'RE DRESSED LIKE THE *GOOD HUMOR* MAN AT A PRIDE PARADE AND YOU'RE GONNA TAKE SHOTS AT *ME?!*
SMART GIRL. KEEPING HIM FOCUSED ON HER.
YOU'RE A FEATHER BOA AND SOME CHAPS AWAY FROM EMCEEING A DRAG SHOW!
I'LL ONLY GET ONE SHOT AT THIS.

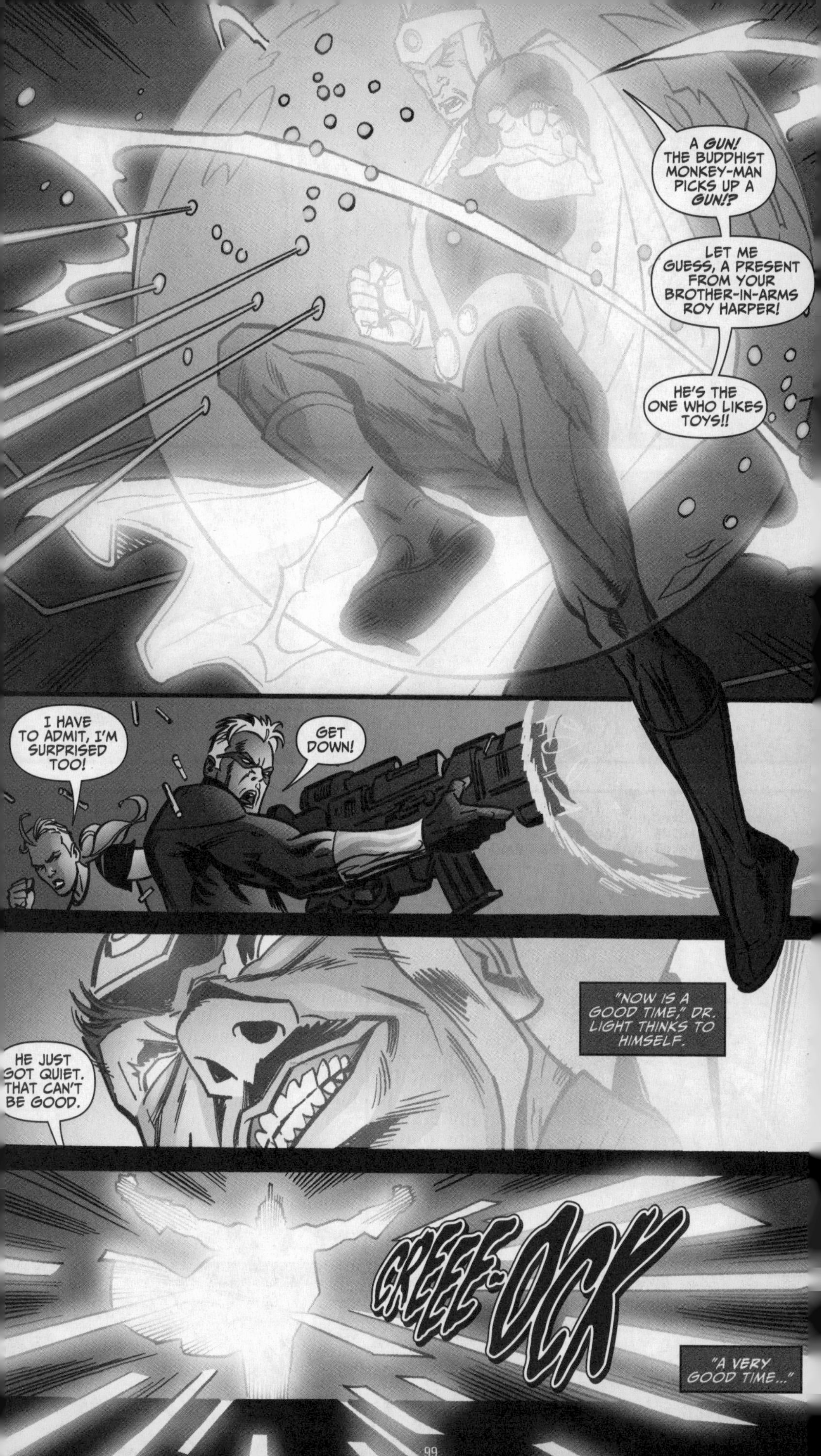
A GUN! THE BUDDHIST MONKEY-MAN PICKS UP A GUN!?
LET ME GUESS, A PRESENT FROM YOUR BROTHER-IN-ARMS ROY HARPER!
HE'S THE ONE WHO LIKES TOYS!!
I HAVE TO ADMIT, I'M SURPRISED TOO!
GET DOWN!
"NOW IS A GOOD TIME," DR. LIGHT THINKS TO HIMSELF.
HE JUST GOT QUIET. THAT CAN'T BE GOOD.
CREEE-OCK
"A VERY GOOD TIME..."

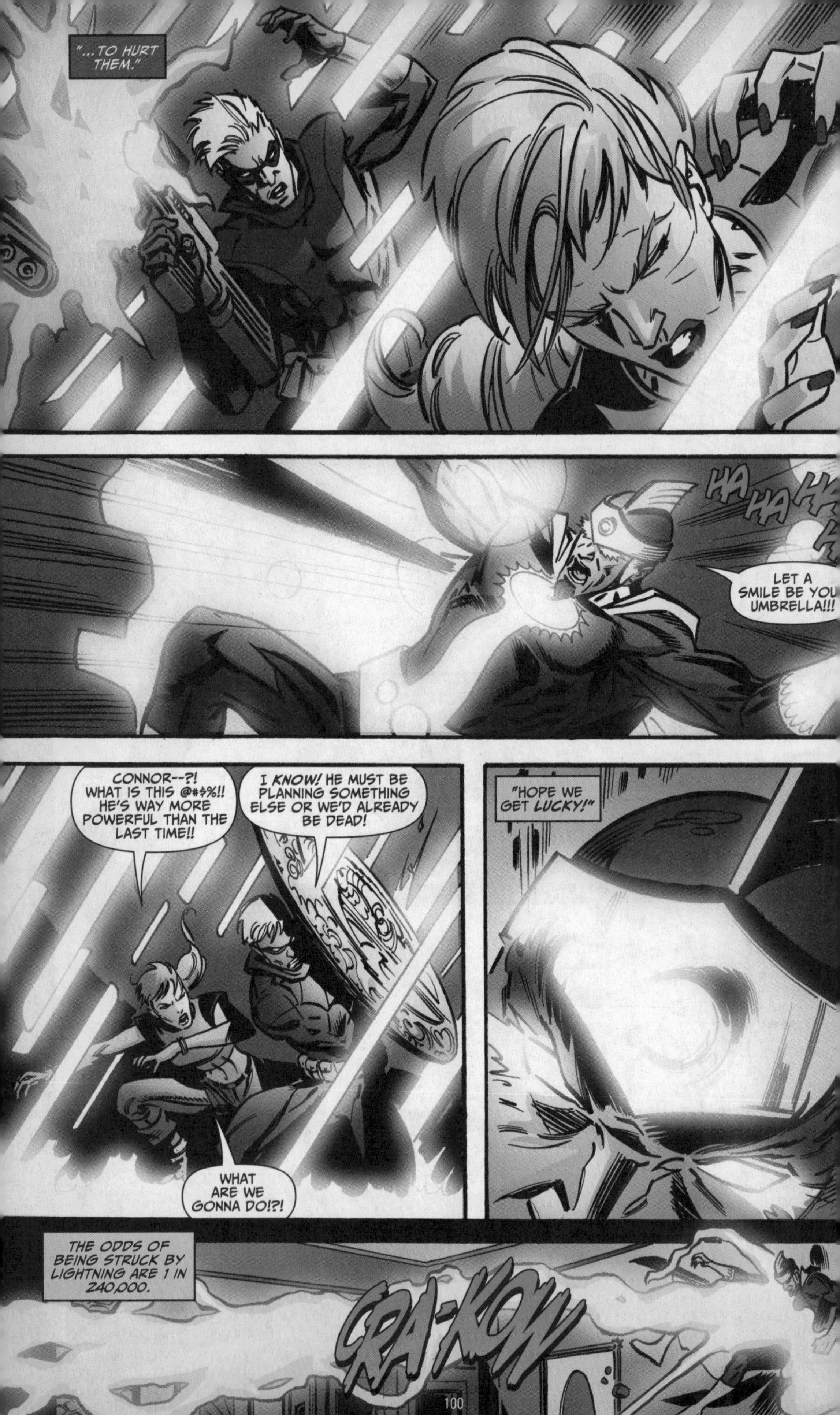
"...TO HURT THEM."
HA HA HA
LET A SMILE BE YOUR UMBRELLA!!!
CONNOR--?! WHAT IS THIS @#$%!! HE'S WAY MORE POWERFUL THAN THE LAST TIME!!
I KNOW! HE MUST BE PLANNING SOMETHING ELSE OR WE'D ALREADY BE DEAD!
WHAT ARE WE GONNA DO!?!
"HOPE WE GET LUCKY!"
THE ODDS OF BEING STRUCK BY LIGHTNING ARE 1 IN 240,000.
CRA-KOW

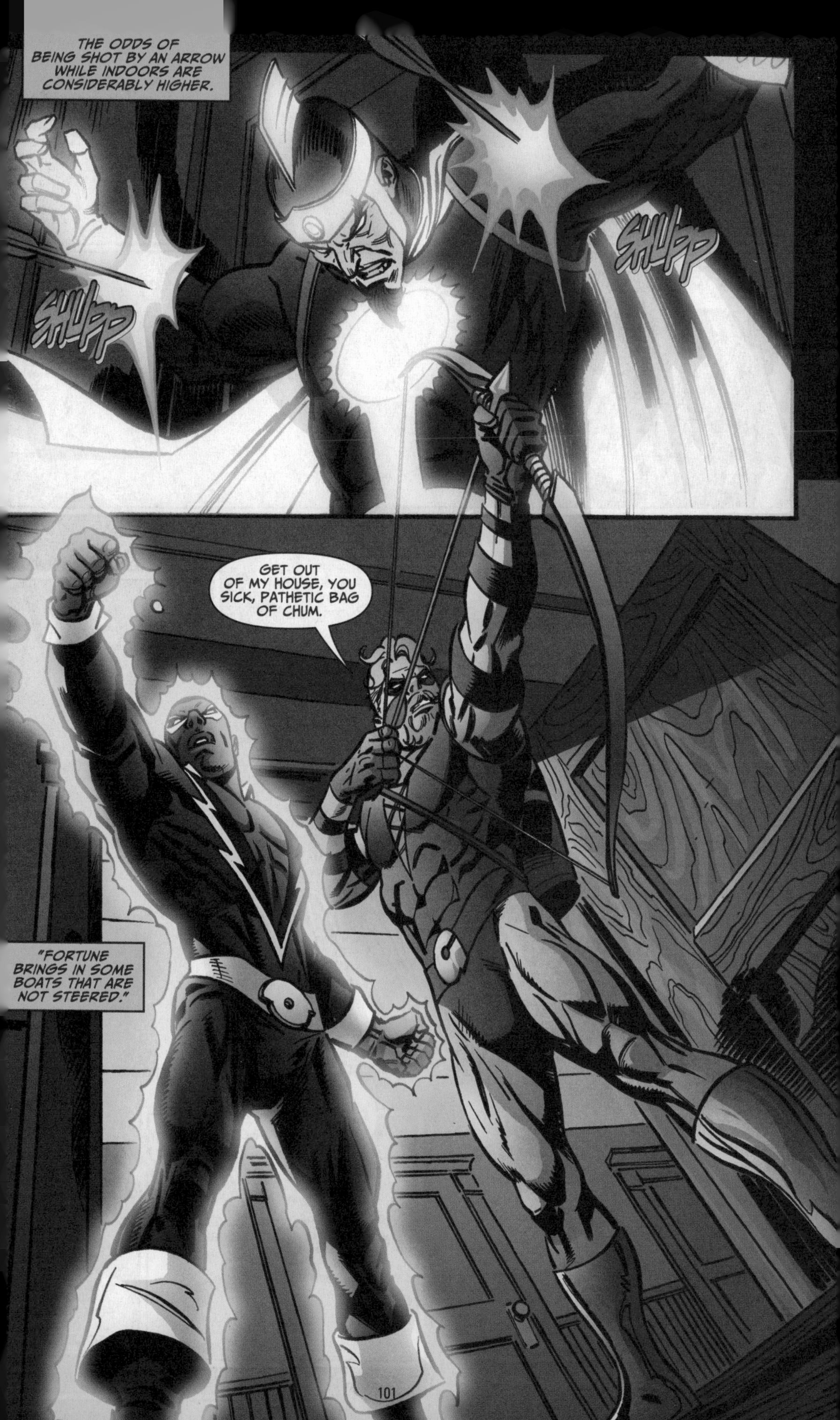
THE ODDS OF BEING SHOT BY AN ARROW WHILE INDOORS ARE CONSIDERABLY HIGHER.
SHUPP
SHUPP
GET OUT OF MY HOUSE, YOU SICK, PATHETIC BAG OF CHUM.
"FORTUNE BRINGS IN SOME BOATS THAT ARE NOT STEERED."

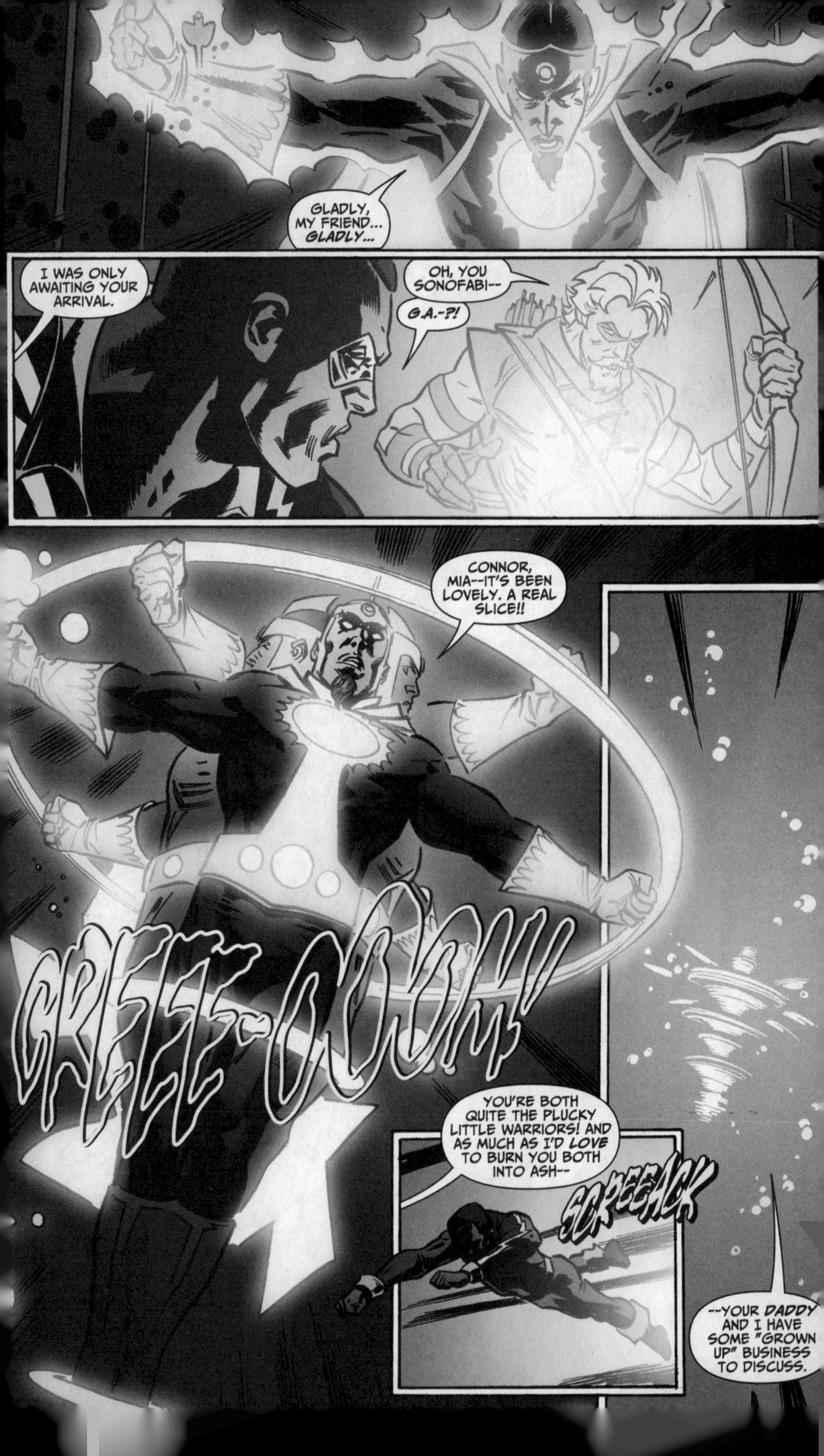
GLADLY, MY FRIEND... GLADLY...
I WAS ONLY AWAITING YOUR ARRIVAL.
OH, YOU SONOFABI--
G.A.-?!
CONNOR, MIA--IT'S BEEN LOVELY. A REAL SLICE!!
CREEE-OOOM!
YOU'RE BOTH QUITE THE PLUCKY LITTLE WARRIORS! AND AS MUCH AS I'D LOVE TO BURN YOU BOTH INTO ASH--
SCREEACK
--YOUR DADDY AND I HAVE SOME "GROWN UP" BUSINESS TO DISCUSS.

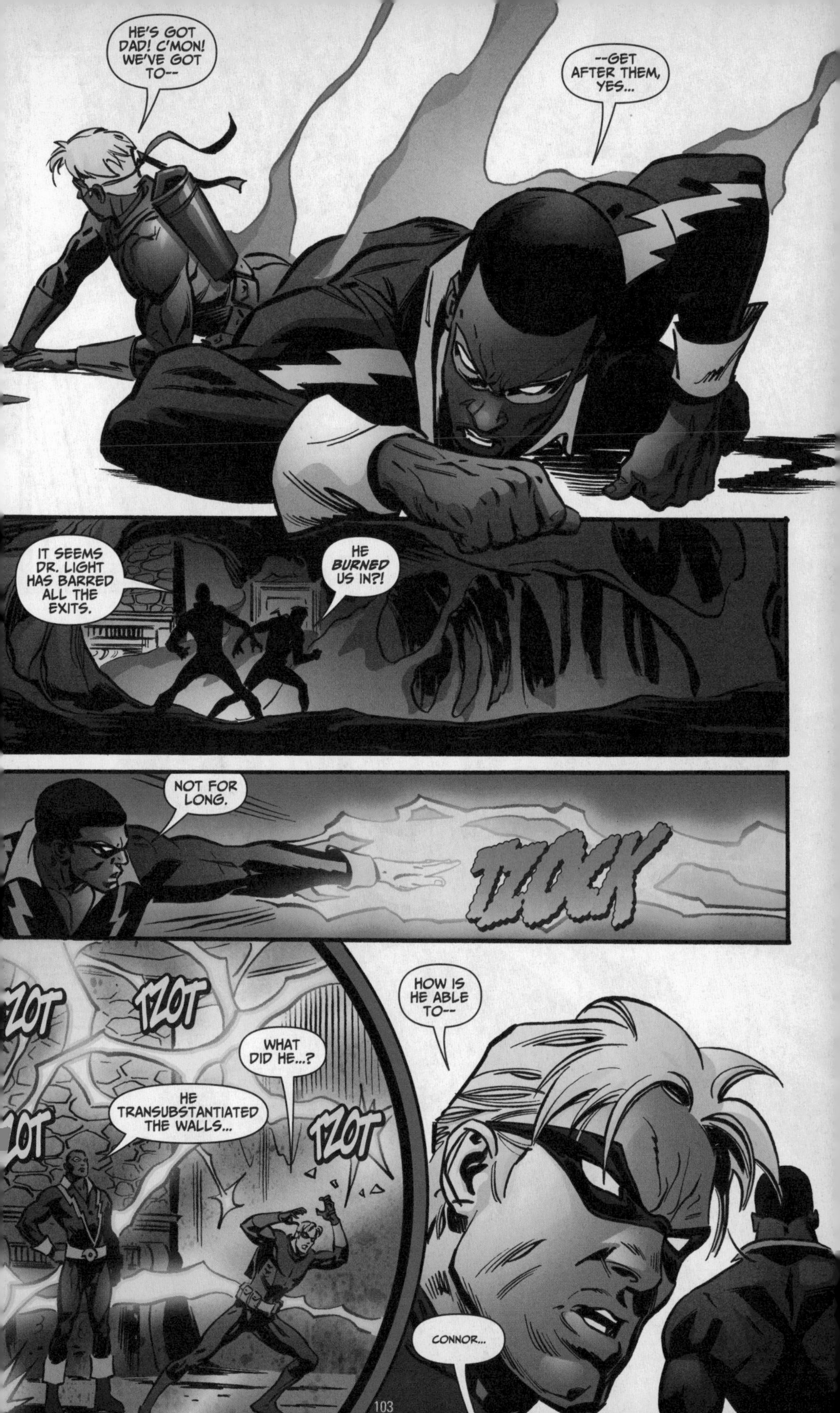
HE'S GOT DAD! C'MON! WE'VE GOT TO--
--GET AFTER THEM, YES...
IT SEEMS DR. LIGHT HAS BARRED ALL THE EXITS.
HE *BURNED* US IN?!
NOT FOR LONG.
TZOCK
TZOT
TZOT
HE TRANSUBSTANTIATED THE WALLS...
WHAT DID HE...?
TZOT
HOW IS HE ABLE TO--
CONNOR...

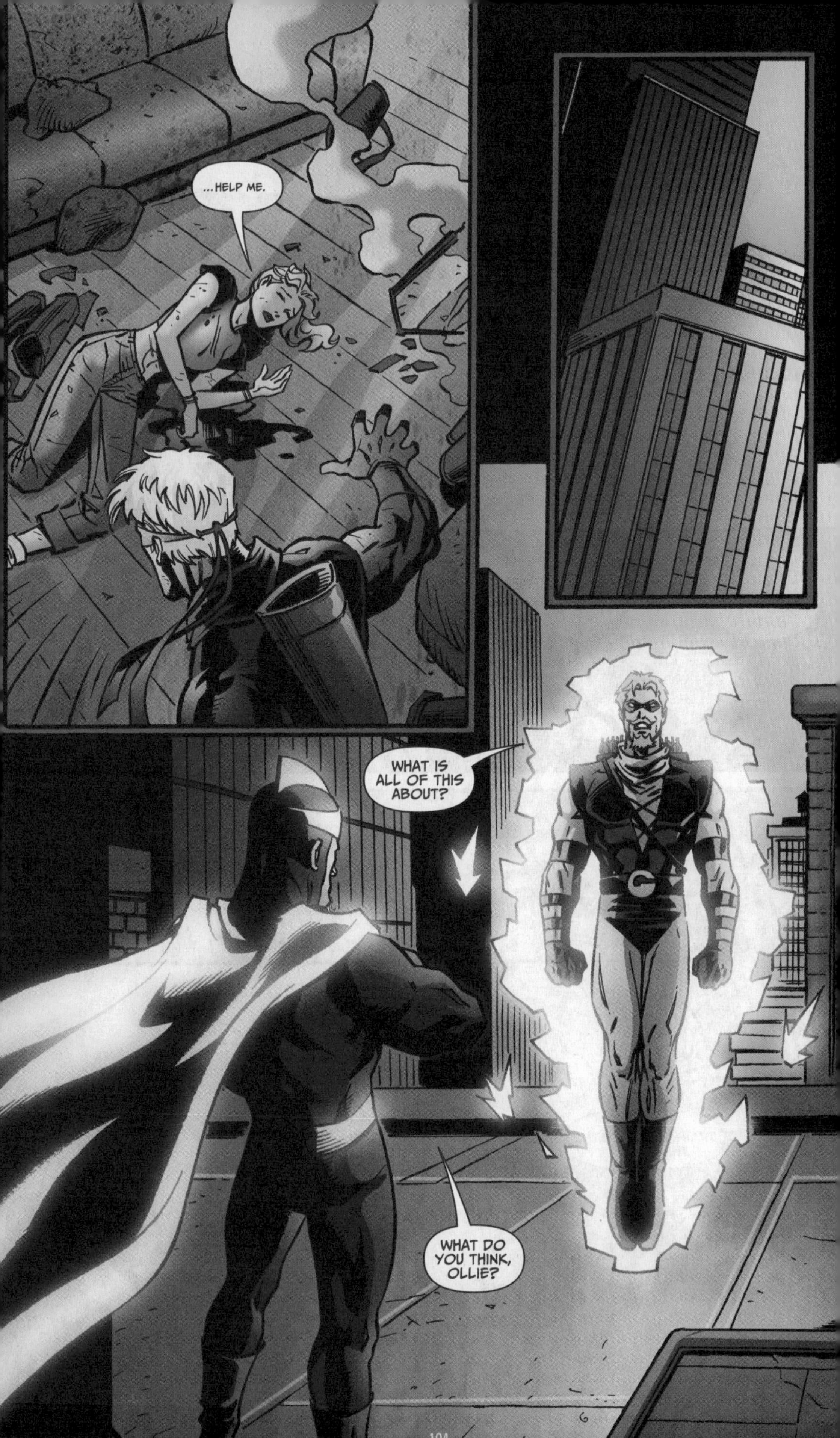
...HELP ME.
WHAT IS ALL OF THIS ABOUT?
WHAT DO YOU THINK, OLLIE?

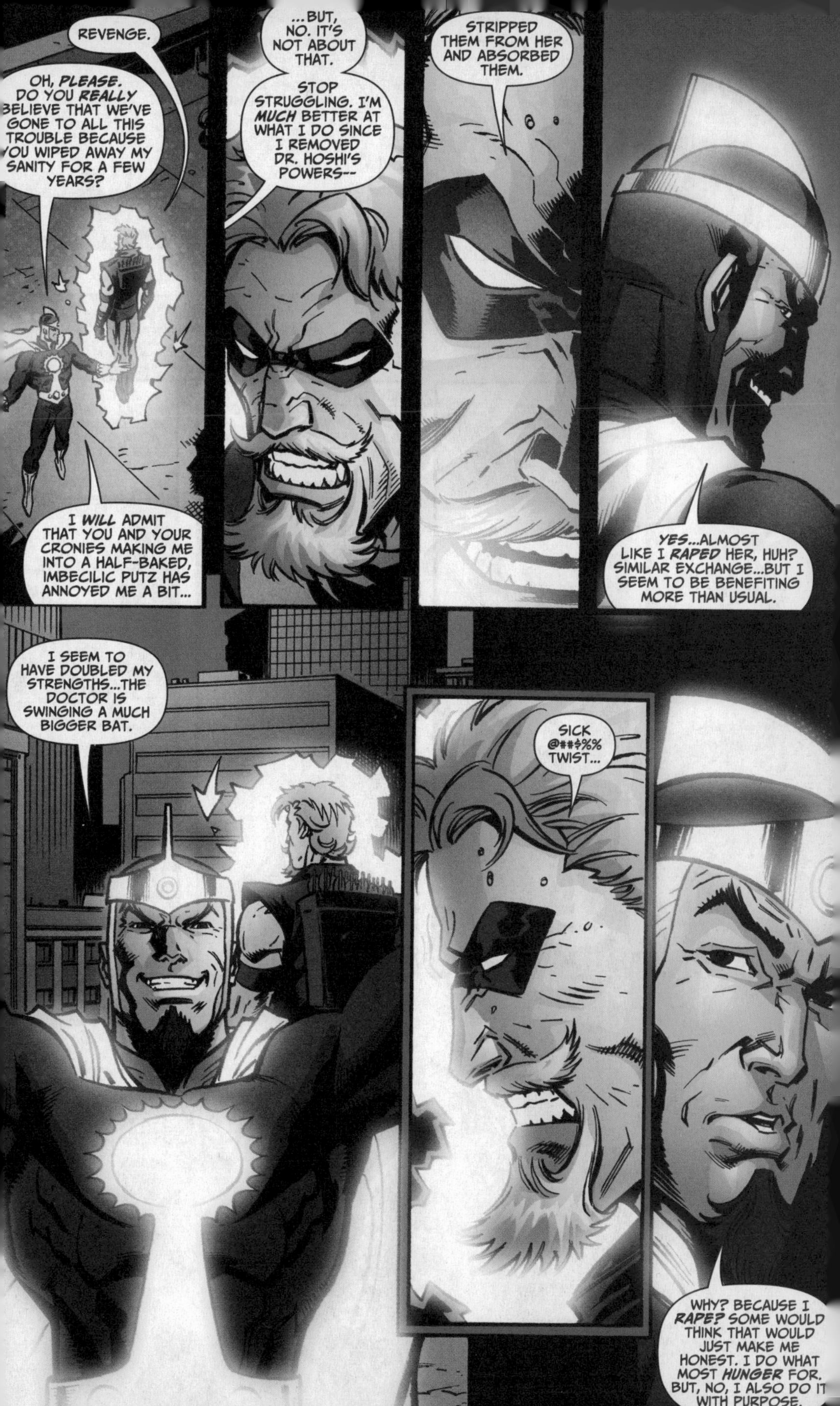
REVENGE.
OH, PLEASE. DO YOU REALLY BELIEVE THAT WE'VE GONE TO ALL THIS TROUBLE BECAUSE YOU WIPED AWAY MY SANITY FOR A FEW YEARS?
I WILL ADMIT THAT YOU AND YOUR CRONIES MAKING ME INTO A HALF-BAKED, IMBECILIC PUTZ HAS ANNOYED ME A BIT...
...BUT, NO. IT'S NOT ABOUT THAT.
STOP STRUGGLING. I'M MUCH BETTER AT WHAT I DO SINCE I REMOVED DR. HOSHI'S POWERS--
STRIPPED THEM FROM HER AND ABSORBED THEM.
YES...ALMOST LIKE I RAPED HER, HUH? SIMILAR EXCHANGE...BUT I SEEM TO BE BENEFITING MORE THAN USUAL.
I SEEM TO HAVE DOUBLED MY STRENGTHS...THE DOCTOR IS SWINGING A MUCH BIGGER BAT.
SICK @##$%% TWIST...
WHY? BECAUSE I RAPE? SOME WOULD THINK THAT WOULD JUST MAKE ME HONEST. I DO WHAT MOST HUNGER FOR. BUT, NO, I ALSO DO IT WITH PURPOSE.

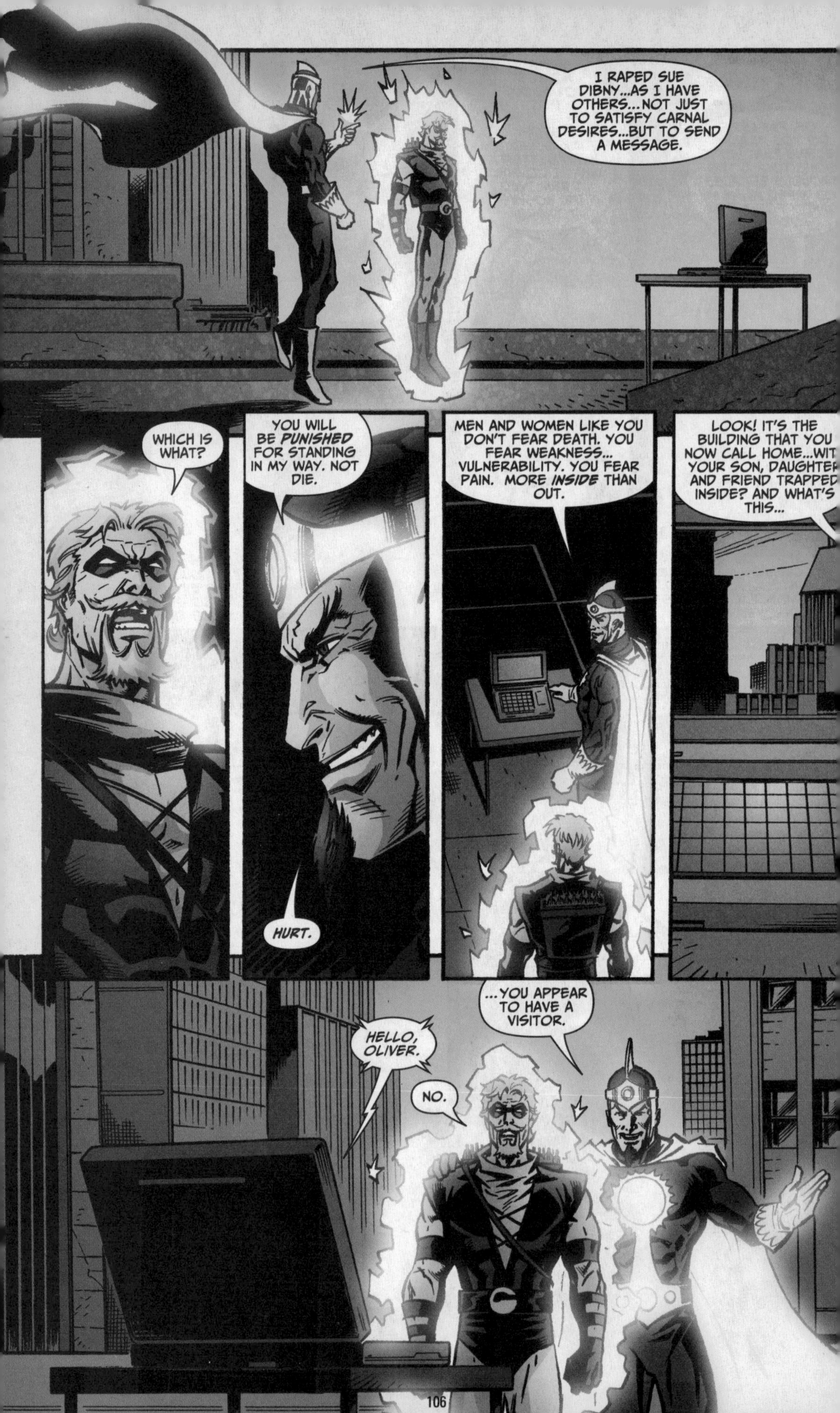
I RAPED SUE DIBNY...AS I HAVE OTHERS...NOT JUST TO SATISFY CARNAL DESIRES...BUT TO SEND A MESSAGE.
WHICH IS WHAT?
YOU WILL BE PUNISHED FOR STANDING IN MY WAY. NOT DIE.
HURT.
MEN AND WOMEN LIKE YOU DON'T FEAR DEATH. YOU FEAR WEAKNESS... VULNERABILITY. YOU FEAR PAIN. MORE INSIDE THAN OUT.
LOOK! IT'S THE BUILDING THAT YOU NOW CALL HOME...WIT YOUR SON, DAUGHTER AND FRIEND TRAPPED INSIDE? AND WHAT'S THIS...
...YOU APPEAR TO HAVE A VISITOR.
HELLO, OLIVER.
NO.

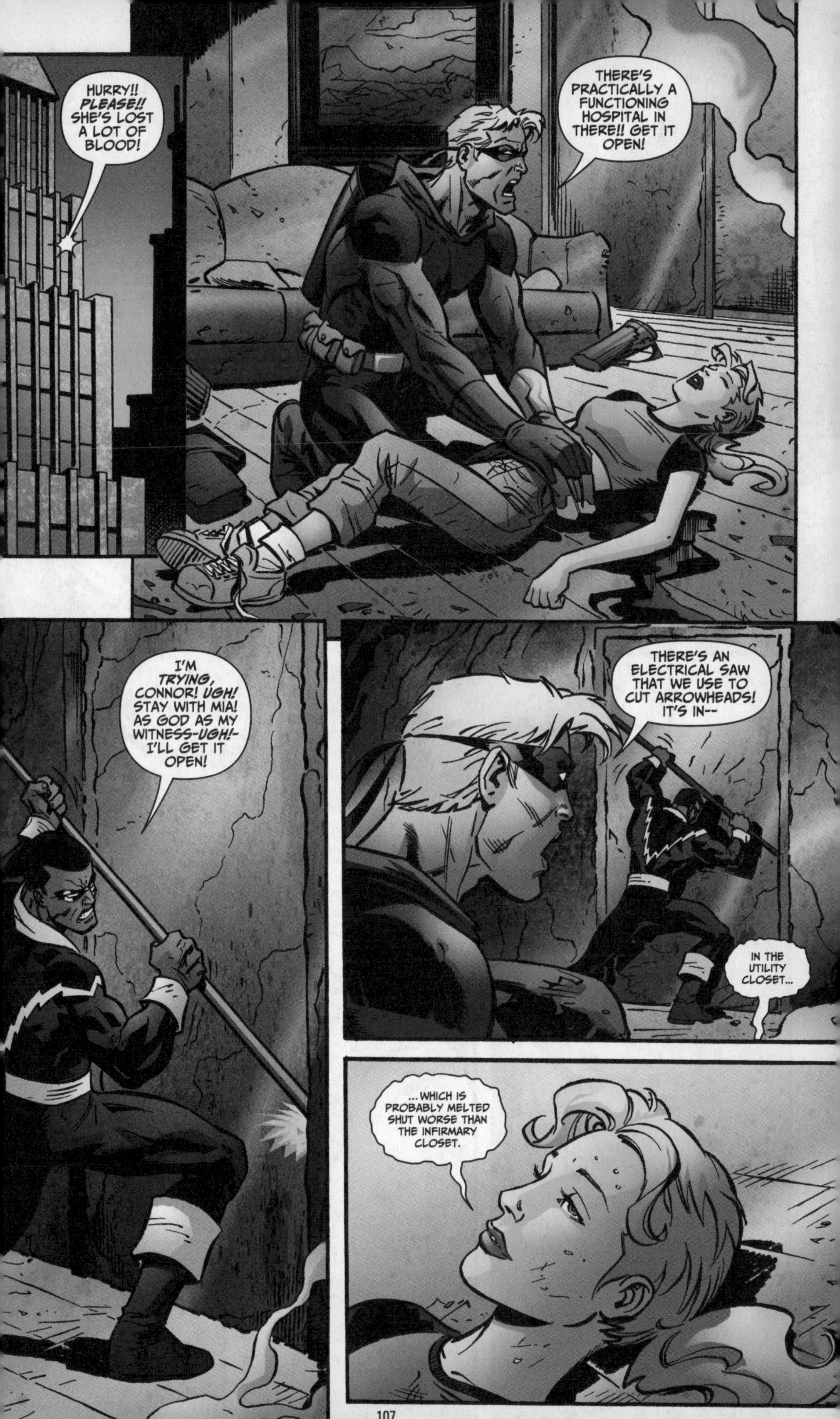
HURRY!! PLEASE!! SHE'S LOST A LOT OF BLOOD!
THERE'S PRACTICALLY A FUNCTIONING HOSPITAL IN THERE!! GET IT OPEN!
I'M TRYING, CONNOR! UGH! STAY WITH MIA! AS GOD AS MY WITNESS--UGH!-- I'LL GET IT OPEN!
THERE'S AN ELECTRICAL SAW THAT WE USE TO CUT ARROWHEADS! IT'S IN--
IN THE UTILITY CLOSET...
...WHICH IS PROBABLY MELTED SHUT WORSE THAN THE INFIRMARY CLOSET.

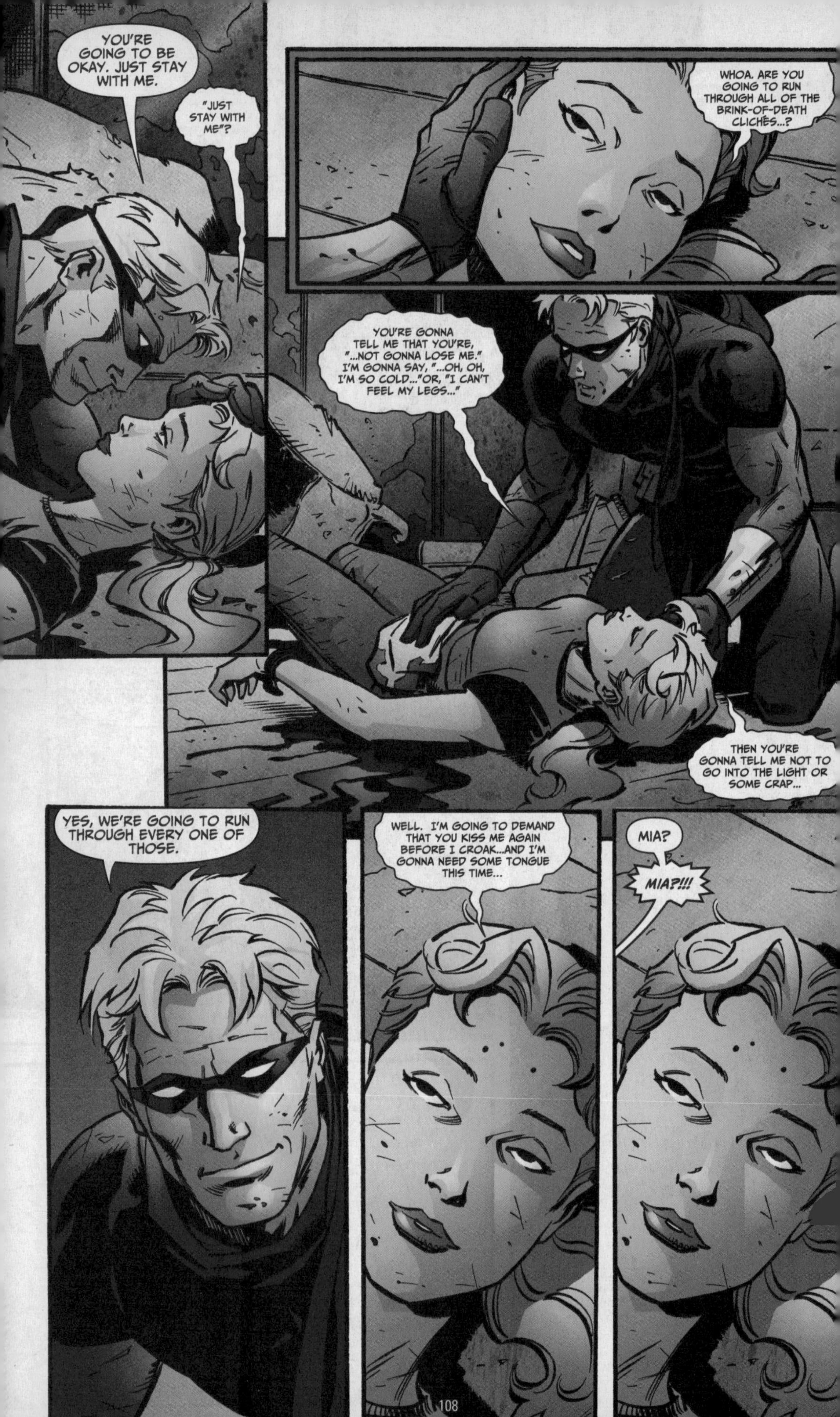
YOU'RE GOING TO BE OKAY. JUST STAY WITH ME.
"JUST STAY WITH ME"?
WHOA. ARE YOU GOING TO RUN THROUGH ALL OF THE BRINK-OF-DEATH CLICHÉS...?
YOU'RE GONNA TELL ME THAT YOU'RE, "...NOT GONNA LOSE ME." I'M GONNA SAY, "...OH, OH, I'M SO COLD..." OR, "I CAN'T FEEL MY LEGS..."
THEN YOU'RE GONNA TELL ME NOT TO GO INTO THE LIGHT OR SOME CRAP...
YES, WE'RE GOING TO RUN THROUGH EVERY ONE OF THOSE.
WELL. I'M GOING TO DEMAND THAT YOU KISS ME AGAIN BEFORE I CROAK...AND I'M GONNA NEED SOME TONGUE THIS TIME...
MIA?
MIA?!!!

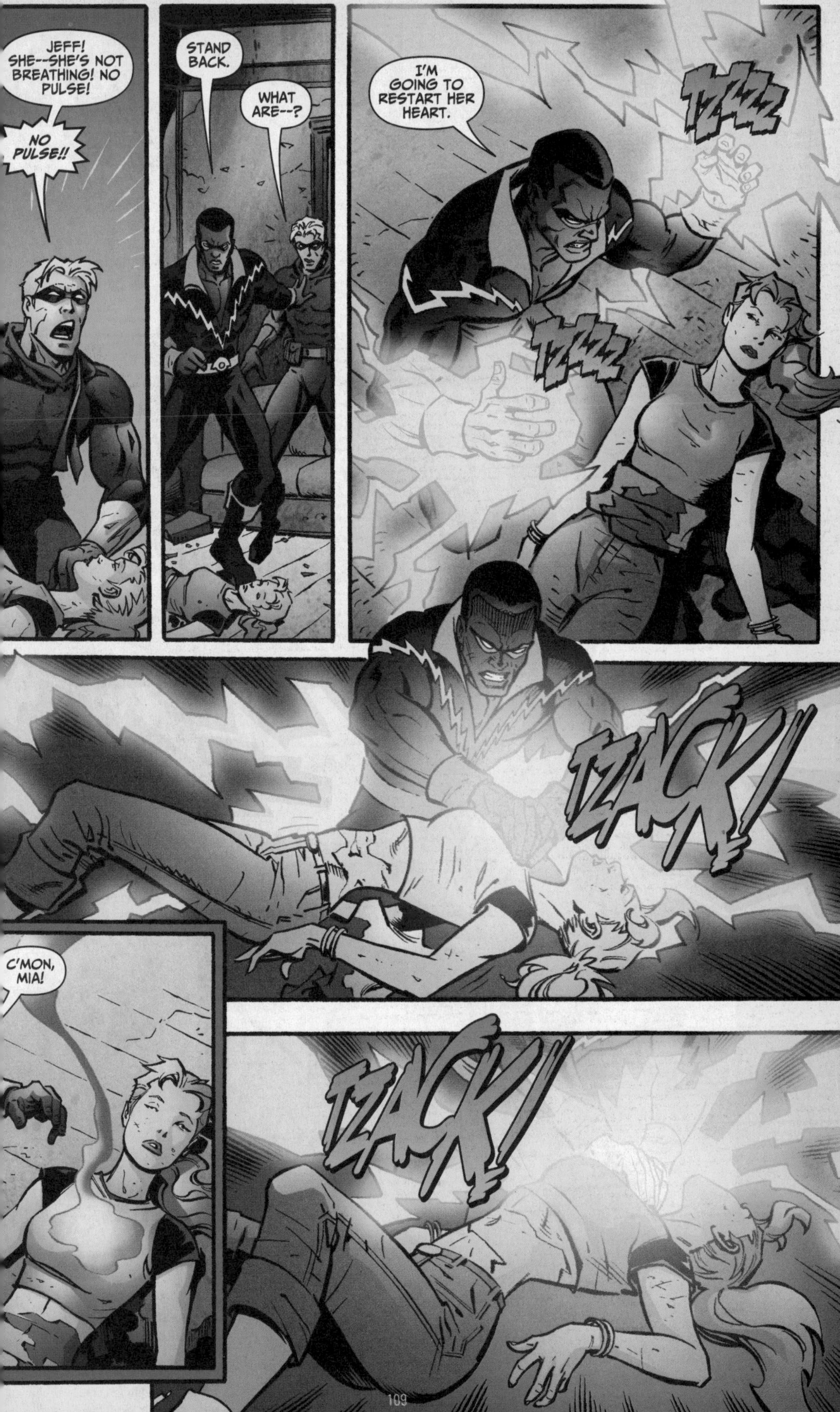
JEFF! SHE--SHE'S NOT BREATHING! NO PULSE!
NO PULSE!!
STAND BACK.
WHAT ARE--?
I'M GOING TO RESTART HER HEART.
TZZZ
TZZZ
TZACK!
C'MON, MIA!
TZACK!

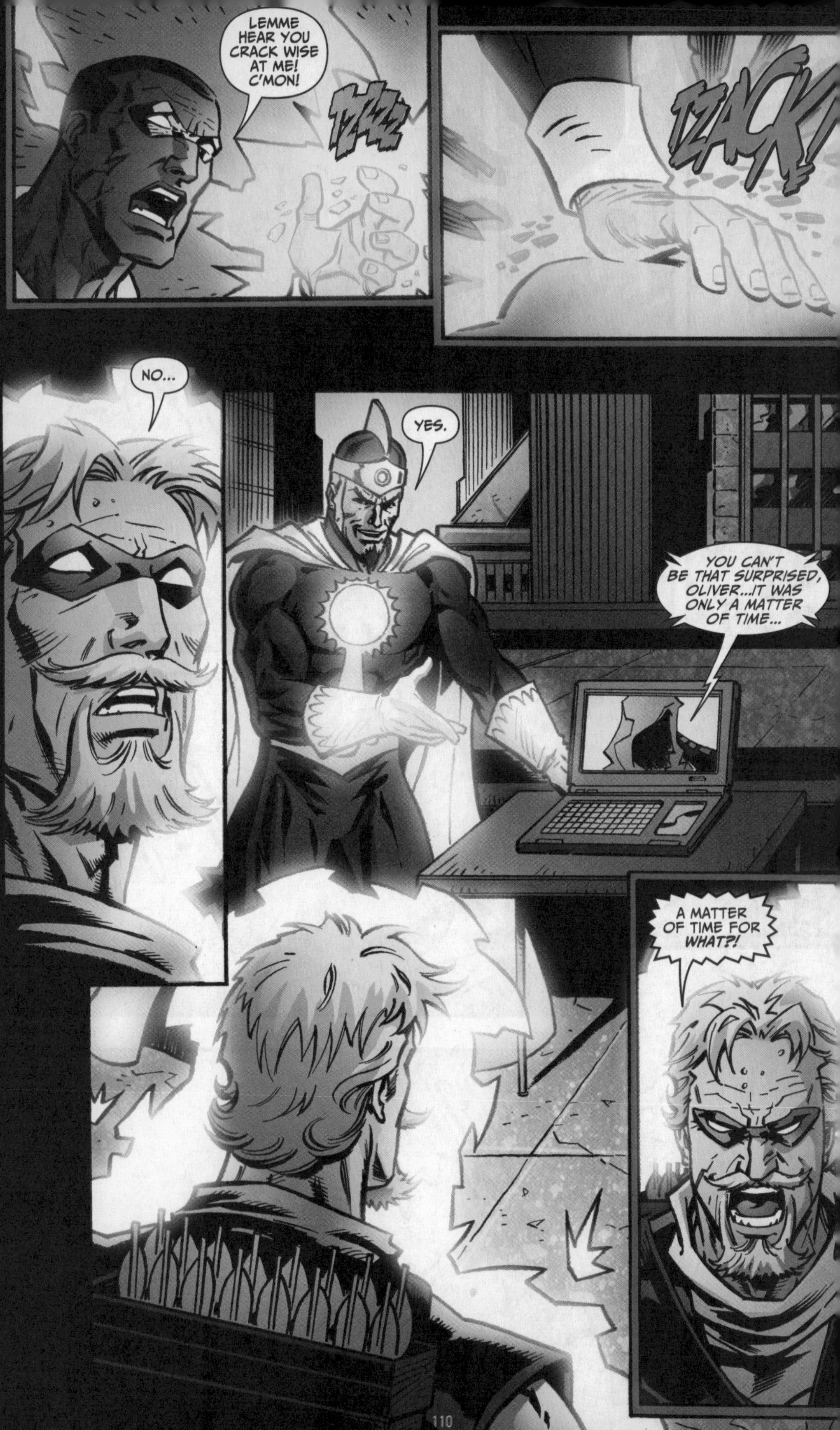
LEMME HEAR YOU CRACK WISE AT ME! C'MON!
TZZZ
TZACK!
NO...
YES.
YOU CAN'T BE THAT SURPRISED, OLIVER...IT WAS ONLY A MATTER OF TIME...
A MATTER OF TIME FOR WHAT?!

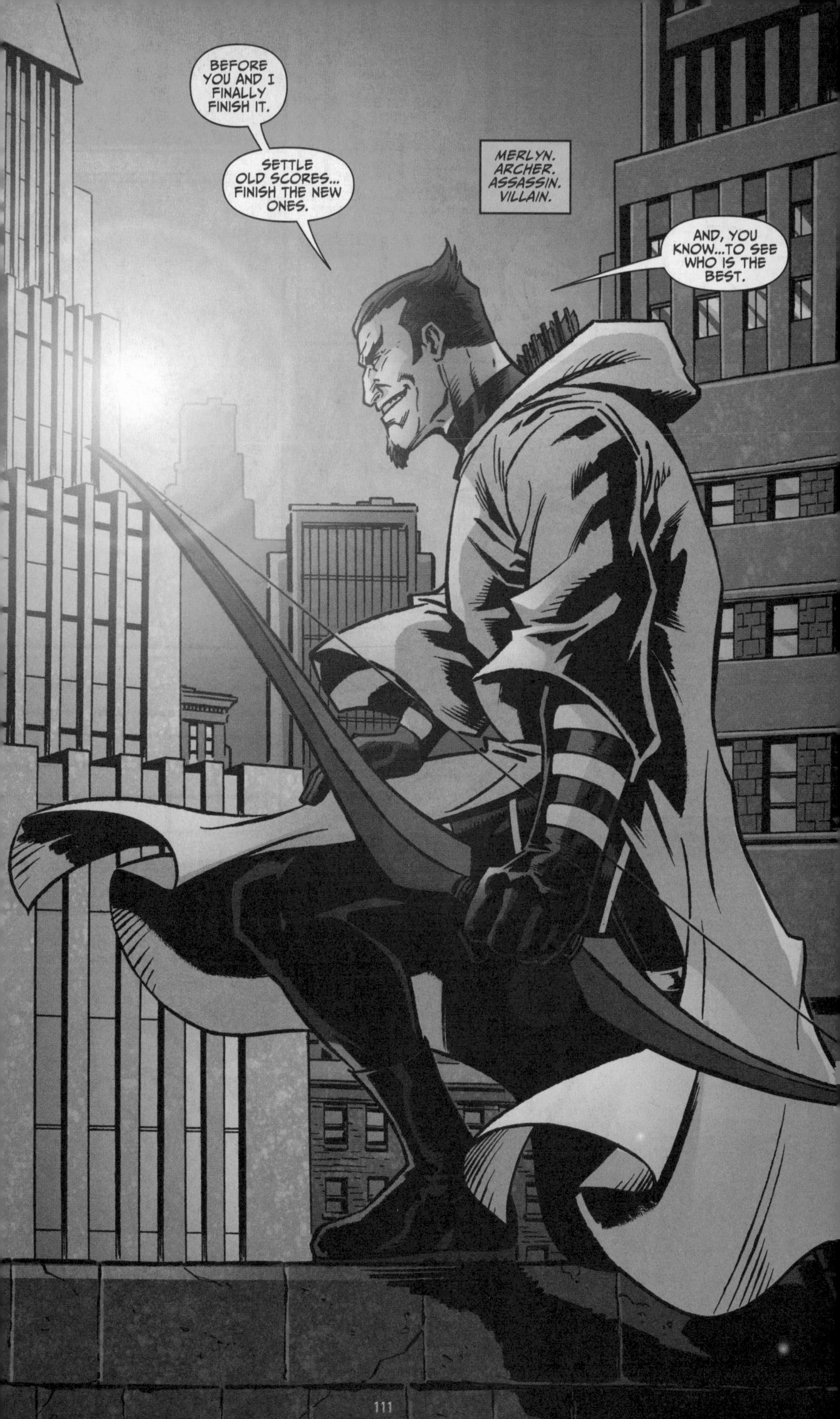
BEFORE YOU AND I FINALLY FINISH IT.
SETTLE OLD SCORES... FINISH THE NEW ONES.
MERLYN. ARCHER. ASSASSIN. VILLAIN.
AND, YOU KNOW...TO SEE WHO IS THE BEST.

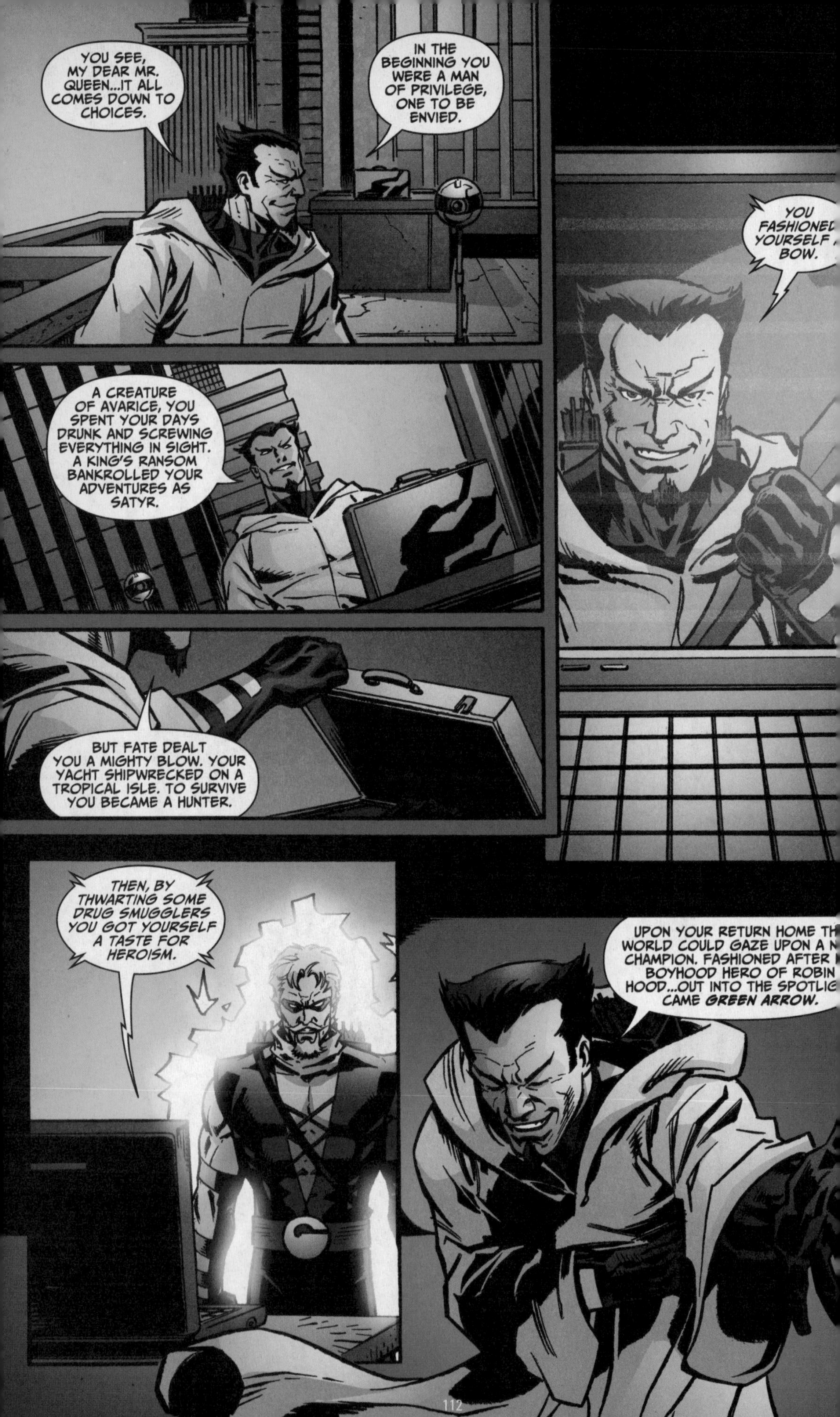
YOU SEE, MY DEAR MR. QUEEN...IT ALL COMES DOWN TO CHOICES.
IN THE BEGINNING YOU WERE A MAN OF PRIVILEGE, ONE TO BE ENVIED.
A CREATURE OF AVARICE, YOU SPENT YOUR DAYS DRUNK AND SCREWING EVERYTHING IN SIGHT. A KING'S RANSOM BANKROLLED YOUR ADVENTURES AS SATYR.
BUT FATE DEALT YOU A MIGHTY BLOW. YOUR YACHT SHIPWRECKED ON A TROPICAL ISLE. TO SURVIVE YOU BECAME A HUNTER.
YOU FASHIONED YOURSELF A BOW.
THEN, BY THWARTING SOME DRUG SMUGGLERS YOU GOT YOURSELF A TASTE FOR HEROISM.
UPON YOUR RETURN HOME THE WORLD COULD GAZE UPON A NEW CHAMPION. FASHIONED AFTER YOUR BOYHOOD HERO OF ROBIN HOOD...OUT INTO THE SPOTLIGHT CAME GREEN ARROW.

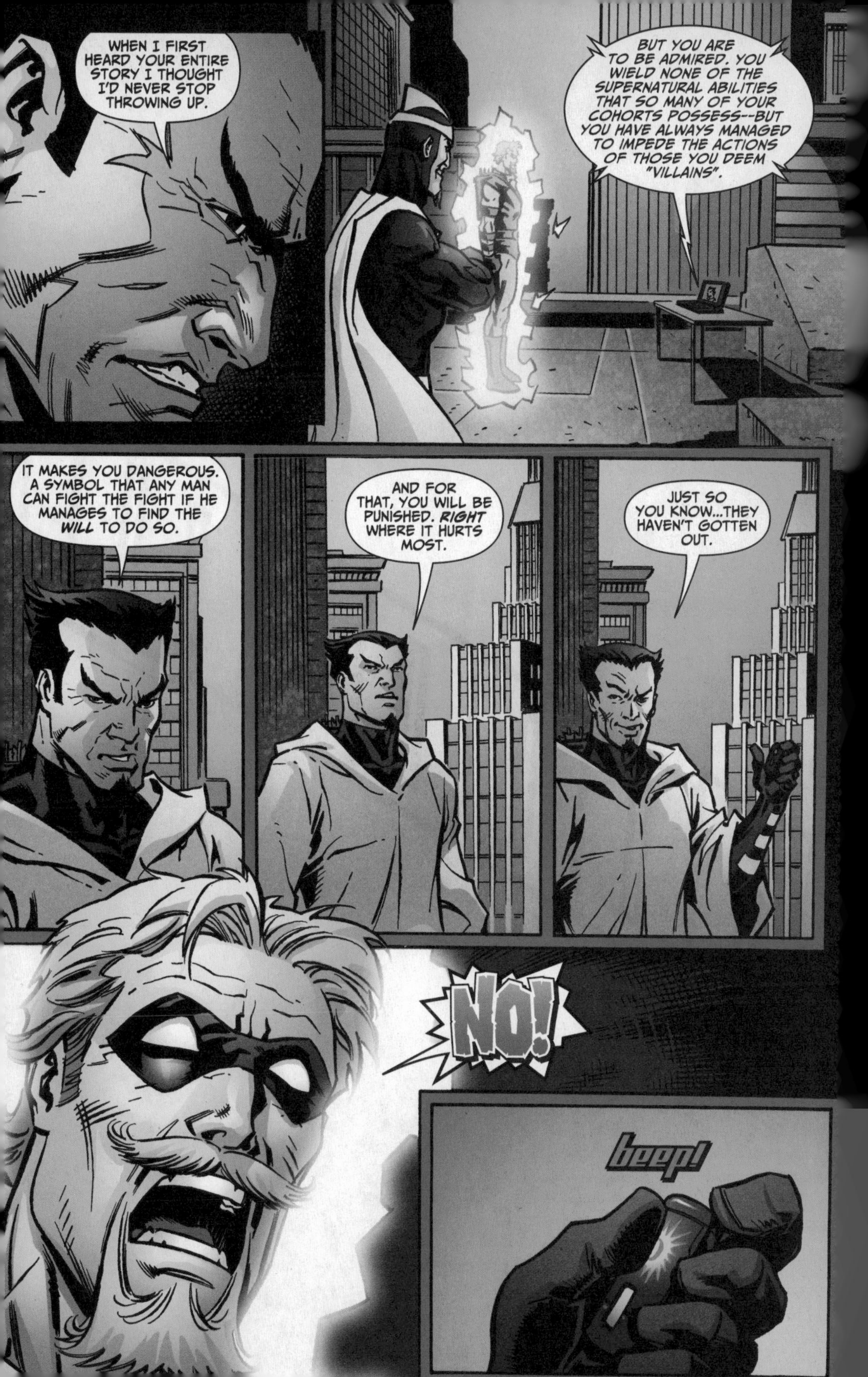
WHEN I FIRST HEARD YOUR ENTIRE STORY I THOUGHT I'D NEVER STOP THROWING UP.
BUT YOU ARE TO BE ADMIRED. YOU WIELD NONE OF THE SUPERNATURAL ABILITIES THAT SO MANY OF YOUR COHORTS POSSESS--BUT YOU HAVE ALWAYS MANAGED TO IMPEDE THE ACTIONS OF THOSE YOU DEEM "VILLAINS".
IT MAKES YOU DANGEROUS. A SYMBOL THAT ANY MAN CAN FIGHT THE FIGHT IF HE MANAGES TO FIND THE *WILL* TO DO SO.
AND FOR THAT, YOU WILL BE PUNISHED. *RIGHT* WHERE IT HURTS MOST.
JUST SO YOU KNOW...THEY HAVEN'T GOTTEN OUT.
NO!
beep!

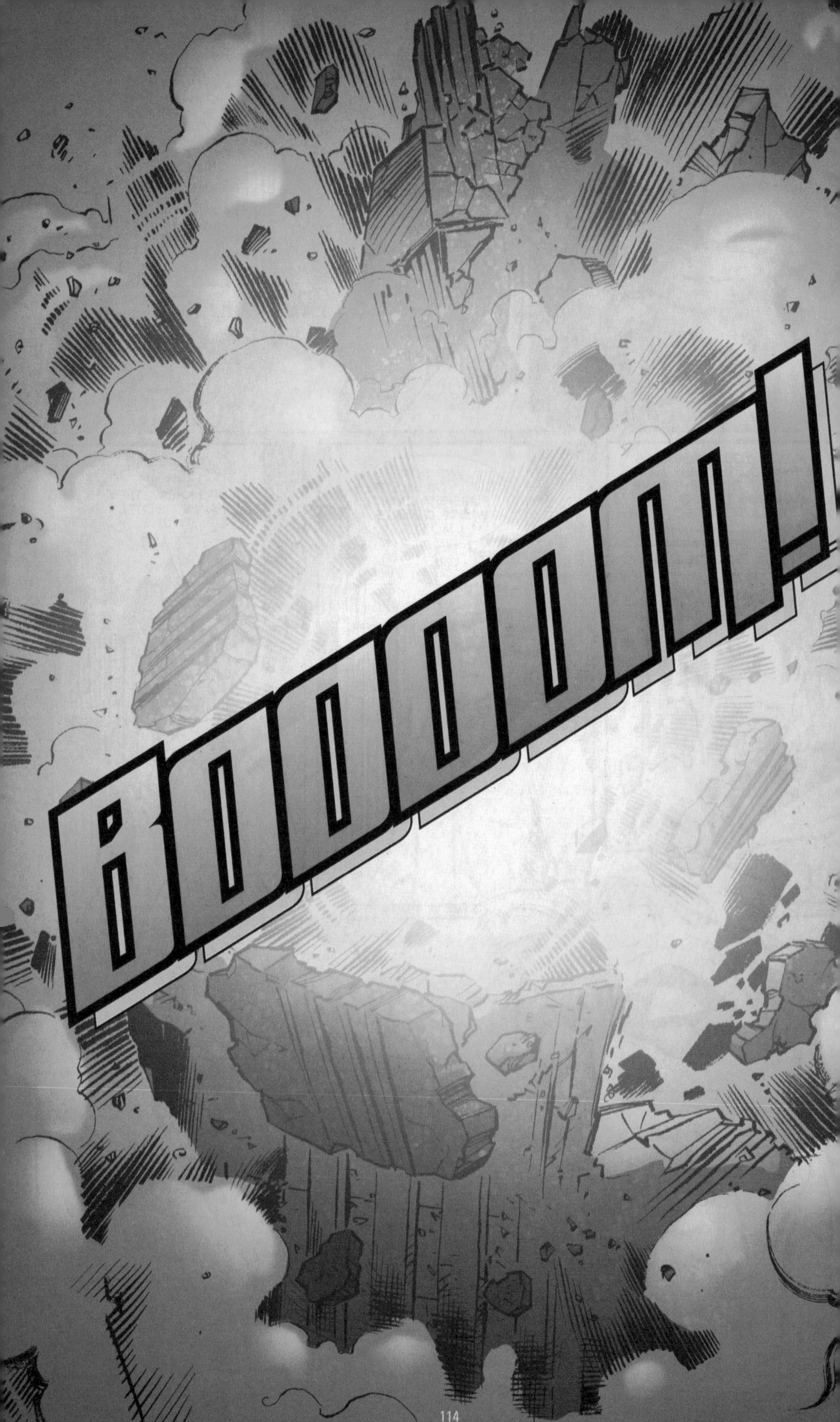
BOOOOM!

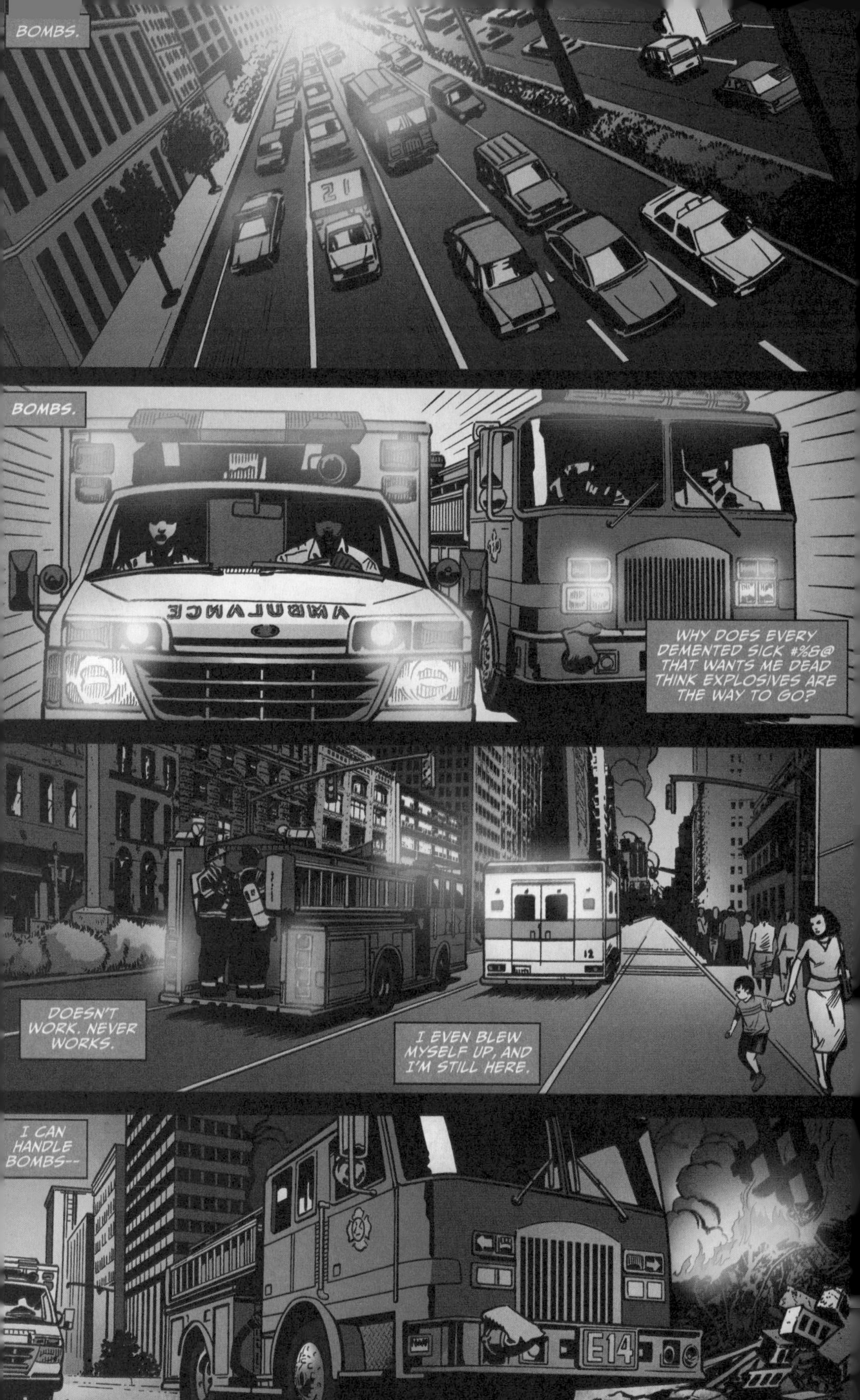
BOMBS.
BOMBS.
AMBULANCE
WHY DOES EVERY DEMENTED SICK #%&@ THAT WANTS ME DEAD THINK EXPLOSIVES ARE THE WAY TO GO?
DOESN'T WORK. NEVER WORKS.
I EVEN BLEW MYSELF UP, AND I'M STILL HERE.
I CAN HANDLE BOMBS--
E14

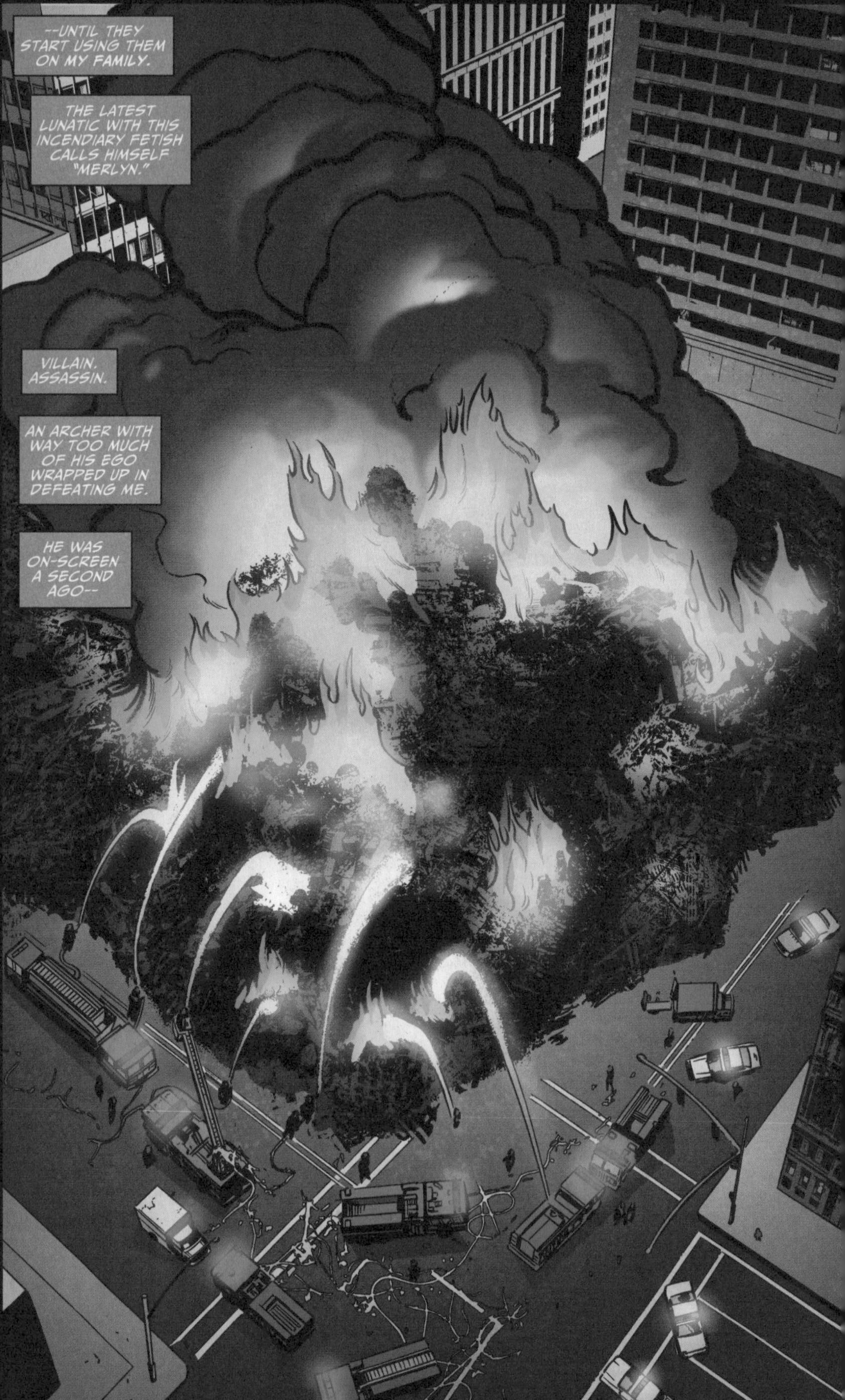
--UNTIL THEY START USING THEM ON MY FAMILY.
THE LATEST LUNATIC WITH THIS INCENDIARY FETISH CALLS HIMSELF "MERLYN."
VILLAIN. ASSASSIN.
AN ARCHER WITH WAY TOO MUCH OF HIS EGO WRAPPED UP IN DEFEATING ME.
HE WAS ON-SCREEN A SECOND AGO--

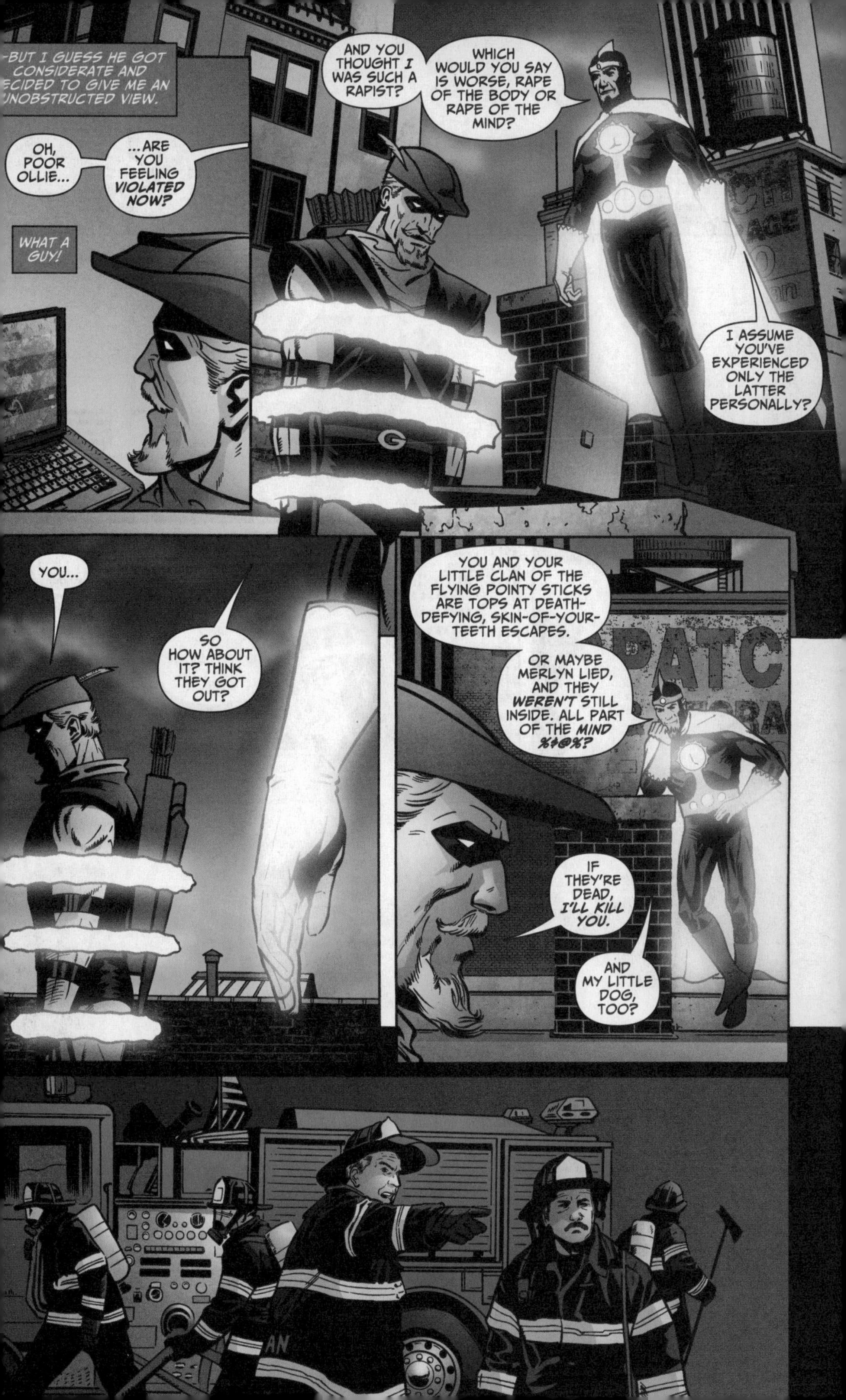
-BUT I GUESS HE GOT CONSIDERATE AND ECIDED TO GIVE ME AN UNOBSTRUCTED VIEW.
OH, POOR OLLIE...
...ARE YOU FEELING VIOLATED NOW?
WHAT A GUY!
AND YOU THOUGHT I WAS SUCH A RAPIST?
WHICH WOULD YOU SAY IS WORSE, RAPE OF THE BODY OR RAPE OF THE MIND?
I ASSUME YOU'VE EXPERIENCED ONLY THE LATTER PERSONALLY?
YOU...
SO HOW ABOUT IT? THINK THEY GOT OUT?
YOU AND YOUR LITTLE CLAN OF THE FLYING POINTY STICKS ARE TOPS AT DEATH-DEFYING, SKIN-OF-YOUR-TEETH ESCAPES.
OR MAYBE MERLYN LIED, AND THEY WEREN'T STILL INSIDE. ALL PART OF THE MIND %$@%?
IF THEY'RE DEAD, I'LL KILL YOU.
AND MY LITTLE DOG, TOO?

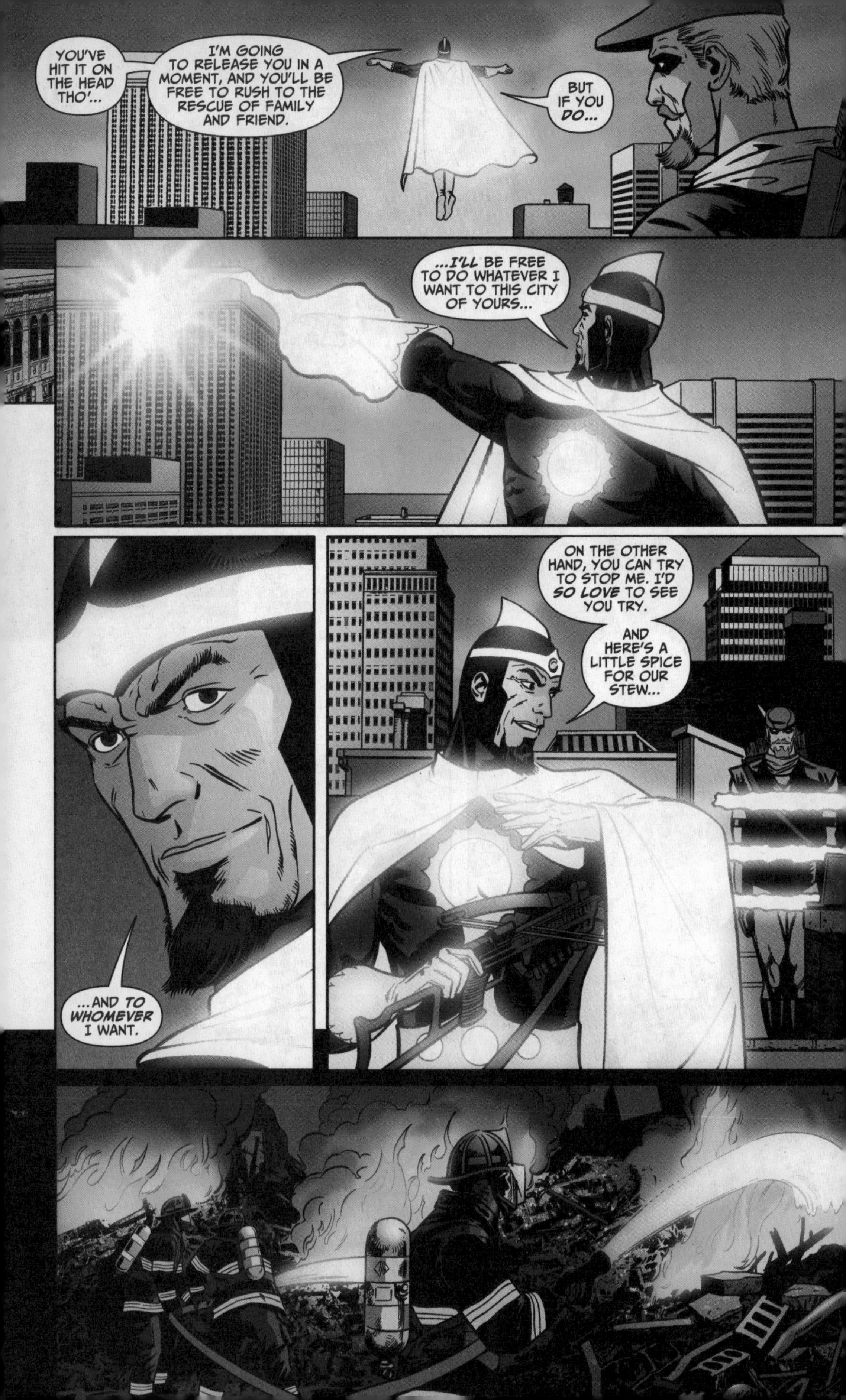
YOU'VE HIT IT ON THE HEAD THO'...
I'M GOING TO RELEASE YOU IN A MOMENT, AND YOU'LL BE FREE TO RUSH TO THE RESCUE OF FAMILY AND FRIEND.
BUT IF YOU DO...
...I'LL BE FREE TO DO WHATEVER I WANT TO THIS CITY OF YOURS...
...AND TO WHOMEVER I WANT.
ON THE OTHER HAND, YOU CAN TRY TO STOP ME. I'D SO LOVE TO SEE YOU TRY.
AND HERE'S A LITTLE SPICE FOR OUR STEW...

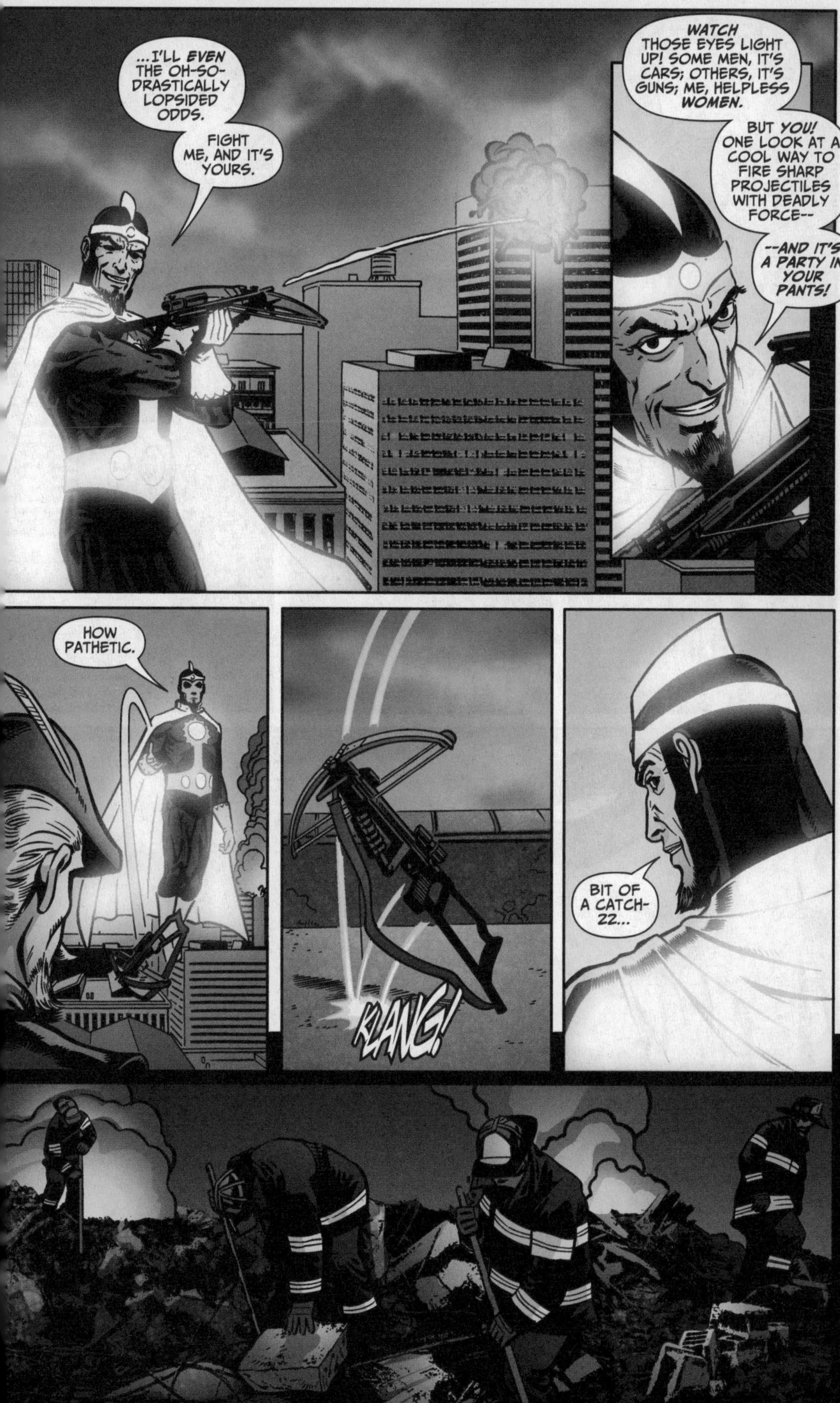
...I'LL EVEN THE OH-SO-DRASTICALLY LOPSIDED ODDS.
FIGHT ME, AND IT'S YOURS.
WATCH THOSE EYES LIGHT UP! SOME MEN, IT'S CARS; OTHERS, IT'S GUNS; ME, HELPLESS WOMEN.
BUT YOU! ONE LOOK AT A COOL WAY TO FIRE SHARP PROJECTILES WITH DEADLY FORCE--
--AND IT'S A PARTY IN YOUR PANTS!
HOW PATHETIC.
KLANG!
BIT OF A CATCH-22...

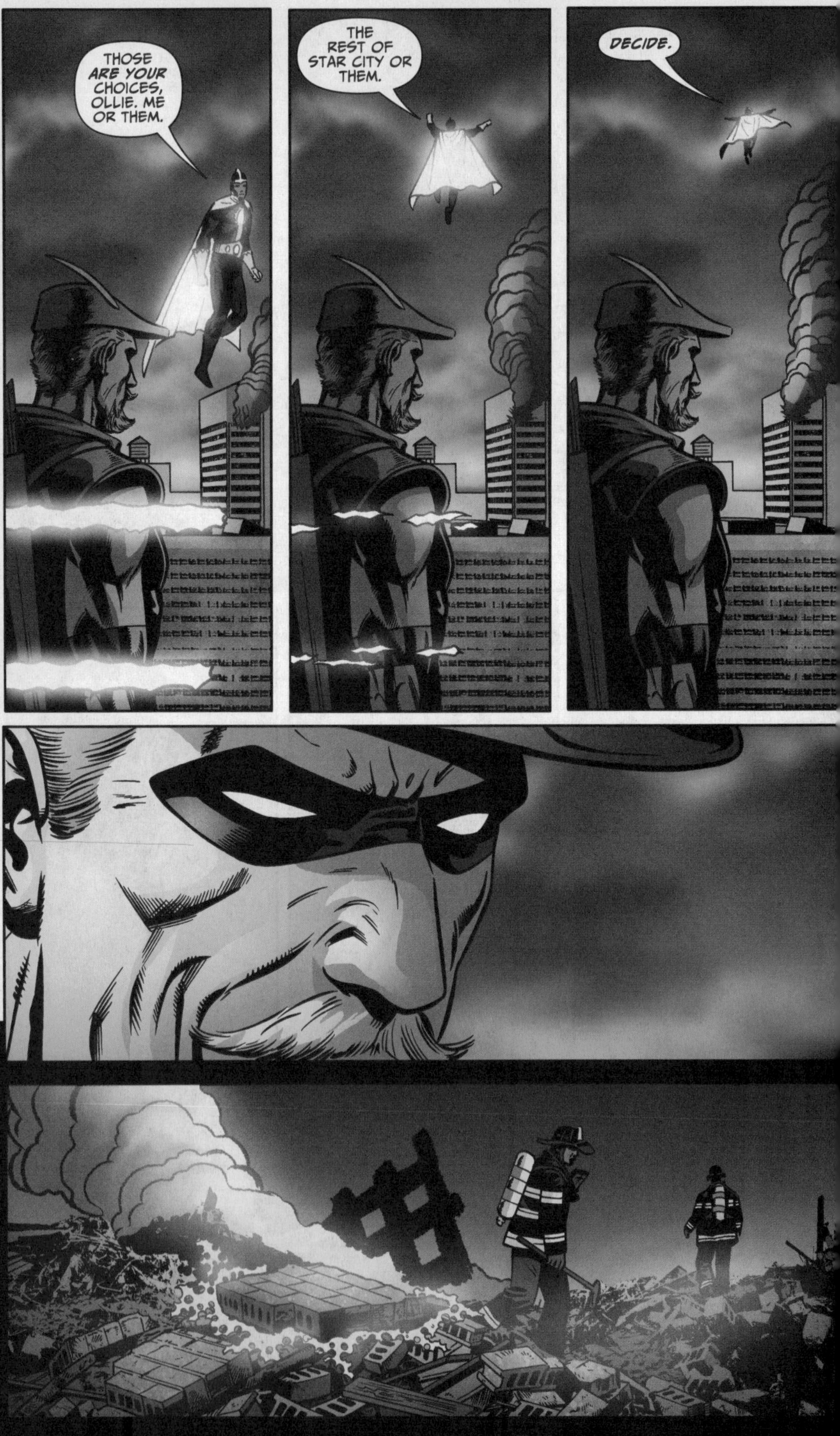
THOSE ARE YOUR CHOICES, OLLIE. ME OR THEM.
THE REST OF STAR CITY OR THEM.
DECIDE.

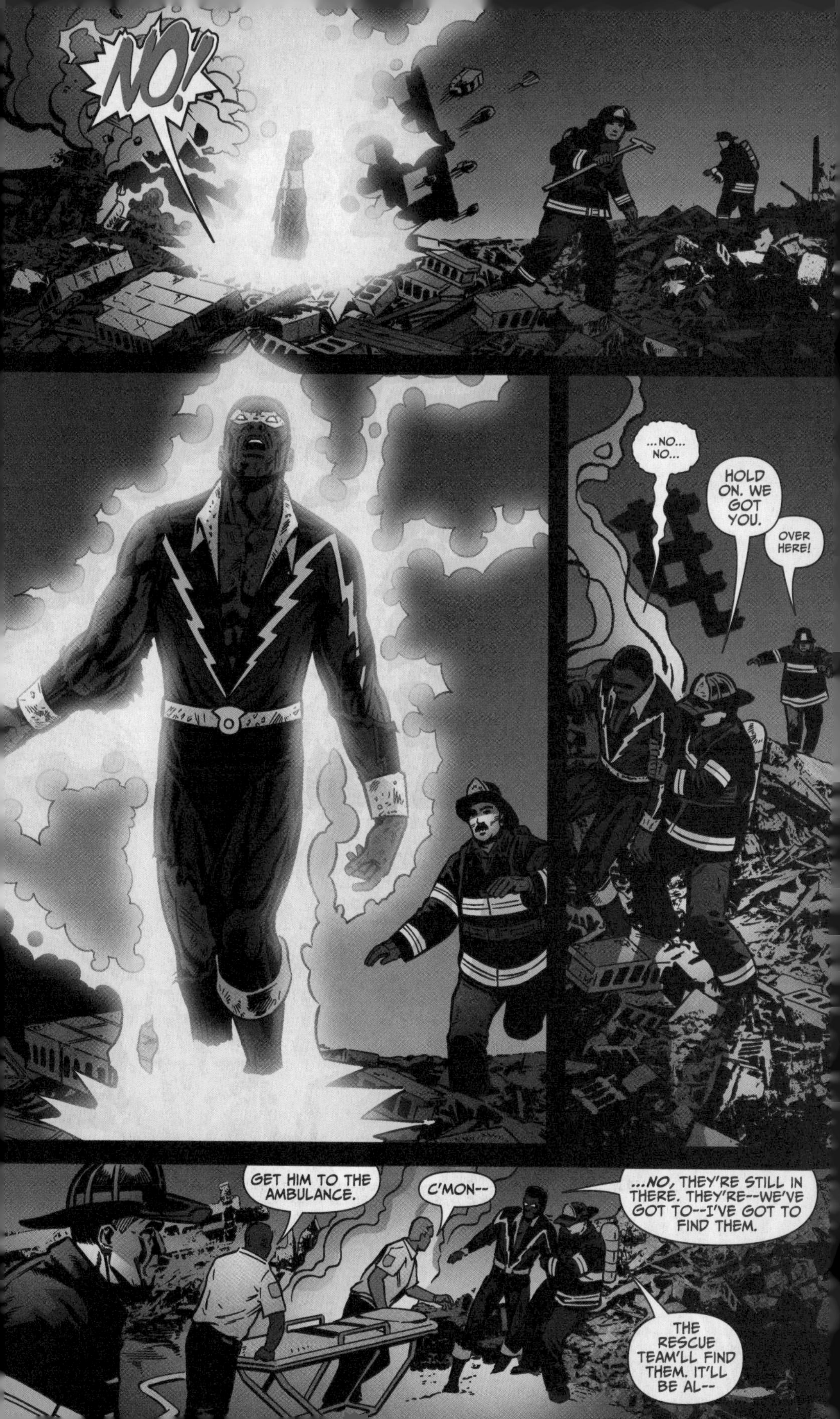
NO!
...NO... NO...
HOLD ON. WE GOT YOU.
OVER HERE!
GET HIM TO THE AMBULANCE.
C'MON--
...NO, THEY'RE STILL IN THERE. THEY'RE--WE'VE GOT TO--I'VE GOT TO FIND THEM.
THE RESCUE TEAM'LL FIND THEM. IT'LL BE AL--

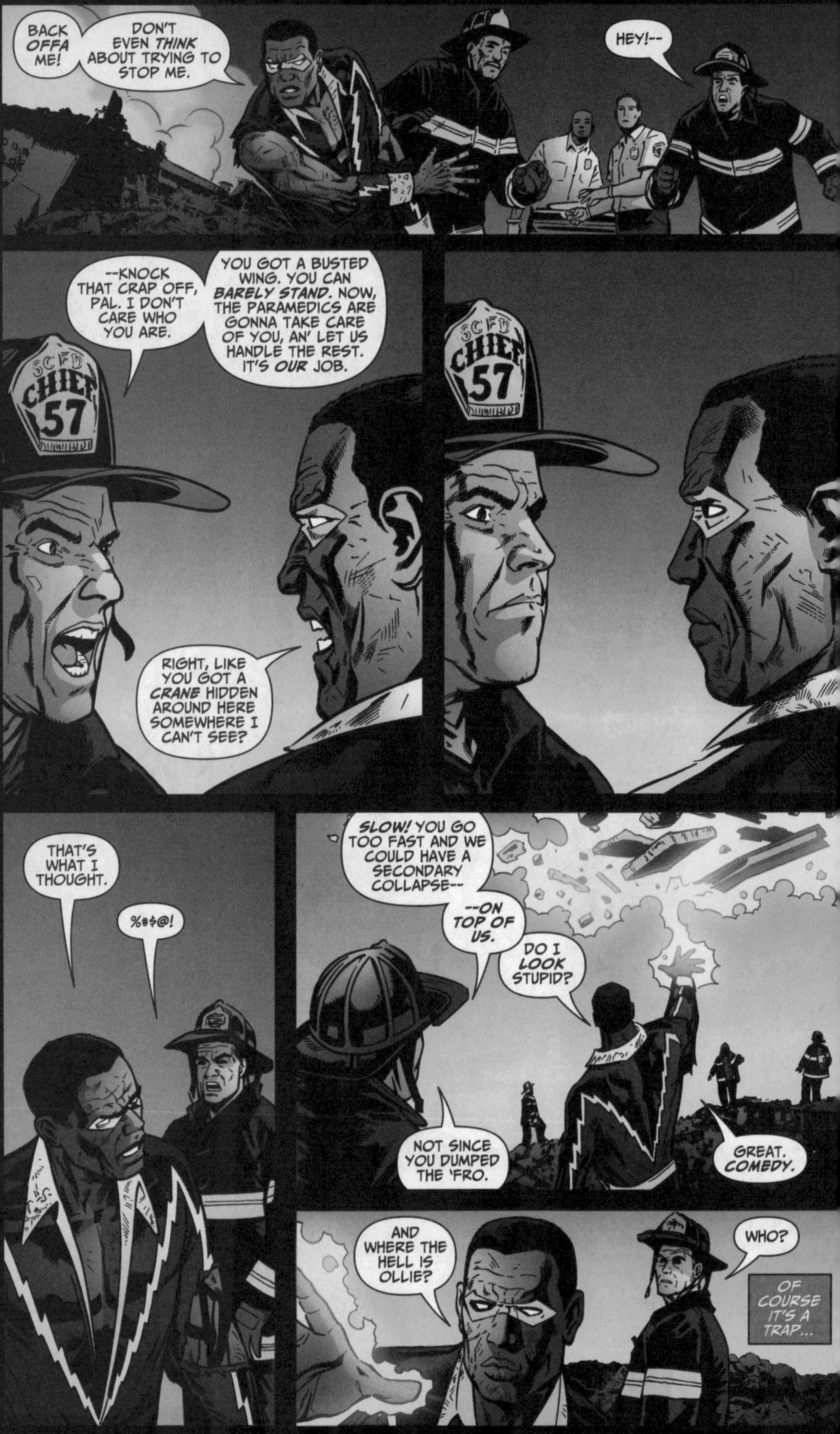
BACK OFFA ME!
DON'T EVEN THINK ABOUT TRYING TO STOP ME.
HEY!--
--KNOCK THAT CRAP OFF, PAL. I DON'T CARE WHO YOU ARE.
YOU GOT A BUSTED WING. YOU CAN BARELY STAND. NOW, THE PARAMEDICS ARE GONNA TAKE CARE OF YOU, AN' LET US HANDLE THE REST. IT'S OUR JOB.
SCFD CHIEF 57
RIGHT, LIKE YOU GOT A CRANE HIDDEN AROUND HERE SOMEWHERE I CAN'T SEE?
SCFD CHIEF 57
THAT'S WHAT I THOUGHT.
%#$@!
SLOW! YOU GO TOO FAST AND WE COULD HAVE A SECONDARY COLLAPSE--
--ON TOP OF US.
DO I LOOK STUPID?
NOT SINCE YOU DUMPED THE 'FRO.
GREAT. COMEDY.
AND WHERE THE HELL IS OLLIE?
WHO?
OF COURSE IT'S A TRAP...

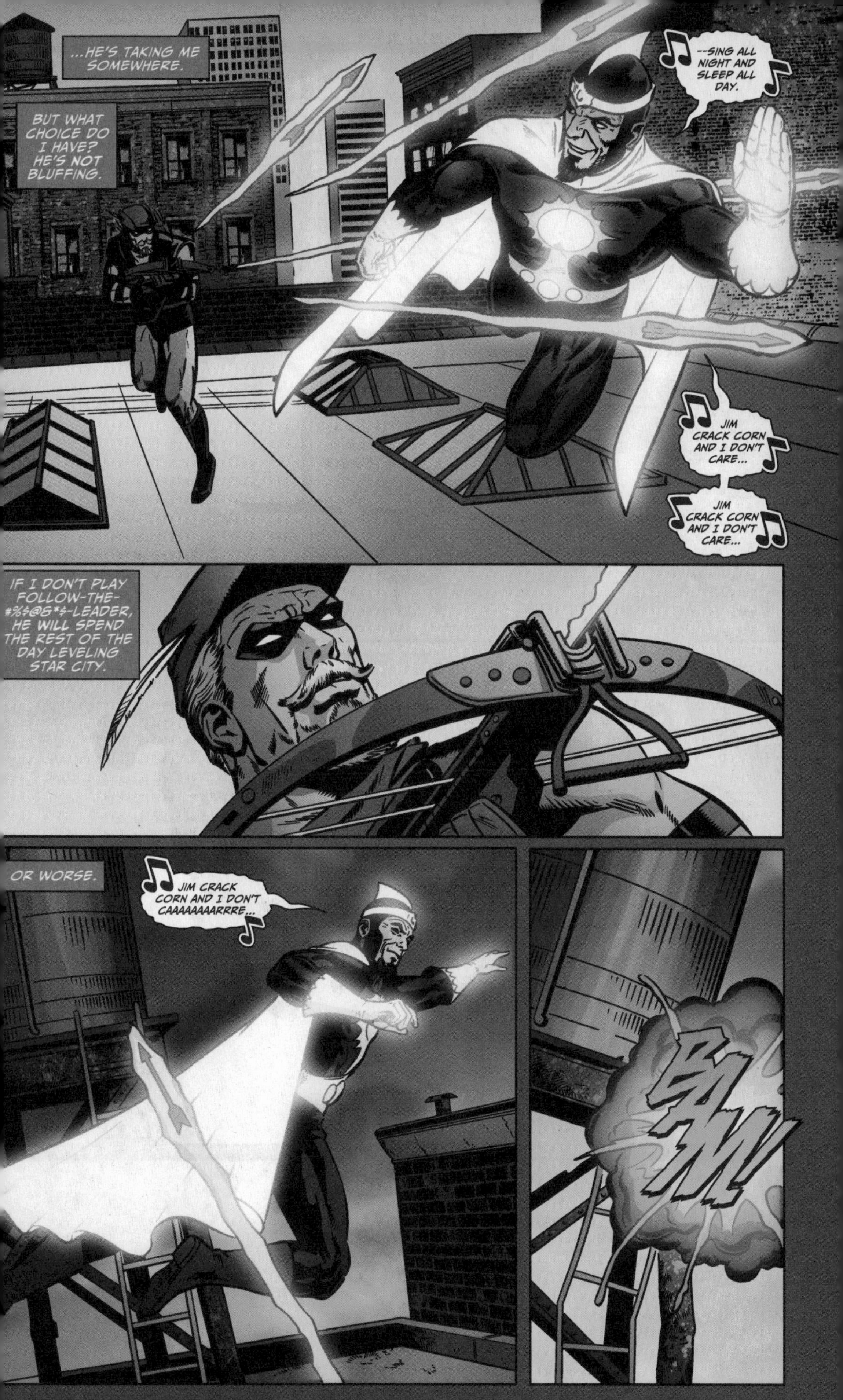

...HE'S TAKING ME SOMEWHERE.
BUT WHAT CHOICE DO I HAVE? HE'S NOT BLUFFING.
--SING ALL NIGHT AND SLEEP ALL DAY.
JIM CRACK CORN AND I DON'T CARE...
JIM CRACK CORN AND I DON'T CARE...
IF I DON'T PLAY FOLLOW-THE-#%$@&*$-LEADER, HE WILL SPEND THE REST OF THE DAY LEVELING STAR CITY.
OR WORSE.
JIM CRACK CORN AND I DON'T CAAAAAAAARRRE...
BAM!

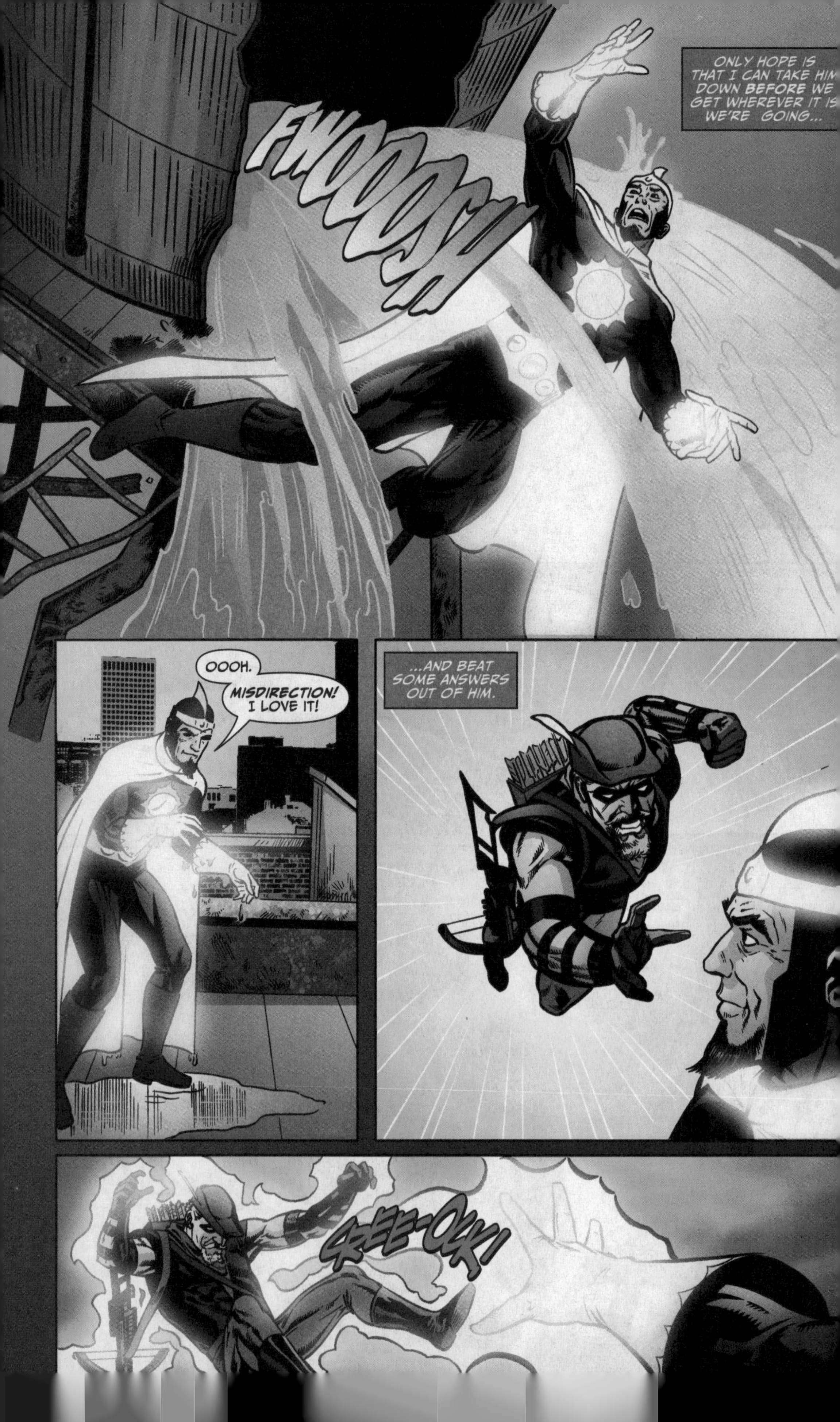
ONLY HOPE IS THAT I CAN TAKE HIM DOWN BEFORE WE GET WHEREVER IT IS WE'RE GOING...
FWOOOSH
OOOH.
MISDIRECTION! I LOVE IT!
...AND BEAT SOME ANSWERS OUT OF HIM.
CREE-OK!

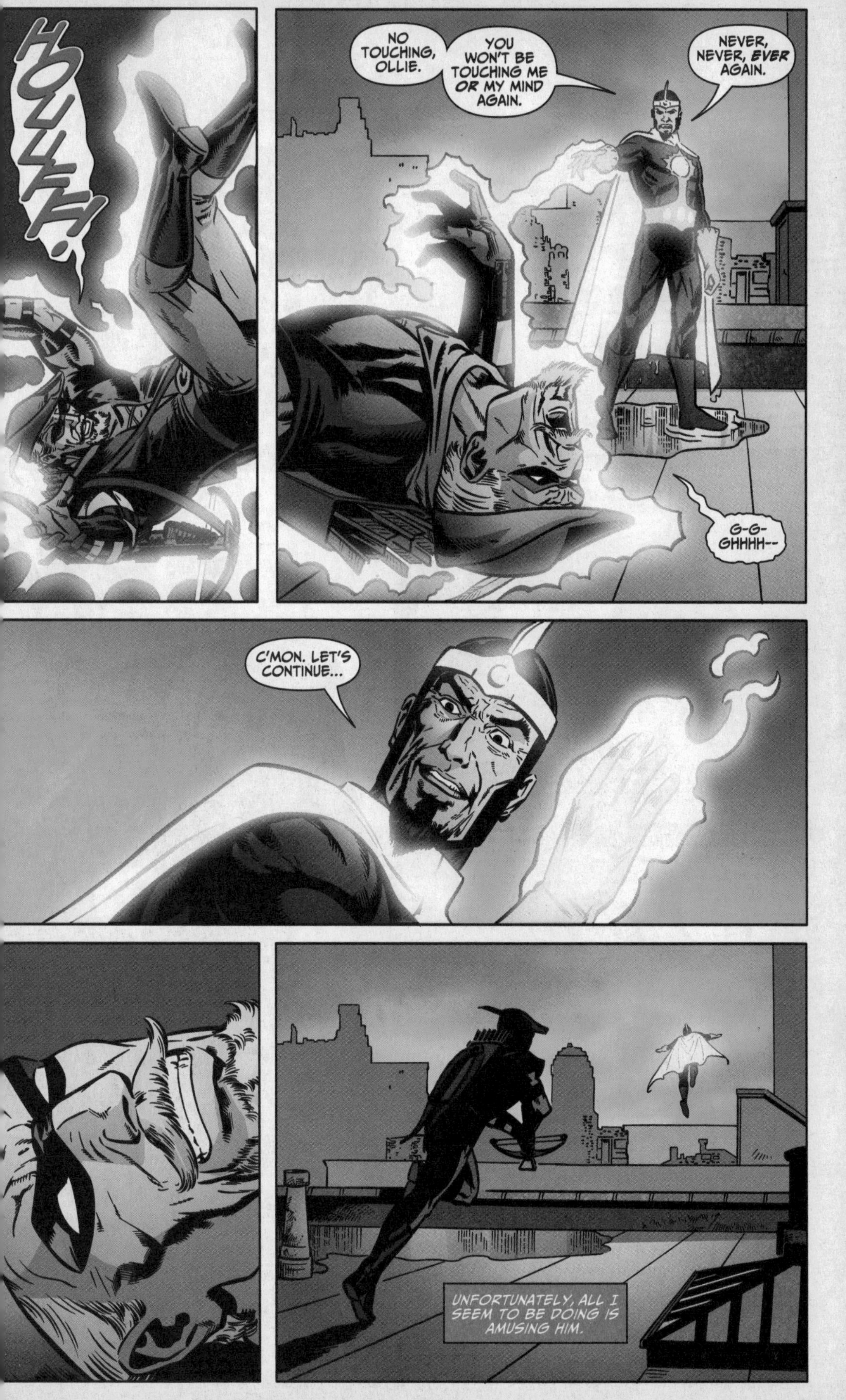
HOOOFFF!
NO TOUCHING, OLLIE.
YOU WON'T BE TOUCHING ME OR MY MIND AGAIN.
NEVER, NEVER, EVER AGAIN.
G-G-GHHHH--
C'MON. LET'S CONTINUE...
UNFORTUNATELY, ALL I SEEM TO BE DOING IS AMUSING HIM.

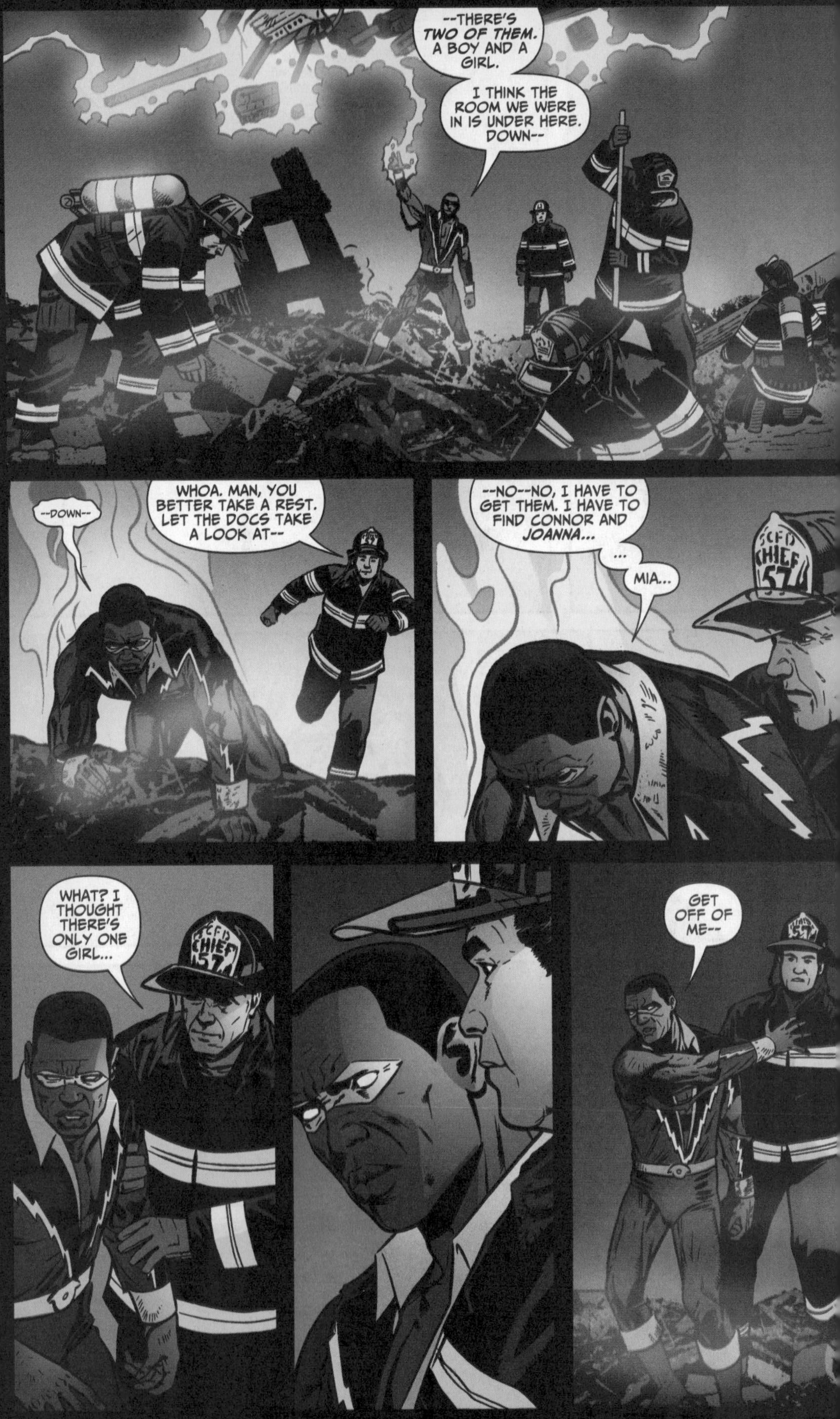

--THERE'S TWO OF THEM. A BOY AND A GIRL.
I THINK THE ROOM WE WERE IN IS UNDER HERE. DOWN--
--DOWN--
WHOA. MAN, YOU BETTER TAKE A REST. LET THE DOCS TAKE A LOOK AT--
--NO--NO, I HAVE TO GET THEM. I HAVE TO FIND CONNOR AND JOANNA...
...
MIA...
SCFD CHIEF 57
WHAT? I THOUGHT THERE'S ONLY ONE GIRL...
SCFD CHIEF 57
GET OFF OF ME--

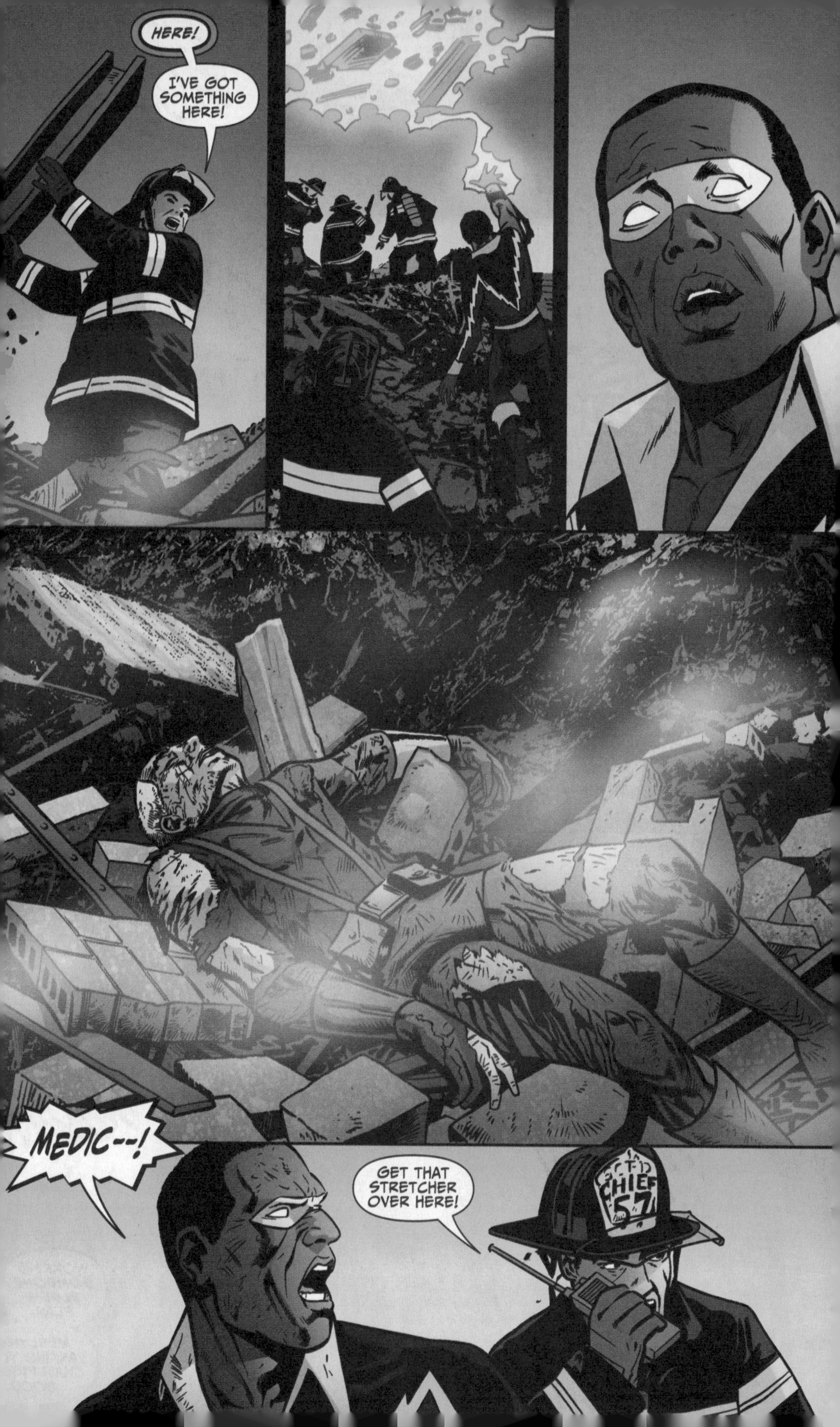
HERE!
I'VE GOT SOMETHING HERE!
MEDIC--!
GET THAT STRETCHER OVER HERE!
CHIEF 57

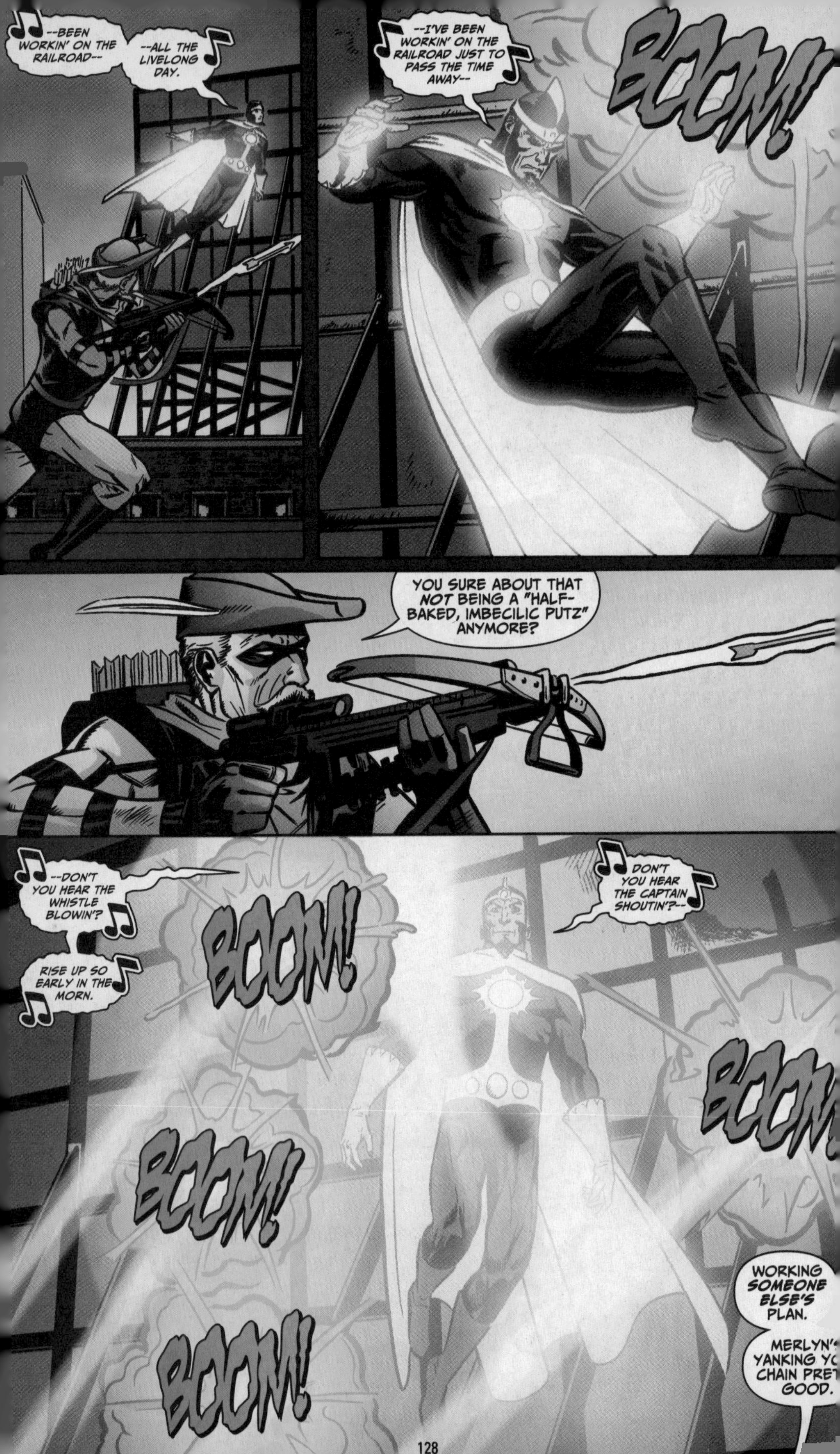

--BEEN WORKIN' ON THE RAILROAD--
--ALL THE LIVELONG DAY.
--I'VE BEEN WORKIN' ON THE RAILROAD JUST TO PASS THE TIME AWAY--
BOOM!
YOU SURE ABOUT THAT NOT BEING A "HALF-BAKED, IMBECILIC PUTZ" ANYMORE?
--DON'T YOU HEAR THE WHISTLE BLOWIN'?
RISE UP SO EARLY IN THE MORN.
BOOM!
DON'T YOU HEAR THE CAPTAIN SHOUTIN'?--
BOOM!
BOOM!
BOOM!
WORKING SOMEONE ELSE'S PLAN.

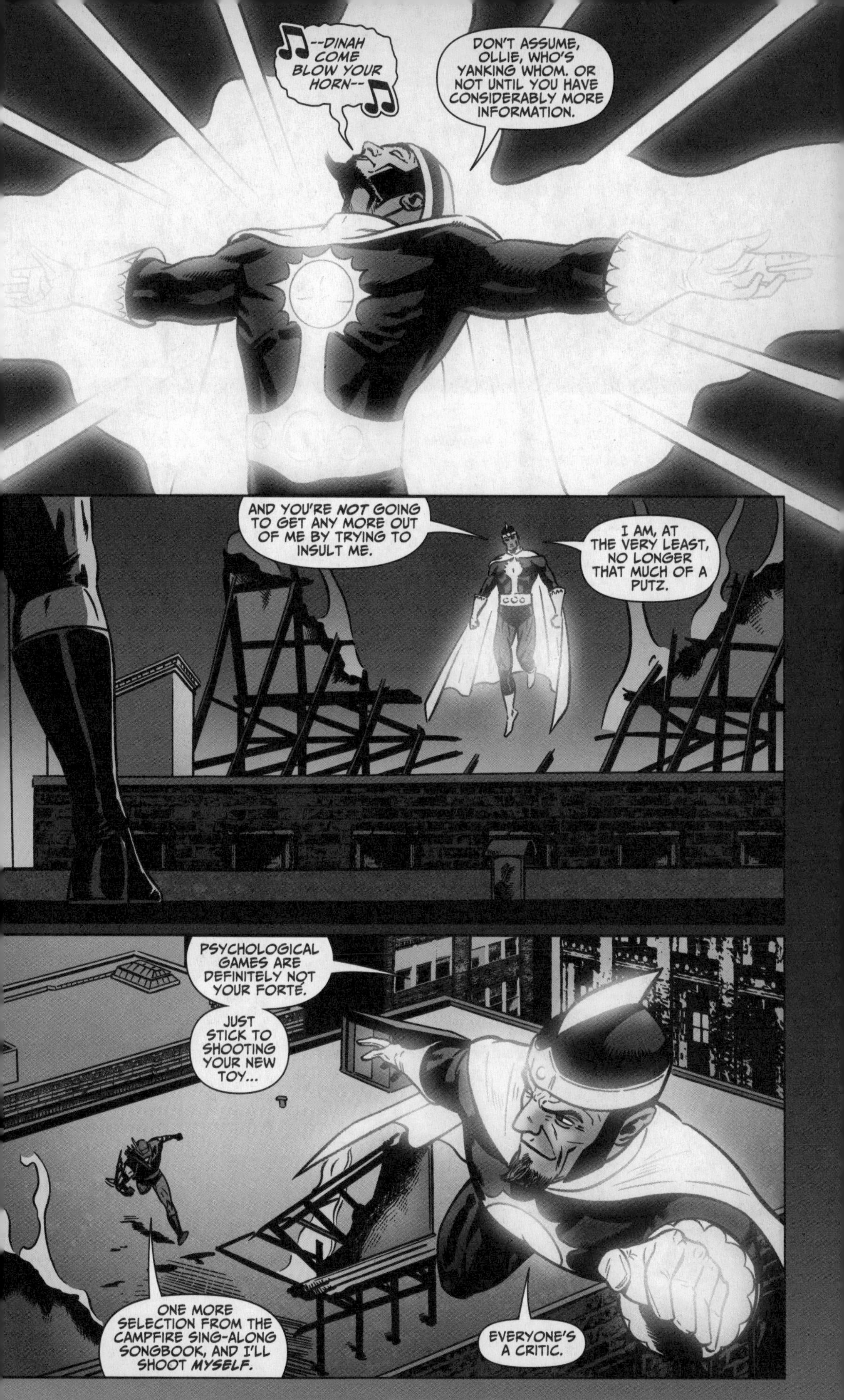
--DINAH COME BLOW YOUR HORN--
DON'T ASSUME, OLLIE, WHO'S YANKING WHOM. OR NOT UNTIL YOU HAVE CONSIDERABLY MORE INFORMATION.
AND YOU'RE NOT GOING TO GET ANY MORE OUT OF ME BY TRYING TO INSULT ME.
I AM, AT THE VERY LEAST, NO LONGER THAT MUCH OF A PUTZ.
PSYCHOLOGICAL GAMES ARE DEFINITELY NOT YOUR FORTE.
JUST STICK TO SHOOTING YOUR NEW TOY...
ONE MORE SELECTION FROM THE CAMPFIRE SING-ALONG SONGBOOK, AND I'LL SHOOT MYSELF.
EVERYONE'S A CRITIC.

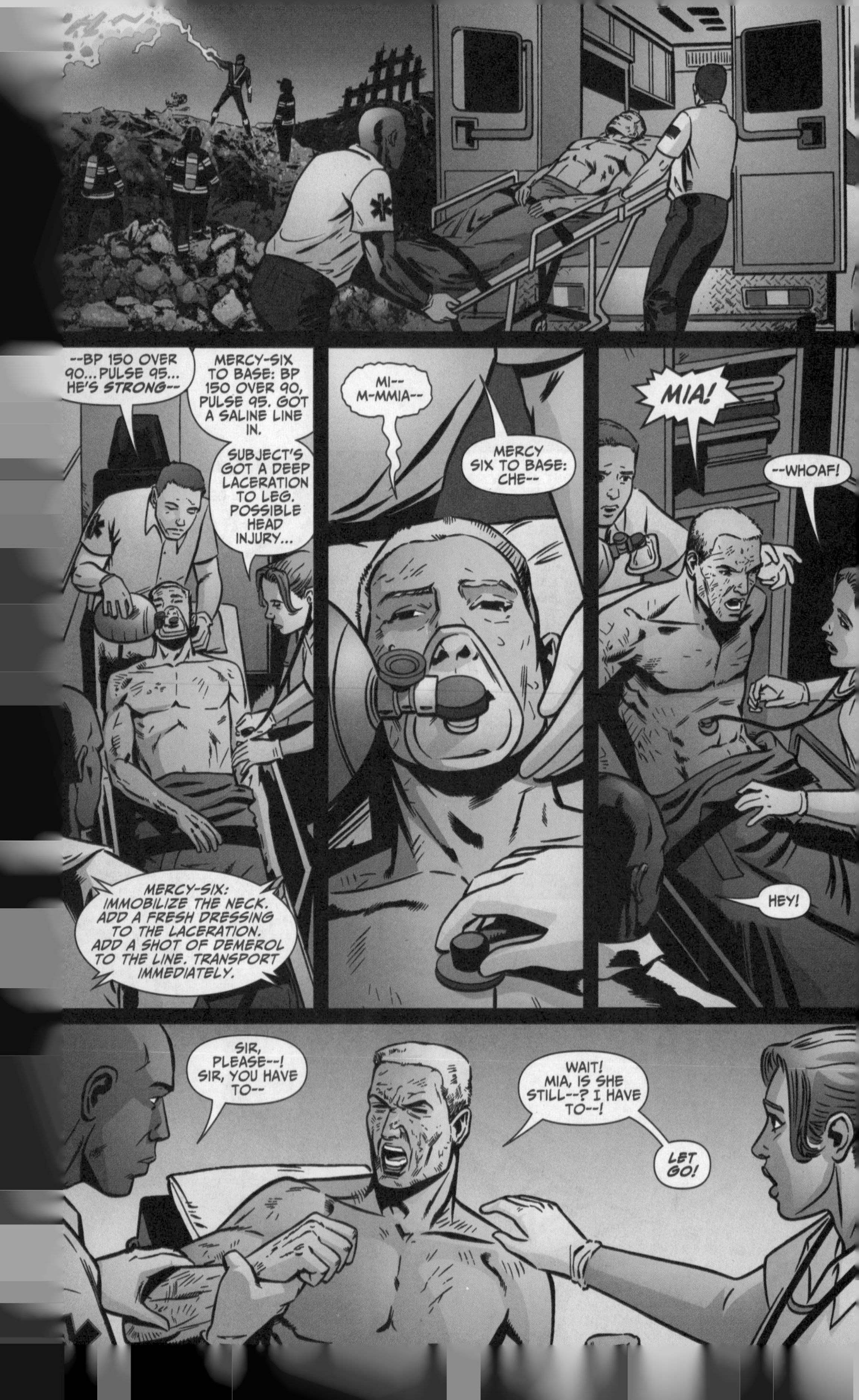

--BP 150 OVER 90...PULSE 95... HE'S STRONG--
MERCY-SIX TO BASE: BP 150 OVER 90, PULSE 95. GOT A SALINE LINE IN.
SUBJECT'S GOT A DEEP LACERATION TO LEG. POSSIBLE HEAD INJURY...
MERCY-SIX: IMMOBILIZE THE NECK. ADD A FRESH DRESSING TO THE LACERATION. ADD A SHOT OF DEMEROL TO THE LINE. TRANSPORT IMMEDIATELY.
MI-- M-MMIA--
MERCY SIX TO BASE: CHE--
MIA!
--WHOAF!
HEY!
SIR, PLEASE--! SIR, YOU HAVE TO--
WAIT! MIA, IS SHE STILL--? I HAVE TO--!
LET GO!

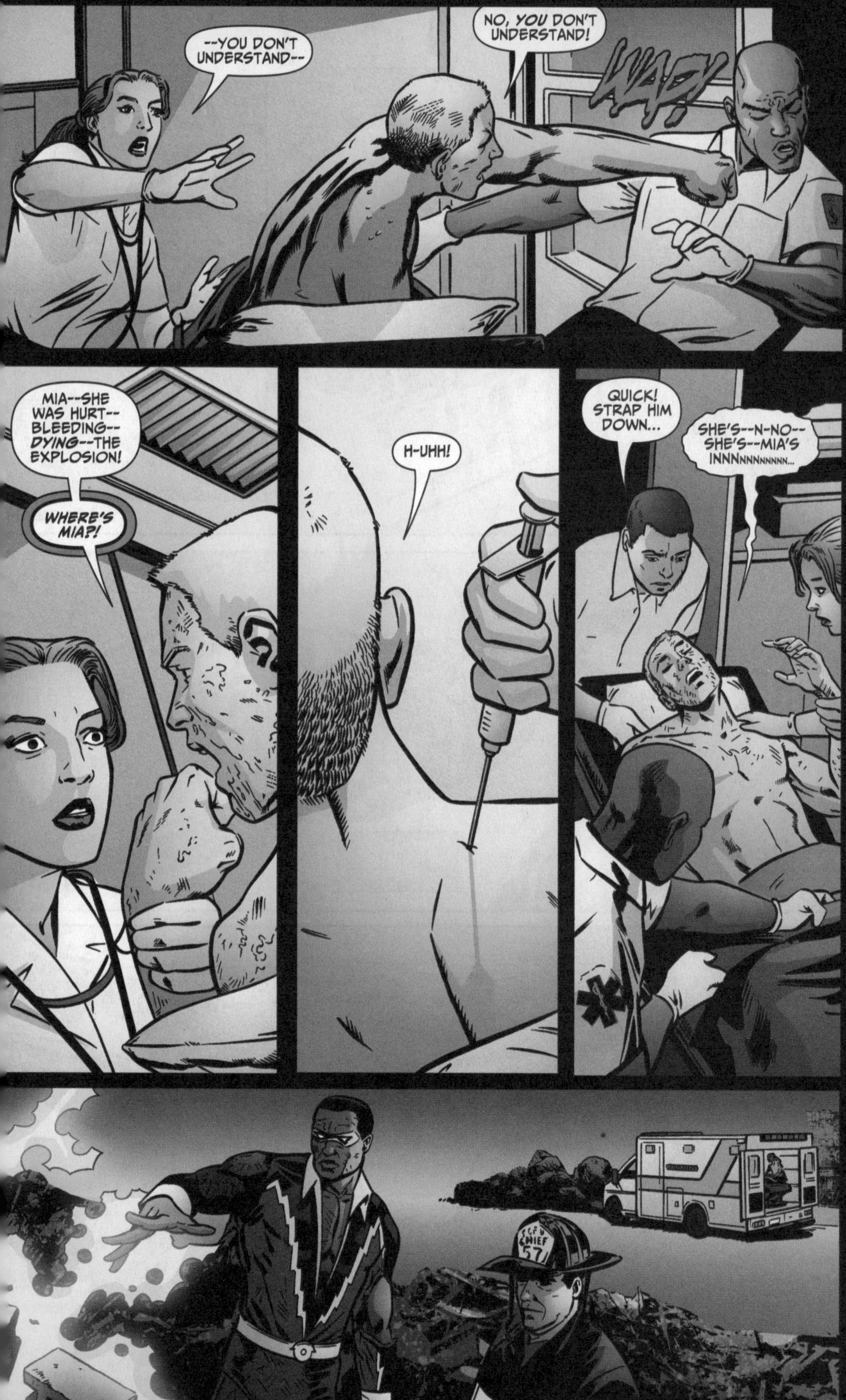
--YOU DON'T UNDERSTAND--
NO, YOU DON'T UNDERSTAND!
WAP!
MIA--SHE WAS HURT--BLEEDING--DYING--THE EXPLOSION!
WHERE'S MIA?!
H-UHH!
QUICK! STRAP HIM DOWN...
SHE'S--N-NO--SHE'S--MIA'S INNNnnnnnnnn...
SCFD CHIEF 57

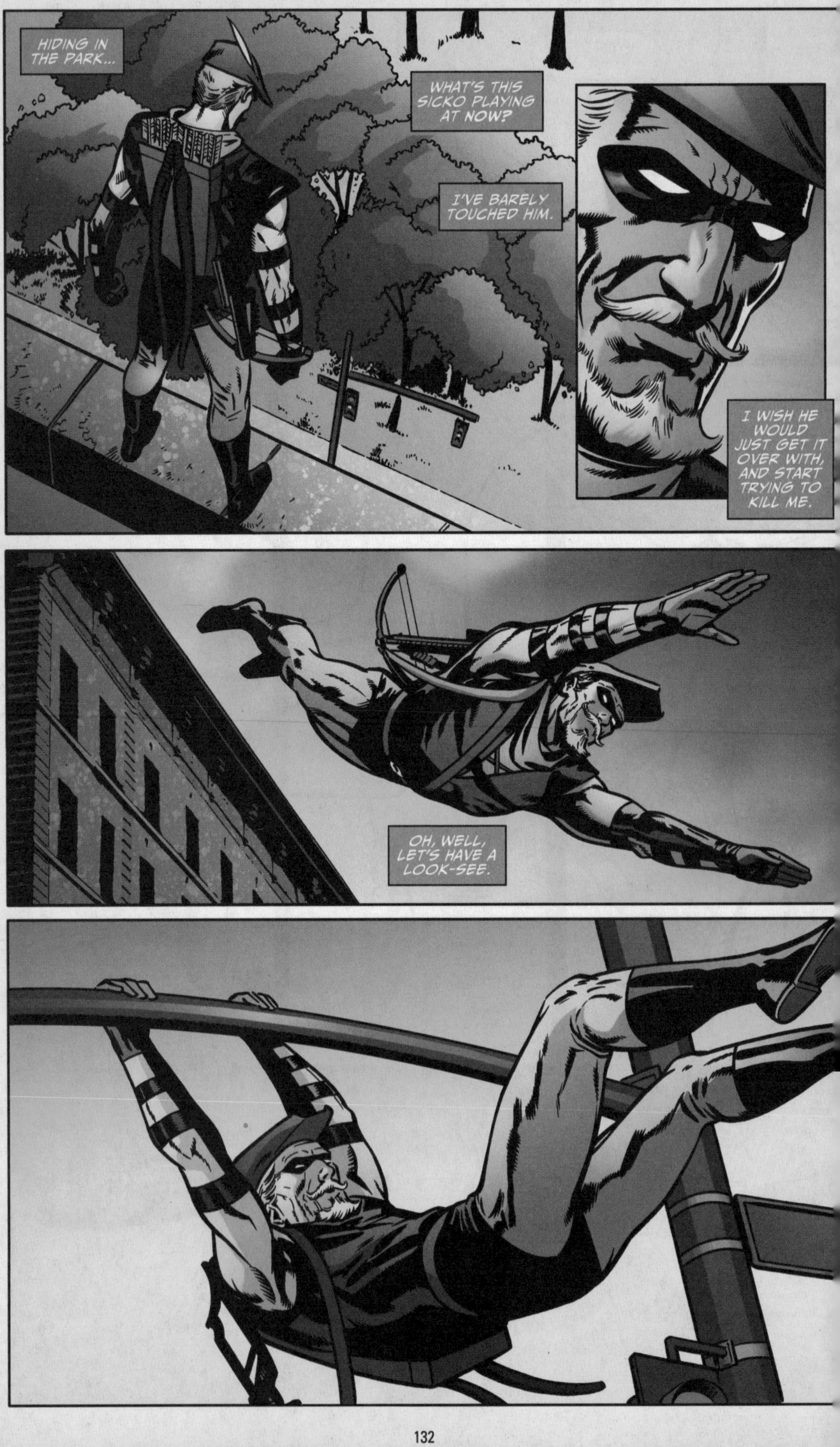
HIDING IN THE PARK...
WHAT'S THIS SICKO PLAYING AT NOW?
I'VE BARELY TOUCHED HIM.
I WISH HE WOULD JUST GET IT OVER WITH, AND START TRYING TO KILL ME.
OH, WELL, LET'S HAVE A LOOK-SEE.

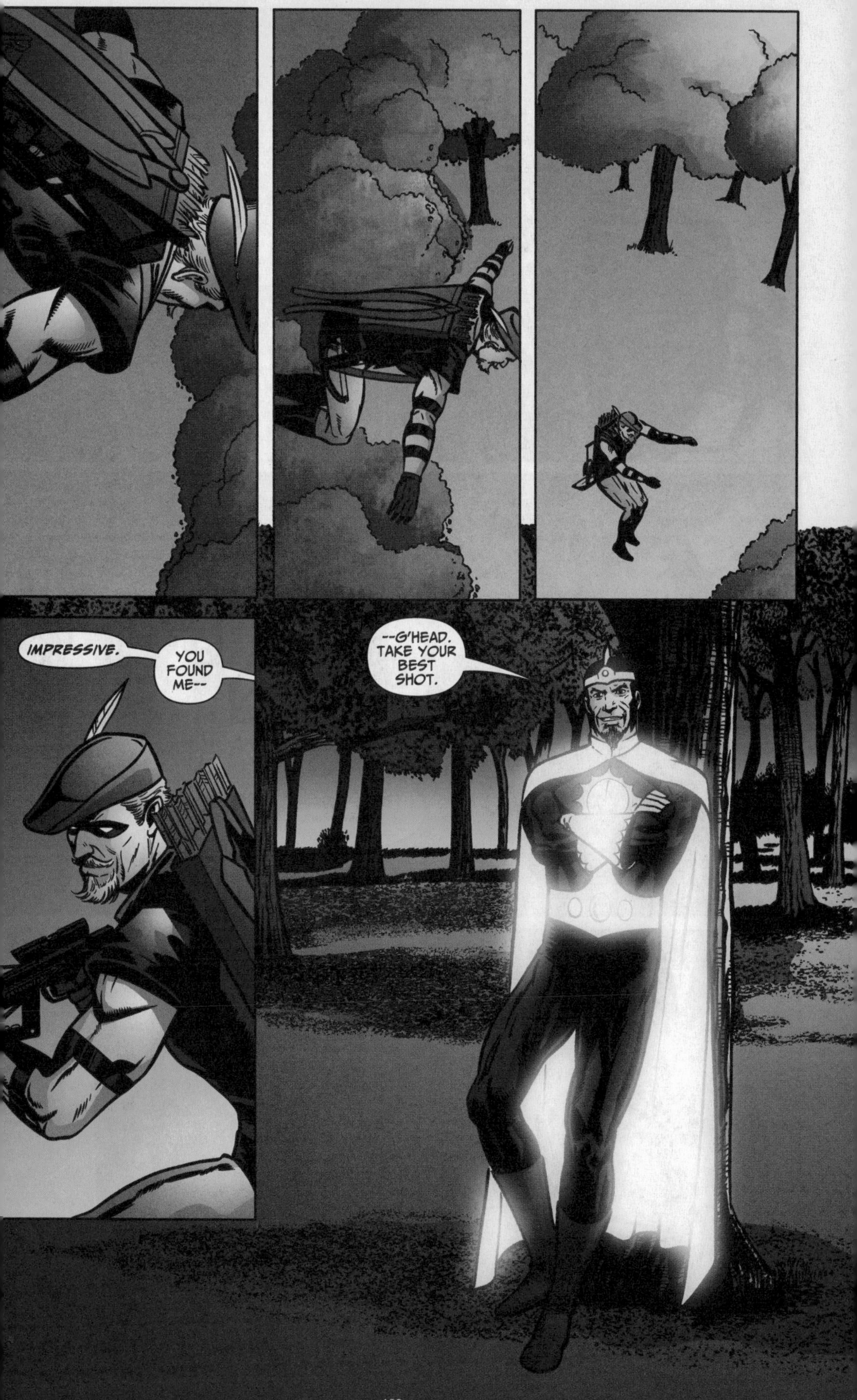
IMPRESSIVE.
YOU FOUND ME--
--G'HEAD. TAKE YOUR BEST SHOT.

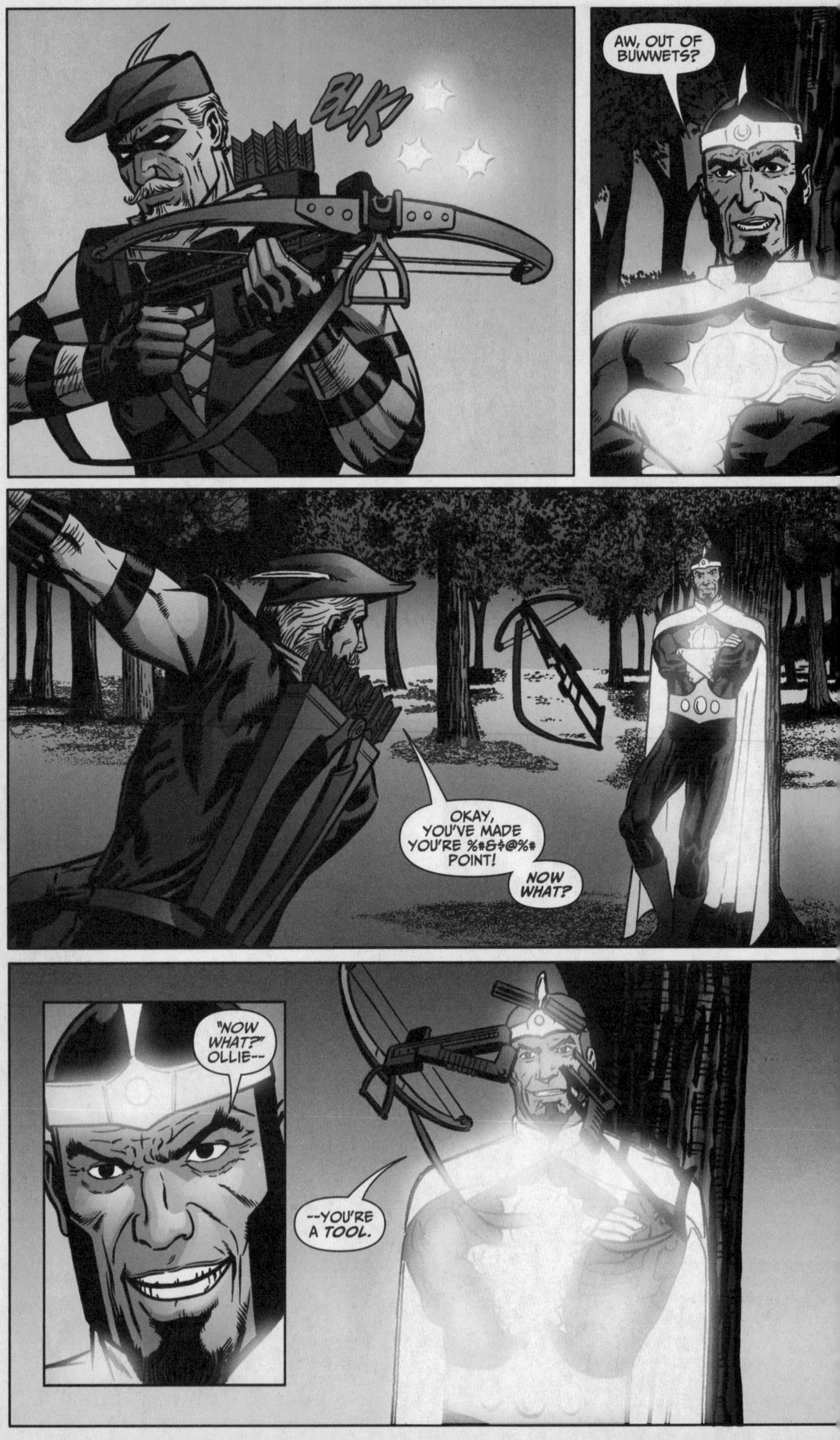
BLIK!
AW, OUT OF BUWWETS?
OKAY, YOU'VE MADE YOU'RE %#&$@%# POINT!
NOW WHAT?
"NOW WHAT?" OLLIE--
--YOU'RE A TOOL.

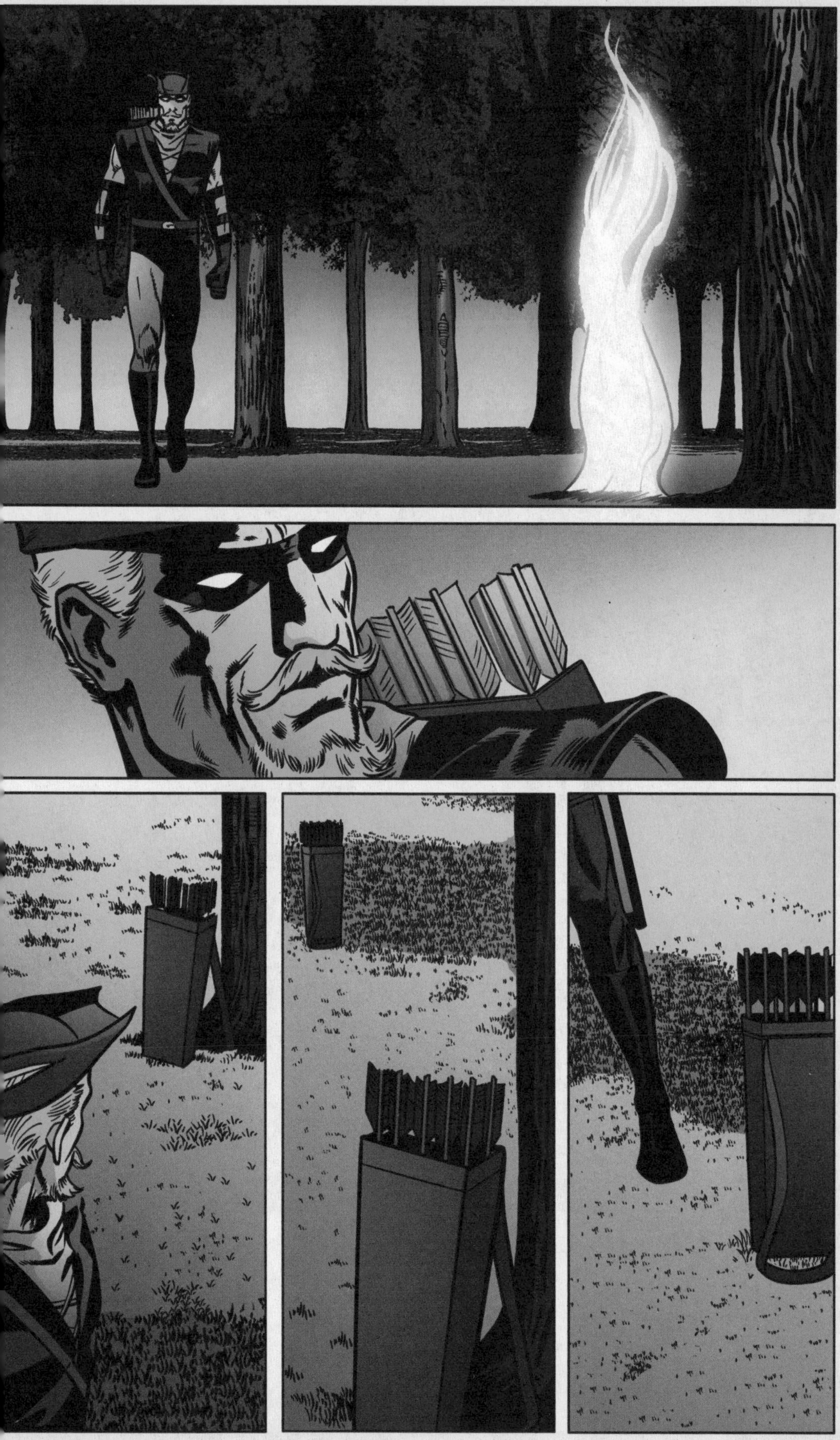

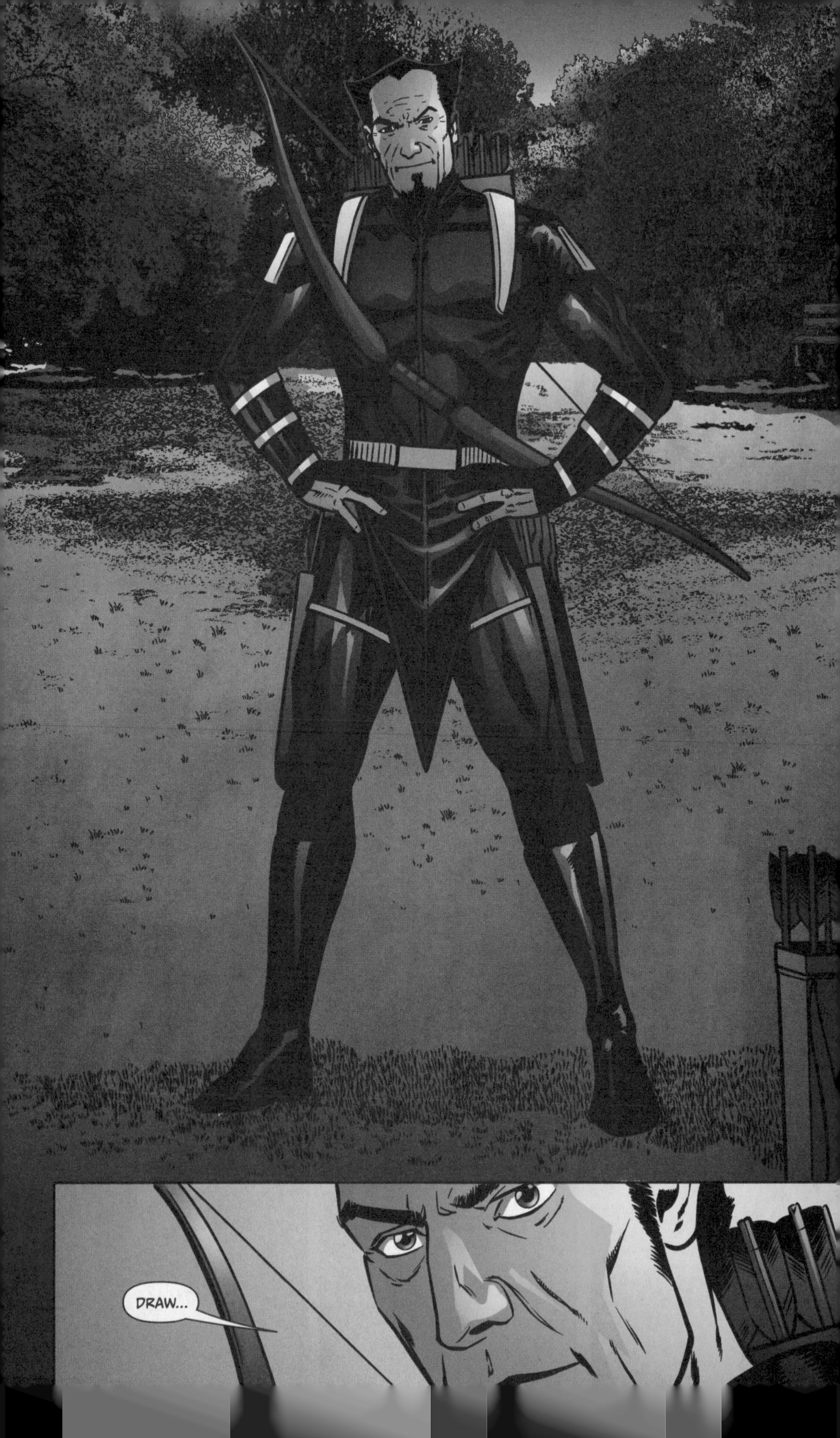
DRAW...

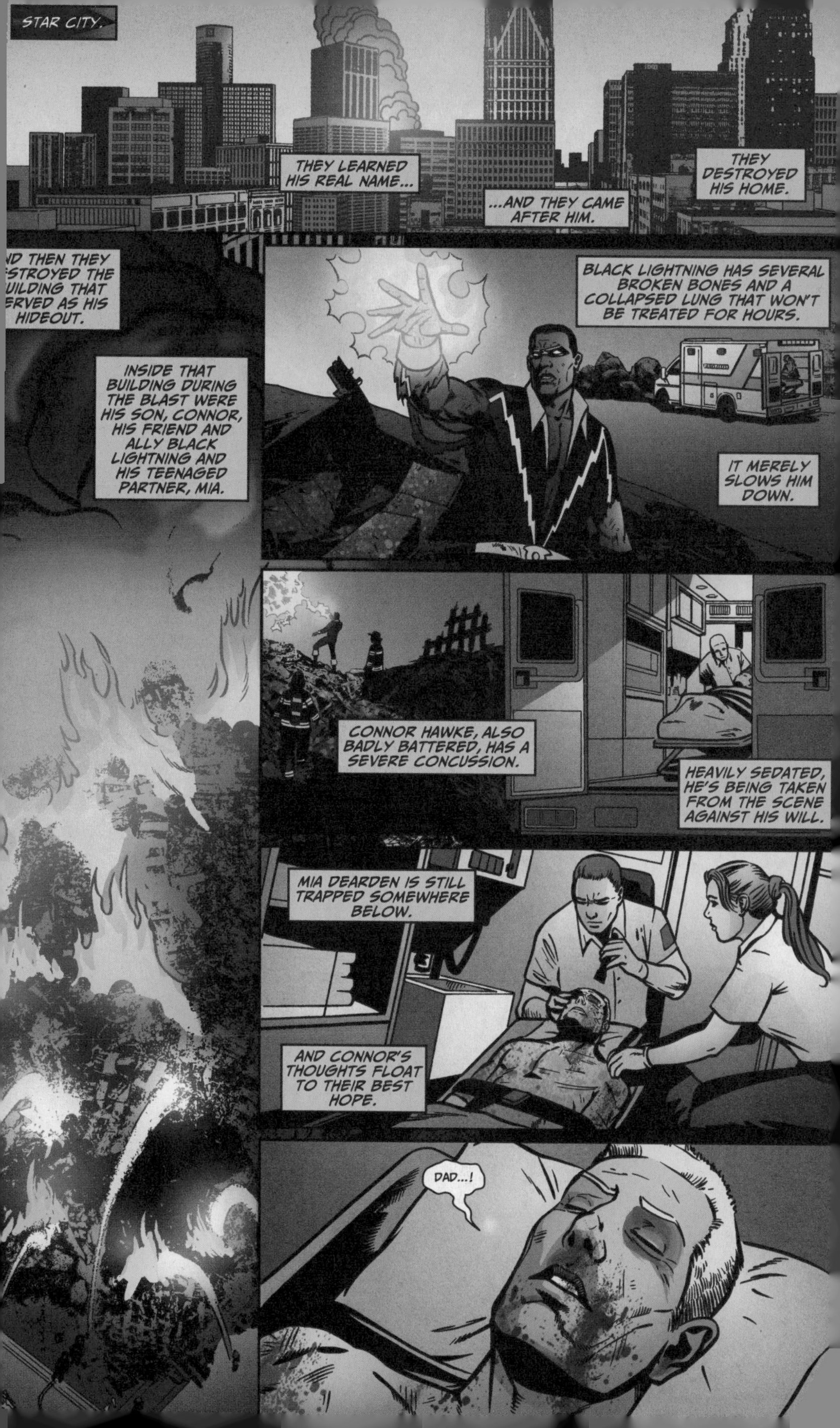
STAR CITY.
THEY LEARNED HIS REAL NAME...
...AND THEY CAME AFTER HIM.
THEY DESTROYED HIS HOME.
ND THEN THEY ESTROYED THE UILDING THAT ERVED AS HIS HIDEOUT.
INSIDE THAT BUILDING DURING THE BLAST WERE HIS SON, CONNOR, HIS FRIEND AND ALLY BLACK LIGHTNING AND HIS TEENAGED PARTNER, MIA.
BLACK LIGHTNING HAS SEVERAL BROKEN BONES AND A COLLAPSED LUNG THAT WON'T BE TREATED FOR HOURS.
IT MERELY SLOWS HIM DOWN.
CONNOR HAWKE, ALSO BADLY BATTERED, HAS A SEVERE CONCUSSION.
HEAVILY SEDATED, HE'S BEING TAKEN FROM THE SCENE AGAINST HIS WILL.
MIA DEARDEN IS STILL TRAPPED SOMEWHERE BELOW.
AND CONNOR'S THOUGHTS FLOAT TO THEIR BEST HOPE.
DAD...!

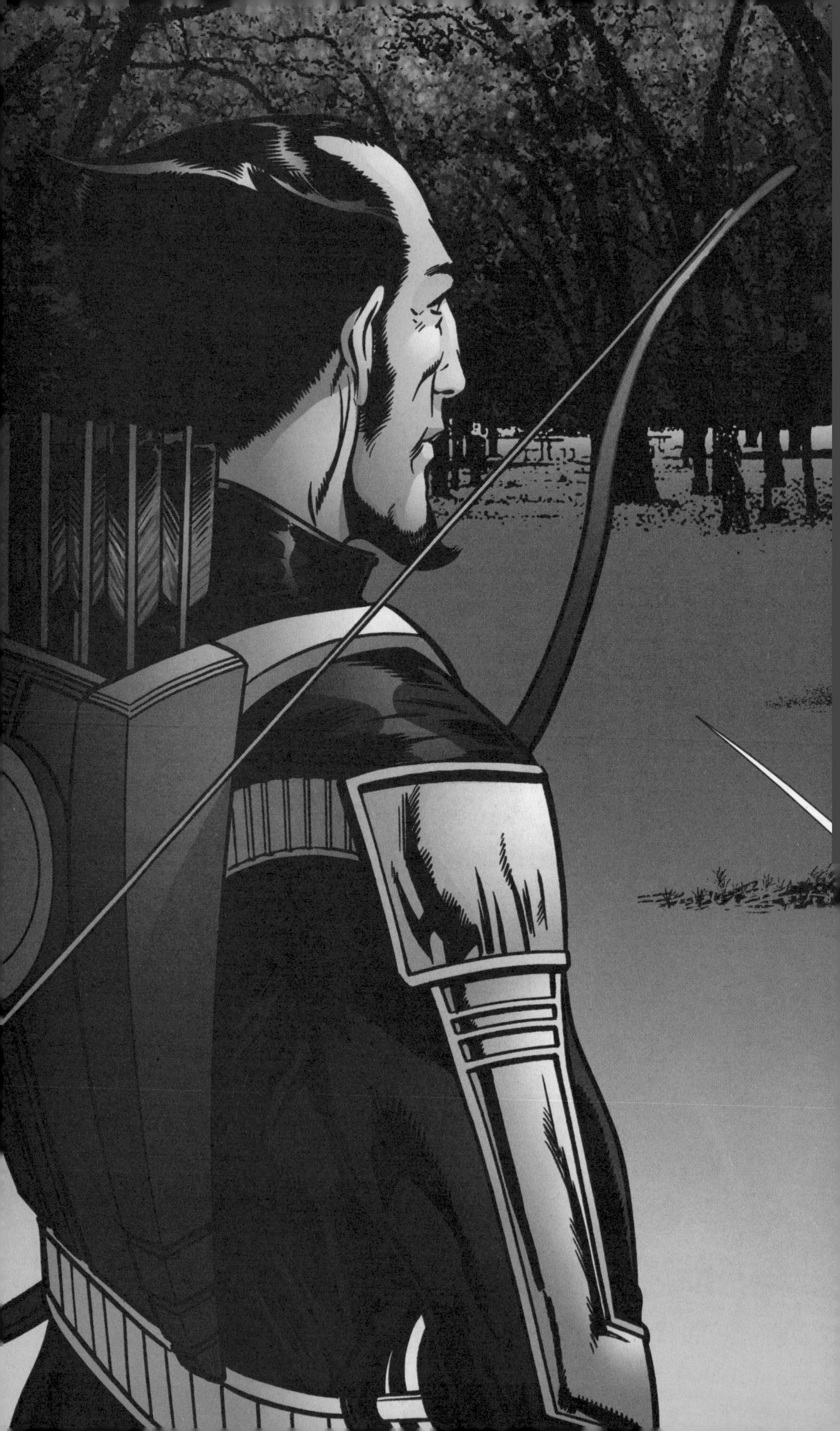

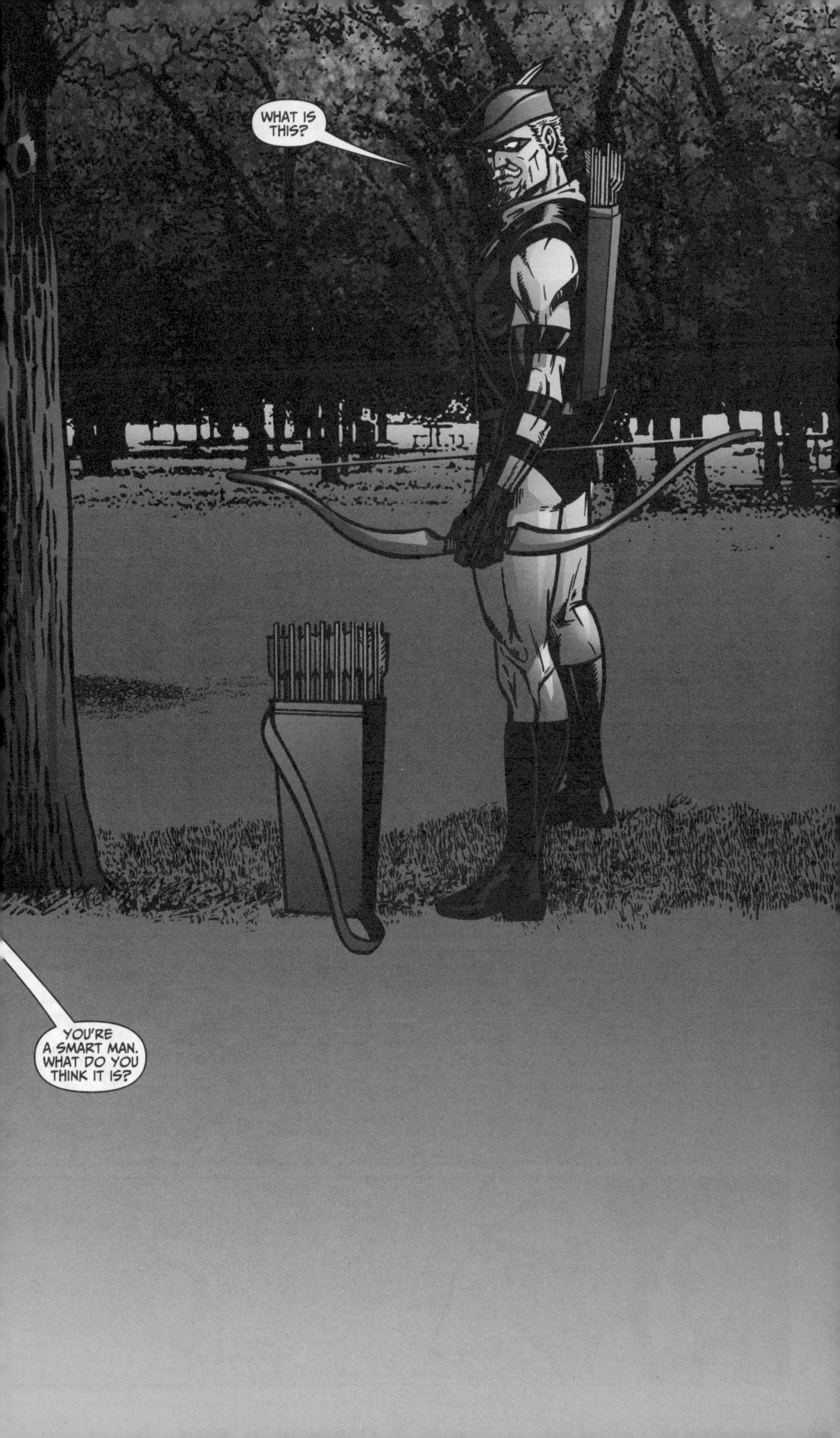
WHAT IS THIS?
YOU'RE A SMART MAN. WHAT DO YOU THINK IT IS?

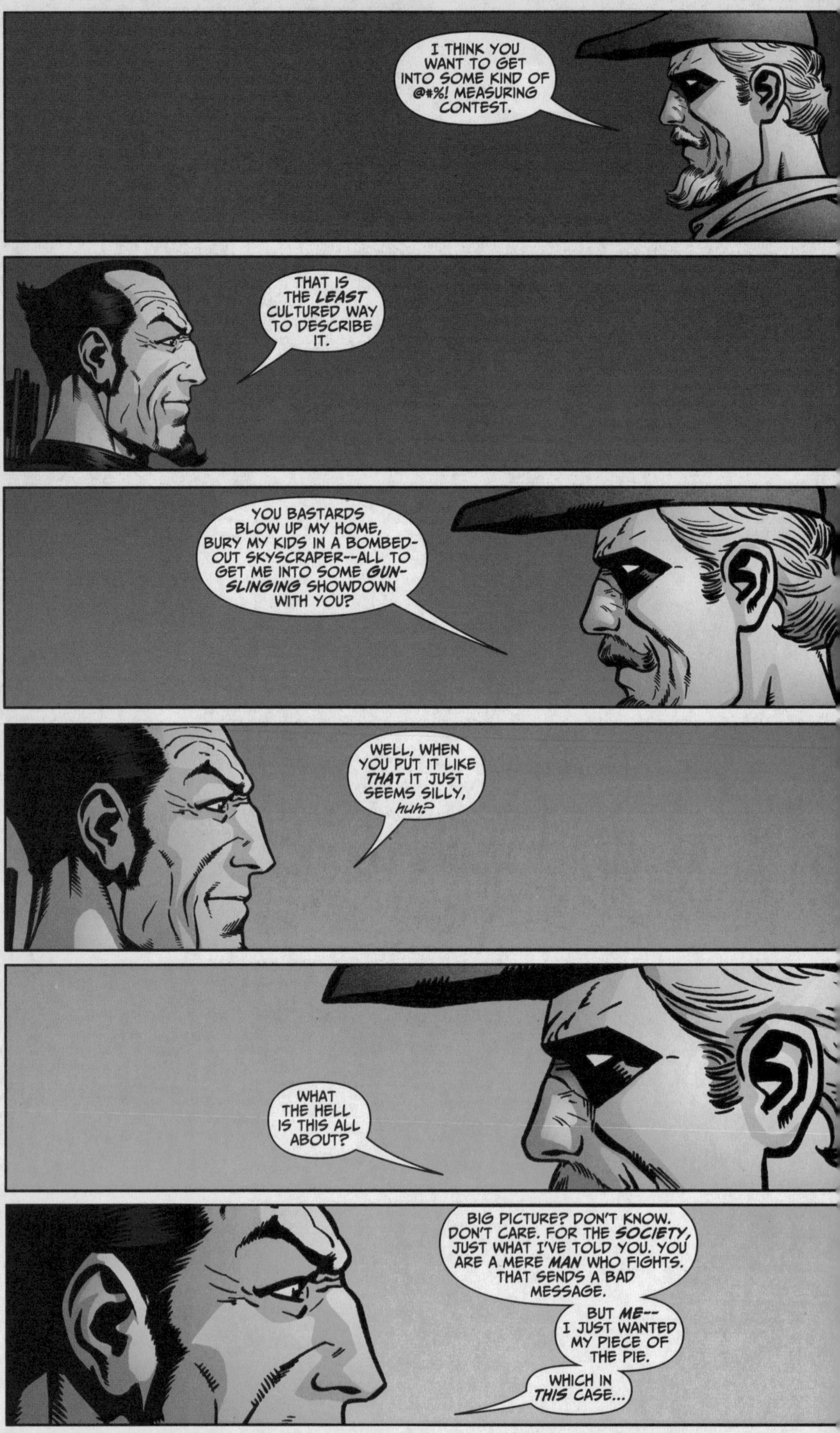
I THINK YOU WANT TO GET INTO SOME KIND OF @#%! MEASURING CONTEST.
THAT IS THE LEAST CULTURED WAY TO DESCRIBE IT.
YOU BASTARDS BLOW UP MY HOME, BURY MY KIDS IN A BOMBED-OUT SKYSCRAPER--ALL TO GET ME INTO SOME GUN-SLINGING SHOWDOWN WITH YOU?
WELL, WHEN YOU PUT IT LIKE THAT IT JUST SEEMS SILLY, huh?
WHAT THE HELL IS THIS ALL ABOUT?
BIG PICTURE? DON'T KNOW. DON'T CARE. FOR THE SOCIETY, JUST WHAT I'VE TOLD YOU. YOU ARE A MERE MAN WHO FIGHTS. THAT SENDS A BAD MESSAGE.
BUT ME-- I JUST WANTED MY PIECE OF THE PIE.
WHICH IN THIS CASE...

...IS YOU.

BARELY SAW HIM REACH.

BUT I DID SEE IT.

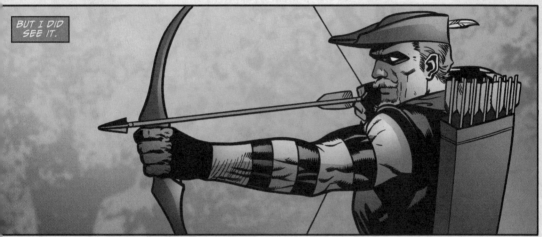

I DON'T KNOW WHO'S FASTER.

I DON'T KNOW WHO HAS THE BETTER EYE.

BUT BEFORE THIS IS OVER...

SHAKK

...I SUPPOSE I WILL.

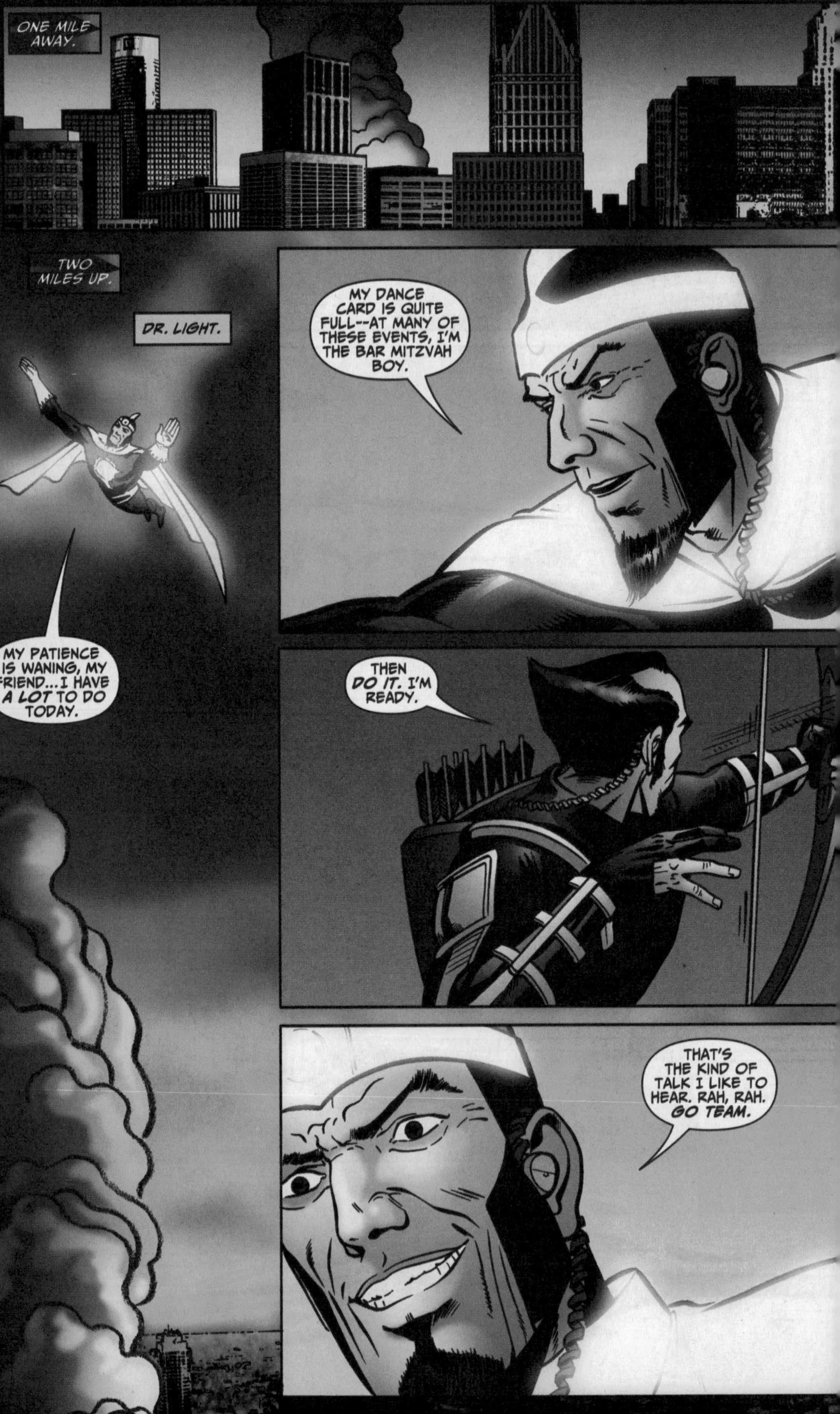
ONE MILE AWAY.
TWO MILES UP.
DR. LIGHT.
MY DANCE CARD IS QUITE FULL--AT MANY OF THESE EVENTS, I'M THE BAR MITZVAH BOY.
MY PATIENCE IS WANING, MY FRIEND...I HAVE A LOT TO DO TODAY.
THEN DO IT. I'M READY.
THAT'S THE KIND OF TALK I LIKE TO HEAR. RAH, RAH. GO TEAM.

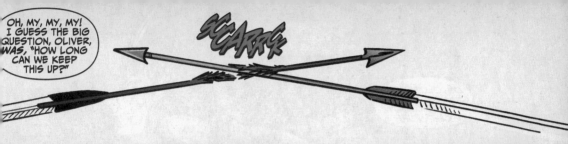

OH, MY, MY, MY! I GUESS THE BIG QUESTION, OLIVER, WAS, "HOW LONG CAN WE KEEP THIS UP?"

SCCARRRK

THE SIMPLE ANSWER WOULD HAVE BEEN UNTIL ONE OF US MISSED OR WE RAN OUT OF ARROWS...

...BUT I DON'T THINK THIS IS *NEARLY* OVER...

I HATE TO DISAPPOINT YOU.

BUT IT IS.

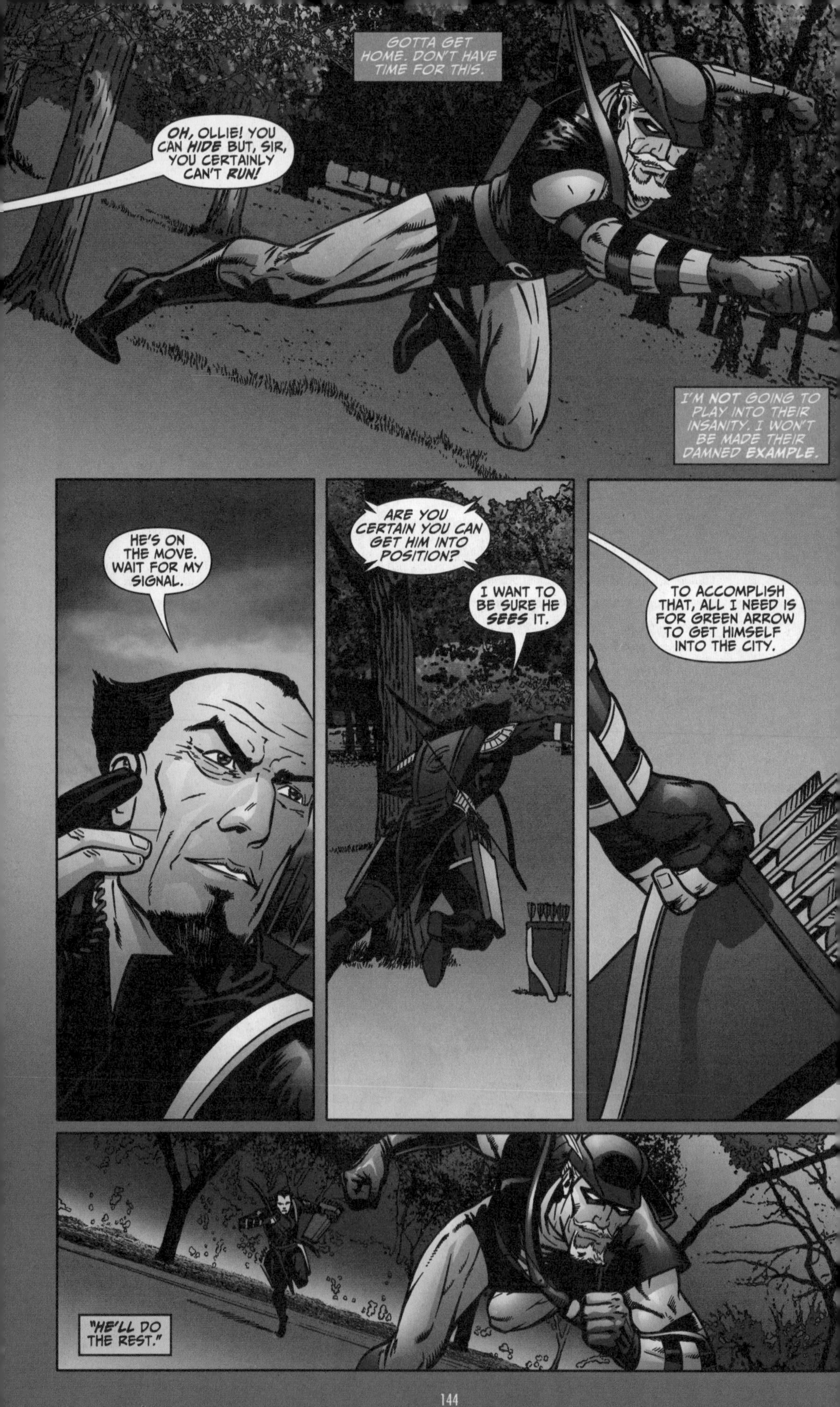
GOTTA GET HOME. DON'T HAVE TIME FOR THIS.
OH, OLLIE! YOU CAN HIDE BUT, SIR, YOU CERTAINLY CAN'T RUN!
I'M NOT GOING TO PLAY INTO THEIR INSANITY. I WON'T BE MADE THEIR DAMNED EXAMPLE.
HE'S ON THE MOVE. WAIT FOR MY SIGNAL.
ARE YOU CERTAIN YOU CAN GET HIM INTO POSITION?
I WANT TO BE SURE HE SEES IT.
TO ACCOMPLISH THAT, ALL I NEED IS FOR GREEN ARROW TO GET HIMSELF INTO THE CITY.
"HE'LL DO THE REST."

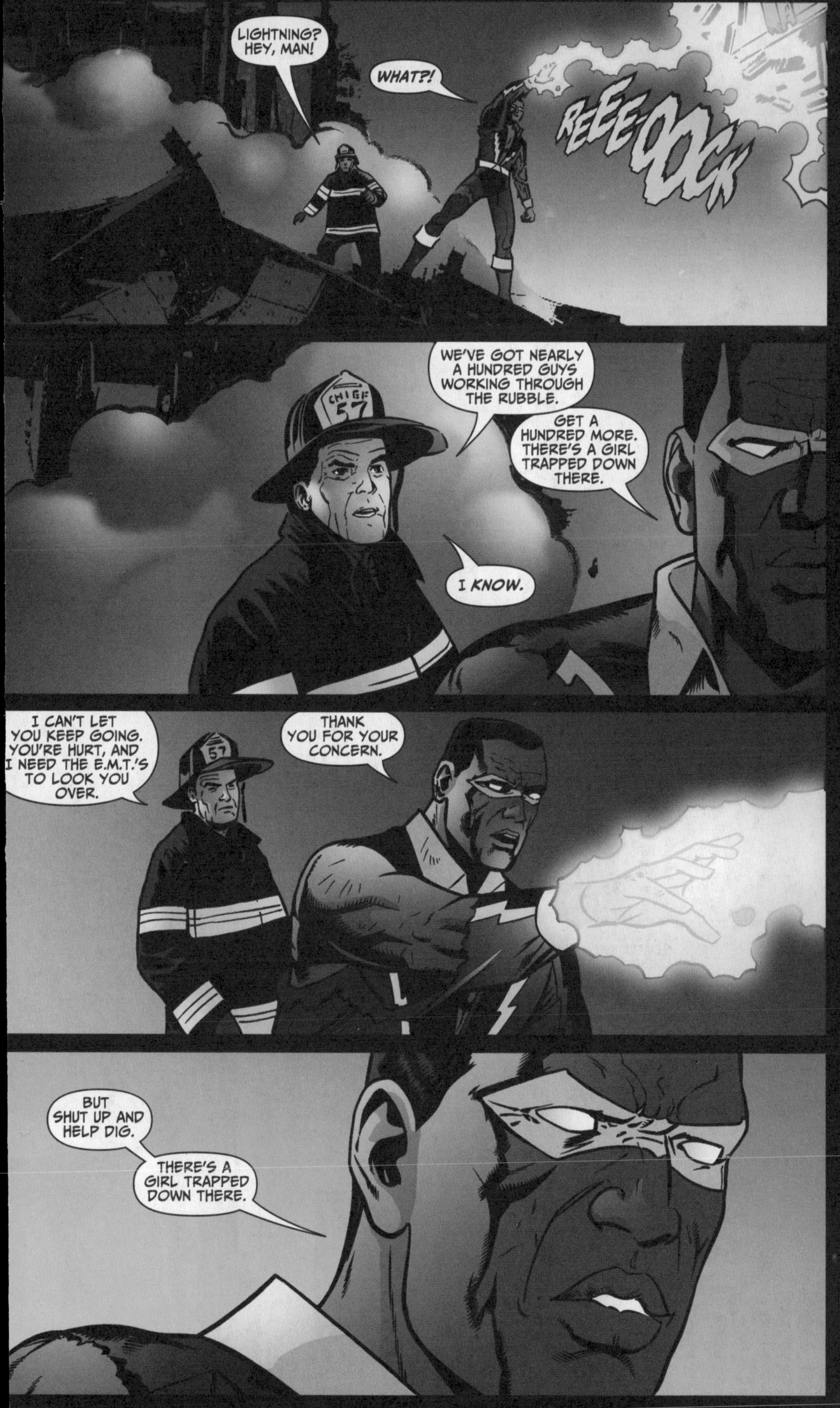
LIGHTNING? HEY, MAN!
WHAT?!
REEEOOCK
WE'VE GOT NEARLY A HUNDRED GUYS WORKING THROUGH THE RUBBLE.
GET A HUNDRED MORE. THERE'S A GIRL TRAPPED DOWN THERE.
I KNOW.
I CAN'T LET YOU KEEP GOING. YOU'RE HURT, AND I NEED THE E.M.T.'S TO LOOK YOU OVER.
THANK YOU FOR YOUR CONCERN.
BUT SHUT UP AND HELP DIG.
THERE'S A GIRL TRAPPED DOWN THERE.

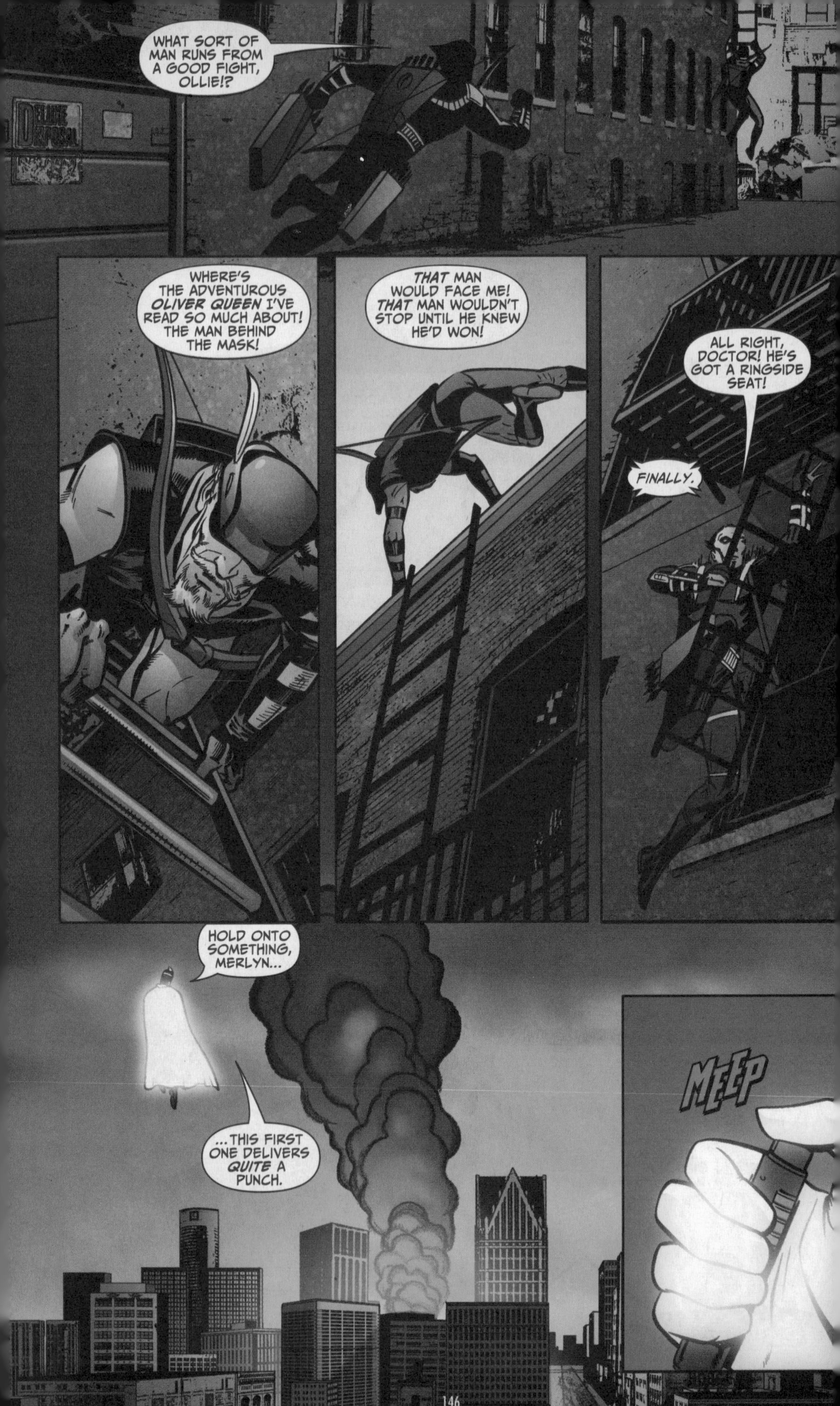
WHAT SORT OF MAN RUNS FROM A GOOD FIGHT, OLLIE!?
WHERE'S THE ADVENTUROUS OLIVER QUEEN I'VE READ SO MUCH ABOUT! THE MAN BEHIND THE MASK!
THAT MAN WOULD FACE ME! THAT MAN WOULDN'T STOP UNTIL HE KNEW HE'D WON!
ALL RIGHT, DOCTOR! HE'S GOT A RINGSIDE SEAT!
FINALLY.
HOLD ONTO SOMETHING, MERLYN...
...THIS FIRST ONE DELIVERS QUITE A PUNCH.
MEEP

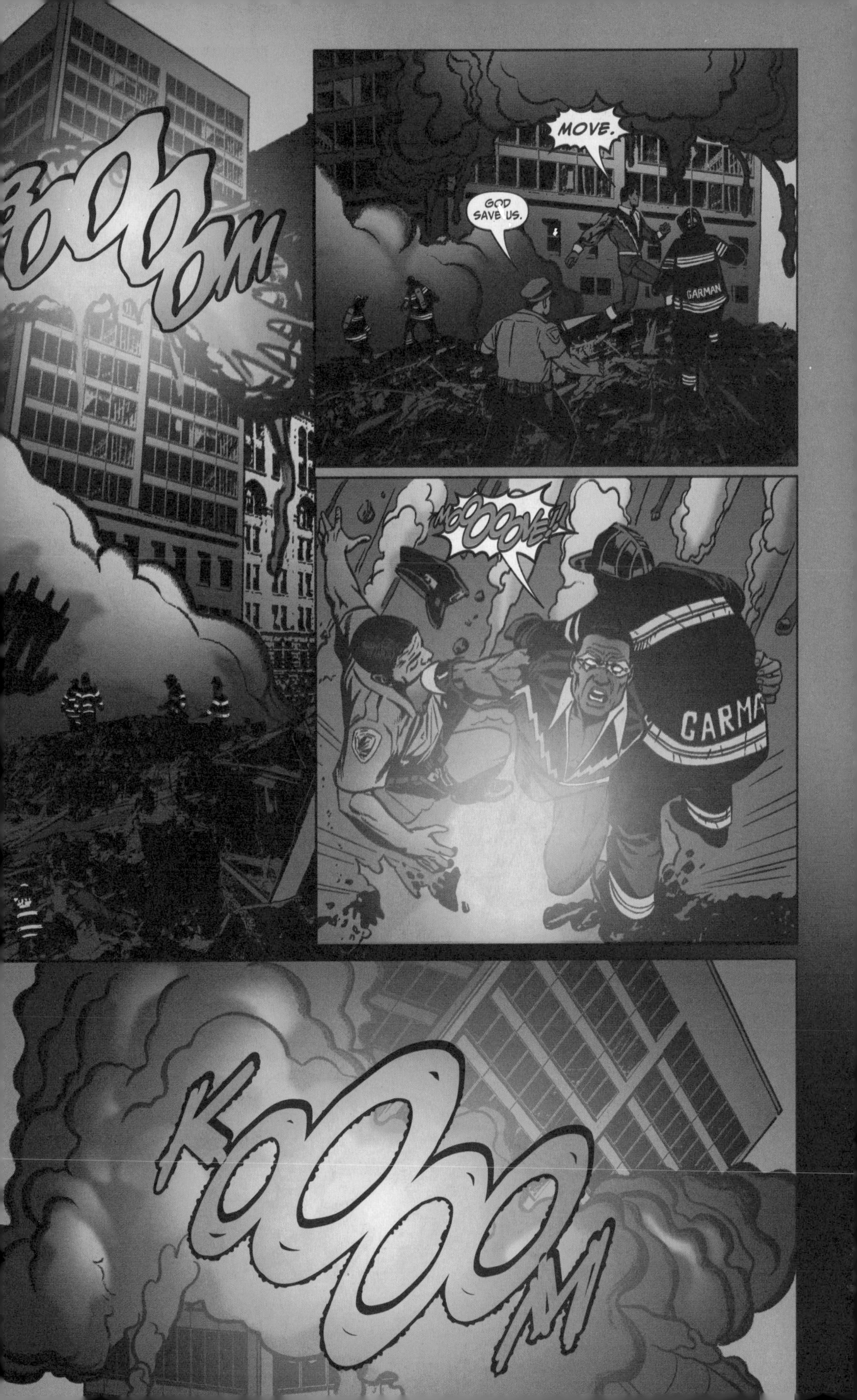
BOOOOM
MOVE.
GOD SAVE US.
GARMAN
MOOOOVE!!
CARMA
KOOOOOM

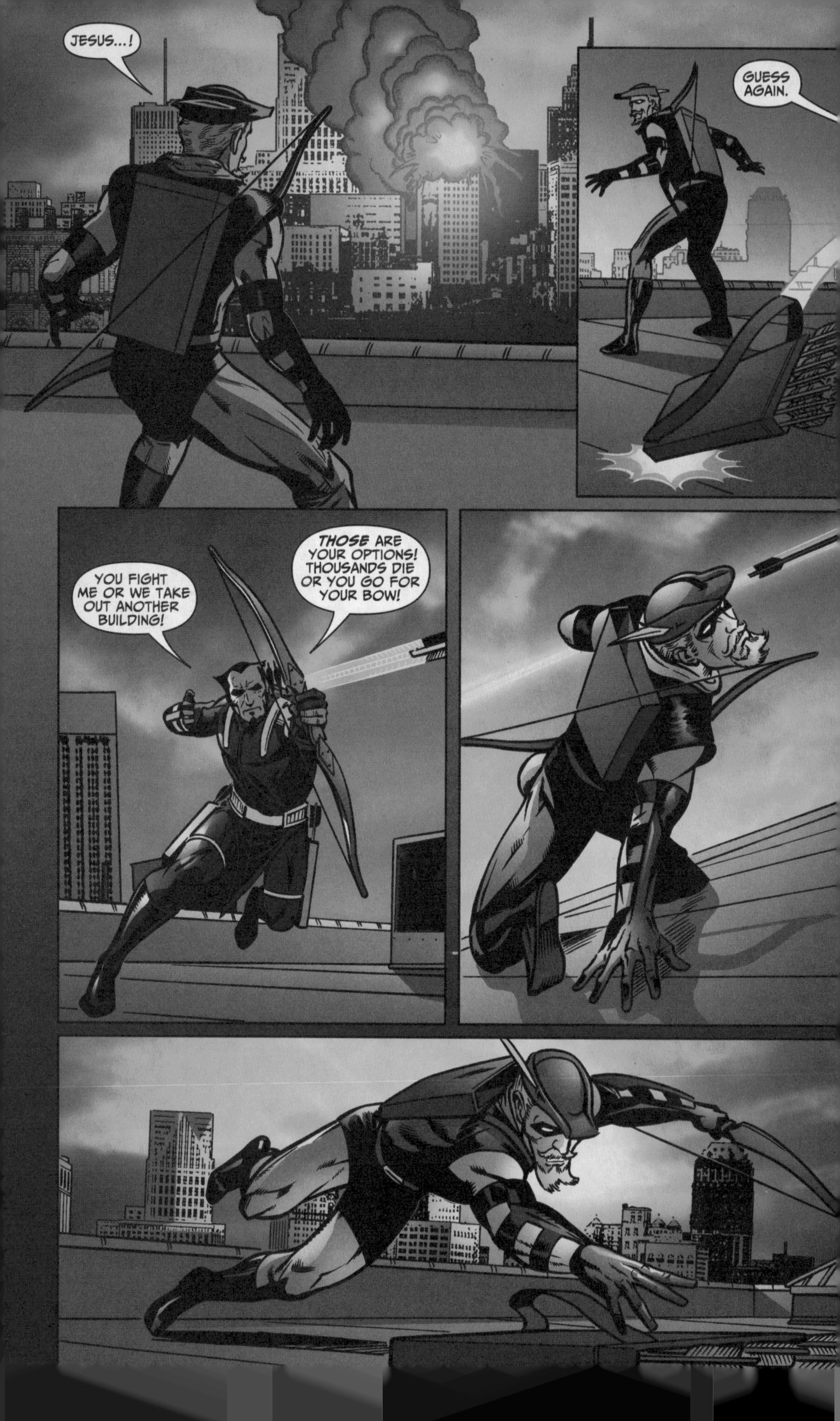
JESUS...!
GUESS AGAIN.
YOU FIGHT ME OR WE TAKE OUT ANOTHER BUILDING!
THOSE ARE YOUR OPTIONS! THOUSANDS DIE OR YOU GO FOR YOUR BOW!

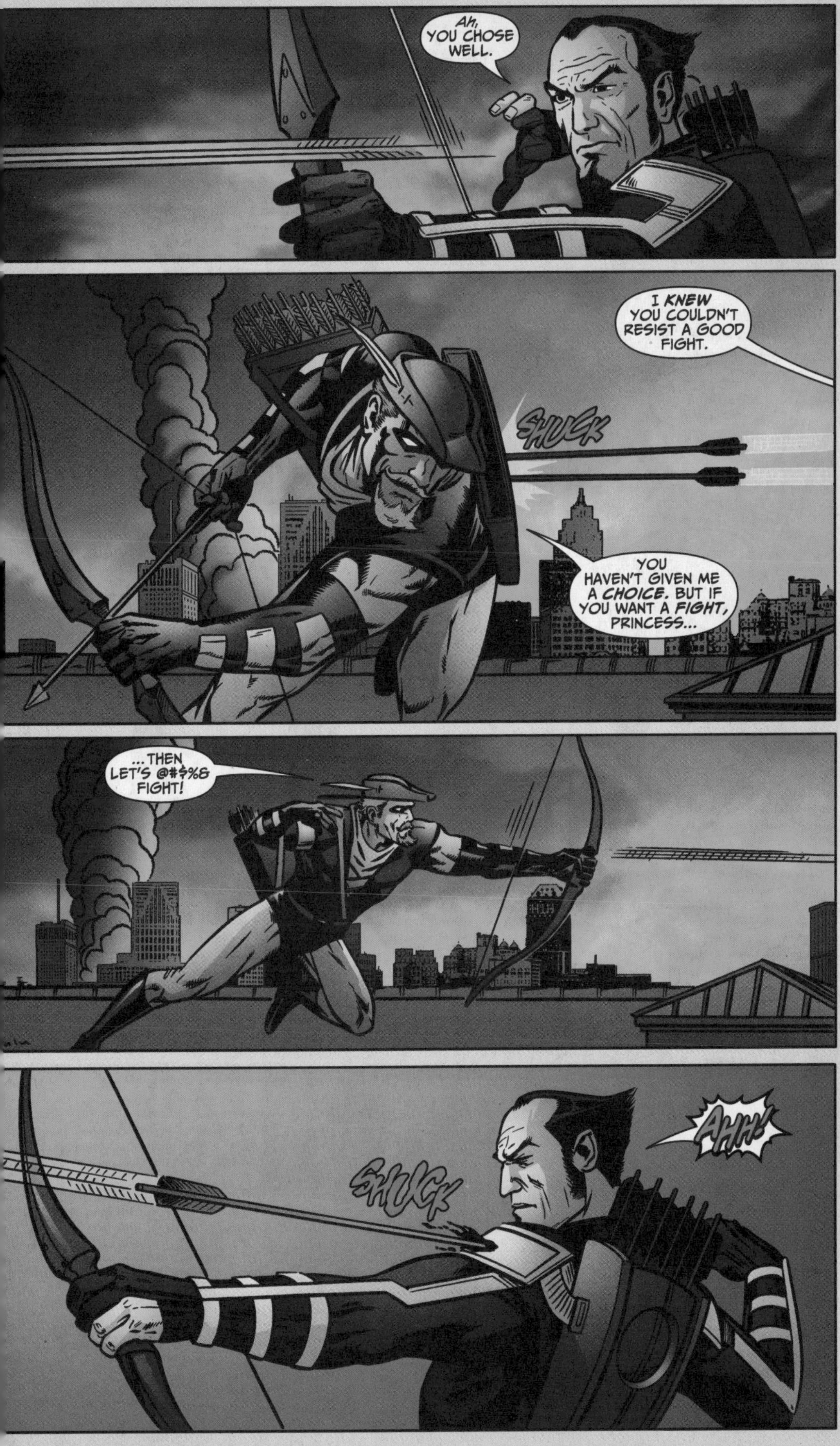

AH, YOU CHOSE WELL.
I KNEW YOU COULDN'T RESIST A GOOD FIGHT.
SHUCK
YOU HAVEN'T GIVEN ME A CHOICE. BUT IF YOU WANT A FIGHT, PRINCESS...
...THEN LET'S @#$%& FIGHT!
SHUCK
AHH!

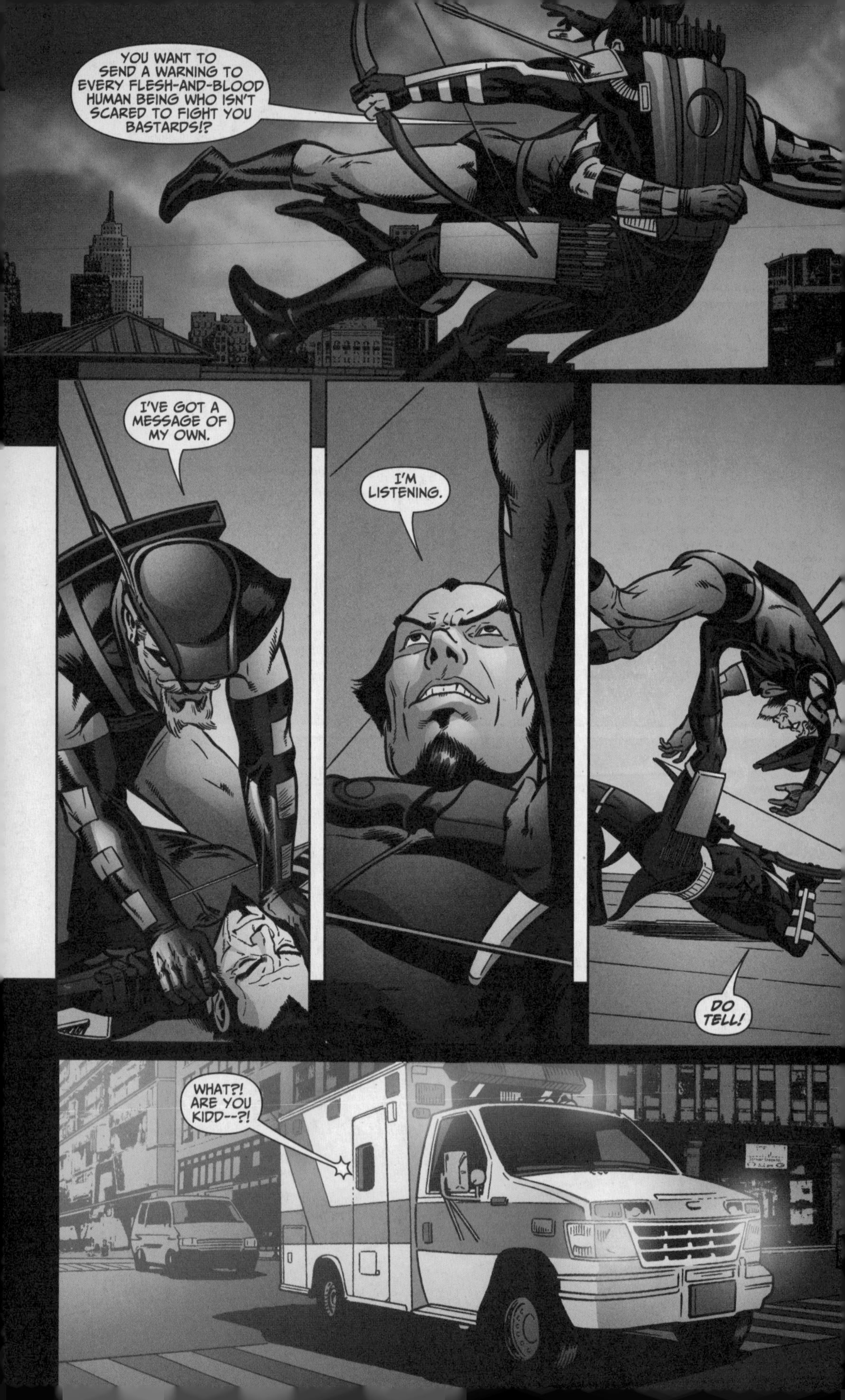
YOU WANT TO SEND A WARNING TO EVERY FLESH-AND-BLOOD HUMAN BEING WHO ISN'T SCARED TO FIGHT YOU BASTARDS!?
I'VE GOT A MESSAGE OF MY OWN.
I'M LISTENING.
DO TELL!
WHAT?! ARE YOU KIDD--?!

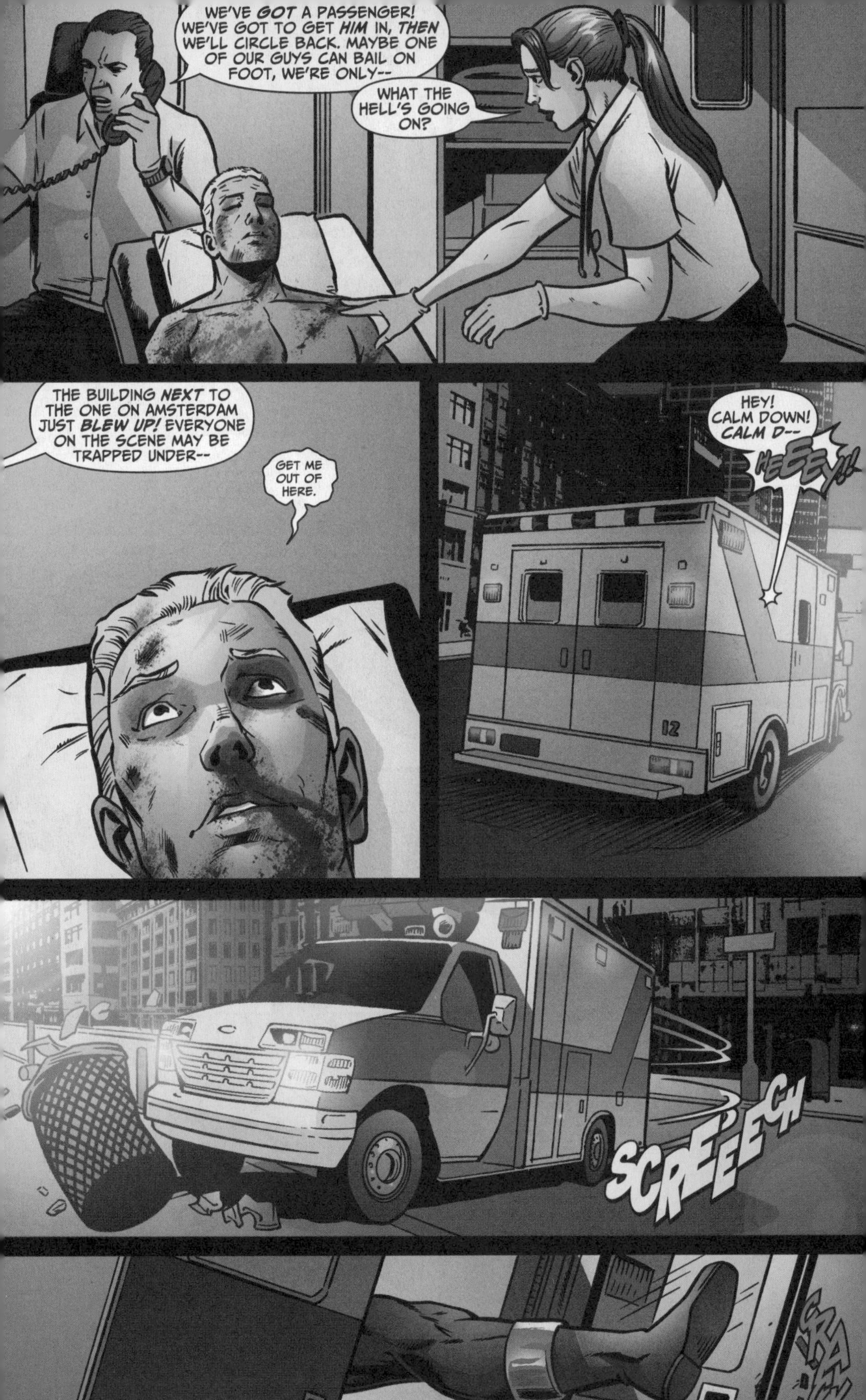
WE'VE GOT A PASSENGER! WE'VE GOT TO GET HIM IN, THEN WE'LL CIRCLE BACK. MAYBE ONE OF OUR GUYS CAN BAIL ON FOOT, WE'RE ONLY--
WHAT THE HELL'S GOING ON?
THE BUILDING NEXT TO THE ONE ON AMSTERDAM JUST BLEW UP! EVERYONE ON THE SCENE MAY BE TRAPPED UNDER--
GET ME OUT OF HERE.
HEY! CALM DOWN! CALM D--
HEEEY!!
12
SCREEEECH
CRACK

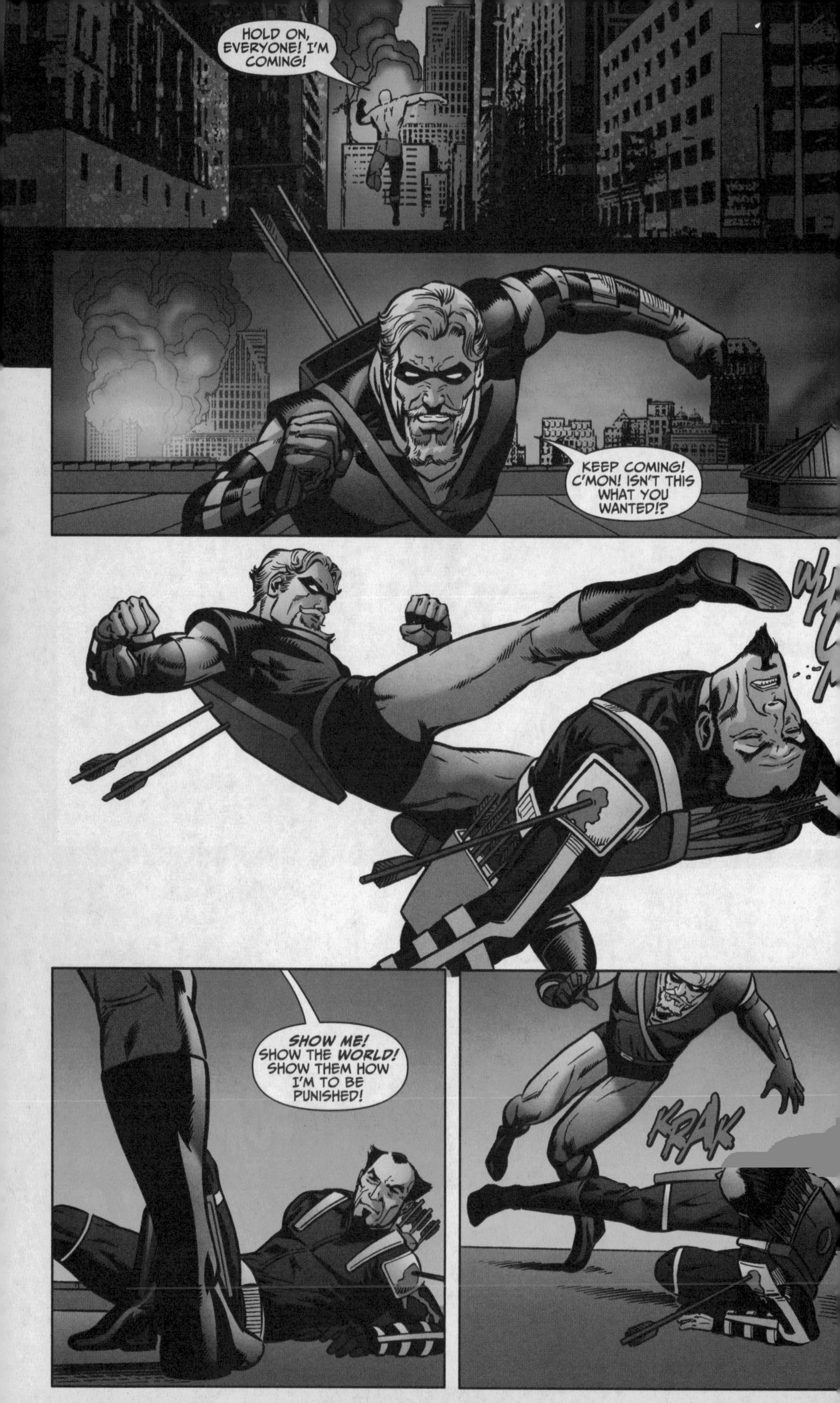
HOLD ON, EVERYONE! I'M COMING!
KEEP COMING! C'MON! ISN'T THIS WHAT YOU WANTED!?
SHOW ME! SHOW THE WORLD! SHOW THEM HOW I'M TO BE PUNISHED!
KRAK

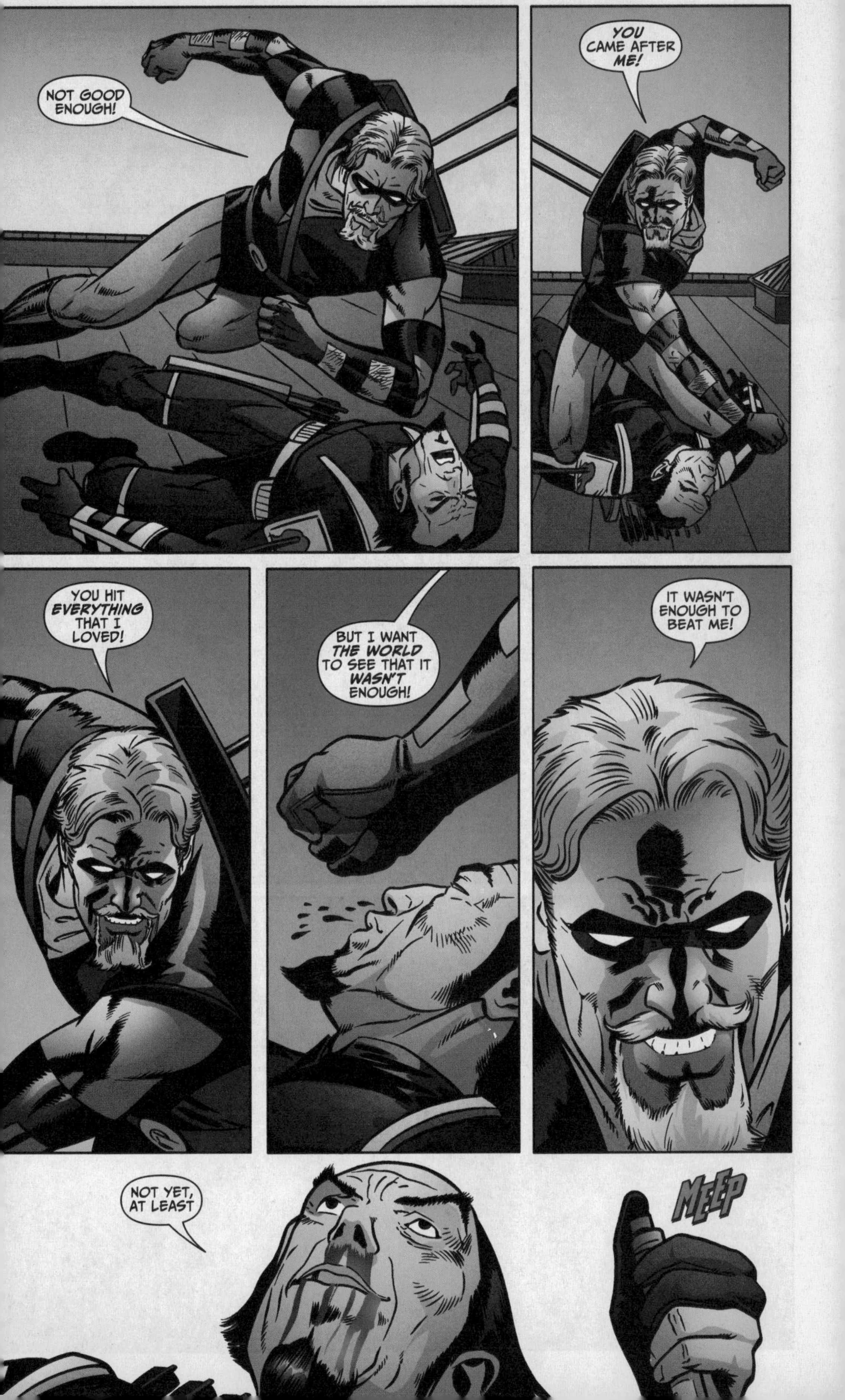
NOT GOOD ENOUGH!
YOU CAME AFTER ME!
YOU HIT EVERYTHING THAT I LOVED!
BUT I WANT THE WORLD TO SEE THAT IT WASN'T ENOUGH!
IT WASN'T ENOUGH TO BEAT ME!
NOT YET, AT LEAST
MEEP

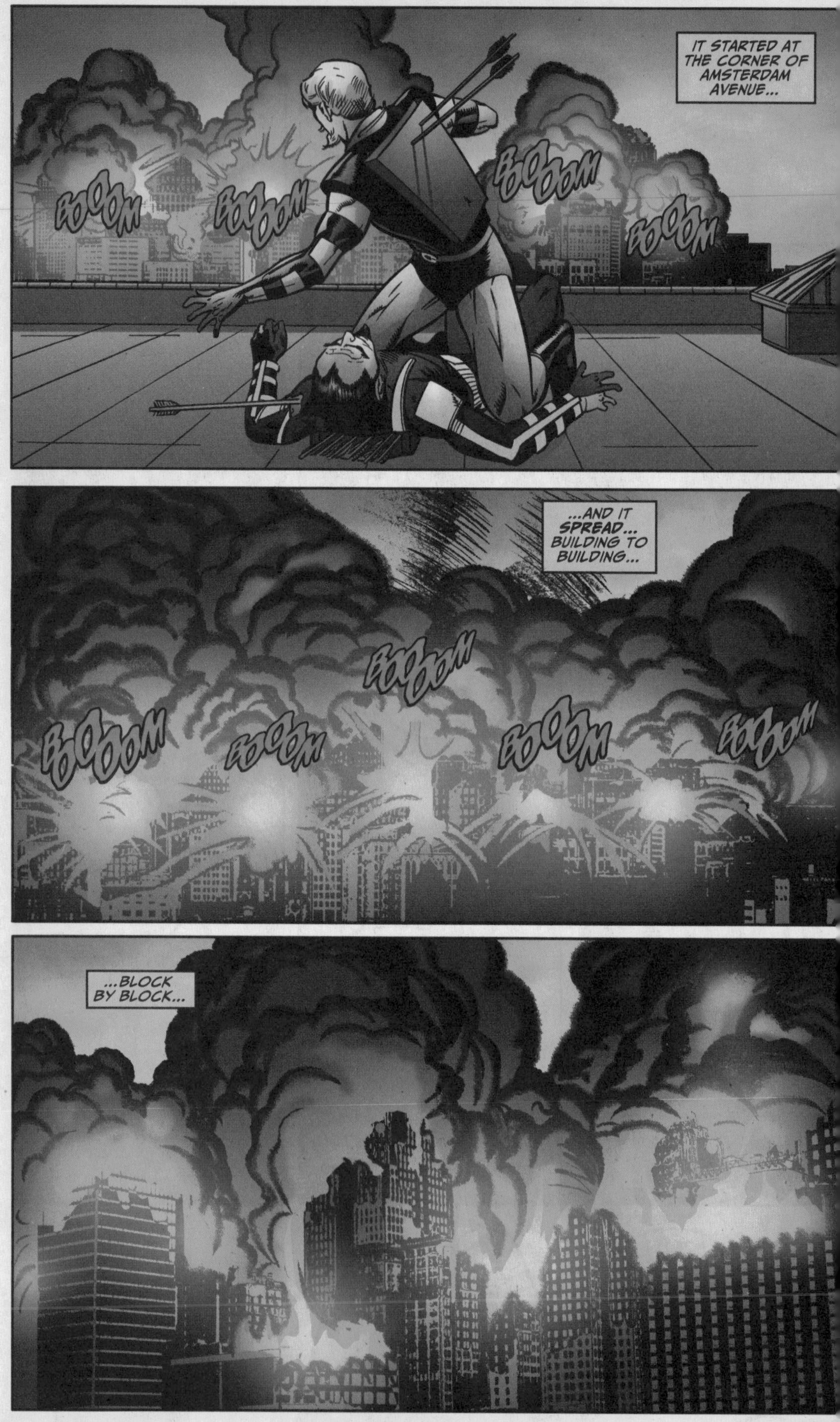
IT STARTED AT THE CORNER OF AMSTERDAM AVENUE...
BOOOOM
BOOOOM
BOOOOM
BOOOOM
...AND IT SPREAD... BUILDING TO BUILDING...
BOOOOM
BOOOOM
BOOOOM
BOOOOM
BOOOOM
...BLOCK BY BLOCK...

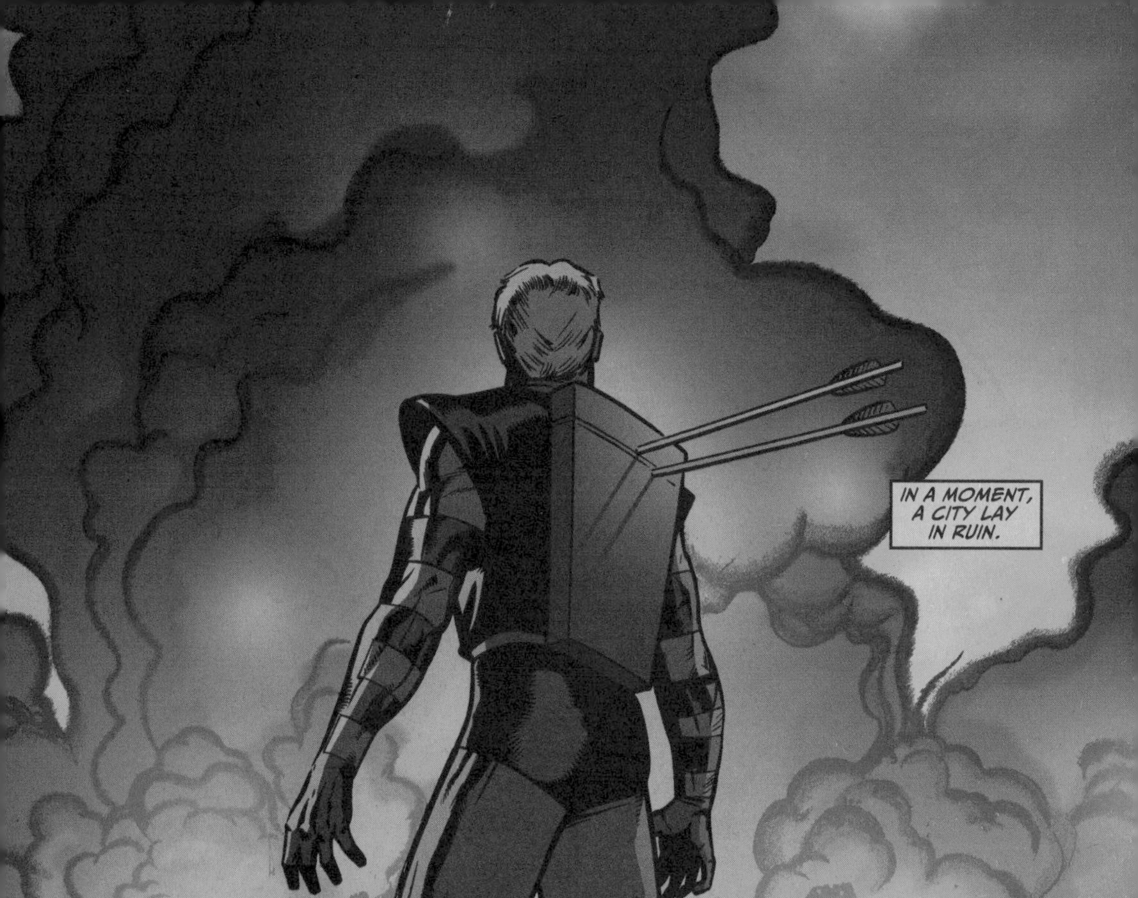
IN A MOMENT, A CITY LAY IN RUIN.

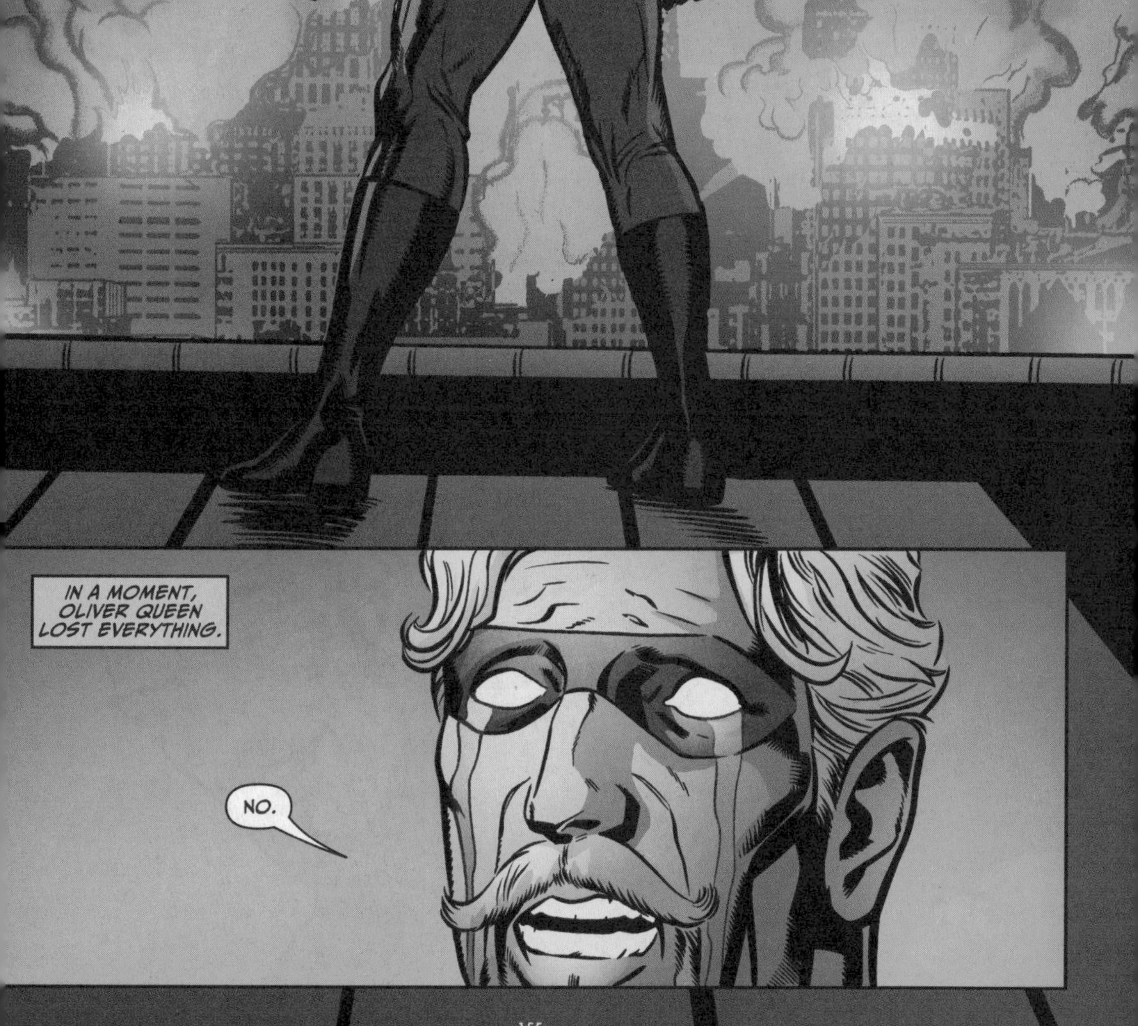
IN A MOMENT, OLIVER QUEEN LOST EVERYTHING.
NO.

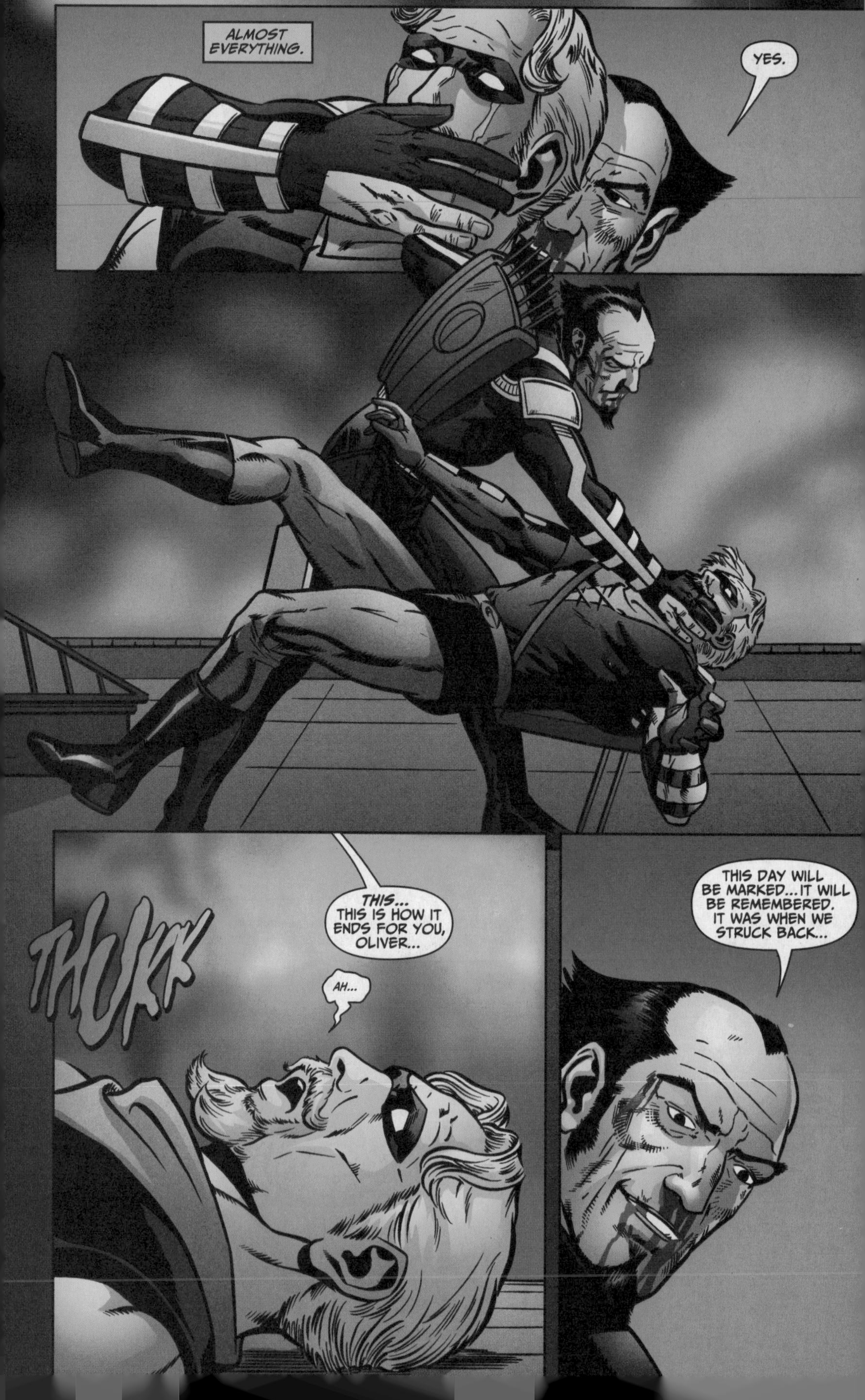
ALMOST EVERYTHING.
YES.
THUKK
THIS... THIS IS HOW IT ENDS FOR YOU, OLIVER...
AH...
THIS DAY WILL BE MARKED...IT WILL BE REMEMBERED. IT WAS WHEN WE STRUCK BACK...

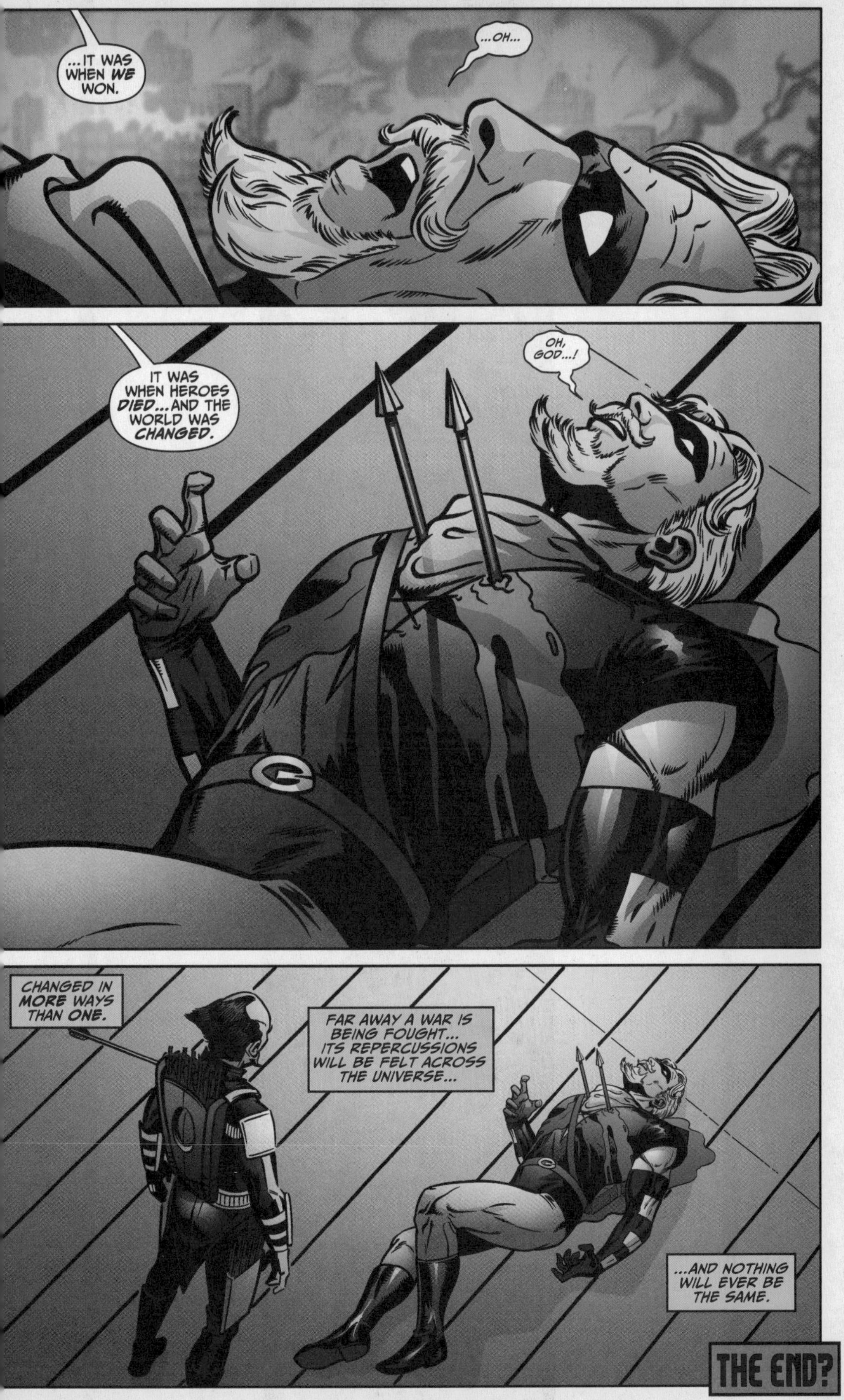

...IT WAS WHEN WE WON.
...OH...
IT WAS WHEN HEROES DIED...AND THE WORLD WAS CHANGED.
OH, GOD...!
CHANGED IN MORE WAYS THAN ONE.
FAR AWAY A WAR IS BEING FOUGHT... ITS REPERCUSSIONS WILL BE FELT ACROSS THE UNIVERSE...
...AND NOTHING WILL EVER BE THE SAME.
THE END?

Green Arrow #52 Cover by Cliff Chiang

Green Arrow #54 Cover by James Jean

Green Arrow #55 Cover by James Jean

Green Arrow #56 Cover by James Jean

Green Arrow #58 Cover by James Jean

Green Arrow #57 Cover by James Jean

Green Arrow #59 Cover by James Jean